The Collected Works of Anne Vaughan Lock

Medieval & Renaissance Texts & Studies

Volume 185

Renaissance English Text Society

Seventh Series
Volume XXI (for 1996)

The Collected Works of Anne Vaughan Lock

Edited by

Susan M. Felch

Arizona Center for Medieval and Renaissance Studies
in conjunction with
Renaissance English Text Society
Tempe, Arizona
1999

Library of Congress Cataloging-in-Publication Data
Lock, Anne Vaughan, ca. 1534–ca. 1590.
[Works. 1998]
The collected works of Anne Vaughan Lock / edited by Susan M. Felch.
p. cm. — (Medieval & Renaissance Texts & Studies ; v. 185)
(Renaissance English Text Society ; vol. 21)
Includes bibliographical references (p.) and index.
ISBN 0-86698-227-2 (acid-free paper)
1. Puritans—England—Early works to 1800. 2. Sermons, English—Early works to 1800. I. Felch, Susan M., 1951- . II. Title. III. Series: Medieval & Renaissance Texts & Studies (Series) ; v. 185 IV. Series: Renaissance English Text Society (Series) ; v. 21.
BX9339.L55A2 1998
280'.4—dc21 98-36936
CIP

This book is made to last.
It is set in Garamond Antiqua,
smythe-sewn and printed on acid-free paper
to library specifications

Printed in the United States of America

For
Doug

The EMBLEM of the Committee on Scholarly Editions indicates that this volume is based on an examination of all available relevant textual sources, that it is edited according to principles articulated in the volume, that the source texts and any deviation of the edited texts from them are fully described, that the editorial principles, the text, and the apparatus have undergone a peer review, that a rigorous schedule of verification and proofreading was followed to insure a high degree of accuracy in the presentation of the edition, and that the text is accompanied by appropriate textual and historical contextual information.

Contents

Illustrations

Tables

Acknowledgments

"My library / Was dukedom large enough" Prospero tells Miranda in the opening act of *The Tempest*. Editors, too, know the expansive pleasures afforded by fine libraries. In particular, I would like to thank the staff at the Folger Shakespeare Library, the Huntington Library, the Library of Princeton Theological Seminary, the British Library, the Bodleian Library, Cambridge University Library, the Angus Library at Regent's College (Oxford), the Library at King's College (Cambridge), the Library of Dulwich College, Edinburgh University Library, and the National Library of Scotland. Although I have benefitted from many knowledgeable professionals, I am especially grateful to Louise Yeoman of the National Library of Scotland for her indefatigable work in tracking down the letters of John Knox to Anne Lock, to Georgianna Ziegler of the Folger Library for her prompt answers to my numerous queries, and to William Harris of the Library of Princeton Theological Seminary for his hospitality. I also owe special thanks to Harry Boonstra, Conrad Bult, Paul Fields, and Kathy Struck of the Heckman Library at Calvin College who cheerfully answered my questions, found elusive resources, and refused to hide when they saw me coming their way.

I could not ask for a more nurturing and challenging environment than that provided by my colleagues at Calvin College. Charlotte Otten offered advice and encouragement, Henry Baron translated Dutch texts, and Mark Williams supplied references to Greek and Latin citations. Kenneth Bratt translated Lock's dedicatory poem to Bartholo Sylva while teaching me the finer points of Latin grammar. John Netland cheerfully read numerous drafts, learning more about Anne Vaughan Lock and the Tudor period than he probably ever cared to know. My student assistants, Gabrielle Darnell, Joy Koning, Kelly Van Andel, Betsy Verduin, and particularly Rebecca Watkins, spent hours carefully checking transcriptions and notes. Sherry Koll Levy and her staff provided secretarial assistance. At the institutional level, I am grateful for a 1995–96 Calvin Research Fellowship and two summer grants from the Calvin College Alumni Association.

I have also benefitted from the wider scholarly community, particularly the lively interaction within the informal circle of Anne Lock scholars: Linda Dove, Charles Huttar, Kel Morin-Parsons, John Ottenhoff, Jill Seal, and Micheline White. Anne Larsen answered questions about sixteenth-century French and corrected my translations. Peter Blayney advised me on the intricacies of early modern printing practices. My editorial committee, Elizabeth Hageman, Steven May, and Anne O'Donnell, meticulously read every line and provided expert advice; this edition is immeasurably better because of them. Erika Olbricht checked the transcriptions and notes. I owe a tremendous debt to Mario Di Cesare who believed in this project from its inception and encouraged me to pursue it. I am also grateful to the National Endowment for the Humanities for a 1995 summer stipend and for sponsoring my attendance at the Folger Institute seminar, "Contextualizing Writing by Early Modern Women," directed by Barbara Lewalski.

My deepest thanks goes to my husband, Doug, for his continuing love and support: Marito carissimo ex dono Susannæ uxoris suæ. 1998.

* * *

The text of *Sermons of John Calvin* (1560) is printed by permission of the Folger Shakespeare Library, Washington, D.C. The text of *Of the Markes* (1590) is printed by permission of The Huntington Library, San Marino, California. The text of Lock's Latin poem (1572) is printed by permission of the Syndics of Cambridge University Library, Cambridge, England. Portions of the material in the introduction were previously published in *Reformation* 2 (1997): 7–38.

Abbreviations

BL	British Library
CUL	Cambridge University Library
OED	*The Oxford English Dictionary*, 2nd ed. prepared by J. A. Simpson and E. S. C. Weiner, 20 vols. (Oxford: Clarendon Press, 1989).
STC	*A Short-Title Catalogue of Books Printed in England, Scotland, and Ireland and of English Books Printed Abroad 1475–1640*, 2nd ed. revised and enlarged by W. A. Jackson, F. S. Ferguson, and Katharine F. Pantzer from materials compiled by A. W. Pollard and G. R. Redgrave, 3 vols. (London: Bibliographical Society, 1976–91).
Tilley	Morris Palmer Tilley, *A Dictionary of the Proverbs in England in the Sixteenth and Seventeenth Centuries* (Ann Arbor: Univ. of Michigan Press, 1950).
UMI	*University Microfilms: Early English Books I, 1475–1640* (Ann Arbor: University Microfilms).
Wing	*Short-Title Catalogue of Books Printed in England, Scotland, Ireland, Wales, and British America and of English Books Printed in Other Countries 1641–1700.* 2nd ed. revised and enlarged from materials compiled by Donald Wing, 3 vols. (New York: Modern Language Association, 1982–1994).

Introduction

Anne Vaughan Lock (c. 1534–after 1590) was born into a London merchant household with strong ties to the court of Henry VIII and to the "new religion," Protestantism. Throughout her life, she moved within the ellipse inscribed by these two foci—the court and the church—while she dedicated herself to promoting Protestantism in England. With her first husband, Henry Lock, she hosted the Scottish reformer John Knox in their London home, even after he became *persona non grata* to the newly crowned Roman Catholic queen, Mary Tudor. Later, she traveled to Geneva, a refuge for English Protestants, and spent nearly two years there until the accession of Elizabeth I.

Lock's first book, printed in 1560 after her return to London, begins with a short discourse on the diagnosis and cure of spiritual illness, followed by a translation of four sermons by John Calvin, and ends with a poetic meditation on Psalm 51, one of the seven traditional penitential psalms. The book holds out the hope that through repentance and faith England and her new queen, Elizabeth, may be restored to spiritual health. Thirty years later, such cautious optimism was replaced by a more realistic assessment. Lock's second book, printed in 1590, addresses the question of how and why Christians must suffer for their faith. It boldly implies that the established Church of England is guilty of persecuting the true heirs of Protestantism, the nonconformists and Puritans among whom Lock counted herself. In the intervening years between her first and second books, Lock remained an active advocate for Protestantism. She corresponded with Knox and acted as an intermediary for him at court. She also contributed a Latin poem to an elegant manuscript presented to Elizabeth I that was apparently designed to win back the queen's favor for Lock's second husband, the Puritan preacher Edward Dering.

Lock thus assumed many roles throughout her eventful life: religious exile, poet, translator, correspondent, and political advocate. These disparate roles, however, coalesced in her determined commitment to promote Protestantism in Tudor England.

* * *

This commitment provides the immediate context for Anne Lock's writings, which are situated within the larger context of England's struggle to define its religious identity. Five terms clarify her own position within that struggle: *Protestant, reformed, Calvinist, nonconformist,* and *Puritan. Protestant* is the most general term, indicating all those who had broken away from the Roman Catholic church. *Reformed* or *Calvinist* refers to those whose theological views were aligned with John Calvin. The doctrinal standard for the Church of England, the Thirty-nine Articles, is Calvinist in its central theological tenets; thus later sixteenth-century English Protestants were, in the doctrinal sense, reformed. By the latter part of the century, however, those who held to reformed teachings in both doctrine and church order began to move away from the episcopalian structure of the Church of England toward a more democratic presbyterianism, although few advocated a complete rupture with the established church. Lock can be numbered among those who wished to be reformed or Calvinist in both doctrine and church order. Although the term *nonconformist* was not used until the seventeenth century, it is now applied by analogy to those English Protestants who considered the established Elizabethan church to be flawed and who refused to conform to such strictures as kneeling at communion, wearing clerical robes, and using *The Book of Common Prayer.* The final term, *Puritan,* is recorded in the *OED* as having first been used in 1572 by various authors to designate the party of nonconformist Protestants who wished to purify the church from its unscriptural and corrupt forms and practices.[1] In that year, the Puritan writers John Field and Thomas Wilcox objected to the term in *An Admonition to the Parliament,* but their opponent, John Whitgift, in *An Answer to the Admonition* insisted that it accurately characterized them, and the designation has been used ever since.[2]

These five words—*Protestant, reformed, Calvinist, nonconformist,* and *Puritan*—delineate Anne Lock's theological commitments. Within their contours, both her life and her works can be situated.

Life

Anne Vaughan Lock was born around 1534 to Stephen Vaughan, a

---

[1] The *OED* does give an earlier reference to "puritan" as a designation for anabaptists and cites the seventeenth-century historian Thomas Fuller to the effect that the term was already used for nonconformists in 1564.

[2] Scholars, however, continue to disagree over the precise definition of the term; for a survey of the debate, see the introduction to Lawrence A. Sasek, ed., *Images of English Puritanism: A Collection of Contemporary Sources, 1589–1646* (Baton Rouge: Louisiana State Univ. Press, 1989), 1–27.

London mercer, and Margaret (or Margery) Gwynnethe (or Guinet), a silkwoman in the Tudor court.[3] Stephen Vaughan was governor of the English Merchant Adventurers in Holland and the crown financial agent in Antwerp. Both the Vaughan and the Gwynnethe families had Welsh connections, but Stephen Vaughan grew up in London; his father may have been Jeffrey Vaughan, known to be master of the merchant tailors of the fraternity of St. John the Baptist in 1523.[4] Anne was the eldest surviving child in a family that included her sister, Jane, and brother, Stephen (b. 4 October 1537).[5] Young Anne grew up in a London household that was tied firmly to both the merchant community and the Henrician court. Her father also showed sympathy for the Protestant cause, particularly in letters he wrote as a young man.

In 1531, Stephen Vaughan was engaged by Henry VIII to persuade William Tyndale to return to England under safe conduct. Tyndale's English translation of the New Testament, completed in 1525 and smuggled into England the following year, had raised Henry's ire and forced the translator to remain in exile. His polemical book, *The practyse of prelates* (1530), did nothing to calm Henry, although *The obedience of a Christen man* (1528), recommended by Anne Boleyn, pleased the king with its argument for the subordination of the church to the state. Henry probably considered it safer to have such a powerful writer under his own eye rather than publishing seditious pamphlets abroad, so he commissioned Vaughan to offer Tyndale safe passage. Vaughan met three times with Tyndale and came away impressed by his learning and dedication to promoting the vernacular Bible. He wrote several favorable letters on Tyndale's behalf to both the king and Thomas Cromwell, who was a member of the privy council, Vaughan's former employer, and an old friend, even after he had been rebuked by Cromwell for showing too much regard for Tyndale.

---

[3] A silkwoman was a skilled seamstress who also may have done embroidery work.

[4] George S. Fry, ed., *Abstracts of Inquisitiones Post Mortem Relating to the City of London, returned into the Court of Chancery,* 3 vols. (1896–1908; reprint, Nendeln, Liechtenstein: Kraus Reprint, 1968), 1:77–8.

[5] For Anne Lock's biography, see Patrick Collinson, "The Role of Women in the English Reformation Illustrated by the Life and Friendships of Anne Locke," in *Godly People: Essays on English Protestantism and Puritanism* (London: Hambledon Press, 1983), 273–87; first published in *Studies in Church History* 2 (1965): 258–72. Collinson's account and W. C. Richardson's monograph, *Stephen Vaughan, Financial Agent of Henry VIII: A Study of Financial Relations with the Low Countries* (Baton Rouge: Louisiana State Univ. Studies, 1953), comprise the major secondary sources for biographical information on Lock and her family.

Ultimately, Vaughan was unsuccessful in bringing the reformer and the crown together; his mission was delegated to Sir Thomas Elyot, who was ordered to apprehend Tyndale.[6]

Despite this rebuff, Vaughan continued to urge the king to read Tyndale's writings for himself, and he also recommended the works of Robert Barnes, a defender of Protestant views, as one who "proves his learning by Scripture, the doctors, and the Pope's law."[7] Accused of heresy in 1531 by George Constantyne, an associate of Tyndale who had been placed in the custody of Sir Thomas More, Vaughan wrote to Cromwell affirming his loyalty to the king, and asserting that he was "neither Lutheran nor Tyndalyn."[8] In the same letter, however, he warns the king to desist from torturing suspected heretics, as such methods only drive people away from England, and he reiterates his own commitment to the Scriptures: "men's learning is not to be trusted; God's learning cannot deceive."[9] The next year, 1532, Vaughan wrote to Cromwell on behalf of Hugh Latimer, another English reformer, suggesting that "it were pity to trouble or cast away a man whom many men have in so good an opinion."[10] Vaughan also continued to sympathize with Tyndale and petitioned Cromwell on behalf of the Merchant Adventurers to spare Tyndale's life during his imprisonment for heresy in 1535–36 since his arrest at the English House in Antwerp had violated a guaranteed immunity.[11] As late as 13 April 1536, just six months before Tyndale's execution, Vaughan was still urging Cromwell to work for his release: "If now yow sende but your lettre to the Pryvey Counsail, I could delyver Tyndall from the fyre, so it came by tyme, for elles it wilbe to late."[12]

Vaughan's patronage of outspoken Protestants extended to commercial ventures as well. After the monasteries were dissolved, Stephen Vaughan received twelve "messuages" (houses and their outbuildings) and one stable that had belonged to the Carthusians' Hospital of St. Mary just outside

---

[6] For a fuller summary of Vaughan's connections with Tyndale, to which this brief account is indebted, see David Daniell, *William Tyndale: A Biography* (New Haven: Yale Univ. Press, 1994), 208–17.

[7] J. S. Brewer, James Gairdner, and R. H. Brodie, eds., *Letters and Papers, Foreign and Domestic, of the Reign of Henry VIII, 1509–1547*, 21 vols. (London, 1862–1910), 5:nos. 303, 533. Barnes was burned at the stake for his Protestant views on 30 July 1540.

[8] Brewer, *Letters and Papers*, 5:no. 574.

[9] Brewer, *Letters and Papers*, 5:no. 574.

[10] Brewer, *Letters and Papers*, 5:no. 957.

[11] Richardson, *Stephen Vaughan*, 34.

[12] Brewer, *Letters and Papers*, 10:no. 663.

Bishopsgate. The Vaughans had lived previously in Cheapside within the city of London, but now they moved to one of these houses in St. Mary Spital in the parish of St. Botolph. Vaughan rented out most of his property to fellow Protestants, including Sir Thomas Wyatt the younger, who was executed in 1554 by Mary Tudor for protesting her projected marriage to Philip II of Spain.[13] In addition to such public displays of his religious affiliation, Stephen Vaughan apparently ordered his own household along the godly lines prescribed by the Protestant reformers. During the period between his first and second marriages, while he was trying to manage his domestic affairs from a distance, he learned that one of the maids, Anne Kydney, had been entertaining male visitors rather too freely. He wrote to William Paget, one of Henry's secretaries of state, asking him to dismiss her, but to do so in such a way that she might be encouraged to repent rather than to despair.[14]

Anne Vaughan Lock's mother had her own connections to the Tudor court and, perhaps, similar Protestant sympathies. Margaret Gwynnethe probably married Stephen Vaughan in 1533; she figures prominently in his letters to Cromwell after May of that year, whether he is asking his friend and former employer to obtain for her a position at court or requesting more money so that he might not be reduced to spending her dowry.[15] While Stephen Vaughan's responsibilities kept him on the Continent for long periods of time, Margaret Vaughan managed their London household with considerable skill and kept her husband informed of the affairs at court.[16] She transferred money, letters, and goods to court officials, accepted receipts, sued for the auditing of Vaughan's accounts, sent him a horse, and took in at least one boarder, Joan Reede.[17]

She was also attached to the court in her own right as a silkwoman, beginning her tenure shortly before Anne Boleyn's coronation in 1533.[18] The position was not without its problems, for the queen was reluctant to pay Margaret for her work. In a letter dated 3 August 1533, Vaughan com-

---

[13] Fry, *Abstracts of Inquisitiones*, 1:85–7. Susanne Woods called this fact to my attention; see her "Anne Lock and Aemilia Lanyer: A Tradition of Protestant Women Speaking," in *Form and Reform in Renaissance England: Essays in Honor of Barbara Kiefer Lewalski*, ed. Amy Boesky and Mary Thomas Crane (Newark: Univ. of Delaware Press, forthcoming).

[14] Brewer, *Letters and Papers*, 20.2:no. 217.

[15] Brewer, *Letters and Papers*, 6:nos. 559, 917, 934, 1082, 1385.

[16] Brewer, *Letters and Papers*, 6:no. 1385; 19.2:no. 724.

[17] Brewer, *Letters and Papers*, 9:no. 330; 13.2:nos. 682, 882; 14.2:no. 782; 19.1:no. 972.

[18] Brewer, *Letters and Papers*, 6:no. 559.

plained to Cromwell: "Help my wife to her business with the Queen, that she may have her fee, or else she had better keep sheep for any gain she will have."[19] Three years later, after the queen's execution, the following outstanding debt was recorded: "Mrs. Vaughanne, silkwoman, 68l. 4s. 1 1/2 d."[20] Margaret Vaughan continued to work at court despite the tardy payments, as is indicated by a memorandum from 1538 stating that "no stuff be delivered by Hewetson, Mrs. Vaughan, Mr. Lok, or any other which ought to be allowed by Mr. Denny without a bill signed by Denny or his deputy."[21] After her death on 16 September 1544, her husband wrote to Paget, asking him to collect £360 that Queen Catherine Parr owed to Margaret for materials and labor; as he reiterated the following January, Margaret "spent her life in labouring and toiling in her Grace's works."[22]

Although little is known of Margaret's religious beliefs, she had connections with both Anne Boleyn and Catherine Parr, the two queens who encouraged a Protestant circle at court. She may have known Katherine Brandon, the duchess of Suffolk and an intimate of Catherine Parr, to whom Lock later dedicated her first book. Margaret also may have known another associate of Catherine Parr, Anne Askew, who was burned at the stake for her Protestant views in 1546.

Anne Lock was probably ten years old when her mother died. Following her death, Stephen Vaughan expended some care in choosing a tutor for his motherless children. His own interest in books and learning date from before his marriage. In a letter of 13 April 1529, he tells Cromwell that he wishes to learn French and asks for help in obtaining a book from John Palsgrave, who refuses to sell him one, "lest his profit as a teacher should be diminished."[23] Apparently Vaughan, with or without the help of Palsgrave's dictionary, taught himself to speak French; on a later diplomatic mission he is commended for his linguistic abilities.[24] Vaughan's

---

[19] Brewer, *Letters and Papers*, 6:no. 934.

[20] Brewer, *Letters and Papers*, 10:no. 914. The name of "William Lok," Anne Lock's future father-in-law, also appears on this list.

[21] Brewer, *Letters and Papers*, 13.2:no. 1201. "Mr Lok" is apparently Anne's future father-in-law, Sir William Lock; Mr. Denny is probably Sir Edmund Denny, chief baron of the exchequer.

[22] Brewer, *Letters and Papers*, 19.2:no. 724; 20.1:no. 27.

[23] Brewer, *Letters and Papers*, 4.3:no. 5459. John Palsgrave was tutor to Henry Fitzroy, Henry VIII's natural son by Elizabeth Blount. He carefully guarded the sale of his *Lesclarcissement de la langue francoyse* (STC 19166), first printed in 1524 but not completed until 1530, to prevent other teachers of French from obtaining copies.

[24] Brewer, *Letters and Papers*, 13.2:nos. 550, 880.

choice for a tutor, then, was a Mr. Cob, a scholar proficient in Latin, Greek, and French, and a man reputed to be of "sober, honest and virtuous life."[25] Cob was probably not a native Englishman but someone born in the Low Countries.[26] He was employed both as a manager for the household and as a tutor to the children, presumably the girls as well as young Stephen, and a son of George Brooke, sixth lord Cobham, who was living with the Vaughans.[27]

In addition to his academic and managerial qualifications, Cob was a dedicated Protestant. He is probably the same Cob, a schoolmaster living in the house of another mercer, John Gouge, who was brought before the Privy Council on 21 April 1543 on charges of having translated "a certeyne Postilla [commentary] upon the Gospelles" filled with erroneous opinions.[28] Catherine Parr sent a servant to intervene on his behalf before the Court of Aldermen in October 1544.[29] A year later, in September

---

[25] Brewer, *Letters and Papers*, 21.2:no. 52; 20.2:nos. 416, 444. He is identified as Stephen Cobbe in Susan Brigden, *London and the Reformation* (Oxford: Clarendon Press, 1989), 346. Kel Morin-Parsons drew my attention to this reference.

[26] Brewer, *Letters and Papers*, 20.2:nos. 217, 416. Vaughan, writing from Antwerp in 1546, describes Cob as "born in these parts," and asks Paget to help the tutor find an "exhibition" (position) at one of the English universities. See Brewer, *Letters and Papers*, 21.2:no. 52. The fact that he is called Mr. (master) Cob, and that Vaughan considered him eligible for a university position, suggests that Cob already had a master's degree from a university on the continent. Furthermore, the name "Stephen Cob" does not appear in lists of Oxford or Cambridge scholars; see John Venn and J. A. Venn, comps., *Alumni Cantabrigienses*, pt. 1, vol. 1 (Cambridge: Cambridge Univ. Press, 1922), 360–1; Joseph Foster, comp., *Alumni Oxonienses*, early series, vol. 1 (London: Parker, 1887), 294–5.

[27] Brewer, *Letters and Papers*, 21.1:no. 1494.

[28] John Roche Dasent, ed., *Acts of the Privy Council of England*, n.s., vol. 1 (London, 1890), 115; Brewer, *Letters and Papers*, 18.1:no. 431. Brigden tentatively identifies the postilla in question as being *A postill or collection of moste godly doctrine* (London, 1550; STC 5806), a translation of the Lutheran Antonius Corvinus's *Postilla in Evangelia Dominicalia* (1536); see Brigden, *London and the Reformation*, 346. The epistle to the reader, however, while commending the book to "the fathers of the houshold, parents and governoures of youth" notes that it has been translated "into our mother and English tong," suggesting that Cob either spoke English as his first language, was not the translator of this book, or perhaps did not write the epistle (A3^r). Although John Gouge is identified in the *Acts of the Privy Council* as a mercer, he may be instead the Protestant printer and stationer. Sir William Reede, curate of Honney Lane, was later examined with Cob; he may be related to Joan Reede, who boarded with the Vaughans. See Dasent, *Acts of the Privy Council*, 126, 128; Brewer, *Letters and Papers*, 18.1:nos. 500, 515.

[29] Brigden, *London and the Reformation*, 359.

1545, Cob, who by this time was employed by Vaughan, was summoned to appear before the chancellor of the bishop of London. Vaughan immediately wrote to William Paget, asking him to assist Cob; unfortunately, by August 1546, matters had deteriorated to the point that Vaughan reluctantly asked Cob to leave his employ. He nevertheless exerted himself to find a new position for the schoolmaster at one of the universities, once again enlisting Paget's help.[30]

Cob's dismissal, while undoubtedly a blow to the Vaughan siblings, did not leave them without adult supervision. Shortly after the death of Margaret, Stephen Vaughan began searching for a new wife, a courtship conducted through various intermediaries since he was still on the Continent. While his letters suggest a sincere affection for Margaret, it is clear that he also sorely missed her managerial skills. On 9 December 1544 he wrote to William Paget: "An honest mind I regard above all other things in a woman; without which I grant it is a pleasant thing to live, but the consideration of my continual shifting from my house, the lack of well nurturing my children, the waste and spoil of my things, draweth me to marry."[31] By early 1546 he had found a new wife; his second marriage, licensed on 27 April 1546, was to Margery Brinkelow, widow of another London mercer, Henry Brinkelow, who had written a pair of polemical Protestant pamphlets.[32] In *The lamentacion of a christian against the citie of London*, Brinkelow equates the Londoners who still observe the "dyrtye dregges and folish ceremonyes" of the Roman Catholic mass with the citizens of Jerusalem who rejected Jesus Christ as their messiah. Furthermore, while Brinkelow argues against the use of force, even to resist a tyrant king, he urges disobedience to ungodly laws on the grounds that one should "rather suffer deeth / than ether resist them bodely with force or streangth of hande / or consent and agree unto their wicked lawes and actes in hert or mouth."[33] Although Vaughan appears to have valued a good manager above all else in his search for a second wife, his choice of Margery Brinkelow shows that he also wished his children to be "well nurtured" in the Protestant faith. She was not only the widow of a man who had been embroiled in partisan politics but was herself a long-time

---

[30] Brewer, *Letters and Papers*, 21.2:no. 52.

[31] Brewer, *Letters and Papers*, 19.2:no. 724.

[32] Henry Brinkelow, *The complaynt of Roderyck Mors for the redresse of certen wicked lawes* ([Strassburg], c. 1542; STC 3759.5); *The lamentacion of a christian against the citie of London, made by R. Mors* ([Bonn], 1542; STC 3764).

[33] Brinkelow, *The lamentacion*, C2^{r}, E2^{r}.

acquaintance of the Vaughan family with the reputation of an honest, pious person.[34]

Anne Vaughan Lock, it is clear, spent her childhood and youth in a reasonably prosperous merchant-class home with strong ties to the Tudor court, surrounded by adults who not only favored, but promoted, the Protestant cause in England. By the time Stephen Vaughan died on 25 December 1549, his daughter was prepared to establish her own household along similar lines.[35] While still in her teens, she married Henry Lock, the son of family friends, probably in 1551.

Henry came from a family that mirrored her own, although they were considerably more wealthy. His father, Sir William Lock, owned numerous houses and shops inside and outside the city of London as well as farms and lands in the countryside.[36] He supplied cloth to the Henrician court, served as a crown agent in Antwerp, was the Sheriff of London in 1548, and sent his eldest son, Thomas, to work with Stephen Vaughan on the Continent. According to the recollections of Sir William's daughter, Rose Lock Hickman Throckmorton, the Lock family bought and read Protestant books during the 1530s that were illicitly smuggled into England from the Continent.[37]

Sir William died 24 August 1550, leaving a substantial inheritance to his fourth son, Henry, including several houses, shops, a farm, and freehold lands.[38] It is unclear to what extent Anne's husband participated in the London nonconformist community as an adult. Nevertheless, in 1552 and 1553 the Scottish reformer and court chaplain John Knox met the Locks and the Hickmans when he came to London and also stayed with them before he fled to the Continent after the accession of Mary. Anne and Henry Lock were of sufficient social stature to host a prominent clergyman when Knox was summoned to preach before Edward VI and of sufficient Protestant sympathies to shelter him when the political and religious winds changed.

---

[34] Brewer, *Letters and Papers*, 21.1:nos. 105, 106, 347.

[35] Stephen Vaughan's will left most of his property to his widow, Margery, and son, Stephen, with the rents on one house in Cheapside going to his daughters, Anne and Jane; see Fry, *Abstracts of Inquisitiones*, 1:85–7.

[36] Fry, *Abstracts of Inquisitiones*, 1:80–3.

[37] "Certaine old stories recorded by an aged gentlewoman a time before her death, to be perused by her children and posterity" (BL Add. MS 43827), fols. 3^v–4^v. Transcribed in Maria Dowling and Joy Shakespeare, "Religion and Politics in mid Tudor England through the eyes of an English Protestant Woman: the Recollections of Rose Hickman," *Bulletin of the Institute of Historical Research* 55 (1982): 94–102.

[38] Fry, *Abstracts of Inquisitiones*, 1:80–3.

John Knox had gained notoriety in the late 1540s for his defense of the reformed doctrines against the established Roman Catholic church in Scotland. In 1549 he came to England to preach, first at Berwick and later at Newcastle, where he attracted large crowds. In 1551 he was appointed one of six chaplains to Edward VI. He preached at Windsor and Hampton Court in the autumn of 1552, and the following year he was one of the Lenten preachers for the young king. When Edward died on 6 July 1553, however, Knox found himself *persona non grata* and escaped to the Continent. After brief stays in other cities, he arrived in Geneva in 1554 where he began a correspondence with Anne Lock that continued for several years.

Anne Vaughan Lock's association with Knox has been noted consistently by Knox biographers and scholars, and, indeed, much of what is known about her life comes from the interest historians have shown in their relationship. Robert Louis Stevenson was the first to suggest that Lock was "the woman [Knox] loved best," although he denied any sexual impropriety in the relationship. Subsequent estimations of Lock by historians have ranged from the critical (a woman "emotional, dissatisfied, seeking in religion an outlet for an eager vanity, a love of drama, of excitement") to the admiring ("a very gifted and enterprising woman").[39]

Whatever may be inferred about Lock's relationship with Knox, their correspondence does provide an intimate portrait of Anne Lock's own character and personality. Unfortunately, the evidence is rendered somewhat problematic by the loss of all the original documents. Because Lock's letters to Knox have not survived in any form, we have only one side of their conversation: his fourteen letters written to her between 1556 and 1562. As a further complication, these letters are preserved only in seventeenth-century transcripts; none of the originals remain. Nevertheless, despite the textual difficulties, the Knox-Lock correspondence remains one of the primary sources of information about Lock's life.

The first letter from Knox, dated 1556 and written from Geneva, is addressed jointly to "Mistress Locke and Mistress Hickman." Along with two other letters addressed to Lock alone and dated that same year, it is preserved in a 1603 folio manuscript of transcripts that belonged to Marga-

---

[39] Robert Louis Stevenson, "John Knox and his Relations to Women," in *Familiar Studies of Men and Books*, vol. 3 of *The Works of Robert Louis Stevenson* (London: Cassell, 1906), 280; George R. Preedy [Marjorie Bowen], *The Life of John Knox* (London: Herbert Jenkins, 1940), 63; Jasper Ridley, *John Knox* (New York: Oxford Univ. Press, 1968), 247–8.

ret Stewart, Knox's second wife.[40] All three letters encourage Lock to leave London and join the exiled Protestant community in Geneva. Mary Tudor was increasing her pressure on the English nonconformists and had already executed several prominent spokesmen including Hugh Latimer and Nicholas Ridley in 1555. While Knox may have been concerned about Lock's physical safety, he primarily worries over her susceptibility to idolatry if she remains in a country that is so perilous to her spiritual health. More intriguingly, as he urges Lock to come to Geneva, he appeals directly to her conscience, despite the fact that her husband apparently was not inclined to leave London. Although Knox acknowledges that Anne owes Henry obedience since her husband is her head, the reformer urges a more primary commitment to God. In fact, he suggests that she "call first for grace by Jesus to follow that whilk is acceptabill in his syght, and thairefter communicat" with her husband, a move that clearly subordinates marriage vows to individual conscience and the active pursuit of God's will.[41] From Knox's perspective, she should first prepare herself for imminent exile and then tell her husband what she has decided to do.

With or without Henry's approval, Anne Lock did manage to leave London; the *Livre des Anglois*, a record of the English exiles in Geneva, notes that "Anne Locke, Harrie her Sonne, and Anne her daughter, and Katherine her maide," arrived in Geneva 8 May 1557. The trip proved costly: within 4 days, "Anne, the doughter of Anne Locke, and Harry

---

[40] This folio volume came into the possession of Robert Wodrow (1679–1734) who collected a large number of manuscripts relating to the Scottish Reformation; it is known as the Wodrow Folio VII and is now at the Glasgow University Library (MS Gen 1219). A later copy of these letters in a quarto manuscript is now housed at the University of Edinburgh (MS La. III. 345). Thomas McCrie (1772–1835), the church historian who owned the quarto volume, thought that it had belonged to Wodrow, but there are significant differences in pagination and content as well as size. For instance, MS La. III. 345 includes more letters from Mrs. Bowes, Knox's mother-in-law, than does MS Gen 1219. David Laing, who borrowed the quarto manuscript (MS La. III. 345) for his edition of Knox's *Works* and then purchased it from Thomas McCrie the younger in 1871 for £10, also thought it had belonged to Wodrow and that misidentification has persisted ever since. See the exchange of letters between Laing and McCrie, February through April 1871, Edinburgh University Library (MS La. IV. 17); see also John Knox, *The Works of John Knox*, ed. David Laing, 6 vols. (Edinburgh: Thomas George Stevenson, 1846–1864), 3:334–5. I am indebted to Louise Yeoman of the National Library of Scotland for her discovery of this misidentification.

[41] Knox, *Works,* 4:219–22. All references to the letters are taken from Laing's edition.

Locke her husband" is recorded as dead.[42] It is possible that Henry Lock may have accompanied his family to the Continent, perhaps staying at Frankfurt while they traveled on to Geneva, but he also may have stayed in London during Mary's reign. By October 1558, and possibly much earlier than that, all three of his older brothers had died, leaving as principal heir to the extensive Lock holdings the nine-year-old son of his eldest brother, Thomas.[43] Henry may have felt compelled to remain in London to oversee the family business.

Anne Lock, however, remained at Geneva for nearly two years with the colony of exiled English. While there is no contemporary record of this period relating to Lock, she may have used the time to translate four sermons of John Calvin, which he had preached in 1557, and possibly also to write the sonnet sequence on Psalm 51. After the death of Mary Tudor in 1558, Lock was free to return to London. She was still in Geneva on 7 February 1559, when she sent a letter to Knox, but she finally arrived home in June 1559.[44]

On 15 January the following year, her first volume, composed of a dedicatory epistle to the duchess of Suffolk, a translation of the Calvin sermons, and sonnets, was entered in the Stationers' Register by John Day. It was printed shortly thereafter, certainly before March 25, since the copy in the British Library bears the inscription: "Liber Henrici Lock ex dono Annæ uxoris suæ. 1559." The inscription, probably written by Henry, suggests that he supported his wife's work and her devotion to the cause of reformed Protestantism.

The correspondence between Knox and Lock, however, resumed in 1559 and continued until 1562 with eleven more letters from Knox.[45] On 7 February 1559, Lock wrote to Knox asking about the appropriateness of

---

[42] *Livre des Anglois, à Genève,* with notes by John Southerden Burn (London, 1831), 9, 17.

[43] Fry, *Abstracts of Inquisitiones,* 1:225–8.

[44] Knox, *Works,* 6:11.

[45] These letters apparently were made available to David Calderwood (1575–1650) who transcribed them into his six unpublished folio manuscript volumes on the history of the Scottish Church. These manuscripts (BL Add. MSS 4734–4739) include a mid-sized version of the history that was used as the basetext for *The History of the Kirk in Scotland* published by the Wodrow Society in 1842–1849, a longer, less ordered version, and a smaller compilation that was published in folio in 1678. By the mid-nineteenth century, when David Laing came to edit the still standard *Works* of Knox, he was unable to locate any of the original letters to Lock and thus reproduced the first three letters from the Edinburgh manuscript (MS La. III. 345) and the remaining letters from Calderwood's manuscripts (BL Add. MSS 4734–4739).

sacraments administered according to the second edition of the *Book of Common Prayer*.[46] She also wanted Knox's advice on the issue of accompanying friends to church in order to witness baptisms or to participate in the Lord's Supper. In his response of 6 April 1559, Knox strongly encourages Lock not to attend services where, he believes, ceremonies outweigh worship and the sacraments are unattended by preaching, but he recommits the matter to her own conscience and discernment: "God grant yow his Holie Spirit rightlie to judge."[47] In addition to acknowledging Lock's spiritual judgement, this letter also seeks her approbation and comfort. Knox was in need of encouragement as he faced criticism for causing political upheaval in Scotland and for writing the intemperate tract, *The first blast of the trumpet against the monstruous regiment of women* (1558), that condemned the reign of Mary Tudor in particular and women rulers in general. Nor was he afraid to ask for reassurance of her friendship: "Yet one thing I ashame not to affirme, that familiaritie once throughlie contracted was never yet brocken on my default. The cause may be that I have rather need of all then that any hath need of me."[48]

The subsequent letters continue to bear out the high regard in which Knox held not only Lock's position but also her advice. Many are accounts, ranging from the exuberant to the despairing, of the ongoing rebellion against Mary Stuart and her French supporters in Scotland, and most rely on Lock to support Knox's cause in London. For instance, he asks her to distribute his letters both to London friends and to those still remaining in Geneva, thus squelching any slanders about the course of events in Scotland. He commits into her care the bearer of a letter, "a poore man unknowen in the countrie, to whome, I beseeche you, shew reasonable favour and kindnes tuiching his merchandise, and the just selling therof."[49] When Lock writes of a painful spiritual struggle or of difficulties in making theological distinctions, Knox responds that he is confident of her ability to remain steadfast and judge wisely.[50] In one strong and clear statement of self-determination, Knox writes,

> And, therefore, Sister, as I will not be a snare to your conscience, to bind me ather to my words, ather yit to my worke, farther than I prove by evident Scripture, so darre I not counsell you to doe that thing which my self am no wise minded to doe. ...

---

[46] Knox notes the date of her letter in his response; see Knox, *Works*, 6:11.

[47] Knox, *Works*, 6:14.

[48] Knox, *Works*, 6:11.

[49] Knox, *Works*, 6:27.

[50] Knox, *Works*, 6:77–9; 6:83–5.

> Nather my penne, nather yit my presence, can prescribe unto you how farre yee are addebted to expone your self to daungers for these imperfectiouns in religioun which ye cannot remedie; but yee, directing your heart to advance God's glorie, sall be instructed by his Holie Spirit how farre yee may condescend, and how farre ye are bound to abstaine.[51]

Knox's confidence in Lock's abilities and position is most clearly demonstrated by a pair of letters he wrote on 18 November 1559.[52] As the financial needs of the Scottish rebellion against Mary Stuart pressed upon him, Knox wrote two urgent appeals for immediate monetary support. The first was to William Cecil, already on his way to becoming the most powerful man in England; the other, expressing his full confidence in her ability to help him, was to Anne Lock. His request reveals not only the strength of Lock's friendship with Knox, but also her access to influential people who reasonably could be expected to support the Scottish reformation. Ten days later she wrote to say that she had not raised the necessary funds; she exhorted Knox to wait on God's providence and pray rather than fight. Although Lock's response must have been disappointing to Knox, his return letter both accepts her rebuke and redirects her attention to God as the only source of comfort in her own difficulties. Her advice, he admits, is "godlie and truelie [given]" and as to her own spiritual questions, he does not think that she "greatlie need[s]" his answers, for "God [will] make your self participant of the same comfort which ye write unto me."[53]

All of these requests, from the assumption that Lock can communicate with far-flung colleagues, to Knox's confidence that she is in a position to help a poor merchant financially, to his reliance on her patronage and theological acuity, reveal the high regard in which Anne Lock was held by Knox and doubtless by others in the nonconformist community.

Within the next three years, the correspondence, or at least what remains of it, comes to a halt, the last two missives being both brief and tantalizing. Nineteen months after his previous letter, on 2 October 1561, Knox writes a short note in which he thanks Lock for a "token" that she sent without a letter. Although Knox acknowledges some "impediment" that apparently prevented her writing, he is unhappy over her silence.[54] The final letter, dated 6 May 1562, laments the dissension among former

---

[51] Knox, *Works,* 6:84.

[52] Knox, *Works,* 6:98–101.

[53] Knox, *Works,* 6:103–4.

[54] Knox, *Works,* 6:129–31.

allies in the Scottish rebellion and is probably only an extract as it does not include any of the expected salutations or concluding personal comments.

Although the materials are admittedly sparse, the portrait of Anne Lock that emerges from these letters reveals a strong woman dedicated to the Protestant cause and actively loyal to it. Her intense devotion, noticeable in her own dedicatory epistles and poems and suggested by Knox's letters, was matched by her practical, public activities: traveling to Geneva and remaining there despite the death of her daughter, performing the role of intermediary for Knox, attempting to raise funds for the reformation in Scotland, and exhorting Knox on the importance of prayer and trust. At the same time, she was managing her own household and raising her children, three of whom appear to have reached adulthood: Henry (baptized 6 September 1553) who followed in his mother's footsteps as a writer of religious sonnets and who married a Cornish cousin, Ann Moyle; Anne (baptized 23 October 1561) who married Robert Moyle, Ann's brother; and Michaell (baptized 11 October 1562).[55]

Henry Lock, Anne's husband, died in 1571, leaving all of his worldly goods to his wife. In 1572, she married the young preacher and gifted Greek scholar, Edward Dering (c. 1540–1576).[56] That same year, Dering, a former fellow of Christ's College in Cambridge, began a course of popular lectures on the Epistle to the Hebrews as a reader at St. Paul's Cathedral. He recognized in Lock the promise of a companion whose spirituality matched his own, and in his proposal letter he wrote that he sought her alone, "whome the grace of God in myne opinion hathe made a good possescion."[57]

Anne and Edward Dering were actively involved with a group of like-minded Calvinists who were becoming known as the Puritans. Of particular interest are their connections with the Cooke sisters: Mildred (1526–

---

[55] Lewis Lupton believed that Michaell died young, but Micheline White has discovered a reference to him as an adult in 1604 in Robert Moyle's will (personal communication). Lupton, after consulting the Register of St. Mary-le-Bow, lists two children in addition to the Anne who died in Geneva and the three who reached adulthood: Anne (baptized 21 December 1559) and Henry (baptized 8 November 1560). It is possible that the Henry born in 1560 is the poet, the first Henry having died, or that he is the child of another Lock family; see Lewis Lupton, *A History of the Geneva Bible*, 25 vols. (London: Olive Tree, 1966–1994), 8:30.

[56] For Dering's life, see Patrick Collinson, "A Mirror of Elizabethan Puritanism: The Life and Letters of 'Godly Master Dering' " in *Godly People: Essays on English Protestantism and Puritanism* (London: Hambledon Press, 1983), 289–323.

[57] Quoted in Collinson, "The Role of Women," in *Godly People*, 283.

1589), Anne (1527/1528–1610), Elizabeth (1528–1609), Katherine (c. 1530–1583), and Margaret (c. 1532–1558).[58] The daughters of Sir Anthony Cooke (1504–1576) and Ann Fitzwilliams, the five sisters were educated at home by their father, a tutor to Edward VI. Anthony Cooke, like Knox and Lock, spent much of Mary Tudor's reign as an exile, finding his haven in Strasbourg. His daughters were well-versed in the Greek fathers of the church as well as in reformed theology. They remained firmly committed to the nonconformist branch of the English church throughout their lives and supported its cause through writing, publishing, and patronage. They were, moreover, connected by marriage to some of the most powerful families in England.

Mildred Cooke, the second wife of William Cecil, Lord Burghley and Queen Elizabeth's Lord Treasurer, translated a sermon by St. Basil from the Greek and dedicated the manuscript (BL MS Royal 17B. XVIII) to another prominent Protestant patron, Anne Seymour, the duchess of Somerset. Anne Cooke, the second wife of Sir Nicholas Bacon, the Lord Keeper of the Great Seal, and the mother of Sir Francis Bacon, allowed her translation of several Italian sermons by Bernardino Ochino to be published around 1550; like Anne Lock, her printer was John Day.[59] In 1564 her translation of John Jewel's Latin treatise, *Apologia ecclesiae anglicanae* (1562), was printed.[60] Throughout the 1570s and 1580s she illegally sheltered nonconformist preachers who had lost their licenses by refusing to

[58] For information about the Cooke sisters, see the following: Roland H. Bainton, "Feminine Piety in Tudor England," in *Christian Spirituality: Essays in Honour of Gordon Rupp*, ed. Peter Brooks (London: SCM Press, 1975), 185–201; Stephen J. Barns, "The Cookes of Gidea Hall," *The Essex Review* 21 (1912): 1–9; Pearl Hogrefe, *Women of Action in Tudor England* (Ames: Iowa State Univ. Press, 1977); Mary Ellen Lamb, "The Cooke Sisters: Attitudes toward Learned Women in the Renaissance," in *Silent But for the Word: Tudor Women as Patrons, Translators, and Writers of Religious Works*, ed. Margaret Patterson Hannay (Kent: Kent State Univ. Press, 1985), 108–25; Marjorie Keniston McIntosh, "Sir Anthony Cooke: Tudor Humanist, Educator, and Religious Reformer," *Proceedings of the American Philosophical Society* 119 (1975): 233–50; Amos C. Miller, *Sir Henry Killigrew: Elizabethan Soldier and Diplomat* (Leicester: Leicester Univ. Press, 1963); A. L. Rowse, "Bisham and the Hobys," in *Times, Persons, Places: Essays in Literature* (London: Macmillan, 1965), 188–218; Louise Schleiner, *Tudor and Stuart Women Writers* (Bloomington: Indiana Univ. Press, 1994), 30–51; Mary Bradford Whiting, "The Learned and Virtuous Lady Bacon," *The Hibbert Journal* 29 (1931): 270–83.

[59] Bernardino Ochino, *Certayne sermons of the ryghte famous and excellente clerk* (London, 1551?; STC 18766).

[60] John Jewel, *An apologie or answere in defence of the Churche of Englande* (London, 1564; STC 14591).

wear clerical robes, taking part in unauthorized prayer and preaching services, and giving improvised homilies. Elizabeth Cooke married first another Marian exile, Sir Thomas Hoby, the translator of Castiglione's *The Courtier*, and later John, Lord Russell, heir of the second Earl of Bedford, who was himself a prominent nonconformist patron. She translated Bishop John Poynet's *Dialecticon de veritate, natura, atque substantia Corporis* (1557) and wrote elegiac verses for the tombs of family members.[61] Katherine Cooke also married a Marian exile, Sir Henry Killigrew, who later became a diplomat for Queen Elizabeth. The youngest sister, Margaret Cooke, died shortly after her marriage to Sir Ralph Rowlet in 1558. As various letters attest, the surviving sisters remained in close contact with one another and continued throughout their lives to support the cause of nonconformist Protestantism in England.

Anne Lock shared similar interests with these religious activists despite differences in social rank. Her own 1560 volume of sermons and sonnets was reprinted in 1569 and 1574 by John Day although no copies remain of these two editions.[62] The Derings were particularly close to the Killigrews; Katherine carried on an extensive correspondence with Edward Dering, and in a letter dated 14 August 1575, Dering mentions how much his own wife longs to see her.[63]

There were also significant connections between Lock and the eldest Cooke sister, Mildred. In 1559 and 1560, while Knox was asking Lock for assistance in the Scottish rebellion against Mary Stuart, Mildred Cecil was also corresponding with Protestant leaders among the Scots including William Maitland, Robert Melville, and James Hamilton, the earl of Arran. Judging from the number and intensity of the letters, and their many expressions of thanks, it appears that Mildred Cecil was an effective spokesperson for the Scottish cause, at least to her husband and possibly to the queen herself.[64] Certainly the Treaty of Edinburgh, signed 6 July 1560 and negotiated chiefly by Cecil and Maitland, opened the door for the parliament of Scotland to establish Protestantism as the national religion. In addition to sharing an interest in promoting the Scottish reformation, Mildred Cecil and Anne Lock were both associated with Kather-

---

[61] Elizabeth Russell, *A way of reconciliation of a good and learned man, touching the nature, of the sacrament* (London, 1605; STC 21455).

[62] For evidence of the 1569 edition, see Andrew Maunsell, *The first part of the catalogue of English printed bookes: which concerneth divinitie* (London, 1595; STC 17669), C2^r^. For the 1574 edition see STC 4451.

[63] Edward Dering, *Certaine godly and comfortable letters* (London, 1597; STC 6683) C7^v^.

[64] Hogrefe, *Women of Action,* 22–8.

ine Brandon Bertie, the dowager duchess of Suffolk to whom Lock dedicated her first volume. William Cecil and the duchess were close friends who exchanged numerous letters. Lock's son, Henry, apparently received some of his education at the Cecil home, along with Peregrine Bertie, the duchess's youngest son.[65] In 1571, William Cecil arranged for Henry Lock to enter the service of Edward de Vere, the seventeenth Earl of Oxford and later Cecil's son-in-law. In addition to these connections, the third Cooke sister, Elizabeth, by her marriage to John Russell, was a sister-in-law to Anne Russell Dudley, the countess of Warwick and the dedicatee of Lock's second volume printed in 1590.

This nonconformist London circle also included women who, like Lock, came from the merchant class. One friend, Mistress Martin, carried letters between Dering and Lock during their courtship. She is probably the same Mrs. Martin who, along with her husband Richard, a goldsmith and master of the Mint, harbored the Puritan scholar Thomas Cartwright during his dispute with the conservative John Whitgift, then vice-chancellor of Cambridge and later archbishop of Canterbury.[66] As Edmund Grindal, the archbishop of York and later the archbishop of Canterbury, complained in a letter to Matthew Parker, Mrs. Martin also acted as "the stationer" (publishing bookseller) for the publication of Cartwright's *A replye to An answere made of M. doctor Whitgifte* (1573).[67] This book was prompted by Whitgift's scathing denunciation of an earlier pamphlet, *An admonition to the parliament* (1572), that Collinson has called "the first popular manifesto of English presbyterianism."[68] She may also be the Dorcas Martin whose prayers and catechism are included in Thomas Bentley's *The monument of matrones* (1582).[69]

Members of this nonconformist group had in common a growing disillusionment with the established church in England. Although Dering had been known as a moderate in the religious controversies of the day, such as the wearing of clerical vestments, he preached a sermon before the queen on 25 February 1570 in which he warned her against spiritual carelessness. Elizabeth took particular umbrage at being compared to "an

---

[65] Lupton, *A History of the Geneva Bible*, 8:35.

[66] Collinson, "The Role of Women," in *Godly People*, 283.

[67] William Nicholson, ed., *The Remains of Edmund Grindal* (1843; reprint, New York: Johnson Reprint, 1968), 347–8; see also A. F. Scott Pearson, *Thomas Cartwright and Elizabethan Puritanism, 1535–1603* (Cambridge: Cambridge Univ. Press, 1925), 118–9.

[68] Patrick Collinson, "John Field and Elizabethan Puritanism," in *Godly People: Essays on English Protestantism and Puritanism* (London: Hambledon Press, 1983), 339.

[69] Micheline White drew this connection to my attention.

untamed and unruly Heiffer" and canceled his preaching privileges.[70] In 1572, the Cooke sisters undertook to rehabilitate his reputation with the queen. They prepared a handsomely illustrated manuscript in Italian of Doctor Bartholo Sylva's *Giardino cosmografico coltivato.*[71] As a compendium of current scientific knowledge, the manuscript did not directly address religious issues. It was, however, dedicated to Robert Dudley, the earl of Leicester, a nonconformist patron and supporter of Dering, and introduced by numerous learned poems in various languages including some written by all four Cooke sisters, Dering, and Lock. Several poems suggest that Sylva had recently become a Protestant convert, possibly through the agency of Dering's preaching, and thus imply that the queen had been mistaken in withdrawing his permit to preach. As Louise Schleiner concludes, "The whole production was to stress without explicit statement that Dering and the reformist party supporting him [were] learned, cultivated, internationally respected, and loyal to the queen—not to be ignored."[72]

Despite the offer of the book, and Dering's own popularity in London, he was examined in May 1573 for his religious views by the Council in Star Chamber and silenced by Queen Elizabeth's command in December of that same year. Lord Burghley and Sir Nicholas Bacon, husbands of the two eldest Cooke sisters, took a leading role in his examination, although they were reluctant to silence him. Leicester himself was unable to restore Dering to the queen's favor. In a Christmas Eve letter to his brother, Dering gratefully reports that Anne had escaped detention, but he comments that "if any fall, God hath made her rich in grace and knowledge to give accompt of her doing," suggesting his confidence in her steadfast faith and ability to defend herself.[73] Edward Dering spent the rest of his life out of the public eye, fighting the tuberculosis to which he succumbed on 26 June 1576.

Sometime before 1583, Lock married Richard Prowse of Exeter, a draper or tailor, who was a man of considerable prominence; he served his city as bailiff (1563), receiver of revenues (1575), sheriff (1576), alderman (1579), and mayor (1578, 1589, 1600). He apparently shared Lock's religious commitments. While a member of Parliament in 1584, he was ap-

---

[70] Edward Dering, *Two godly sermons* ([Middelburg, 1590]; STC 6732), A5^r.

[71] CUL MS Ii.5.37, described by Schleiner, *Tudor and Stuart Women Writers*, 39–45, 256 notes 10–11.

[72] Schleiner, *Tudor and Stuart Women Writers*, 41.

[73] Dering, *Certaine godly and comfortable letters*, A5^v.

pointed to a committee that was promoting a bill to encourage appropriate sabbath observance, a reform supported by the Puritans.[74]

Although nothing is known of Anne Lock between 1576 and 1583, she may have been helping John Field, an indefatigable promoter of nonconformist causes, gather Dering's writings, which were published as collected works around 1590.[75] In 1583, Field published one of Knox's sermons, dedicating the book to "The Vertuous and my very godly friend, Mres. Anne Prouze of Exeter."[76] Field had obtained the previously unprinted sermon on Matthew 4 from Lock and apparently published it without her permission, but his dedication to her is significant. Field compliments Lock on being "no young scholler" in the school of Christ and recalls her steadfastness during the Marian exile. He also invokes her second husband, noting that he is keeping Dering's "writings, labors and letters" close at hand.[77] The dedication suggests that despite Lock's removal from London, she was still considered a prominent figure within the nonconformist community. Nor were the compliments meant as idle flattery. In much the same way that Lock, in her 1590 epistle to the Countess of Warwick, praises her patron only to remind her of greater responsibilities, Field also calls on Lock to perform her duty as a matriarch of the church. Specifically, he wishes her to share other Knoxian memorabilia, and perhaps by extension various Dering papers, with the church at large.[78] Perhaps she succumbed to this plea and gave her letters from Knox to Field. He, in turn, may have passed them on to one of the Scottish reformers such as James Carmichael, John Davidson, or James Melville, who spent some time in exile in England during 1584. From there the letters found their way to David Calderwood, the seventeenth-century Scottish historian.[79]

Lock's continued prominence within the nonconformist community is further highlighted by other events that occurred in 1583. On 1 September, Christopher Goodman, a cofounder with John Knox of the English congregation at Geneva in the 1550s and a friend of Lock's since that time, was invited to preach at St. Peter's Church in Exeter. Collinson argues that perhaps Anne Lock was instrumental in issuing the invitation to Goodman

---

[74] P. W. Hasler, ed., *The History of Parliament: The House of Commons 1558–1603*, vol. 3 (London: The History of Parliament Trust, 1981), 256.

[75] Edward Dering, *Maister Derings workes* (Middelburg, 1590?; STC 6676).

[76] John Knox, *A notable and comfortable exposition of M. John Knoxes, upon the fourth of Mathew* (London, 1583; STC 15068), A2^r. Knox apparently had sent Lock this manuscript more than twenty years earlier.

[77] Knox, *A notable and comfortable exposition,* A3^r.

[78] Knox, *A notable and comfortable exposition,* A2^v–3^r.

[79] Knox, *Works,* 6:7.

whose remarks that Sunday were certainly consistent with her own beliefs.[80] Goodman proclaimed in his sermon that religious authorities could require obedience only so far as "the Worde, and example of the godly, and of Jesus Christe our lord doth limitte and appoint."[81] He went on to be more explicit, calling for a reform of the liturgy and the Prayer Book "accordinge to the right rule of gods holy word."[82]

Meanwhile, that same month, John Whitgift became the Archbishop of Canterbury. He immediately drew up a set of articles that enforced ecclesiastical uniformity by demanding, among other things, a pledge of fidelity to *The Book of Common Prayer.* Nonconformists were outraged, and tensions escalated between the prelatical party, led by Whitgift, and the increasingly radical Puritan faction. The skirmishes escalated over the next five years, culminating in the publication of seven pamphlets signed by a pseudonymous "Martin Marprelate, Gentleman." The Marprelate Tracts (1588–89) satirically attacked the concept of the episcopacy as well as the character of particular bishops and resulted in the prosecution of many nonconformist ministers.

As Micheline White has argued, it was in the face of such pressure from the authorities that Lock made a final contribution to her religious community with the translation of Jean Taffin's *Of the Markes of the Children of God,* which was printed in 1590 by Thomas Orwin for Thomas Man.[83] A treatise that could be read as both comforting the nonconformists during a period of persecution and rebuking the established clergy for their aggressive stance against ongoing reformation, *Of the Markes* offered Lock another opportunity to promote her religious beliefs and strengthen the English Puritan movement.

Lock may have died soon after the publication of *Of the Markes*; there is no mention of her in Richard Prowse's will of 1607. She had lived, however, through the reigns of four Tudor monarchs during a time when her nation was struggling to establish its political and religious identity. As poet, translator, political activist, and committed nonconformist, Anne

---

80 Collinson, "The Role of Women," in *Godly People*, 285.

81 Albert Peel, "A Sermon of Christopher Goodman's in 1587 [sic]," *Journal of the Presbyterian Historical Society of England* 9 (1949): 85. Transcript of sermon from Huntington Library, Ellesmere MS 34/C/2, No. 34. Linda Dove provided the copy of this transcript.

82 Peel, "A Sermon," 88.

83 See Micheline White, "Renaissance Englishwomen and Religious Translations: The Case of Anne Lock's *Of the markes of the children of God*," *English Literary Renaissance* 29 (forthcoming).

Lock played her part in that struggle, aligning herself to the end with the cause of reformed Protestantism in England.

Works

Although separated by thirty years, Anne Vaughan Lock's two books, *Sermons of John Calvin, upon the songe that Ezechias made after he had bene sicke, and afflicted by the hand of God, conteyned in the 38. Chapiter of Esay* (1560) and *Of the markes of the children of God, and of their comforts in afflictions* (1590), are remarkably similar. Each is an octavo volume, and each begins with a dedicatory epistle to a prominent Protestant noblewoman, continues with the translation of a French text that elucidates the meaning of suffering for true believers, and concludes with a poetic work. Lock also wrote a short Latin poem that is included in a manuscript dedicated to the earl of Leicester (1572).

Anne Lock wrote under the names A. L. (*Sermons of John Calvin)*, Anna Dering (Latin manuscript poem), and Anne Prowse (*Of the Markes*). The spelling of "Lock" is uncertain, given the vagaries of sixteenth-century orthography. The only contemporary witness, the inscription in the London copy of the *Sermons of John Calvin*, does give the family name as "Lock." The Knox letters variously call her Anne Lock, Anna Lock, and Anna Locke, but, given their transmission history, they are of little value in determining her own preference. Historians have generally called her Anne Locke, while recent literary scholars tend toward Anne Lok, perhaps in an attempt to connect her with her son whose name is usually spelled Henry Lok. My decision to call her Anne Vaughan Lock in the title of the present volume acknowledges her birth family and primary authorial identity and accedes to the authority of the 1560 inscription.[84]

The Epistle to the Duchess of Suffolk

The dedicatory epistle that introduces the 1560 volume develops a familiar religious conceit: the soul, diseased by sin and oppressed by despair,

[84] For "Locke," see Patrick Collinson and most biographies of John Knox. For "Lok," see Margaret P. Hannay, " 'Unlock my lipps': the *Miserere mei Deus* of Anne Vaughan Lok and Mary Sidney Herbert, Countess of Pembroke," in *Privileging Gender in Early Modern England,* ed. Jean R. Brink, Sixteenth Century Essays and Studies 23 (Kirksville, Mo.: Sixteenth Century Journal Publishers, 1993), 19–36; Susanne Woods, "The Body Penitent: A 1560 Calvinist Sonnet Sequence," *American Notes and Queries* 5 (1992): 137–40. For "Lock," see Michael R. G. Spiller, *The Development of the Sonnet: An Introduction* (London and New York: Routledge, 1992), 92–3.

can be healed only through the application of God's medicinal word. The epistle is addressed to Katherine Willoughby Brandon Bertie, the dowager duchess of Suffolk (1520–1580), a Marian exile herself and an important patroness of Protestant literature.[85] *Sermons of John Calvin* was one of fourteen books dedicated to the duchess, many of them printed by John Day.[86] Lock's own work was certainly congruent with the reformist agendas of both her dedicatee and her printer. She may even have known the duchess personally: their sons, Peregrine Bertie and Henry Lock, were later acquaintances and perhaps friends, having been educated together at the home of the duchess's friend, William Cecil.

The epistle itself demands special attention for the insights it gives into Lock's own literary style and the flexibility of mid-century nonconformist literature. Despite her unswerving commitment to reformed and anti-Papist sentiments, Lock's epistle is not iconoclastic. In both its allegorical use of biblical materials and conservative rhetoric, it remains firmly embedded in the tradition of English devotional writings. Yet, at the same time, Lock demonstrates an easy familiarity with the medical ideas of her day, as well as a determination to look encouragingly into the future of a new England, made spiritually healthy by the application of true doctrine. Although she was unable as a woman to hold an official position either in the state or in the church, Lock betrays no sense of powerlessness but rather writes with a confident authorial hand. Along with other mid-sixteenth-century nonconformist writers, she is engaged in the process of working out a Protestant aesthetic that is intimately connected with the orthodox Christian tradition even as it forges a sense of its own identity.

Lock's choice of vocabulary in the epistle is, in many ways, unremarkable. As befits an author dedicated to the reformed cause, she consistently employs words favored by the Protestant writers who preceded her. Roman Catholics are "papistes" (line 99) who abandon the clear teaching of God's word for "superfluous workes" and "devised service" (lines 101, 103), while Protestants are "trewe belevyng Christians" (line 72) or "th'elect" (line 96) who find their hope in "Gods holye testament" (line

---

[85] For further discussion of the duchess's patronage, see John N. King, *English Reformation Literature: The Tudor Origins of the Protestant Tradition* (Princeton: Princeton Univ. Press, 1982), 105–6 and "Patronage and Piety: The Influence of Catherine Parr," in *Silent But for the Word: Tudor Women as Patrons, Translators, and Writers of Religious Works*, ed. Margaret Patterson Hannay (Kent: Kent State Univ. Press, 1985), 55–9.

[86] For a list of books dedicated to the duchess, see Franklin B. Williams, Jr., *Index of Dedications and Commendatory Verses in English Books before 1641* (London: Bibliographical Society, 1962), 23.

139) and his "eternall decree" (line 181). Conversely, a single lexical choice alerts us to the fact that even ardent nonconformity flowed in channels that were deeply hewn by the traditional religion of the English medieval church. As Lock describes the horror of a soul cast into hell through misplaced trust in Roman Catholic doctrine, she alludes to the parable of the rich man and Lazarus recorded in Luke 16:19–31: "they which taught him to trust of salvation by mans devises have set his burnyng hert in that place of flames, where th'everlasting Chaos suffreth no droppe of Godes mercye to descende" (lines 114–116). In the Vulgate, the unbridgeable breach between heaven and hell that prevents Lazarus from offering even a drop of water to the tormented rich man is translated *chaos magnum* from the Greek *mega chasma*. Lock transliterates the Latin *chaos* and adds her own adjectival description: it is not merely a great chaos, but an everlasting chaos that separates heaven from hell. Lock's fidelity to the Latin text may be contrasted with her compatriots' decisions not to follow the Vulgate's rendition of *mega chasma* in their vernacular translations. Wyclif translates the term as "derke place," Tyndale as "greate space," and the Genevan scholars as "great gulfe," adding "swallowing pit" as a marginal reading. Lock's echo of the Vulgate is not an isolated example, and it is indicative of the continuity her epistle retains with the patristic and medieval tradition of exhortation.

If Lock's religious vocabulary reflects that of a nonconformist molded by the catholic Christian tradition, her medical vocabulary is impressively contemporary. The entire dedicatory epistle develops the conceit of a diseased mind restored to health through the action of the heavenly physician. While the notion that good words provide good medicine was an ancient trope, both classical and biblical, Lock's reworking of this material shows a knowledge not just of conventional formulations but of recent medical developments as well. The most striking example of this awareness occurs in her discussion of scorpion's oil. Alluding to the fact that God both causes and cures spiritual disease, she remarks that "beyng stong with the stinge of the scorpion [the believer] knoweth howe with oyle of the same scorpion to be healed agayne" (lines 126–128). This brief comment embraces numerous traditions, including Pliny's observation, frequently reiterated, that a scorpion's sting can be cured only by recourse to its own flesh and Augustine's comment on Numbers 21:4–9 that God cured "death by death" by means of the brass serpent.[87] The more imme-

---

[87] Pliny, *Natural History*, 29.29. Edited and translated by W. H. S. Jones, Loeb Classical Library (Cambridge: Harvard Univ. Press, 1963), 8:242–3; William Turner, *A new booke of spirituall physik for dyverse diseases of the nobilite and gentlemen of Eng-*

diate source for Lock's observation, however, is probably the unusual woodcut on the title page of the 1557 Geneva Psalter that shows a skull topped by a palm branch (a symbol of life) and resting on a scorpion (Fig. 1).[88] The bordering inscription, *MORS MORTIS MEDICINA ET VICTORIA* [Death is death's cure and conqueror], reminds the reader that the cure for death lies in death itself.

The reference to oil of scorpion, however, comes directly from contemporary medicine. The distillation of curative oils was recent medical technology in the mid-sixteenth century, embraced not only by Paracelsan but by Galenic pharmacologists as well, and imported from the Continent to England.[89] Conrad Gesner's popular *Thesaurus euonymus philiatri* (1555) provided drawings of distilling "furnaces" as part of a project to reform the art of pharmacology, and the 1559 English translation by Peter Morwyng devoted five pages to recipes for and uses of scorpion oil.[90] Although it is not possible to uncover the original source of Lock's introduction to oil of scorpion, many Protestants championed the vernacular-writing Paracelsus and the new chemical experiments as complementary to their own religious reformation, even before Robert Bostocke's defense of this view in *The difference betwene the auncient phisicke, and the latter phisicke* (1585).[91]

---

lande ([Emden], 1555; STC 24361), M2^r; Augustine, *The City of God*, 10.8. Translated by Marcus Dods, The Nicene and Post-Nicene Fathers, First Series, vol. 2. Edited by Philip Schaff (1886; reprint, Grand Rapids, MI: Eerdmans, 1993), 185. Tilley does not record the use of "oil of scorpion" until 1634, S153.

88 *The psalmes of David tr. accordyng to th'Ebrue, wyth annotacions moste profitable* (Geneva, 1557; STC 2383.6). Lupton identifies the "Death of Death" device as a mark used by the Genevan printers Conrad Badius and Michel Blanchier; Lupton, *A History of the Geneva Bible*, 4:74.

89 For a discussion of the rediscovery of distillation techniques in the sixteenth century, see R. J. Forbes, *Short History of the Art of Distillation* (Leiden: E. J. Brill, 1948). *The vertuose boke of distyllacyon* (London, 1527; STC 13435), a translation of Hieronymus von Brunschweig's 1512 *Liber de arte distillandi*, was one of the earliest books in English on the art of distillation.

90 *The treasure of Euonymus, conteyninge the secretes of nature, to destyl medicines* (London, 1559; STC 11800), BB3^r–CC1^r.

91 For an example of Protestant interest in the new medicine, see William Bullein, *A newe booke entituled the governement of healthe* (London, 1558; STC 4039). For further discussions see Charles Webster, "Alchemical and Paracelsian medicine," in *Health, medicine and mortality in the sixteenth century*, ed. Charles Webster (Cambridge: Cambridge Univ. Press, 1979), 301–34; Catherine Cole Mambretti, "William Bullein and the 'Lively Fashions' in Tudor Medical Literature," *Clio Medica* 9 (1974): 285–97.

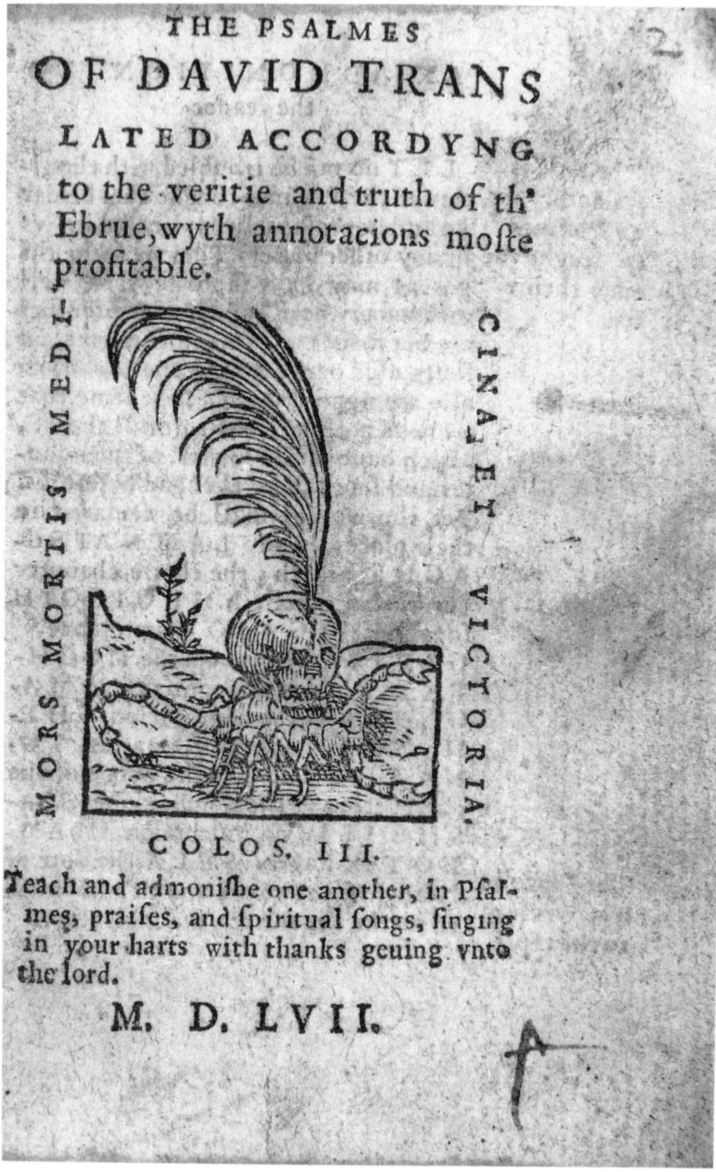

THE PSALMES
OF DAVID TRANS
LATED ACCORDYNG
to the veritie and truth of th'
Ebrue, wyth annotacions moſte
profitable.

MORS MORTIS MEDI- CINA, ET VICTORIA.

COLOS. III.
Teach and admoniſhe one another, in Pſalmes, praiſes, and ſpiritual ſongs, ſinging in your harts with thanks geuing vnto the lord.

M. D. LVII.

Figure 1. Title page from the Genevan translation of the Psalms (1557).

Oil of scorpion, however, is not the only evidence that Lock was familiar with contemporary medical practice. She accurately uses many medical terms: "receipt" (recipe or prescription), compound, "well drawynge" plasters, diet, conserve (an innovative remedy concocted from plant parts preserved with sugar), "lyvely moisture," humors. References to the Galenic humors and to the new chemically distilled remedies reflect the eclectic and essentially pragmatic nature of English medical practice at this time, although it may be significant that, for Lock, the more traditional humors are associated with Roman Catholic disorders. In four cases, her medical usage is either the earliest *OED* reference or predates the earliest citation by more than twenty years. She describes inadequate dressings as those that "so overheale the wounde that it festreth and breaketh oute afreshe" (lines 62–63), the first documented use of "overheale" as a verb. In the context of decrying papist medicine, Lock calls it "unholsome stuffe" (line 104). While "stuff" can be used generically to mean simply "material," it seems here to indicate liquid medicine, particularly in light of its subsequent designation as medicine "to drincke" (line 113) or as "poisonous potions" (line 120).[92] The emphasis on the deleterious effects of an evil liquid medicine may reflect the reformed antipathy toward the presumed salvific benefits of the Roman Catholic mass. Later, in describing physical illness, Lock uses two common terms—fits and passions—but then adds a third, "alterations" (line 146), which by the seventeenth century was an accepted synonym for distempers.[93] Finally, she also uses the word "prescribeth" (lines 189–190) in its technical sense as ordering a medicine.[94]

In addition to these terms, when Lock designates God as the physician and Calvin as the apothecary, she acknowledges two of the three official categories of medical practitioners (physicians, surgeons, apothecaries) and correctly ranks them according to the accepted hierarchy of the day. But of even greater interest is her comment that cures are formulated either by "skilfull men by arte, or honest neyghbours havyng gathered . . . by theyr owne experiment" (lines 36–38). Here Lock seems to make a distinction between university-educated doctors with their liberal arts curriculum and

---

[92] The *OED* gives the first medical citation as occurring in Shakespeare's *Cymbeline*, 5.5.255 (1611; first folio STC 22273); see *OED* "stuff" *sb.*[1] III 6b.

[93] The earliest *OED* citation is from Robert Burton's *The anatomy of melancholy* (1621; STC 4159); see *OED* "alteration" 3.

[94] The earliest *OED* citation is taken from book two of George Pettie's translation, *The civile conversation of M. Steeven Guazzo* (1581; STC 12422), although Turner had earlier used the term in his *A new booke of spirituall physik* (1555), K1[v]; see *OED* "prescribe" 3a.

the nonbaccalaureate practitioners, who maintained a strong presence in London as well as in the countryside throughout the sixteenth century.[95] An act of 1512 required physicians without a university degree to be licensed by the bishop of the diocese in which they practiced (or, in London, by the dean of St. Paul's) in consultation with four degreed doctors, although evidence indicates that the law was imperfectly enforced. Another act of 1542, however, specifically recognized the medical competence of unlicensed men and women and allowed them to practice as long as they refrained from charging fees for their work.[96] Lock tellingly designates such practitioners as honest neighbors rather than using the more opprobrious term, "empirics."

Lock probably provided medical care for her friends and family. Her own maternal uncle, John Gwynnethe, was noted for his medical expertise despite the fact that he was not a licensed physician.[97] There was certainly no social stigma attached to such activity, and upper-class women seem regularly to have dispensed advice and treatments to members of their communities. Furthermore, throughout the sixteenth century significant numbers of women practiced as both licensed and unlicensed physicians as well as midwives.[98] For instance, in 1568 two women were licensed for surgery, one by the bishop of Exeter and one by the bishop of Norwich. In the former case, this was one of only two licenses granted in the diocese during the entire year. Also, women often were paid by the parish to provide medical attention to the poor.[99]

Whatever Lock's official status as a practitioner, her lexical choices indicate a knowledge of contemporary medicine, and they also illustrate her skill in developing overlapping medical and theological arguments. Her rhetorical strategies, similarly, demonstrate a skilled authorial voice as shown in the design of the dedicatory epistle and in her use of balanced constructions, affective language, and well-developed images.

---

[95] For a further discussion of doctors and practitioners, see Margaret Pelling and Charles Webster, "Medical practitioners," in *Health, medicine and mortality in the sixteenth century*, ed. Charles Webster (Cambridge: Cambridge Univ. Press, 1979), 165–235.

[96] F. N. L. Poynter, "The Influence of Government Legislation on Medical Practice in Britain" in *The Evolution of Medical Practice in Britain*, ed. F. N. L. Poynter (London: Pitman Medical, 1961), 9.

[97] Brewer, *Letters and Papers*, 8:no. 300.

[98] Pelling and Webster, "Medical practitioners," 182–8; 222–3; 233–5.

[99] For a further discussion of women practitioners, see R. M. S. McConaghey, "The History of Rural Medical Practice," in *The Evolution of Medical Practice in Britain*, ed. F. N. L. Poynter (London: Pitman Medical, 1961), 124–6.

The epistle, arranged in three parts, begins with a pair of tightly constructed scenes. On the one hand, Lock draws a picture of those who suffer from poverty, adversity, and sickness but, because their minds are "armed and fournished with prepared patience" neither give in to such calamities nor even stoop to be miserable (lines 6–13). This picture might very well remind the duchess of her own recent exile during the reign of Mary Tudor. On the other hand, Lock evokes a contrary image of those who, while peaceful, healthy, and seemingly blessed in every way, nevertheless are vexed by even the smallest disagreeable changes in their circumstances. From these two scenes, Lock concludes that diseases find their root cause not in the body but in the mind (or soul, two terms that she uses interchangeably) and, therefore, that the physician who can cure the mind deserves more thanks than the one who cures only the body.

With her initial exemplum firmly in place, Lock now offers her little book to the duchess in a striking chiastic structure that demands her patron's thanks (and possibly a material reward) but then diffuses that payment into a graceful compliment. The physician who offers the curative recipe is none other than God himself, says Lock. But God works both through an earthly apothecary, John Calvin, and through an assistant, Lock herself, who has put the cure "into an Englishe box" that is presented to "you" (lines 48–49). In the space between that final "you" and the "My" of the following sentence, the duchess, having been so well instructed, presumably expresses her gratitude. Lock, however, immediately begins both to accept and to disperse this thanks as she retreats in a chiastic motion away from the duchess towards herself, Calvin, and, finally, God himself. For herself, "My thankes are taken away and drowned by the greate excesse of duetie that I owe you" (lines 49–50). Having thus canceled the duchess's gratitude with her own debt, Lock also dismisses the thanks owed to the preacher, claiming that Calvin only desires people to use the medicine he has compounded. Although she directs patronage away from the human benefactors, Lock admits that the duchess does owe gratitude to one person, the heavenly physician. But since he can never be recompensed for his pains, being owed continual thanks, the patron is transformed into a devout petitioner, a position that, Lock gracefully adds, the duchess already exemplifies by her godly life. Although Lock presents herself modestly as the mere packager of the verbal medicine, her rhetorical moves are powerful: she rather audaciously demands patronage, but then promptly redistributes it. Furthermore, by relieving the duchess of obligations to herself and Calvin, but redirecting her more firmly to God, Lock verbally creates a community of spiritual equals comprised of administrator, apothecary, and patient who together owe their allegiance to God and his curative word.

The second part of the dedication continues to exhibit Lock's confident sense of design as she develops the conceit of illness by introducing two biblical exemplars, Hezekiah and David. Although she focuses on Hezekiah, the subject of Calvin's sermons, the reference to David surely anticipates the sonnet sequence. The true debilitating illness from which both kings suffered, and which Lock recognizes as a contemporary and pestilent ailment, is not physical, but spiritual: the fear that since God hates sin and is a just God, he must also hate those whose sin he so justly punishes with suffering. This spiritual despair, Lock recognizes, "is daungerous and hard to be cured" because all the elements of the syllogism are, in fact, true. God is just and he does hate sin; even true believers are sinners and they do suffer (lines 88–99). The logic, however, is incomplete and the missing element is precisely the crucial ingredient in the effective medicine that she offers: a sense of "the determined providence of almyghtie God, whiche ordreth and disposeth all thynges to the best to them that truste in him" (lines 69–71). As Lock goes on to argue at some length, despair is cured not by trusting in the false medicine of good works that the Papists offer but in the assurance of God's purpose "that whome God hath from eternitie appointed to live, shal never die, howsoever sicknesse threaten" (lines 130–132).

As Lock concludes her dedication, she returns, in the third part, to the efficacy of her own "litle boke" in administering the medicine of God's providence to those suffering from spiritual despair. Her book, she claims, not only contains the medicine "brought from the plentifull shop and storehouse of Gods holye testament," but also provides an example both of the disease and of the cure (lines 138–143).

In addition to its careful design, Lock's preface offers ample evidence of a skilled and confident author who effectively exploits the power of balanced constructions, affective language, and developed images.

One sophisticated use of balanced construction is illustrated in the chiastically arranged delivery of medicine from God to the duchess and of thanks from the duchess to God. Similarly, Lock has a penchant for constructing sentences that are balanced in twos and threes. For instance, the calm soul is nevertheless "oppressed with povertie, tossed with worldlye adversitye, tourmented with payne" (lines 7–8). This set of three phrases is not uncommon for Lock: the unholy trinity set against the true physician is composed of the philosopher, infidel, and papist (lines 65–66). But near-tautological doublets, that is, the coupling of nearly synonymous words, are even more widespread, as illustrated by the italicized pairs in the following sentence:

> He knoweth that his safetie is much more surely reposed in Gods moste *stedfast and unchangeable* purpose, and in the most

> *strong and almightye* hande of the *alknowynge and alworking* God, than in the *wavering will and feble weaknes* of man. (lines 133–136)

Lock's use of doublets, along with the periodicity of her sentences, argues for the deliberate employment of a conservative, traditional rhetoric, but one that is pressed into the service of an ardent Protestantism.[100] She does not enrich the semantic range of English by pairing an older word with a newer one, but rather uses the doublets for rhythmic and rhetorical balance. The effectiveness of her language is demonstrated by a single sentence (Table 1) in which the author enacts the despair of the sick man, piling up the symptoms of his distress into an overwhelming heap, before concluding, "alas what helpe remaineth in this extremitie?" (lines 98–99).

Lock is able to create the effect of despair precisely because she knows how to handle her rhetorical figures: grammatically parallel clauses (*parison*) tumble over each other without either intervening conjunctions (*asyndeton*) or the calming effect of near-tautological doublets; a sense of doom is engendered by anaphoric repetition ("no soundnes, no strength, no helpe"); the antitheses are multiplied (man/God; strength/weakness; grace/wound); exactly parallel clauses (*isocolon*) emphasize the spiritual cause of the illness ("that God's displeasure hath laide upon him/that Gods anger hath left in his conscience"). Yet these tropes and schemes are not used mechanically but in the service of an affective and sensuous rhetoric. As the sick one feels, hears, and sees his weakened condition, so the reader is drawn into, and wearied by, the sentence itself. The inconclusive triad of participles at the end leads only to the damning perplexity of the final question, "alas what helpe remaineth in this extremitie?" Instead of giving a positive answer, however, Lock increases the affective tension by leaving the anguished patient dangling in distress while she goes on to describe in intricate detail the nature and effects of the bad medicine that Papists have to offer.

This sensual image of desperate illness is only one of many that Lock uses to develop her central conceit—that the medicine offered by her book will cure suffering souls. It is not simply that good doctrine is good medicine, but that this medicine comes tangibly to a sick soul through the efforts of a heavenly physician who writes a formula, an earthly pharmacist who mixes it, and a loving servant who packages it in an appropriate box. The reader is not told merely that Hezekiah is a good example but

---

[100] For a discussion of the pervasive use of doublings in the fourteenth and fifteenth centuries, see Janel M. Mueller, *The Native Tongue and the Word: Developments in English Prose Style 1380–1580* (Chicago: Univ. of Chicago Press, 1984), 147–61.

Table 1. Sentence from *Sermons of John Calvin* (1560), A4^{v}.

For when the wretched man

findyng all helpe of man not able to uphold him from perishing,

being striken with the mightie hande of God,

feleth him selfe unable to stande,

no soundnes in his bodye,

no strength in his limmes,

no helpe of nature

to resist the violence of that disease

that Gods displeasure hath laide upon him,

seeth no signe of Gods grace in his soule,

but the deep woundes

that Gods anger hath left in his conscience,

perceiveth no token

to argue him

th'elect of God and

partaker of the death of his Saviour,

hearyng pronounced that the soule which sinneth shall die,

knowyng him selfe to have sinned, and

felying him selfe dying:

alas what helpe remaineth in this extremitie?

is made to feel him "nowe fresing, now fryeng," to see his "gastly eyen, starynge wyth horrour" and his "white and blodles hand" reaching up toward heaven and even to hear his gasping "unperfect soundes" (lines 158, 164, 168, 170). In each case, Lock develops her images into a presence that can be physically experienced.

This imagistic skill is also demonstrated by her use of biblical allusions, particularly the way in which she links the concept of spiritual cure with three examples of medicinal oil. In the first allusion, she compares the Roman Catholic doctrine of supererogation, that is the attributing of the superfluous good works of the saints to those less godly, to the parable of the virgins' oil in Matthew 25:1–13 (lines 99–105). In that story, the five foolish virgins forget to bring an extra supply of oil as they await the return of the bridegroom at midnight. When their lamps go out, they beg oil of the five wise virgins but are rebuffed because "there wil not be ynough for us and you," and so are left weeping in darkness while the wise virgins go in to enjoy the wedding feast. Although the biblical oil is fuel rather than medicine, the allusion to this parable succinctly illustrates Lock's point. At one stroke she consigns Papists to outer darkness, points out the foolishness of their doctrine that promises a cure but provides only an empty container, and labels those who offer a false medicine as "papisticall soulesleaers [soulslayers]" (line 104).

As she moves from the negative example to the positive in the next paragraph, however, Lock offers a counter example of oil, this time the homeopathic medicine of the scorpion's oil that heals its own sting. Although Lock does not make a specific allusion to a biblical text, the conjunction of scorpion and snake in Deuteronomy 8:15 and Luke 10:19, the repeated reference to raising up, and the emphatic conclusion that God provides both judgment and pardon, all point to Numbers 21:4–9. In that account, God punishes the Israelites for their disbelief by sending fiery serpents that sting them to death. The Israelites' only hope of relief comes from looking up at a brass serpent that Moses raises on a pole. In an exegetical tradition beginning with the Wisdom of Solomon 16:6–7, this serpent was recognized as a symbol of salvation and was explicitly identified with the crucified Christ in John 3:14–15. Although none of the biblical texts mentions oil, Lock's conjunction of a recent medical discovery with the scriptural tradition neatly links the christological salvific cure with the oil available only to the faithful virgins but falsely promised by a doctrine of good works.

Christ as the heavenly physician, as well as the link between the Old Testament and the New Testament, is confirmed by Lock's third and final image of oil. Looking at Hezekiah returned to health, she says,

> we se the heavenly Physician anoynt him with the merciful Samaritans oyle, purge the oppressing humors with true repentaunce, strengthen his stomack with the holsome conserve of Gods eternall decree, and expell his disease, and set hym on foote with assured faith of Gods mercy, and staieng his yet unstedy pace and foltring legges with the swete promyses of Gods almyghtye goodnes. (lines 178–184)

Drawing on the parable of the good Samaritan (Luke 10:25–37), traditionally seen as an image of Christ, she re-enacts its story in the life of Hezekiah as she visualizes him anointed with oil, fed the life-giving wine, and set, not on a donkey, but on his own feet again by the power of God. With the conjunction of these three images of healing oil, Lock, in an amazingly compact space, not only develops her own conceit of the heavenly medicine, but also explicates a reformation doctrine of salvation that emphasizes the effective and affective nature of God's providence and grace.

Although this dedicatory epistle displays an impressive grasp of *inventio*, *dispositio*, and *elocutio* as Lock gathers her materials and deploys them artfully, there is no doubt that she marshals this rhetorical skill in order to present the truth plainly. Yet Lock's imaginatively developed analogy of the three medicinal oils contradicts Calvin's treatment of the same New Testament texts in his commentaries. In the case of the virgins' oil, Calvin insists that the text simply asserts the need for unwearying perseverance and decries the "great ingenuity over the lanterns, the vessels, the oil."[101] Even more forcibly, Calvin objects to embellishments of the Good Samaritan parable including the

> allegory which has won such regard that nearly everyone comes down in its favour like an oracle. In this, they make out the Samaritan to be Christ, because He is our protector: they say that wine mixed with oil was poured into the wound because Christ heals us with repentance and the promise of grace. . . . Anyone may see that these speculations have been cooked up by meddlers, quite divorced from the mind of Christ.[102]

This stripping of allegorization is one element of the Protestant plain style, yet Lock apparently sees no conflict between the styles of her epistle and translation (or even Calvin's own theory of sacred rhetoric) since both are

---

[101] John Calvin, *A Harmony of the Gospels: Matthew, Mark and Luke*, vol. 3 of *Calvin's New Testament Commentaries,* trans. A. W. Morrison and ed. David W. Torrance and Thomas F. Torrance (Grand Rapids, Mi.: Eerdmans, 1972), 110.

[102] Calvin, *A Harmony of the Gospels*, 39.

used for the same end, to draw believers to God.

Thus, with self-assured skill, Lock gathers a number of diverse elements into her "litle boke": references to contemporary medicine and everyday life, biblical allusions knitted together by a common metaphor into a short narrative, a plain translation of plain sermons about the plain biblical text, and a set of intensely personal devotional lyrics. While these cannot be limited to a single rhetorical paradigm, they do share a set of common assumptions: that God speaks, primarily in his word but also in the world, that one's first responsibility is to hear the word of God and be drawn to him, and that the goal of religion is not simply knowledge of, but love for and obedience to, God. Theological precision, however, does not result in generic rigidity. Indeed, Lock's stylistic flexibility complements the range of Protestant writing in this period, which includes English and Latin dramas, historiography and hagiography, and metrical paraphrases, to mention just a few genres.

Furthermore, although she firmly excludes Roman Catholics, Lock just as clearly constitutes a new community beginning with the duchess, Calvin, and herself, that extends outward to embrace all those who acknowledge God's providence in their lives. Although she may use traditional materials (Ciceronian periodicity, the appeal to patronage, allegorical moral tales), she consistently shapes the genre to conform to her own reformed sensibilities. In the same way, newer modes of cultural exchange (distilled medicine, plain sermons, sonnet form) are engaged not for their novelty but for their appropriateness. Indeed, Lock takes her place among the generation of nonconformists who, by reforming genres and providing a fresh gloss for the vernacular scriptures, were consciously creating a new consensual community.

Sermons on Isaiah 38

John Calvin preached four sermons on the song of Hezekiah found in Isaiah 38 on Friday and Saturday, 5 and 6 November 1557 and on Monday and Tuesday, 15 and 16 November 1557. Lock herself was in Geneva at this time, having arrived the previous May.

From 1549 through 1560, Denis Raguenier, a professional stenographer, recorded Calvin's sermons as he spoke, taking down approximately six thousand words an hour in his own carefully designed shorthand system. These notes were later transcribed into a longhand manuscript from which additional copies were made and circulated.[103] The printed French

[103] For a further discussion of the transcriptions, see T. H. L. Parker, *Calvin's Preaching* (Louisville, Ky.: Westminster/John Knox Press, 1992), 65–71.

edition of these sermons, with minor revisions to the transcribed manuscript version, was published in 1562.[104] According to the editors of the manuscript, there are 450 variants between the manuscript version and the printed edition, most of which involve improvements in grammar or style. A few variants indicate the use of direct speech or correct biblical citations. Only ten slightly change the meaning of the text itself, suggesting "a desire to give a warmer message than is found in the manuscript" or "to insinuate a slightly more optimistic colouring."[105] Lock apparently made her translation from an early copy of the revision, since her text almost always follows the 1562 edition rather than the manuscript version when there is a difference between the two; the eleven instances where Lock follows the 1557 manuscript all occur in the first two sermons and are indicated in the textual notes.

Lock invokes the notion of plainness in the dedicatory epistle to explain her philosophy of translation: "Concernyng my translation of this boke, it may please you to understand that I have rendred it so nere as I possibly might, to the very wordes of his text, and that in so plaine Englishe as I could expresse" (lines 202–204). Her translation does exhibit a scrupulosity about following the original as closely as possible, often preferring, for instance, to transliterate the French. For example, on a single page the following cognates occur: *glorifié*/glorified, *estendre*/extende, *abolie*/abolished, *ordonnez*/ordeined, *estat*/estate, *declarant*/declaryng (The First Sermon, lines 9, 11, 14, 16). In seeking a close, literal translation, Lock was following the precedent for translating the Bible established by Wyclif and Purvey in the fourteenth century and Calvin's own expressed preference for plain speech.[106] Furthermore, the English appreciation for Calvin was predicated precisely upon what was perceived as his fidelity to scripture and clarity of language. Thus, for instance, Rouland Hall, printer of a 1561 volume of sermons, commends Calvin's writings to the English reader because their matter is worthy, the style is plain and simple, and the scriptures are handled reverently, thereby showing their power "when it is most naked and bare and void of that painted sheathe that men would

---

[104] The 1562 printed edition is found in John Calvin, "Sermons sur le Cantique D'Ezechias," in *Joannis Calvini Opera Quae Supersunt Omnia*, ed. G. Baum, E. Cunitz, and E. Reuss, vol. 35 (Brunswick: Schwetschke, 1887), 525–80; the manuscript version is found in John Calvin, *Sermons sur le Livre d'Esaïe Chapitres 30–41*, ed. Francis M. Higman, Thomas H. L. Parker, and Lewis Thorpe, Supplementa Calviniana III (Neukirchen-Vluyn: Neukerchener Verlag des Erziehungsvereins, 1995), 412–48.

[105] Higman, Parker, and Thorpe, *Sermons*, xviii–xix.

[106] For a discussion of Wycliffe's translation principles, see David Norton, *A History of the Bible as Literature*, vol. 1 (Cambridge: Cambridge Univ. Press, 1993), 78–84.

put upon it."[107] Yet Hall, like Lock, praises simplicity with an elegant image: "all his sermons seme nothyng els but the swete licour of the scriptures and lively word of god set furth before our eyes in Christalline vessels."[108]

Calvin's expositions on Isaiah already enjoyed a substantial connection with the English church. In 1550, Calvin dedicated the first edition of his Latin commentary on Isaiah to Edward VI, challenging the young king to restore the church to its pristine condition by following God's instructions as given through his prophet. Ten years later, Calvin dedicated the revised commentary to Elizabeth I in honor of her accession to the throne, again reminding a new monarch of her duty to restore the Protestant church and especially to welcome home the exiles who had fled England during Mary Tudor's reign.

As one of those returning exiles, Lock had good reasons for choosing to translate this particular set of sermons from Isaiah. They centered around King Hezekiah, a popular reformation hero, who was often praised for destroying the brass serpent that had degenerated from a source of healing to an object of adoration. The reformers saw a parallel between the brass serpent, which had originally been sanctioned by God, and certain religious practices and artifacts that had lost their spiritual meaning. Thus, the first *Forme of Prayers*, developed by the English congregation at Geneva, specifically cited Hezekiah as a precedent for breaking with the "idolatrie" fostered by the Roman Catholic church:

> For if Ezechias was commended by the holy ghoste, for breaking in pieces the brasen serpent, which Moses had erected by gods commandement, and now had continued above 800. yeres, which thing of it self was not evell, but rather put men in remembrance of gods benefit: yet becawse it began to minister occasion to the people to committ idolatrie was not to be borne withall: how muche more oght we to take heed, that through our occasion men committ not idolatrie with their owne imaginations and phantasies?[109]

Yet the sermons from Isaiah 38 focus on Hezekiah's failures and afflictions rather than on his triumphs. As a hero who nevertheless found

---

[107] John Calvin, *Four godlye sermons agaynst the pollution of idolatries, comforting men in persecutions* (London, 1561; STC 4438), A2^{r}.

[108] Calvin, *Four godlye sermons*, A2^{v}.

[109] *The forme of prayers and ministration of the sacraments, etc. used in the Englishe congregation at Geneva: and approved, by J. Calvyn* (Geneva, 1556; STC 16561), A6^{v}–A7^{r}.

himself in need of repentance and God's grace, Hezekiah provided Lock with the requisite model for a Protestant England newly emerging from the turmoil of Mary's reign into the (as yet unformed and unstable) Elizabethan age. While there was reason to hope that the nation, like Hezekiah, would be restored to full health, there was no room for complacency.

Several themes run throughout the sermons, usually taking the form of paired truths. On the one hand, Hezekiah's illness can be traced to his own sin, for which he is justly punished. On the other hand, his illness is ordained by a loving Lord not as reproof but as a means of teaching the king how to trust in God. Similarly, although suffering causes believers to see their own failures more clearly, it also brings them closer to God as they recognize their utter dependence on him and his unfailing mercy towards them. The temptation, to which Hezekiah almost succumbs, is to fall into despair when faced with affliction. But, again, Christians are brought back to a double truth: suffering is a humbling experience, but it does not drive a true believer to despair; rather, it forces him or her into the arms of God, the loving heavenly father.

Lock interweaves these themes, as well as other details from the sermons, into her epistle to the duchess of Suffolk. The dominant medical imagery of the epistle is, of course, consonant with the tenor of Hezekiah's song, but it is also specifically linked to Isaiah's application of a plaster of figs to the king's body at the conclusion of the song (The Fourth Sermon, lines 423–465). In the sermon, the prophet Isaiah administers God's medicine to the sick king; in the epistle, the "prophet" Calvin and his assistant, Lock herself, offer the same medicinal word, now placed in "an Englishe box," to a nation desperately in need of its curative powers. Furthermore, Lock's contrast between the good medicine of God's word and the unwholesome medicine of the Papists develops Calvin's own blast against works of supererogation (The Thirde Sermon, lines 436–441).

The sonnets that follow also appear to draw on the sermons. Although Calvin only briefly mentions Psalm 51 (The Fourth Sermon, lines 100–101), he consistently links Hezekiah with David throughout all four sermons. More importantly, both the second and the third sermons develop at length the imagery of a trial in which God appears as a terrifying, but ultimately merciful, judge with Hezekiah as the penitent, and almost despairing, plaintiff. As Calvin notes in the third sermon, it is appropriate that we contemplate our own position before God as adumbrated in this courtroom scene. The opening five sonnets, which preface the paraphrase of Psalm 51, provide just such a meditation.

Sonnets on Psalm 51

The 1560 volume concludes with a twenty-one sonnet paraphrase on Psalm 51 prefaced by five introductory sonnets. Together the twenty-six poems comprise the earliest known sonnet sequence in English.[110] The entire sequence is given the title, "A Meditation of a Penitent Sinner: Written in Maner of a Paraphrase upon the 51. Psalme of David." The psalm sonnets are preceded by a shortened title, "A Meditation of a penitent sinner, upon the 51. Psalme." The prefatory sonnets are introduced by a headnote that asserts that they are not included "as parcell of maister Calvines worke, but for that it well agreeth with the same argument, and was delivered me by my frend with whom I knew I might be so bolde to use and publishe it as pleased me" (A Meditation, lines 8–10). The most natural reading of this phrase, "delivered me by my frend," would attribute these poems to an acquaintance of Lock. Some scholars have suggested John Knox as the author, although we know of no other poetry that he wrote.[111] Other possibilities include published poets such as William Kethe or William Whittingham whom Lock undoubtedly met in Geneva. More recent scholars, however, have claimed that Lock herself is the primary author.[112] This claim is supported by Lock's authorship of the Latin poem in the Silva manuscript and her probable authorship of the poem on suffering that concludes the 1590 volume, *Of the Markes of the Children of God.*

Furthermore, substantive connections can be made between the 1560 dedicatory epistle and the sonnets in terms of images and lexical choices. Lock introduces David in the epistle as a king who, like Hezekiah, experienced both illness and God's restorative power. Her sensuous depictions of desperate illness in the epistle are reiterated in the sonnets, and her explicit use of contemporary medical practice in the allusion to scorpion's oil is picked up by the distilling furnace of the second prefatory sonnet. The abstract notion of despair, made concrete in the epistle with reference to

---

110 Linda Dove, however, argues that the twelve-line stanzas recounting the fall of King Edward IV in William Baldwin's revised *A myrroure for magistrates* (London, 1559; STC 1247) may claim the honor of being the first sonnet sequence written in English; see Linda Dove, "Women at Variance: Sonnet Sequences and Social Commentary in Early Modern England" (Ph.D. diss., University of Maryland at College Park, 1997).

111 Collinson, "The Role of Women," in *Godly People*, 280.

112 Thomas P. Roche, Jr., *Petrarch and the English Sonnet Sequences* (New York: AMS Press, 1989), 155; Spiller, *The Development of the Sonnet*, 92; Hannay, " 'Unlock my lipps'," 21–2.

a dying man, is personified in the third prefatory sonnet as a prosecuting attorney.

Unusual lexical choices also link the sonnets with the epistle, as well as with Lock's translation of Calvin's sermons. Lock, for instance, favors "all" with a present participle: "all sufficing" and "allpearcing" in the sonnets (lines 73, 146); "alknowynge" and "alworking" in the epistle (line 135). She uses the participial adverb "yeldyngly" in the epistle (line 166) and the participial adjective "yelding/yeldyng" in the sonnets (lines 75, 315). "Corrupted," as a participial adjective, is used in both the epistle (line 120) and the sonnets (line 301); "refused" is similarly used in both the translation of the first sermon (line 179) and in the sonnets (line 47). What makes these word choices particularly significant is that, in each case, the use of the participle antedates the earliest recorded *OED* usage. Furthermore, there are twenty-five first usages of the participle construction in the sonnets alone (see the textual notes), suggesting Lock's fondness for this lexical form. Finally, the "Chaos" that separates heaven from hell in the epistle (line 115) is personalized in the sonnets: "My Chaos and my heape of sinne doth lie, / Betwene me and thy mercies shining light" (lines 139–140).

Although such congruences are suggestive, they cannot be taken as definitive, since the tropes and rhetoric of the epistle, translations, and poems were common currency among nonconformist writers. If, indeed, Lock did write the poems, there still remains the problem of the headnote. One possible resolution is to consider the note as an example of the modesty *topos*, in which Lock disclaims authorship while still presenting her poems to the public.[113] Yet the evidence of the epistle and the translation points toward a confident authorial voice that is at odds with such self-deprecation. A second possibility is that the headnote was written not by Lock but by John Day, the printer.[114] Day uses the same term, "publish," elsewhere; for instance, in *The treasure of euonymus* (1559) he promises that if this book is well received, he will also "publishe" the work of other continental medical writers (+2^{v}). Lacking any other viable candidate, it seems reasonable to assign the authorship of the sonnet sequence to Anne Lock. Certainly, it is through her efforts that the poems have been preserved for and presented to subsequent readers.

The five prefatory sonnets present a tightly interlocked set of images in which the principal characters are a God who is at once both threatening and gracious, a desperate narrator overwhelmed by sin, and Despair, who assumes the role of a prosecutor. These sonnets, in the words of the

---

[113] Woods, "The Body Penitent," 137–8.

[114] Hannay, " 'Unlock my lipps'," 21.

title, express "the passioned minde of the penitent sinner"; that is, they explore the psychological state of the person who will utter the cries for mercy that make up Psalm 51.

In the first sonnet, the narrator's eyes take in two appalling sights: a stained life and the wrath of God, represented as a double-edged sword. The language and imagery are urgent, dynamic, and horrifying, dramatically capturing that moment after the pleasure of eating the forbidden fruit has vanished, the eyes are open, and the realization of guilt has opened a gaping hole in the soul. As a consequence of this knowledge, the body becomes a distilling furnace, overflowing the eyes with briny tears that first diminish and then totally eradicate the sense of sight.

The focus of energy in the second sonnet moves from the eyes to the body of the sinner who is unhorsed in an uneven jousting match. With God's shining light only a distant memory, the speaker's blind body is shown in incessant motion, groveling, groping, and finally gathering up enough breath to cry, "Mercy, mercy." The intensity of this voice, characterized as a shrieking cry and a braying bootless noise, is amplified in the middle sonnet. Despair, enacting his connection with the law, prosecutes the speaker using the Protestant language of election. In the fourth sonnet, however, Despair is no longer necessary, as the persona's own conscience becomes prosecutor, jury, and executioner. Disabled, insentient, dragged into the very throat of hell, the narrator finds a voice again in the fourth sonnet, although it is nearly drained of any right to speak. In the final sonnet, the cries for mercy become a piteous plaint accompanied by woeful "smoking sighes," groans, bitter penitence, faltering knees, and hands that collapse in the very act of supplication.

Despite this pitiful condition, however, two more positive biblical images underlie this final picture of the penitent sinner. The first is signaled by the phrase "to crave the crummes," a reminder of the Syro-Phoenician woman who persisted in asking Jesus for grace even after she, an outsider, had been rebuffed (Matt. 15:21–28; Mark 7:24–30). The second is signaled by the sighs and groans of the inarticulate cry for mercy, a sign that the Holy Spirit has taken over the plea for mercy when the resources of the human tongue fail (Rom. 8:26). Both these biblical subtexts suggest that, although the narrator is still tossed with the pangs and passions of despair, mercy, while delayed, ultimately will not be denied.

In the paraphrase of Psalm 51 that follows, the voice of the penitent sinner is still clearly heard, but there is much less exploration of the internal state, and, therefore, less dramatization. The narrative of the preface gives way to an explicative paraphrase that imitates the shift from the imagery of the epistle to the "plain rendering" of Calvin's sermons. The movement in the prefatory sonnets is linear: from the realization of sin, through confrontation with Despair, to a supplicant's posture. The movement in the remaining twenty-one sonnets, however, is circular—reenacting a repetitive cycle of complaint, repentance, and hope.

The rhetorical style of the paraphrased sonnets centers on the repetition and elaboration of key words along with the careful exposition of theological doctrines. This elaboration of key words can be seen, for instance, in the tenth sonnet of the paraphrase where the distinction is drawn between hearing the gospel and hearing the law. Rather than the more common image, "pierce my heart," Lock inserts "pearce myne eares," a graphic clause that both aptly extends the metaphor of hearing and captures the violent action of grace needed to restore the penitent sinner. Theological distinctions are also carefully drawn. The emphasis on simplicity in the eighth sonnet of the paraphrase extends the contrast made in the epistle between the plain teaching of master Calvin and the "papisticall" superstitions of the Roman church, a commonplace complaint among Protestants.

There is, as well, the continuing theme from the prefatory sonnets of the intimate connection between God's law and the individual conscience. It is the conscience, rather than the explicit voice of God, that originally threatens the narrator in the first five sonnets; similarly, in sonnet ten of the paraphrase, the conscience acts as an echo chamber for God's voice. In this sonnet, Lock sets up a series of parallels between her inner being and the outside world. With her ears, she has heard the "dredfull threates and thonders of the law," presumably in the words of the Scripture as they are read aloud. Yet, dreadful as this external voice is, Lock's true anguish stems from the fact that her conscience, her "gylty minde," concurs with the accusation of guilt. This "redoubled horror," compounded of God's voice and her own guilty conscience, almost overwhelms her inner being, the soul who is listening to the gentle voice of grace. In the middle of this internal struggle, Lock finds the strength to call more loudly for mercy, as indeed she previously had found her voice in the prefatory sonnets. God graciously silences her guilty conscience, replacing the resounding echo of sin with the merciful sound of the gospel.

The prose version of Psalm 51, printed in the margins alongside the sonnets, is Lock's own original translation of this familiar biblical passage. It is not identical to any known translation, although nearly every phrase finds a counterpart in one or the other English translation printed before 1560.[115]

---

[115] I have compared the marginal prose translation with the following versions: *The psalter of David in Englishe tr. aftir the texte of ffeline* ([Antwerp], 1530; STC 2370; George Joye's translation of Martin Bucer's Latin psalter); *Ortulus anime. The garden*

Such similarities, however, do not mean that Lock patched together her translation from various sources. Rather, they point to a single common source for many of the English translations, including Lock's own, namely the Gallican version of the Latin psalms.[116] Lock's translation never deviates from the Latin text and, on the English side, most nearly resembles the Coverdale and Great Bible versions that were themselves dependent, to some extent, on the Vulgate. Where her phrasing differs from Coverdale or the Great Bible, it is often similar to other Latin-based translations such as those found in the parallel Latin-English psalter (1540). More convincingly, Lock does not follow the translations of either the 1557 Geneva Psalter or the 1560 Geneva Bible, both of which worked with the Hebrew text, when these deviate from the Vulgate.

Lock was not alone in her decision to compose her own translation. Despite the reformers' emphasis on the Bible, sixteenth-century Protestants were remarkably cavalier about precise quotations, drawing freely on a variety of translations and paraphrases.[117] As the translators of the Geneva Bible commented, "some translations read after one sort, and some after

---

of the soule: or the englisshe primers newe corrected and augmented ([Antwerp], 1530; STC 13828.4; commonly known as the Reformed Primer); *Davids psalter, diligently and faithfully tr. by G. Joye with breif arguments* ([Antwerp], 1534; STC 2372; George Joye's translation of Ulrich Zwingli's Latin psalter); the translation included in *An exposition after the maner of a contemplacyon upon the .li. psalme, called Miserere mei Deus* (London, 1534; STC 21789.3; William Marshall's translation of Girolamo Savonarola's exposition of Psalm 51); *A paraphrasis, upon all the psalmes of David* (London, 1539; STC 2372.6; Miles Coverdale's translation of Johannes Campensis's Latin psalter); the Coverdale Bible ([Cologne?], 1535; STC 2063); the Great Bible ([Paris and London], 1539; STC 2068); *The psalter or boke of psalmes both in Latyn and Englyshe, with a kalendar, and a table* (London, 1540; STC 2368); *The psalmes of David tr. accordyng to th'Ebrue, wyth annotacions moste profitable* (Geneva, 1557; STC 2383.6; the first Geneva psalter); the Geneva Bible (Geneva, 1560; STC 2093). The 1557 Geneva psalter retains much of the language of the Great Bible, with some revisions from the Hebrew that are carried over into the 1560 Geneva Bible.

[116] There are two versions of the Vulgate Psalter, both of which originate with St. Jerome. Jerome's translation from the Hebrew text, the "Hebrew" Psalter, predominates in manuscripts up to the ninth century. Late in the eighth century, however, Alcuin (c. 735–804), as part of his liturgical reforms for Charlemagne, replaced the Hebrew Psalter with the text commonly used in Gaul, the so-called "Gallican" Psalter. This Gallican Psalter, a revision of the Old-Latin Psalter on the basis of the Hexapla made by Jerome before he translated the Hebrew Psalter, became the accepted text in the manuscripts after the ninth century and was the version with which the English church was most familiar.

[117] Norton, *History of the Bible*, 1:118–9.

another, whereas all may serve to good purpose and edification."[118] In Lock's case, it appears that the Latin Bible, along with that of the vernacular translations, provided a rich source of images and language. This macaronic effect can be seen not only in the prose translation of Psalm 51 but also in her use of the phrase "th'everlasting Chaos" in the dedicatory epistle.

That the reading of the Vulgate continued to be a common practice, even among Protestants, is suggested by the 1559 Articles of Visitation that list the requirements parish churches were expected to meet. The fifty-six items forbid such Roman Catholic practices as the saying of mass, the accumulation of images, the promotion of pilgrimages, and the use of Latin in the public worship services, but include the following question to be asked of parish priests: "Item, whether they do discourage any person from readynge of any parte of the Byble, eyther in latyn or englyshe, and do not rather comforte, and exhort every person to read the same at convenient times, as the very lively word of god and the speciall fode of mans soule."[119]

The printed format of the sonnets—a poetic paraphrase with accompanying marginal prose translation—was followed by Lock's son, Henry, in his 1597 version of the book of Ecclesiastes.[120] Although Henry employs a rime royal form, he includes two stanzas for each biblical verse, a combination that yields fourteen lines of iambic pentameter and visually resembles a sonnet.[121]

The Latin Poem

Lock's single surviving Latin poem is found in a beautifully illustrated manuscript at the Cambridge University Library (MS Ii.5.37). It features an encyclopedia of scientific knowledge, the *Giardino cosmografico coltivato*, divided into eight books and written in Italian by Doctor Bartholo Sylva,

---

[118] *The Geneva Bible: A facsimile of the 1560 edition*, intro. Lloyd E. Berry (Madison: Univ. of Wisconsin Press, 1969), ***4r.

[119] *Articles to be enquyred in the visitation, in the fyrste yeare of the raygne of Elizabeth* (London, 1559; STC 10118), A2v.

[120] Henry Lok, *Ecclesiastes, otherwise called the preacher. Abridged, and dilated in English poesie. Whereunto are annexed sundrie sonets* (London, 1597; STC 16696).

[121] In his prose translation, however, he follows the 1560 Geneva version almost exactly; for instance, in the first chapter there are only two minor variations, in verse 6 where the *es* is dropped from *circuites* (A8r), and verse 18 where the Geneva Bible reads first *grief* and then *sorowe*, while Henry Lok uses *griefe* in both cases (B3r).

an émigré from Turin.[122] The first eight leaves, however, are devoted to introductory material, including a dedication to Robert Dudley, the earl of Leicester, one of Queen Elizabeth's favorite courtiers and a patron of nonconformist literature. Sylva himself contributes an opening sonnet, addressed to the reader and written in Latin (fol. 1^v), a prose epistle to the earl written in Italian and dated 24 May 1572 (fols. 2^r–3^v), and a second Italian prose epistle addressed to the readers (fol. 4^r–4^v). These epistles are followed by eight pages of complimentary poems written in Greek, Latin, Italian, English, Spanish, and French.

The first page of poems (fol. 5^r) consists of Greek verses written by Edward Dering, Elizabeth Cooke Hoby, and Mildred Cooke Burghley. The verso page is devoted to two Latin poems, the second one attributed to Anna Dering. A Latin poem by Pietro Bizari, an exiled Italian historian and poet who had converted to Protestantism and was a protégé of the earl of Leicester, fills the next page (fol. 6^r).[123] The following three pages (fols. 6^v–7^v) include a Latin epigram, an Italian sonnet, a Spanish sonnet, and fourteen lines of rhymed fourteeners written in English by a George Stanley. The dedicatory poems conclude with two Latin poems by Anne Cooke Bacon and Katherine Cooke Killigrew (fol. 8^r) and a French poem by a Doctor Pierre Penna (fol. 8^v).

The entire elegant manuscript may have been designed to appeal to the queen, as well as Leicester, and to convince them that the partisan Puritans were worthy of consideration at court.[124] Lock's four-line poem, punning on Sylva's name, praises the doctor for providing as much delight for his readers as they might experience on a walk through a shady grove of trees.

The Epistle to the Countess of Warwick

Eighteen years after this Latin poem, Anne Lock completed her final work, a translation of Jean Taffin's *Of the markes of the children of God* (1590), and dedicated it to Anne Russell Dudley, the countess of Warwick.

---

[122] The manuscript measures 205 x 280 mm. and consists of 106 numbered leaves plus six flyleaves. It is written in the same hand throughout, although the Greek verses may be the work of another copyist. The poem was located and first transcribed by Schleiner, in *Tudor and Stuart Women Writers*, with an English translation by Connie McQuillen, 256 n.11.

[123] For a discussion of Bizari and another example of his poetry, see Eleanor Rosenberg, *Leicester: Patron of Letters* (New York: Columbia Univ. Press, 1955), 139.

[124] For further development of this argument, see Schleiner, *Tudor and Stuart Women*, 39–41.

It is not difficult to understand Lock's attraction to Taffin's work, which addresses two consuming questions for the sixteenth-century Protestant: how can I be assured that I am one of the elect, and why, if I am elect, do I experience so much suffering? Although Taffin's original audience was a persecuted minority in a foreign country, Lock frames the situation rather differently for her readers. Her announced goal in preparing this book is to awaken the English church from its "*Halcyon* daies ... [of] rest and pleasure" (lines 11–13) and to prepare it "to the day of trial" (line 10). For the epistle, Lock takes as her central text Hebrews 12:6, that the Lord chastens everyone whom he loves, and as her primary audience three groups of people: those who have never experienced affliction and so might be startled when they are confronted by it, those who have grown lazy and lethargic in their Christian profession, and those who are already afflicted and need the comfort of understanding the purpose for their suffering.

England's halcyon days certainly seemed at an end, at least to Lock's nonconformist community.[125] Archbishop Whitgift's pressure toward ecclesiastical uniformity, beginning with the articles of 1583, had been countered by the movement towards presbyterianism and attempts were made in Parliament in 1585 and again in 1587 to adopt both a Genevan prayer book and a presbyterian form of government.[126] General conferences or synods, which many hoped would lead to the establishment of local presbyteries, were held in several parts of the country, and Walter Travers, a Puritan minister who had spent years in Geneva, edited a book of church discipline to serve as a model for newly formed presbyterian congregations.[127] By 1588, however, it appeared that such moderate efforts toward reform were meeting with little success.

On 16 April of that year, the authorities confiscated, and later destroyed, the press of Robert Waldegrave after he had printed a satirical

---

[125] For the importance of the religious-political controversies to Lock's work, see White, "Renaissance Englishwomen and Religious Translations."

[126] For a discussion of the presbyterian movement, see Patrick Collinson, *The Elizabethan Puritan Movement* (Berkeley: Univ. of California Press, 1967), 273–329; M. M. Knappen, *Tudor Puritanism: A Chapter in the History of Idealism* (Chicago: Univ. of Chicago Press, 1939), 283–94; Scott Pearson, *Thomas Cartwright*, 236–63.

[127] This book of discipline, "Disciplina Ecclesiae Dei Verbo Descripta," survives only in manuscript copies; Thomas Cartwright's translation was printed in 1644 as *A directory of church government* (London, 1644; Wing T2066). It was based on Travers's *Ecclesiasticae Disciplinae et Anglicanae Ecclesiae* (1574), translated by Thomas Cartwright, *A full and plaine declaration of ecclesiasticall discipline* (Heidelberg, 1574; STC 24184). For a fuller discussion of Travers's importance, see S. J. Knox, *Walter Travers: Paragon of Elizabethan Puritanism* (London: Methuen, 1962).

dialogue on the state of England by John Udall, a preacher at Kingston-on-Thames.[128] Waldegrave and his wife managed to save much of the type, however, and within three months an underground press began producing a spate of works including six tracts and one broadside against the episcopacy written by a fictitious and highly satirical Martin Marprelate.[129] The illegal press was harbored by a series of sympathizers, including Elizabeth Crane of East Molesey, Sir Richard and Lady Elizabeth Seymour Knightley of Fawsley, and Mr. and Mrs. Roger Wigston of Wolston.[130] The press was captured in August 1589, all copies of the penultimate tract, *More Worke for Cooper*, were destroyed, and the printer and his assistants were arrested. Job Throckmorton and John Penry, leaders in the Marprelate controversy, managed to print a final tract before the press was abandoned.[131]

Books, however, were not the only target of Whitgift's attack. The printer who had succeeded Waldegrave, John Hodgkins, was imprisoned and tortured. Throckmorton was indicted by a grand jury in October 1590, although his case was later suspended, and Penry and Waldegrave fled England for Scotland.[132] Elizabeth Crane, Sir Richard Knightley, and Roger Wigston were held in the Fleet prison and, along with Mrs. Wigston, were heavily fined.[133] Although many Puritans, such as Whitgift's old adversary Thomas Cartwright, denounced the Marprelate tracts, a

---

[128] John Udall, *The state of the church of Englande, laide open in a conference betweene Diotrephes a Byshop, Tertullus a Papist*, etc. (London, 1588; STC 24505).

[129] For a further discussion of the Marprelate tracts see Leland H. Carlson, "Martin Marprelate: His Identity and His Satire," in *English Satire: Papers Read at a Clark Library Seminar, January 15, 1972* (Los Angeles: William Andrews Clark Memorial Library, 1972), 1–53; Collinson, *The Elizabethan Puritan Movement*, 391–7; William Pierce, *An Historical Introduction to the Marprelate Tracts* (London: Clarke, 1908), 135–95.

[130] Elizabeth Crane was the widow of Anthony Crane, master of the queen's household; for her identification see Julia Norton McCorkle, "A Note Concerning 'Mistress Crane' and the Martin Marprelate Controversy," *Library*, 4th ser. 12 (1931–2): 276–83. Elizabeth Seymour Knightley was the youngest daughter of Edward Seymour, the duke of Somerset, and Anne Stanhope. Roger Wigston was the squire of Wolston.

[131] Job Throckmorton's father Clement, himself a prominent Protestant, was first cousin to Rose Lock Hickman's second husband, Simon Throckmorton.

[132] Penry, however, was arrested and hanged when he returned to England in 1593.

[133] Mrs. Wigston appears to have been more committed to the nonconformist cause than her husband, a fact taken into account by the court, which fined her £1000 but her husband only 500 marks; see Pierce, *An Historical Introduction,* 187–9; 207. For Crane's sentence, see Collinson, *The Elizabethan Puritan Movement*, 418.

number of nonconformist ministers, including Cartwright himself, were imprisoned while others were killed or defrocked. The deaths of the earl of Leicester, to whom the Silva manuscript had been dedicated, and the earl of Warwick, Anne Russell Dudley's husband, weakened the reformed party's influence at court. Threatened with such duress, it is understandable that Lock should choose to translate a book that would encourage those who were suffering, remind them that they were, indeed, the true—if not the established—church, and also serve to summon the established church hierarchy back to its reformed roots.

If Lock's choice of text reveals her spiritual sensitivity to the issues of the day, her choice of a dedicatee shows her political acuity. Anne Russell Dudley (d. 1604) had an impeccable Protestant pedigree. She was the eldest daughter of Francis, the second earl of Bedford, who had traveled abroad during Mary Tudor's reign and lent his support to Protestant exiles. Her brother was John Russell, the second husband of Elizabeth Cooke. She herself was the third wife of Ambrose Dudley, the earl of Warwick, and sister-in-law to Robert Dudley, the earl of Leicester, both of whom were patrons of Puritan writers. A younger Dudley brother, Guildford, had been executed by Mary Tudor along with his wife, the Lady Jane Grey, who was memorialized by John Foxe as a Protestant martyr. More importantly, as a longtime companion to Queen Elizabeth, Anne Russell Dudley was in a position to help the nonconformists at court, as indeed she already had. In 1586 she "interfered" on behalf of John Udall, who had been called to account for his preaching of Puritan doctrines; other supporters had failed to convince the authorities to restore his preaching privileges, but Thomas Cooper, the bishop of Winchester, told Udall that "he was beholden to the Countess."[134] Like the duchess of Suffolk, the countess was also the recipient of numerous dedications, twenty-four in all, most of them religious works.[135]

That Lock intended the countess to use her political influence at court is made clear in the preface. While Lock pays Anne Dudley the compliment of being "not onlie a professour, but also a lover of the trueth," she

---

[134] Albert Peel, ed., *The Seconde Parte of a Register*, vol. 2 (Cambridge: Cambridge Univ. Press, 1915), 40.

[135] Williams, *Index of Dedications*, 57. The other book dedicated to the countess in 1590, also printed by Thomas Orwin, was *The excellencie of the mysterie of Christ Jesus* (STC 18247), written by Peter Muffet, younger brother of the well-connected Paracelsian physician and author, Thomas Muffet [Moffet]. For an analysis of the earl of Warwick and his countess as nonconformist patrons, see Rosenberg, *Leicester*; White, "Renaissance Englishwomen and Religious Translations."

also reminds her that a privileged position at court makes her responsible to "give light unto manie" (lines 42–45). Lock's epistle recognizes the difficult position in which members of the reformed party found themselves. The nonconformists needed every friend they could muster, and Lock was not afraid to remind the countess of her duty.

For herself, Lock realizes that her own influence may be limited because she is a woman: "great things by reason of my sex, I may not doo" (line 50). Yet such an acknowledgement is no excuse for failing to act. Lock completes the sentence with a ringing affirmation of her own responsibility—"and that which I may, I ought to doo" (lines 50–51)—before returning to a familiar Protestant metaphor, the building of the walls of Jerusalem: "I have according to my duetie, brought my poore basket of stones to the strengthning of the walles of that Jerusalem, whereof (by grace) wee are all both Citizens and members" (lines 51–53). Although the Jerusalem to which all true believers owe their allegiance is heavenly, Lock summons herself and her reader to an earthly task, reforming the present church. Moreover, as an earthly task, it must be performed within the appropriate structures of social and spiritual hierarchy. Men and women both have a duty to pursue active obedience to God, but men may do "great things" while women bring their "poore basket of stones." Similarly, Lock, as a member of the middle class, may encourage and exhort Christians to do their duty, but the countess, as a member of the ruling class, has a greater responsibility to let her light shine in the court. Mutual spiritual duties must be performed within the rankings of a real social world.

The situation of persecution as well as the intervening thirty years of emphasis on plain Protestant rhetoric may account for the striking rhetorical differences between this dedication and the one addressed to the duchess of Suffolk in 1560. The 1590 dedicatory epistle does include some balanced constructions and doublets reminiscent of the Suffolk dedication, but it is nearly bereft of imaginative imagery. In the place of elaborate medical conceits and biblical stories, Lock substitutes a tissue of scriptural citations and allusions. The cautious optimism of the 1560 epistle also gives way here to a prophetic certainty that England must soon endure the chastening hand of God if she is to remain a true Protestant child.

Of the Markes of the Children of God

Lock's "poore basket of stones," which she brings to edify the church, is her translation of Jean Taffin's *Des Marques des enfans de Dieu et des consolations en leurs afflictions*. Although John Calvin's name is well-known to modern readers, Jean Taffin's (c. 1529–1602) is now recognized only by theological and historical specialists.[136] Yet, during his lifetime he was an influential Continental reformer who studied in Geneva, signed the 1561 reformed Belgic Confession of Faith, became a chaplain to the Protestant prince William of Orange, and pastored French-speaking churches in the Low Countries. He wrote three major works that were translated into English, Dutch, Latin, and German; they continued to be reprinted for over fifty years after his death.[137]

---

[136] For biographies of Taffin see Cornelia Boer, *Hofpredikers van Prins Willem van Oranje: Jean Taffin en Pierre Loyseleur de Villiers* (The Hague, 1952); S. van der Linde, *Jean Taffin: Hofprediker en raadsheer van Willem van Oranje* (Amsterdam: Bolland, 1982) and "Jean Taffin: Eerste Pleiter voor 'Nadere Reformatie' in Nederland," *Theologia Reformata* 25 (1982): 6–29; Charles Rahlenbeck, "Jean Taffin, un Réformateur Belge du XVIe Siècle," *Bulletin de la Commission pour l'histoire des Eglises Wallonnes* 2 (1887): 117–79; Christiaan Sepp, *Drie Evangeliedienaren uit den tijd der Hervorming* (Leiden: E. J. Brill, 1879), 1–81. Important encyclopedia entries include A. J. van der Aa, ed., *Biographisch Woordenboek der Nederlanden*, vol. 19 (Haarlem, 1876), 8–9; R. Apers, "Jean Taffin" in *Biographie Nationale publiée par l'Académie Royale des Sciences, des Lettres et des Beaux-arts de Belgique*, vol. 24 (Brussels, 1929), 476–82; Hans J. Hillerbrand, ed., *The Oxford Encyclopedia of the Reformation*, vol. 4 (New York: Oxford Univ. Press, 1996), 143. Additional information on Taffin's life and work may be found in Phyllis Mack Crew, *Calvinist Preaching and Iconoclasm in the Netherlands 1544–1569* (Cambridge: Cambridge Univ. Press, 1978); C. de Clercq, "Jean et Jacques Taffin, Jean d'Arras et Christophe Plantin," *De Gulden Passer* 36 (1958): 125–36; Heinrich Heppe, *Geschicte des Pietismus und der Mystik in der Reformirten Kirche, namentlich der Niederlande* (Leiden: E. J. Brill, 1879), 95–8; Andrew Pettegree, *Emden and the Dutch Revolt: Exile and the Development of Reformed Protestantism* (Oxford: Clarendon Press, 1992); F. Ernest Stoeffler, *The Rise of Evangelical Pietism* (Leiden: E. J. Brill, 1965), 121–6. My discussion is drawn from these sources and reflects a mediation of conflicting accounts.

[137] The only twentieth century edition of his work appears to be a 1977 Dutch translation of *Des Marques* by K. Exalto, *De kenmerken der Kinderen Gods*, published at Urk; see Linde, "Jean Taffin," 29 n. 28.

Taffin's second major work, *Instruction contre les erreurs des Anabaptistes* (1589), is a polemical tract that identifies Anabaptists as dangerous enemies of Protestantism along with atheists and political anarchists. Taffin's third work, *Traicté de l'amendement de vie, comprins en quatre livres* (1594), was another popular piece, translated into English as *The amendment of life, comprised in fower bookes* by Georg Bishop (London, 1595; STC 23650) as well as into Dutch, German, and Latin. Later editions of *Traicté de l'amendement* often were bound with *Des Marques*.

In addition to these three major works, a single example of Taffin's sermons survives, in a 1591 Dutch translation entitled *Vermaninghe tot liefde ende aelmoesse, ende van de schuldighe plicht ende troost der armen* (Admonitions to love and almsgiving both of the obligation to and comfort of the poor). The work probably originated as a French sermon although there is no record of a French original; there is no indica-

Des Marques des enfans de Dieu, the earliest of these works, was probably first issued in 1586.[138] It was written during a difficult voyage from Germany to the Netherlands where Taffin was to assume the leadership of the French-speaking church in Haarlem. The assassination of William of Orange two years earlier and the failure of the earl of Leicester to drive the Roman Catholic Spanish forces out of the Low Countries had discouraged the reformed churches. In this context, Taffin writes a book of encouragement, assuring his readers that suffering is a mark of God's favor, not his disapproval.

In *Des Marques des enfans de Dieu*, Taffin wears his considerable learning lightly, integrating his quotations from the church fathers and historians into the fabric of his argument. He deliberately cultivated the common touch, writing to his friend Vulcanius: "Do not wait for a learned work from me; I work only for the people."[139] Yet, his earlier scholarly life shows through. He took as his motto *A Dieu ta vie, En Dieu ta fin* (To God your life; in God your end) with its deliberate pun on his last name. He apparently owned, or had access to, the Frobenius brothers' ten volume set of Augustine, as indicated by marginal references that specify the volume in which a particular treatise is found. In addition to

tion that Taffin wrote Dutch, although he may have spoken it. This tract was translated by C. Cotton and published in English as *The practice of charity. Pressed upon the conscience by sundry effectuall and forcible arguments* (London, 1625; STC 23656.5).

Taffin may also have worked with Philipp van Marnix on a new edition of Adriaan Corneliszoon van Haemstede's martyrology, *De Gheschiedenisse ende den doodt der vromer Martelaren* (1559) after the Synod of Dordrecht in 1578 declared it an official book. He wrote poetry, as exemplified by the prefatory and concluding verses in his published works, and may also have collaborated in publishing ventures with the Plantin family. Jean Taffin the younger, son of Taffin's brother Jacques, also published two books, which has led to some bibliographic confusion as they are occasionally attributed to Taffin himself. These are *L'estat de l'église, avec le discours des temps dépuis les apostres jusqu' à présent* (Bergen-op-Zoom, 1605) and *Claire exposition de l'apocalypse ou révelation de St. Jean, avec déduction de l'histoire et chronologies* (Flissingue, 1609).

[138] The most reliable bibliographic sources are H. J. Laceulle-Van de Kerk, *De Haarlemse Drukkers en Boekverkopers van 1540 tot 1600* (The Hague: Martinus Nijhoff, 1951) and Cornelia Boer, *Hofpredikers van Prins*. These sources often refer to citations in E. W. Moes and C. P. Burger, Jr., *De Amsterdamsche Boekdrukkers en Uitgevers in de zestiende eeuw*, vol. 2 (Amsterdam, 1907). All the biographical sources enumerate various editions, but none of the lists agree in their details. Although 1584 is given as the date of the first edition in some sources (see Rahlenbeck, "Jean Taffin," 174), this earlier date does not correspond with biographical or internal textual evidence.

[139] Quoted in Rahlenbeck, "Jean Taffin," 179.

his patristic and biblical references, Taffin frequently draws on homey metaphors to make his point. For instance, to explain God's tender care for his children he says:

> What prayer maketh the little Infant to his mother? Hee weepeth and cryeth, not beeing able to expresse what hee lacketh. The Mother offereth him the breast, or giveth him some other thing, such as shee thinketh his necessitie requireth. Much more then the heavenly father heedeth the sighes, the groanes, the desires and teares of his children. (Chapter 4, lines 403–408)

Or to illustrate that suffering makes us more vigilant in our spiritual lives, he paints a dramatic vignette:

> For as it hapneth to him that is quiet and at his ease, that he falleth soone asleepe, and having an apple or anie other thing in his hand, it falleth, or is easely taken from him: so the ease of the flesh bringeth us a sleep in the world, and causeth us to leese the spiritual good things and to suffer them to fall to the ground. On the contrarie side, the more one forceth to take away a staffe which I holde in my hand while I am awake: so much the faster I shut it in, and hold it the harder, that it may not be taken away from me. (Chapter 9, lines 162–170)

Throughout the entire volume, his focus remains steadily on the comfort that God offers to his children in the midst of their suffering.

Des Marques des enfans de Dieu went through at least two editions before Taffin revised and augmented the book in 1588. The augmented edition was printed that same year in both French and Dutch, and it is this French edition that Lock uses for her translation.[140]

---

[140] The title page of the 1588 augmented edition reads "Troisieme Edition." The only remaining copy of this edition is at the University Library, Amsterdam. There are no extant copies of the earlier, nonaugmented editions. Of subsequent French editions, I have been able to verify existing copies only from 1597 (fifth edition), 1601, and 1606 (also labeled as the fifth edition). But various bibliographic sources also mention French editions from 1592, 1593, 1596, 1612, 1614, 1616, 1621, 1628, and 1659 although none of the sources provides complete bibliographic information, transcribes the title pages, or indicates the location of existing copies.

Existing Dutch editions include those from 1588, 1589, 1590, 1598, and 1659, although Boer claims that there are at least nine Dutch editions and possibly as many as eleven; see Boer, *Hofpredikers van Prins*, 164. There appear to be German editions from at least 1593 and 1602, while a Latin edition appeared in 1601. Only Rahlenbeck insists on Flemish editions beginning with 1588, but he is probably confusing the aug-

Lock's translation belongs to a long-standing tradition of cooperation between Protestants in England and the Netherlands. Both Edward VI and Elizabeth I encouraged the establishment of Dutch congregations in London (as well as other English cities) to provide a model of Calvinist rigor for the budding English church and to increase the pool of skilled textile workers. Twenty-five Netherlands ministers visited England during the 1550s and 1560s and the flow of correspondence and visits continued throughout the century. Taffin's own brother, Nicholas, came to London in 1568, and his printer, Gillis Rooman, practiced his trade briefly in England, registering with the Company of Stationers on 3 October 1580.[141] Lock's father, Stephen Vaughan, was the English governor of the Merchant Adventurers' factory in Antwerp from 1538 to 1546. Peregrine Bertie, the son of her first patron, distinguished himself as commander of the English forces in the Low Countries after the earl of Leicester was recalled in 1587, and Lock's old friend, Henry Killigrew, was a councillor of state in the Netherlands from 1585 to 1589. Taffin himself corresponded with the Brownists, a separatist Puritan sect, in 1599 and is considered one of the founders of the *Nadere Reformatie* (Second Reformation), a pietistic movement in the Netherlands influenced by English Puritanism.[142] Lock's translation thus provided one more link in the on-going relationship between reformed Protestants in England and those in the Low Countries.

"The necessitie and benefite of affliction"

Lock elaborates on Taffin's theme of suffering with her concluding poem of one hundred and twenty-four lines, written in ballad-style quatrains rhyming *abab*. In the absence of any attribution or denial of authorship, it seems reasonable to assume that the verse is from her own hand. Lock substitutes this poem for Taffin's quotations from the New Testament and Augustine's *City of God* that conclude *Des Marques des enfans de Dieu* (see the textual notes).

The poem eschews the rich sensual imagery of the sonnets for a

---

mented French edition with a Flemish translation; see Rahlenbeck, "Jean Taffin," 126. Micheline White, Charles Huttar, and James Tanis assisted in identifying these editions.

141 The entry in the Stationers' Register, which is struck out, reads: "master myddleton. Gyles Romayn. Admytted a brother of this Cumpanye. yt is agreed that he shall paie x^{s} whereof v^{s} in hand and ye Rest by xij^{d} a weeke." Edward Arber, ed., *A Transcript of the Registers of the Company of Stationers of London; 1554–1640*, 5 vols. (London and Birmingham, 1875–94), 2:683.

142 Linde argues for seeing Taffin as the father of the *Nadere Reformatie*, while Boer sees him as a precursor.

simpler dualistic structure: eternal heavenly joys are to be preferred over temporal earthly pleasures, but since believers find it difficult to believe this truth, God ordains afflictions to turn their attention away from the earth toward heaven. From the many biblical and historical examples of persecuted believers that Taffin cites, Lock chooses two as her models: Job and David. In chapter eight, Taffin conjoins Job and David as examplars of those who have suffered afflictions (line 169); in chapter nine, he again links them as those who, through suffering, have learned to submit themselves to God (lines 259–261). Lock's poem, following Taffin's lead, describes Job and David as those who, falling under God's "scourging rod" (line 117), yet learned through suffering to appreciate his "mercie, kindnes and . . . love" (line 51). In the context of the difficulties being experienced by the nonconformist community and the unnamed trial that must soon erupt in England, Job and David provide exemplary models for believers to follow. Furthermore, Lock's emphasis on the fleeting nature of worldly pleasures and the Christian's need to relinquish them recalls key themes from the writings of Edward Dering, her second husband. Dering's letters often conclude with a reminder to deny "impietie and worldly concupiscence" and to "live soberly, purely, and godly in this present life" looking "for the blessed hope that shall be revealed."[143]

The dedicatory epistle, translation, and poem of 1590 thus work together as a call for the English church to turn from its persecution of the Puritan faction, reform itself, and return to the promise of a truly Protestant church, which Lock had foreseen in her 1560 epistle to the duchess of Suffolk. Although Lock's disappointment with the established church is palpable in this 1590 volume, equally evident is her unabated commitment to the cause of reformed Protestantism.[144]

---

143 Dering, *Certaine godly and comfortable letters*, A3^{v}.

144 Her translation may also have influenced later Puritan works such as "The Comforte of Adoption" (Dd4^{r}–Ff6^{v}) included in *Bromleion. A discourse of the most substantial points of divinitie* (London, 1595; STC 14057), which was written by S. I. and dedicated to Sir Francis Newport of Shropshire. This collection also includes prayers by Edward Dering, a translation of Theodore Beza's *Summa totius Christianismi*, and a dedicatory letter to Alexander Nowell, dean of St. Paul's and almoner to Mildred Cooke Cecil. The collection in its entirety is dedicated to Sir Henry Bromley, son of Sir Thomas Bromley who was lord chancellor of England and the protégé of both William Cecil and Nicholas Bacon. Steven May drew my attention to the similarities between *Markes* and "The Comforte of Adoption."

Texts

Sermons of John Calvin (1560)

Sermons of John Calvin, upon the songe that Ezechias made after he had bene sicke, and afflicted by the hand of God, conteyned in the 38. Chapiter of Esay (STC 4450) was entered in the Stationers' Register on 15 January 1560 and printed that year by John Day in London. The title page, like the rest of the book, is relatively unadorned, appearing without borders or designs, and includes the statement that the text is "Newly set fourth and allowed, accordyng to the order appointed in the Quenes Majesties Injunctions." The dedicatory epistle to "Katharine, Duchesse of Suffolke" (A2^{r}–A8^{r}) is printed in 80-point italic typeface with the running title "THE EPISTLE." in roman letters on both recto and verso leaves. The epistle begins with a decorative woodcut *I* and is signed simply "A. L."

Lock's translations of Calvin's four sermons on Isaiah 38 (B1^{r}–G7^{r}) are printed in 62-point textura typeface with the opening text for each sermon printed in italics and some, but not all, of the direct quotations from Isaiah 38 within the sermons also printed in italics. The running title, in 96-point roman typeface, on both the recto and the verso is "The first sermon.", "The seconde sermon.", etc., along with page numbers that are frequently incorrect. Biblical references are indicated in the shoulder-notes and are printed in italics. The first letter of each sermon is decorated with a woodcut. Page numbers are placed on the upper left-hand corner of the verso pages and on the upper right-hand corner of the recto pages.

The volume concludes with a sonnet sequence of twenty-six poems on Psalm 51 (Aa1^{r}–Aa8^{r}) printed in the same black-letter type as the sermons. The sequence is introduced with its own title, "A Meditation of a Penitent Sinner: Written in Maner of a Paraphrase upon the 51. Psalme of David." with the following proviso, "I have added this meditation folowyng unto the ende of this boke, not as parcell of maister Calvines worke, but for that it well agreeth with the same argument, and was delivered me by my frend with whom I knew I might be so bolde to use and publishe it as pleased me." The first five sonnets are given their own title, "The preface, expressing the passioned minde of the penitent sinner." with the running title, "The Preface." The remaining twenty-one sonnets are entitled "A Meditation of a penitent sinner, upon the 51. Psalme." with the verso running title, "A meditation of a sinner" and the recto running title, "upon the 51. Psalme." The shoulder-notes provide a prose rendering of the psalm printed in italics. The gathering is numbered inconsistently with no signature on the title page, A.ii. on the second leaf, Aa.3 on the third leaf, and no subsequent signature markings; there are no page numbers.

Only two copies of the 1560 text are known:

F Folger Shakespeare Library, Washington, D.C. Previously owned by Alexander Moffatt (1863–1921) of Abercromby Place, Edinburgh.

L British Library, London; Pressmark 696.a.40. An inscription in an English hand imitating *italianate cancellaresca* on the verso flyleaf facing the title page reads "Liber Henrici Lock ex dono Annæ uxoris suæ. 1559" [A book of Henry Lock by gift of Anne his wife. 1559].[145] UMI Reel 491.

Another edition was printed in 1574 by John Day, but the single surviving copy (STC 4451) held by the British Museum was destroyed during the Second World War. Although there is no physical description of this edition, citations from it are given in the *OED*, which indicate no substantive alterations from the 1560 text. Andrew Maunsell in *The first part of the catalogue of English printed bookes* (1595) registers *Sermons of John Calvin* among the books on Isaiah and the books by John Calvin. In the main entry, Maunsell gives the title as *Sermons upon the song that* EZechias *made after that he had beene sicke, and afflicted by the hand of God on* Esay 38. *ver.* 9. *to the end of the Chapter* and the publication date as 1569. If this citation is accurate, and there is no reason to believe that it is not, there were at least two printings subsequent to the original 1560 edition. All three editions were printed by John Day.

In the 1560 edition, F and L are apparently both from the same print run but show evidence of correction during the printing process. The most obvious difference between the two copies occurs on the last leaf of the third sermon (F3^{v}) where F includes an erroneous running head (The fourth sermon) and twenty-five lines printed upside down on the lower two-thirds of the page. Peter W. M. Blayney suggests the following scenario:[146] Apparently, the compositor selected the lines of type from formes that were in the process of being distributed in order to create a bearer that would keep the type even and prevent the wet paper from sinking down into the print bed. This bearer type, however, was not properly patched with a frisket and so at least one, and probably several, sheets were printed before the mistake was noticed and corrected. F includes the uncorrected page, while L has a later state of the same forme.

---

145 See the example of humanistic cursive in Michelle P. Brown's *A Guide to Western Historical Scripts from Antiquity to 1600* (Toronto: Univ. of Toronto Press, 1990), 134–5.

146 Peter W. M. Blayney, personal communication, 8 June 1994. The collation of F and L was carried out by Dr. Blayney and the discussion of the press variants is entirely indebted to him.

The first ten lines of inverted text [A] come from the beginning of F3^{r} (lines 1–10). The next nine lines [B] are taken from the middle of F5^{r} (lines 15–23). The following line [C] consists of the direction line from F4^{v}, which consists mostly of large spaces with the catchword "fied [from glorified] in." Three more lines [D] are again taken from F5^{r} (lines 12–14). The final two lines [E] come once again from F3^{r} (lines 22–23).

Blayney surmises that this apparently haphazard arrangement of previously used type can be accounted for by imagining that the compositor simply filled the foot of F3^{v} (part of the inner forme) with blocks of text that came easily to hand from the outer forme of sheet F. Blayney theorizes that one possible logical explanation could be as follows: After the outer columns and headlines had been transferred from the outer forme of sheet F to the inner forme, Compositor 2 began to distribute the type of the outer forme, first emptying F6^{v}. In the meantime, "Compositor 1 places a piece of wooden 'furniture' below the text on F3^{v} to prevent accidents, and begins to fill the foot of the page with upside-down text. He starts with the first 10 lines of the nearest outer-forme page, F3^{r} (block A). While he's dealing with it, Compositor 2 finds that there are now *two* incomplete pages, and starts distributing the foot of F3^{r}. Compositor 1 therefore takes the next most convenient piece of text, block B (F5^{r}, lines 15–23). To hold those lines steady while he removes the piece of furniture he adds the direction line from F4^{v} (consisting mainly of large spaces except for the catchword)—the only direction line left on this side of the bench. After removing the furniture he once again finds the bottom of part-page F5^{r} accessible, and takes three more lines (block D = F5^{r}, lines 12–14). Needing two more, he finds that Compositor 2 is temporarily out of the way and takes what are now the last two lines of part-page F3^{r} (block E = F3^{r}, lines 22–3)."[147] The point that Blayney makes is not that this scenario is correct, but that there can be "a perfectly logical explanation" for the apparent random selection of text.[148]

While it is likely that the printer would have caught and corrected the error on F3^{v}, a more significant discrepancy occurs on C4^{r}, where a double transposition seems to indicate an authorial change that was overlooked during the correction process, but later changed during the print run of

[147] Blayney, personal communication, 8 June 1994.

[148] Another example of type used for a bearer in which the frisket-patch was mistakenly omitted is shown in copies of Giovanni Giorgio Trissino's *De la volgare eloquenzia*. See John R. Turner, "The printing of Trissino's *De la volgare eloquenzia*" *The Library*, 6th ser., 4 (1982): 307–13 with a corrective response by Peter W. M. Blayney, "Trissino's *De la volgare eloquenzia:* A Question of Bearing," *The Library*, 6th ser., 5 (1983): 175–6.

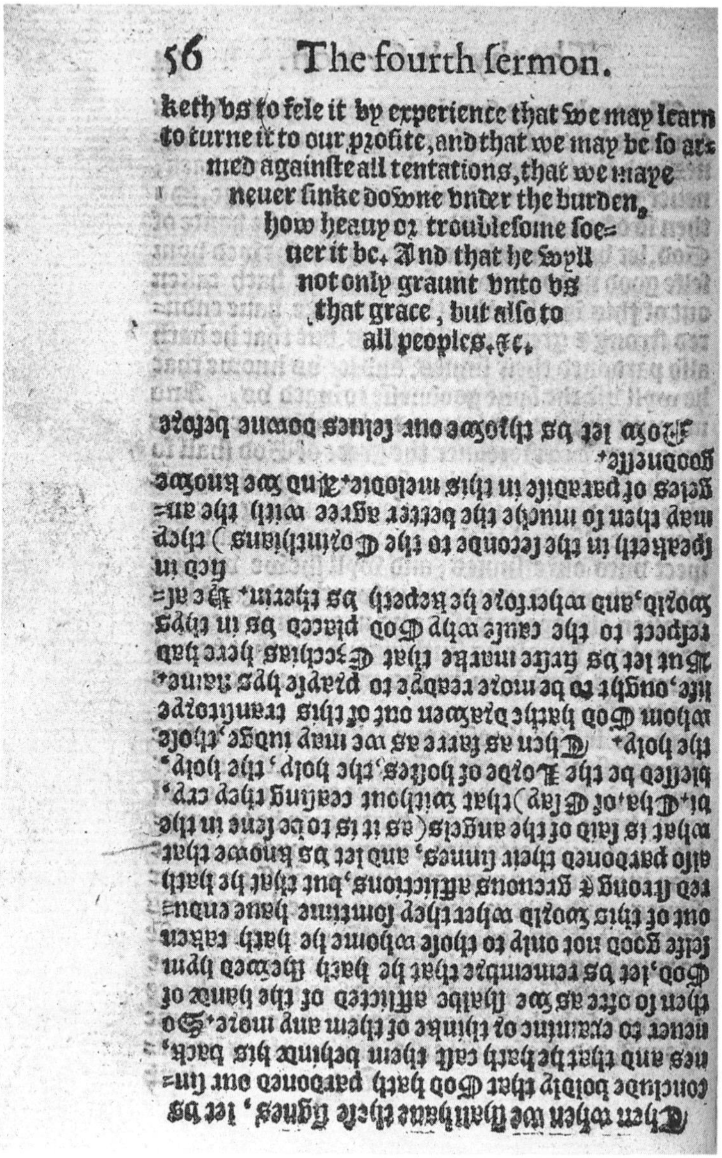
56 The fourth sermon.

keth vs to fele it by experience that we may learn
to turne it to our profite, and that we may be so armed againste all tentations, that we maye
neuer sinke downe vnder the burden,
how heauy or troublesome soe-
uer it be. And that he wyll
not only graunt vnto vs
that grace, but also to
all peoples. &c.

Then when we shall haue these signes, let vs
conclude boldly that God hath pardoned our sinnes and that he hath cast them behinde his back,
neuer to examine or thinke of them any more. So
then so ofte as we shalbe afflicted of the hande of
God, let vs remembre that he hath shewed hym
selfe good not only to those whome he hath taken
out of this world wher they somtime haue endured strong & greuous afflictions, but that he hath
also pardoned their sinnes, and let vs knowe that
what is said of the angels (as it is to be sene in the
vi. Cha. of Esay) that without ceasing they cry,
blessed be the Lorde of hostes, the holy, the holy,
the holy. Then as farre as we may iudge, those
whom God hathe drawen out of this transitorye
life, ought to be more readye to prayse hys name.
But let vs firste marke that Ezechias here had
respect to the cause why God placed vs in thys
world, and wherfore he kepeth vs therin. He as-
sied in
speaketh in the seconde to the Corinthians) they
may then so muche the better agree with the angeles of paradise in this melodie. And we knowe
goodnesse.
Now let vs throwe our selues downe before

Figure 2. Facsimile of misprinted page from *Sermons of John Calvin* (1560), F3v.

Table 2. Misprinted text from *Sermons of John Calvin* (1560), F3^{v}.

[A] Then when we shall have these signes, let us
conclude boldly that God hath pardoned our sinnes and that he hath cast them behinde his back,
never to examine or thinke of them any more. So
then so ofte as we shalbe afflicted of the hande of
God, let us remembre that he hath shewed hym
selfe good not only to those whome he hath taken
out of this world wher they somtime have endured strong and grevous afflictions, but that he hath
also pardoned their sinnes, and let us knowe that
[B] what is said of the angels (as it is to be sene in the
vi. Cha. of Esay) that without ceasing they cry,
blessed be the Lorde of hostes, the holy, the holy,
the holy. Then as farre as we may judge, those
whom God hathe drawen out of this transitorye
life, ought to be more readye to prayse hys name.
But let us firste marke that Ezechias here had
respect to the cause why God placed us in thys
world, and wherfore he kepeth us therin. He as-
[C] fied in
[D] speaketh in the seconde to the Corinthians) they
may then so muche the better agree with the angeles of paradise in this melodie. And we knowe
[E] goodnesse.

Now let us throwe our selves downe before

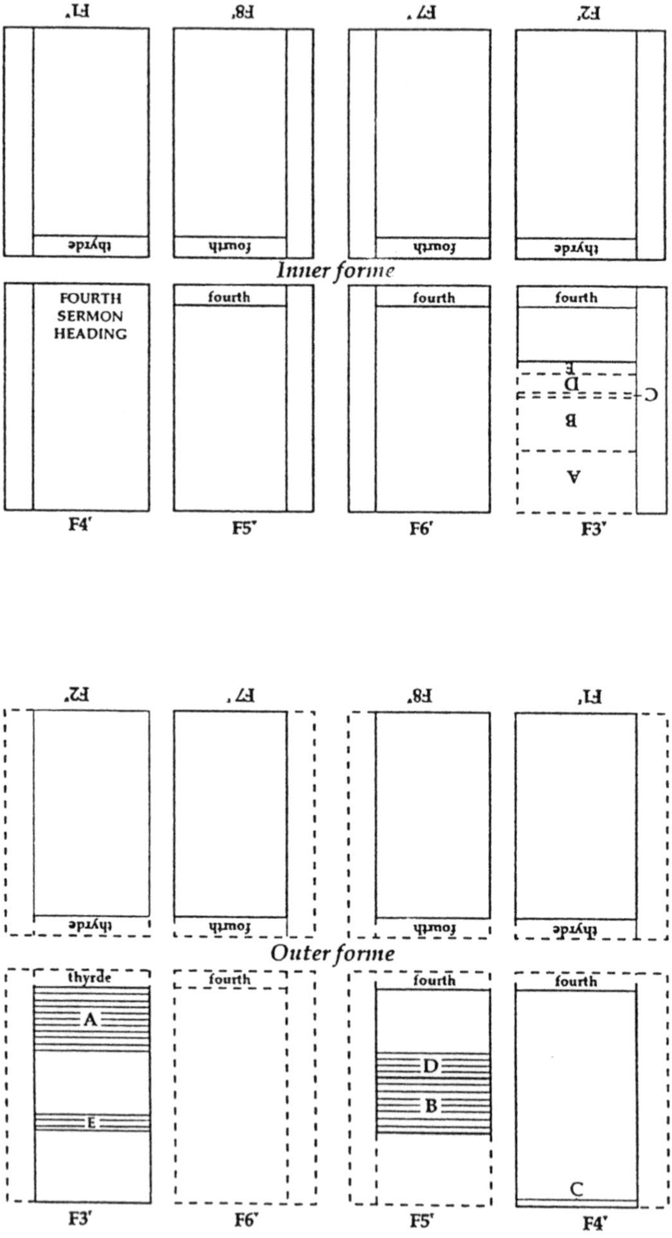

Figure 3. Inner and Outer Formes of Sheet F from *Sermons of John Calvin* (1560).

that page. From the correction of typographical errors ("shall shalbe" is changed to "shalbe" [Sermon One, line 435] and "boyng" is changed to "bowyng" [Sermon Two, line 174]), it appears that L has the earlier state of gathering C. In L, the penultimate paragraph of the first sermon reads:

> And yet alwaye lette us runne to oure God, and although it semeth that he persecuteth us, and that hys hande be verye roughe and dreadfull unto us, yet let us not cease to approche unto hym, and magnifie hys goodnesse: beynge assured that it shall very well surmount farre, and exccade all oure faultes and offences. (Sermon One, lines 516–520)

In F, however, the same paragraph reads:

> And yet alwaye lette us runne to oure God, and although it semeth that he persecuteth us, and that hys hande be verye roughe and dreadfull unto us, yet let us not cease to approche unto hym, and magnifie hys goodnesse: beynge verye well assured that it shall farre, surmonte and exccade all oure faultes and offences. (Sermon One, lines 516–520)

The movement of "verye well" and the transposition of "surmount/ surmonte" and "farre" argue for an authorial, rather than a printer's, correction since there is no reason, other than improvement of the translation, for making it. The original reads *estans asseurez qu'elle surmontera toutes nos fautes et offenses.*[149] By making "very well" modify "assured," rather than "surmount," Lock is able to emphasize both "assured" ("very well assured") and "surmount" ("farre surmount") rather than placing all the emphasis simply on "surmount." The Folger copy has the superior English rendition, and the retention of the comma after "farre" can be accounted for by the compositor's moving the entire word plus punctuation from its place following "surmount" to the antecedent position. The error in "exccade" ("exceade") remained uncorrected.

Although there is no way to prove that Lock herself supervised the printing and proofing of her own book, the evidence of this page suggests authorial intervention, a role not incompatible with what is known of Lock's public activities and personal status. Moreover, it seems that the Day printshop did host authors who proofread their own books. In William Baldwin's satirical *Beware the Cat*, the storytelling divine, Gregory Streamer, describes Day's house at Aldersgate as the place where he often

---

[149] Calvin, "Sermons sur le Cantique D'Ezechias," 538. The manuscript version is identical except that *fautes* is spelled *faultes*.

Table 3. Press Variants from *Sermons of John Calvin* (1560).

Section and Line in this edition	*Signature and Line in original edition*	*L*	*F*
Epistle. 17	A2^{r} catchword	fortune$_{s}$	fortunes
Ser. 1.316	B7^{v}33 shoulder -note	*Psalm 73.*	. [frisket bite]
	C Signature Outer Forme		
Ser. 1.435	C2^{v}9	When (I say) we shall shalbe	When (I saye) we shalbe
Ser. 1.451	33	of	f [frisket bite]
Ser. 1.452	34	xxv.	xv. [frisket bite]
Ser. 2.174–175	C8^{v}33	|boyng . . . afflictiõ,|	|bowyng . . . afflic=|
Ser. 2.175	34	|but	|tion, but
	C Signature Inner Forme		
Ser. 1.423	C2^{r}25	besid we $\overset{t}{\dot{y}}$ may	besid $\overset{t}{\dot{y}}$ we may
Ser. 1.519	C4^{r}31	as=|	ve=|
Ser. 1.519	32	|sured that it shall very well surmount farre	|rye well assured that it shall farre, surmonte
	F Signature Inner Forme		
Ser. 3.436	F2^{r}1	Lo^{e}	Loe
Ser. 3.453	25	and iugle	& inagled
Ser. 3.456	30	know	kuow
Ser. 3	F3^{v} running-title	thirde	fourth
Ser. 3	10ff	[blank]	inverted lines

stayed, "sometime for lack of other lodging, and somtime as while my Greeke Alphabets were in printing, to see that it might bee truly corrected."[150]

In addition to mechanical accidents on A2^{r} and B7^{v}, there are press variants in three printers' formes.

Of the Markes (1590)

The first English translation of Jean Taffin's *Des Marques des enfans de Dieu et des consolations en leurs afflictions* was entered in the Stationers' Register on 30 October 1587, licensed to Edward Aggas under the title *the Tokens of the children of GOD. and comfortes in their afflyctions.* Seven other French titles were registered to Aggas that same year, including at least three that had not yet been translated into English. This entry may refer to a translation of the 1586 nonaugmented Taffin edition prepared by Aggas himself, who translated other French Protestant texts such as *A caveat for France, upon the present evils that it now suffereth* (1588). If a translation of Taffin by Aggas was printed, it is apparently no longer extant.

Lock's translation of the 1588 augmented French text, *Of the markes of the children of God, and of their comforts in afflictions,* was entered in the Stationers' Register on 26 March 1590, licensed to Thomas Man. It was printed by Thomas Orwin. The dedicatory epistle to the Countess of Warwick (A2^{r}–A5^{v}) is set in 93-point roman typeface. The translation of *Des Marques des enfans de Dieu et des consolations en leurs afflictions* (A6^{r}–R4^{r}), set in 82-point roman typeface, includes Taffin's epistle "To the Faithfull," dated 15 September 1586 at Harlem and set in 82-point italic typeface, and the table of contents, set in 67-point roman typeface. The running titles throughout the main text are set in 82-point italic typeface and read "*Of the markes*" on the verso and "*of the children of God.*" on the recto. The book concludes with a poem, set in 82-point italic typeface, entitled "The necessitie and benefite of affliction" (S1^{r}–S3^{r}). Woodcuts are used for the initial letters of Lock's epistle, the letter from Taffin, and each of the subsequent thirteen chapters. Folio numbers are placed on the upper right-hand corner of the recto pages.

Four copies of the 1590 text (STC 23652) are extant:

---

150 William Baldwin, *A marvelous hystory intitulede, Beware the cat* (London, 1570; STC 1244), A4^{v}. Also noted by C. L. Oastler in *John Day, the Elizabethan Printer,* Occasional Publication no. 10 (Oxford: Oxford Bibliographical Society, 1975), 29.

HN Huntington Library, San Marino, California; Pressmark 14578. Nineteenth-century binding. Lacks S4. Purchased from the Robert Pariser Sale at the Anderson gallery Dec. 1920, no. 571. UMI Reel 358.

F Folger Shakespeare Library, Washington, D.C. Nineteenth-century binding. Purchased from the Harmsworth Library. Part of the Britwell Court Sale, May 1920, Lot #441.

L British Library, London; Pressmark c.119.dd.41. Sixteenth-century binding of limp vellum with holes punched for a tie. An inscription in cursive script, "John Lufman his Booke" is written across the spine from the end page onto the inside cover; beneath, in the same hand, is inscribed "Thomas a dams," possibly the printer (d. 1620?) who was admitted as a freeman of the Stationers' Company on 15 October 1590. Eighteenth-century inscriptions on the verso page facing the title page and the title page itself are those of Hugh Lacy and Jeremiah Holloway. Purchased in December 1879 at the auction of David Laing.

PN^2 The Library of Princeton Theological Seminary, Princeton, New Jersey. Nineteenth-century binding. Title page inscription: "John Wilson his Book." Purchased by Alexander Balloch Grosart (1827–1899) for the Princeton Seminary Library and part of its Puritan Collection.

Exemplars of seven subsequent editions of *Of the Markes* are extant, all of them octavo volumes. The following list indicates the copies of those editions recorded in the STC:

1591 King's College, Cambridge; Pressmark C.66.26. STC 23652.3. Printed by Richard Field for Thomas Man. Rebound with bookplate of George Thackeray (1777–1850) provost of King's College from 1814 to 1850. Signatures $A1^r$–$R8^v$. R8 blank. UMI Reel 1859.

1597 Folger Shakespeare Library, Washington, D.C. STC 23652.5. Printed by Robert Robinson for Thomas Man. Nineteenth-century binding. Inscription "Francis Clark's his book 1691" on $Q5^r$. Signatures $A1^r$–$R8^v$. R8 blank. Folger purchase from the Harmsworth Library. Previous property of Garnet W. Holt, Esq., acquired from the library of Tanderagee Castle, property of the Duchy of Manchester, Irish estates and sold in Lot 159 at Sothebys to the Folger on 4 July 1928. Bookseller's mark, "W. A. F."

1599 Dulwich College, London; Pressmark L.4.31. STC 23652.7. Printed by Felix Kingston for Thomas Man. Sixteenth-century binding of limp vellum with holes punched for a tie. The title page inscription reads "Benchingham [or Renchingham] 1606." Signatures

A1^{r}–P8^{v}. Probably given to the school by the London actor turned bookseller William Cartwright (d. 1687) in 1680 as part of an annuity in exchange for a lifetime guarantee of bed and board (Cartwright died, however, before he could actually move to the college). The book is listed in the first catalog of Dulwich College library begun by James Hume in 1729.

1608L British Library, London; Pressmark 4410.f.41. STC 23653. Printed by T[homas]. E[ast]. for Thomas Man. Nineteenth-century binding. Signatures A1^{r}–R7^{v}. R8 lacking. 23 July 1868 acquisition. UMI Reel 1695.

1608O^{28} Regent's Park College, Angus Library, Oxford. STC 23653. Printed by T. E. for Thomas Man. Nineteenth-century binding. Signatures A1^{r}–R8^{v}. R8 blank.

1608MCG McGill University, Montreal. A ghost copy that seems not to exist.

1609F Folger Shakespeare Library, Washington, D.C., STC 23654. Printed by T[homas]. C[reede]. for Thomas Man. Nineteenth-century binding. Signatures A1^{r}–R8^{v}. R8 blank. Purchased by the Folger from the Harmsworth collection. Previously owned by Frederic A. Hapley (or Kapley) June 1886; passed through hands of booksellers, J. and J. Leighton, Jan. 1921. UMI Reel 667.

1609O Bodleian Library, Oxford; Pressmark Vet. A2. f. 266. STC 23654. Printed by T. C. for Thomas Man. Seventeenth-century binding of limp vellum with holes punched for a tie. Well-used, underlined, and annotated volume. Signatures A1^{r}–R7^{v}. R8 lacking.

1615C University Library, Cambridge; Pressmark Syn. 8.61.53. STC 23655. Printed by Thomas Snodham for Thomas Man. Seventeenth-century binding of limp vellum with holes punched for a tie. Inscription on the second flyleaf recto reads "John Whincop 1618 Non iuvat amisso claudere septa grege" [It is no good shutting the enclosure after the herd is already lost].[151] Signatures A1^{r}–R8^{v}. R8 blank. Acquired in 1715 from the royal library of George I; formerly in the library of John Moore, Bishop of Ely. UMI Reel 1782.

---

[151] The inscription is a variant on the common proverb, "When the steed is stolen, shut the stable door." See Tilley, S838; Bartlett Jere Whiting and Helen Wescott Whiting, *Proverbs, Sentences, and Proverbial Phrases from English Writings Mainly before 1500* (Cambridge, Mass.: Harvard Univ. Press, 1968), S697; Hans Walther, *Proverbia Sententiaeque Latinitatis Medii Aevi*, vol. 3 (Göttingen: Vandenhoeck & Ruprecht, 1965), no. 16744.

1615O Bodleian Library, Oxford; Pressmark 8° F 144 Th. STC 23655. Seventeenth-century binding of limp vellum with holes punched for a tie. Signatures A1^r–R8^v. R8 blank.

1634 British Library, London; Pressmark 4400.m.17. STC 23656. Printed by the assignes of Thomas Man, Paul Man, and Jonah Man to be sold by John Grismond. Octavo rebound into a quarto volume with signatures gathered in twelves. Signatures A1^r–O12^v. Acquired 1 March 1887. Note on back cover: microfilmed 1987, 10073. UMI Reel 1695.

Andrew Maunsell in *The first part of the catalogue of English printed bookes* (1595) lists the 1591 edition of *Of the Markes* four times, under the heading "Of *Adversitie* and *Affliction*," and alphabetized under *M* for *Markes*, *P* for "An Prowsse her translation," and *T* for Taffin. The separate heading for "Prowse" as translator suggests that Lock's name was widely recognized and that she continued to hold a prominent position within the nonconformist community.

The publication rights to *Of the Markes* were held by Thomas Man through the 1615 edition. Subsequently they passed, as part of a block of titles, to Paule and Jonas Man from Thomas Man (3 May 1624); to Benjamyn ffisher from Jonah Man (6 July 1629); and to Benjamin ffisher and Widow Mann from Thomas, Paul, and Jonah Man (27 October 1634, but registered 12 August 1635).[152] These printers were a tightly knit group. Joan Orwin, whose husband printed the 1590 edition of *Of the Markes*, was the mother of Felix Kingston (1599 edition), Thomas East (1608 edition) passed his business to Thomas Snodham (1615 edition) around 1608, and Benjamin Fisher managed the printshop of Thomas Man from 1622 to 1625 and worked closely with Man's widow and sons thereafter.[153]

This edition is based on the copy in the Huntington Library; variants among the 1590 copies are given in the textual notes. The majority of these occur on G1^r, G1^v, G8^r, and G8^v where leaves G1 and G8 in L have been replaced by leaves from the 1597 edition.[154] I have not recorded the differences in printing impressions; the shoulder notes show the greatest variation in ink distribution, with the clarity of the impression varying from

---

[152] Arber, *A Transcript of the Registers*, 4:117, 215, 344.

[153] Jill Seal brought these connections to my attention.

[154] Perhaps this copy, with two damaged leaves, was part of the unbound stock still owned by Thomas Man in 1597. During the printing of the 1597 edition, the printer simply ran an extra sheet of the G signature and completed the copy for sale.

page to page. As a general rule, HN presents the clearest copy and PN^2 the faintest.

Among the subsequent editions, the first copy of each edition listed has been examined and all substantive variants in that copy are indicated in the textual notes. Significant accidental variants that clarify the printing history of the various editions have also been included. In the case of the 1608 edition, copies from both the British Library and the Angus Library at Regent's Park College have been examined and the variants noted.

It seems clear that the 1590 edition (STC 23652) is the first edition because it retains the most accurate translation of Taffin's 1588 augmented French text. The subsequent editions, however, appear to share a common ancestor, a nonextant second edition [β], that corrects some obvious grammatical and orthographic errors but introduces other mistakes. This second edition makes its revisions without recourse to the French text, and, therefore, probably was not made by Lock (a point that may argue for her death in 1590). This missing second edition may have been printed in 1590 or it may be the 1591 edition noted by Maunsell.

Table 4 summarizes the relationships among the editions, as determined through a comparison of all the variants.

Table 4. Stemma for *Of the Markes*.

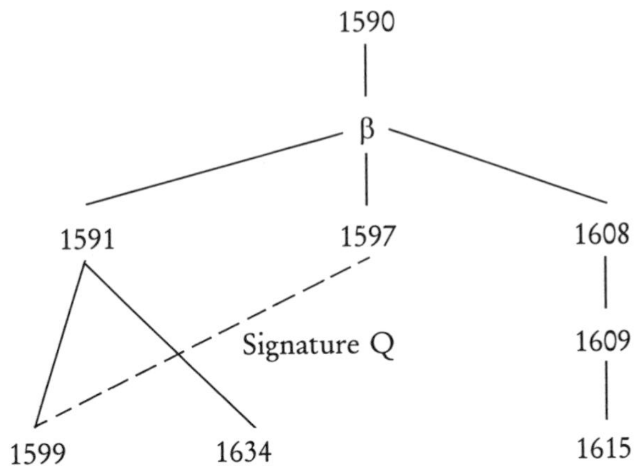

As Table 4 and the textual notes show, all the editions after 1590 follow the missing second edition [β] and fall into three family groups: 1591, 1599, 1634; 1597; and 1608, 1609, 1615. The 1599 edition follows the 1591

edition except in the Q signature where it relies on the 1597 edition (see Table 6). These distinct family groups may be seen most clearly in the variations of line 112 in the concluding poem, "The necessitie and benefite of affliction." This line in the 1590 edition reads: "*for ever it can have.*" The 1591 edition and its successors (1599 and 1634) read: "*in many we atchieve.*" The 1597 edition copies the line that is directly opposite on the verso page: "*more folly did esteeme.*" Finally, the 1608 edition and its successors (1609 and 1615) read: "*which they full soone shall leave.*" This wide variation suggests that line 112 may have been lacking or obscure in β, but confirms the family relationships among the editions noted in Table 4.

Table 5, which gives the substantive variants between the 1590 edition and the missing second edition [β] as determined by the unanimous readings of the 1591, 1597, and 1608 editions, clearly shows the superiority of the 1590 edition in terms of its fidelity to the French original; the variant readings of the subsequent editions, following β, most often represent agreement in error. Where the missing second edition [β] is superior, it usually corrects mistakes that are obvious in the English translation. The anomaly of the 1597 edition agreeing with the 1590 edition against all the other editions in 14 percent of the cases may be explained by the printer working from a composite copy of pages drawn from both the first and the second editions. The agreements between the 1590 and the 1615 editions may be explained as changes made by the compositor without recourse to the 1590 edition, for example changing "should not" to "would not" (12.97).

The change from "dissipations, assailed" (1590) to "disputations, assaulted" (all subsequent editions) in Taffin's preface, "To the Faithfull," (lines 7–8) may have been made for dogmatic reasons, to emphasize the conflicts within the English church and to align the nonconformists with the true Church.

As has already been noted, all the editions after 1590 follow the missing second edition [β] and fall into three family groups: 1591, 1599, 1634; 1597; and 1608, 1609, 1615 (see Table 4). All the editions, even those within family groups, show significant variations from one another in orthography and punctuation.

The 1591 edition, printed by Richard Field, has the same number of leaves as the 1590 edition but does not have the same line-breaks or page-breaks as the first edition and uses twenty-six lines of type per page (excluding the catchword line) rather than the twenty-seven lines used in the 1590, 1597, 1599, and 1634 editions. The 1599 edition, printed by Felix Kingston, follows the 1591 edition but condenses the type, with the result that it is one signature smaller than its source text. It does deviate from the 1591 edition in Chapters 12 and 13 where it follows the unique readings of

Table 5. Variants between *Of the Markes* (1590) and missing edition β.

An asterisk indicates the reading that is closer to the French original.

Chapter and Line	*1590 Edition*	*β Edition (established by the unanimous readings of the 1591, 1597, and 1608 editions)*
To the Faithfull.7–8	*dissipations, assailed	disputations, assaulted
1.72 note #27	*1. Thess. 4.17.	2. Thess. 4.17
1.268 note #68	*Joh. 16.22.	Joh. 15.22
2.24	accompted	accounted
2.168	feare God	*feare of God
2.174	childen	*children
3.108	*Marie [& 1597]	Mary
3.151	*to put thee	put to thee
4.111	*so is	so it is
4.250	*But thou (¶) [& 1615]	But thou (no ¶)
4.350 note #73	Mar. 17.5.	*Matth. 17.5.
4.572–573	*yet it can	yet can
5.77	unto	to
5.167	*that he	as he
7.26	afflictions	*affliction
7.125 note #24	*Act. 14.22.	Actes. 14.
8.27	eyes. Did they escape [& 1597]	eyes, they did escape
8.77	seditious [& 1597]	*seditions
8.96	*tormens	torments
8.151	people *Israel*	*people of *Israel*
8.177	sheepe	*sheepes
8.230	*welbeloved one [& 1597]	welbeloved ones
9.95 note #18	*2. In	3. In
9.162	*tribulations	tribulation
9.163	*at his ease	at ease
9.204	compt [& 1597]	count
9.211–212	*to subject	subject
9.290	*pieces of wood [& 1597]	a piece of wood
10.18 note #9	of the God	*of God
10.153	*this reward	their reward
10.157 note #31	*2. Cor. 4.17	1. Cor. 4.17.

10.181 note #33	*2. Sam. 16 12	2. Sam. 12.16
10.211–212	*our afflictions	afflictions
10.241	*of man	of a man
10.253	*80. yeres	80.
11.25	*renowme [& 1597]	renowne
11.38 note #7	decla- claring [& 1597]	*declaring
11.50	*supposts	suppost
11.102	*goodlie [& 1597]	godlie
11.120	*the honours	honours
11.154	compteth	counteth
12.4	**to pray*	*pray*
12.7	*or to be	or be
12.46–47	shall not it	shal it not
12.47	accompt	account
12.57	*it is as a	it is a
12.75 note #8	**Ja.* 5.11.	Jam. 5.1.
12.97	would not [& 1615]	should not
12.118	compt [& 1597]	count
12.152	*Let us put off	Let us cut off
12.197	into the land [& 1615]	in the land
12.234	**Nicodemites*	*Nicodemoies* [& variants]
12.241 note #33	*2. Cor. 7.1	1. Cor. 7.1 [& variants]
12.361	*lusts	lust
12.365–366	*reproofe	proof
12.383	*yee	we
12.398 note #85	*1. Pet. 4.10	1. Pet. 10.
12.412	*offend	offended
12.476	faithfull	faithfully
13.4	*the troubles	thy troubles
13.6	but forasmuch	but as much [& variants]
13.7	*thi wrath	his wrath
13.11–12	*wee are worthie to bee rejected of thee	[omitted]
13.33	*our God	ô God
13.56	*thy Word	the Word
13.110	at tone	*at one
13.143	lift	*life
Poem.33	These	The
Poem.35	Then	The
Poem.88	mere [& 1615]	more
Poem.112	for ever it can have	[various readings]
Poem.124	infinite the gain	infinite is the gain

Table 6. Use of the 1597 Q Signature in the 1599 Edition.

Chapter and Line	*1591 Edition*	*1597 Q Signature*	*1599 Edition*
12.328 note #61	Gal. 5.24.	Gal. 5.24.	Gal. 5.22.
12.329 note #62	[omitted]	Gal. 5.25.	Gal. 5.25.
12.331	if ye	if we	if we
12.332	If yee	If wee	If we
12.399 note #86	1. Pet. 4.8	1. Pet. 8.4.	1. Pet. 8.4.
12.429	heape	heade	head
12.461	your	our	our
13.6	as much	in asmuch	in as much

Table 7. Anomalies in the 1615 Edition.

Chapter and Line	*1609 Edition*	*1615 Edition*
7.37	(saith he) to his Apostles	(saith hee to his Apostles)
7.38	amongst	among
7.48–49	sayeth Saint *Peter*	(saith Saint *Peter*,)
12.97	should not	would not
12.197	in the land	into the land
12.384	bowell	bowells
Poem.88	more	mere

Table 8. Miscellaneous Anomalies in Editions of *Of the Markes*.

Chapter and Line		*All other Editions*
	1590, 1597, 1608 Editions	
4.61	forsaken	forsaken me
	1615, 1634 Editions	
4.492	others	other
	1608 Edition	
9.142	the flesh	of the flesh
	1590, 1599 Editions	
11.79	he hath	he had
	1590, 1599, 1634 Editions	
13.4	the troubles	thy troubles

the 1597 Q signature (see Table 6). The 1591 edition is also clearly the source text for the 1634 edition, which replicates its unique readings. This final edition, the longest at 334 pages, presents an entirely new page layout with the text boxed in by ruled lines and gatherings in twelves.

The 1597 edition, printed by Robert Robinson, introduces numerous new errors that are not followed in subsequent editions. Its line-breaks and page-breaks, however, are nearly identical to those in the 1590 edition. As shown in the textual notes, the L copy of the 1590 edition contains two leaves, G1 and G8, taken from the 1597 edition. These two leaves in 1590L are identical in spelling, punctuation, and typeface to the surviving 1597 edition. Similarly, as Table 6 shows, anomalous readings in the 1599 edition can be explained by the presence of a 1597 Q signature in the basetext from which the 1599 compositor was working.

The 1608 edition, printed by Thomas East, introduces a number of lexical changes and more paragraph divisions. Its pagination is nearly identical to that of the 1590 edition, although it uses twenty-six lines per page rather than twenty-seven. The 1609 edition, printed by Thomas Creede, is nearly an exact copy of the 1608 edition including almost identical page-breaks and line-breaks. The slight changes made in the 1609 edition are followed in the 1615 edition, printed by Thomas Snodham. The 1615 edition again modernizes some words, for instance substituting "count" for "compt," and adds more paragraph divisions. Lineation and pagination are almost identical with the 1609 edition in the body of the book but not in the prefatory material or concluding poem. The 1615 edition includes seven variants that appear to follow one of the earlier editions, rather than the 1609 edition, but all of these can be explained as changes initiated by the compositor when the type was being set without recourse to earlier editions. Table 7 shows these anomalies.

The remaining anomalies that might argue against the stemma described in Table 4 can also be attributed to printing errors, as shown in Table 8.

Editorial Procedure

All the listed copies of the 1560 and 1590 volumes have been collated for this edition with F as the basetext for *Sermons of John Calvin* and HN as the basetext for *Of the Markes*. All variants among the listed copies of the original edition are given in the textual notes, but only substantive variants in the later printings of *Of the Markes* are so indicated.

The original spelling, punctuation, and paragraphing remain intact, except for the following changes: I have regularized spacing between words, for example modifying "shallnot" to "shall not" but have not combined separations such as "him self" or "in stead"; corrected obvious printing errors (such as turned or substituted letters); followed modern orthographic conventions for *i, j, u, v, w*, and the long *s*; and expanded the following abbreviations: & to *and*, y^e to *the*, y^t to *that*, and w^t to *with*. A tilde over a vowel has been expanded to *m* or *n* as needed. These emendations are made silently except for the printing errors, which are listed in the textual notes. Damaged or worn type (most frequently seen in the letters *m*, *e*, and *i*) has not been noted. I have not indicated the substitution of type, except where there are variants among copies of the original edition. All of these substitutions occur in *Of the Markes* and are usually of the following types: oversize S. for Saint, italicized parentheses and punctuation marks, black-letter colons and periods, and small capital G for God as in God. In *Of the Markes*, when the divine name is spelled out in capital letters, it is always spaced as follows: G O D. The common printing practice of justifying lines by increasing or decreasing spaces between words and before and after punctuation marks has not been noted.

Signature indications and page numbers are given in the text between square brackets. Lock's shoulder-notes are reproduced as footnotes and are keyed to the first word in the relevant line of the original. Where the placement of the shoulder-note is unclear, it has been matched with the upper line of the text. Scripture references in the shoulder-notes have not been emended; erroneous citations are corrected in the textual notes. I have not followed prose lineation and have omitted hyphens where they serve only to divide a word at the end of a line. When a word is broken across a page, I have ignored the hyphen and placed the complete word after the signature mark.

Selected Bibliography

Bainton, Roland H. "Anne Locke." In *Women of the Reformation: From Spain to Scandinavia*. Minneapolis: Augsburg, 1977.

Beilin, Elaine V. *Redeeming Eve: Women Writers of the English Renaissance.* Princeton: Princeton Univ. Press, 1987.

Brewer, J. S., James Gairdner, and R. H. Brodie, eds. *Letters and Papers, Foreign and Domestic, of the Reign of Henry VIII, 1509–1547.* 21 vols. London: Longman, 1862–1910.

Calvin, John. *Sermons of John Calvin, upon the songe that Ezechias made after he had bene sicke, and afflicted by the hand of God, conteyned in the 38. Chapiter of Esay.* 1560. Translated by Anne Lock. Facsimile, with notes by Lewis Lupton. London: Olive Tree Press, 1973.

Collinson, Patrick. *The Elizabethan Puritan Movement.* Berkeley: Univ. of California Press, 1967.

——. *Godly People: Essays on English Protestantism and Puritanism.* London: Hambledon Press, 1983.

Donawerth, Jane. "Women's Poetry and the Tudor-Stuart System of Gift Exchange." In *Women, Writing, and the Reproduction of Culture in Tudor and Stuart Britain.* Edited by Mary E. Burke, Jane Donawerth, Linda Dove, and Karen Nelson. Syracuse: Syracuse Univ. Press. 1999.

Dove, Linda. "Women at Variance: Sonnet Sequences and Social Commentary in Early Modern England." Ph.D. diss., University of Maryland at College Park, 1997.

Felch, Susan M. "Curing the Soul: Anne Lock's Authorial Medicine." *Reformation* 2 (1997): 7–38.

——. " 'Deir Sister': The Letters of John Knox to Anne Vaughan Lok." *Renaissance and Reformation/Renaissance et Reforme* 19, no. 4 (1995): 47–68.

——. "The Rhetoric of Biblical Authority: John Knox and the Question of Women." *Sixteenth Century Journal* 26 (1995): 805–22.

Fry, George S., ed. *Abstracts of Inquisitiones Post Mortem Relating to the City of London, returned into the Court of Chancery.* 3 vols. 1896–1908. Reprint, Nendeln, Liechtenstein: Kraus Reprint, 1968.

Greene, Roland. *Post-Petrarchism: Origins and Innovations of the Western Lyric Sequence.* Princeton: Princeton Univ. Press, 1991.

Hannay, Margaret Patterson, ed. *Silent But for the Word: Tudor Women as Patrons, Translators, and Writers of Religious Works.* Kent: Kent State Univ. Press, 1985.

Hannay, Margaret P. "'Strengthning the walles of... Ierusalem': Anne Vaughan Lok's Dedication to the Countess of Warwick." *American Notes and Queries* 5 (1992): 71–75.

——. "'Unlock my lipps': the *Miserere mei Deus* of Anne Vaughan Lok and Mary Sidney Herbert, Countess of Pembroke." In *Privileging Gender in Early Modern England.* Edited by Jean R. Brink. Sixteenth Century Essays and Studies, vol. 23. Kirksville, Mo.: Sixteenth Century Journal Publishers, 1993.

——. "'Wisdome the Wordes': Psalm Translation and Elizabethan Women's Spirituality." *Religion and Literature* 23, no. 3 (1991): 65–82.

Huttar, Charles A. "Translating French Proverbs and Idioms: Anne Locke's Renderings from Calvin." *Modern Philology* 96 (1998): 158–83.

Knox, John. *The Works of John Knox.* Edited by David Laing. 6 vols. Edinburgh: Thomas George Stevenson, 1846–1864.

Locke, Anne. *A Meditation of a Penitent Sinner: Anne Locke's Sonnet Sequence.* Edited and with an introduction by Kel Morin-Parsons. Waterloo, On.: North Waterloo Academic Press, 1997.

Lupton, Lewis. *A History of the Geneva Bible.* 25 vols. London: Olive Tree, 1966–1994.

Morin-Parsons, Kel. "'Loose my speche': Anne Locke's Sonnets and the Matrilineal Protestant Poetic." Ph.D. diss., University of Ottawa, 1999.

Prowse, Anne Lock, trans. *Sermons of John Calvin, upon the songe that Ezechias made*, by John Calvin; and *Of the markes of the children of God*, by John Taffin; and Elizabeth Russell, trans. *A Way of Reconciliation of a good and learned man*, by John Ponet. Introduced by Elaine V. Beilin. The Early Modern Englishwoman: A Facsimile Library of Essential Works. Edited by Betty S. Travitsky and Patrick Cullen, pt. 2. Brookfield, Vt.: Scolar Press, 1998.

Richardson, W. C. *Stephen Vaughan, Financial Agent of Henry VIII: A Study of Financial Relations with the Low Countries.* Louisiana State University Studies. Edited by Richard J. Russell. Baton Rouge: Louisiana State Univ. Press, 1953.

Roche, Thomas P., Jr. *Petrarch and the English Sonnet Sequences.* New York: AMS Press, 1989.

Schleiner, Louise. *Tudor and Stuart Women Writers.* Bloomington and Indianapolis: Indiana Univ. Press, 1994.

Seal, Jill. "Psalms, Sonnets, and Spiritual Songs: Some Traditions and

Innovations in English Religious Poetry, c. 1560–1611." Ph.D. diss., University of Nottingham, 1997.

Spiller, Michael R. G. *The Development of the Sonnet: An Introduction*. London and New York: Routledge, 1992.

——. "A literary 'first': the sonnet sequence of Anne Locke (1560)." *Renaissance Studies* 11 (1997): 41–55.

Stevenson, Robert Louis. "John Knox and his Relations to Women." In *Familiar Studies of Men and Books*. Vol. 3 of *The Works of Robert Louis Stevenson*. London: Cassell, 1906.

White, Micheline. " 'Cunning in Controversies': Protestant Women Writers and Religious and Literary Debates, 1580–1615." Ph.D. diss., Loyola University Chicago, 1998.

——. "Renaissance Englishwomen and Religious Translations: The Case of Anne Lock's *Of the markes of the children of God*." *English Literary Renaissance* 29. Forthcoming.

Woods, Susanne. "Anne Lock and Aemilia Lanyer: A Tradition of Protestant Women Speaking." In *Form and Reform in Renaissance England: Essays in Honor of Barbara Kiefer Lewalski*. Edited by Amy Boesky and Mary Thomas Crane. Newark: Univ. of Delaware Press. 1999.

——. "The Body Penitent: A 1560 Calvinist Sonnet Sequence." *American Notes and Queries* 5 (1992): 137–40.

The Collected Works of Anne Vaughan Lock

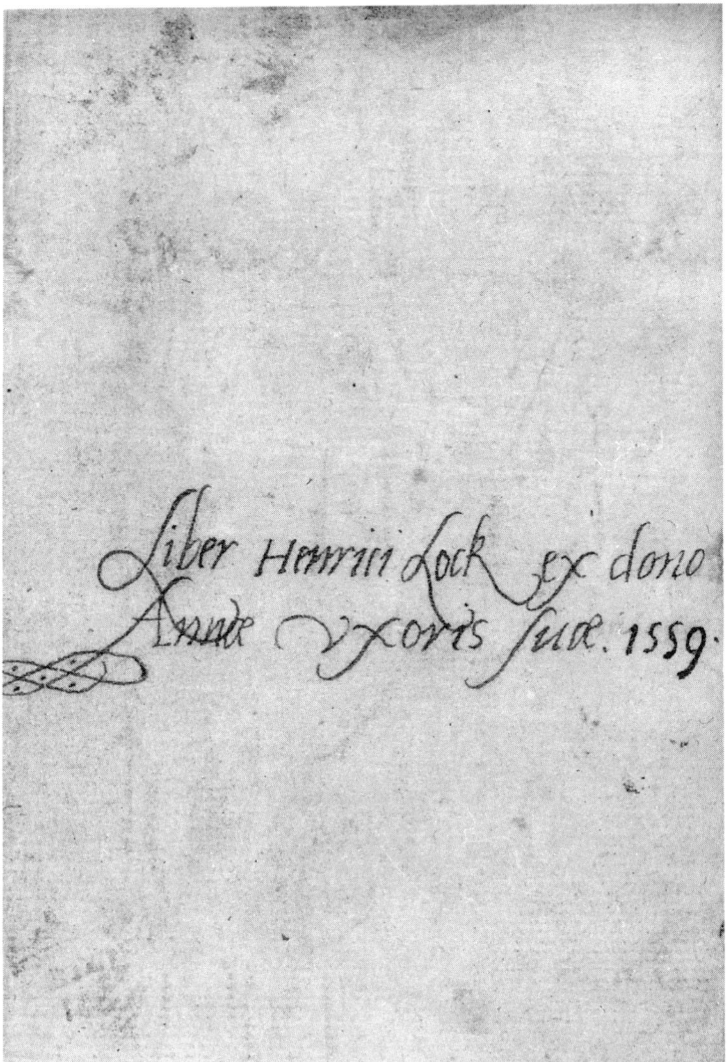

Figure 4. Inscription from *Sermons of John Calvin* (1560).

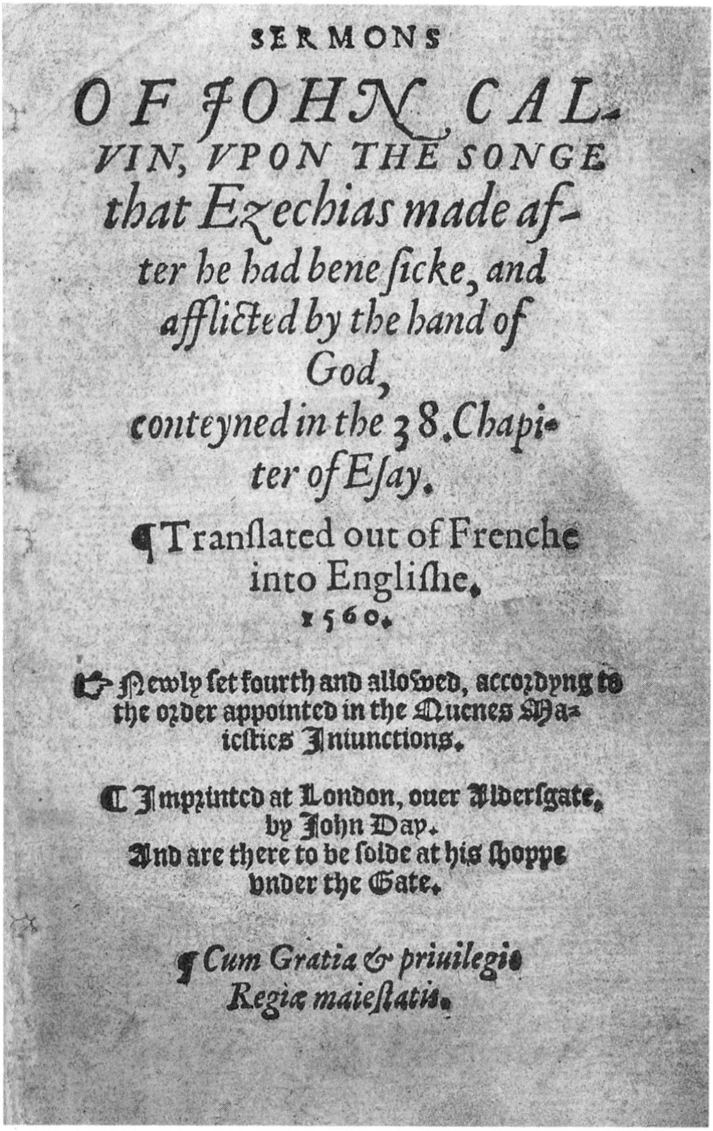

SERMONS
OF JOHN CAL-
VIN, VPON THE SONGE
that Ezechias made af-
ter he had bene ſicke, and
afflicted by the hand of
God,
conteyned in the 38.Chapi-
ter of Eſay.

¶Tranſlated out of Frenche
into Engliſhe.
1560.

☞ Newly ſet fourth and allowed, accordyng to
the order appointed in the Quenes Ma-
ieſties Iniunctions.

¶ Imprinted at London, ouer Alderſgate,
by John Day.
And are there to be ſolde at his ſhoppe
vnder the Gate.

¶ Cum Gratia & priuilegio
Regiæ maieſtatis.

Figure 5. Title page from *Sermons of John Calvin* (1560).

SERMONS

OF JOHN CAL-
VIN, UPON THE SONGE
that Ezechias made af-
ter he had bene sicke, and
afflicted by the hand of
God,
conteyned in the 38. Chapi-
ter of Esay.

Translated out of Frenche
into Englishe.
1560.

Newly set fourth and allowed, accordyng to
the order appointed in the Quenes Majesties Injunctions.

Imprinted at London, over Aldersgate,
by John Day.
And are there to be solde at his shoppe
under the Gate.

Cum Gratia and privilegio
Regiæ majestatis.

[A2r]

TO THE RIGHT HONORABLE, AND Christian Princesse, the Lady Katharine, Duchesse of Suffolke.

IT often falleth out in experience (my gracious and singular good Lady) that some men beynge oppressed with povertie, tossed with worldlye adversitye, tourmented with payne, sorenes, and sicknes of body, and other suche common matters of griefe, as the world counteth miseries and evils: Yet having theyr myndes armed and fournished with prepared patience, and defence of inward understandyng, all these calamities can not so farre prevaile, as to make them fall, nor yet once stoupe into the state of men to be accompted miserable: but they beare them with suche constaunce, as if suche afflictions were not of such nature as other commonly do fele them, or as if those men were suche upon whome those troubles coulde not worke theyr naturall propertie. On th'other side we se some that flowyng in earthly wealth and suffisance, free from [A2v] fortunes crueltie, healthy in bodye, and every waye to the worldes seming blessed: yet with mynde not well instructed, or with conscience not well quieted, even upon such small chaunces as other can lightly beare, are vexed above measure with reasonlesse extremitie. Wherby appeareth that the greves of body and calamities of fortune do so farre onely extende, to afflict, or make a man miserable, as they approch to touch the mind, and assaile the soule. Which proveth that the peines and diseases of minde and soule are not only the most grevous, and most daungerous, but also they onely are peinfull and perillous, and those of the body and fortune are such as the mynde useth, and maketh them. So as to a sicke stomacke of mynde, all bodylie matters of delite and worldely pleasures are lothesome and displeasant, as on th'other side the power of a healthy soule easely digesteth and gathereth good nouriture of the hard peines, and bitter tormentes of the body and fortune. He then, that cureth the sicke minde, or preserveth it from disease, cureth or preserveth not onely minde, but bodye also: and deserveth so much more praise and thanke, than the bodies Physicion, as the soule excelleth the bodie, [A3r] and as the curing, or preservation of them both is to be preferred before the cure of the bodye alone. But we se dayly, when skilfull men by arte, or honest neyghbours havyng gathered understandyng of some specyall dysease and the healing therof by theyr owne experiment, do applie their knowledge to the restoring of health of any mans body in any corporall sicknesse, howe thankfully it is taken, howe muche the releved patient accompteth him selfe bound to him by meane of whose aide and ministration he findeth him self holpen or eased.

What then deserveth he, that teacheth such a receipt, wherby health both of body and mynde is preserved, and wherby if health be appaired, it may be restored, yea whereby sicknes and common miseries continuyng shall not have so muche power to trouble a man as to make him sicke, or miserable? This receipte God the heavenly Physitian hath taught, his most excellent Apothecarie master John Calvine hath compounded, and I your graces most bounden and humble have put into an Englishe box, and do present unto you. My thankes are taken away and drowned by the greate excesse of duetie that I owe you: Master Calvine thinketh his paynes [A3v] recompensed if your grace or any Christian take profit of it: bicause how much soever is spent, his store is neverthelesse. And for God, recompensed he can not be: but how he is continually to be thanked, your graces profession of his worde, your abidyng in the same, the godly conversation that I have sene in you, do prove that your selfe do better understand and practise than I can admonishe you.

And that you maye be assured, that this kinde of medicine is not hurtfull: two moste excellent kinges, Ezechias and David, beside an infinite numbre have tasted the lyke before you, and have founde health therin, such healthe as hathe cured them for ever, and not as common or naturall reasons of Philosophie doe cure a sicke or soore mynde, which with easie and weake not well drawynge or cleansinge plasters, so overheale the wounde that it festreth and breaketh oute afreshe wyth renewed and doublye encreased danger.

Suche remedye as here is conteined can no Philosopher, no Infidele, no Papist minister. For what perfite helpe can they geve to a dyseased mynde, that understande not, or [A4r] beleve not the onely thyng that muste of nedefull necessitie be put into all medicines that maye serve for a tourmented soule, that is to say, the determined providence of almyghtie God, whiche ordreth and disposeth all thynges to the best to them that truste in him?

This Physicke resteth onely amonge trewe belevyng Christians, who are perswaded that whatsoever betideth unto us, his hie wisdom that sent it, and that seeth all thynges, sent it of hys good pleasure and decreed purpose, and that for oure benefite if we love and beleve hym, thoughe oure weake understandynge knoweth not howe it shoulde be profitable, but naturally judgeth it hurtefull and unpleasaunt. And necessarye it was that he whiche by understandynge of Godes hatred of synne and felynge of hys justice, is subject to fall into the moste perillous peine and tourment of conflicte with sinne and desperation, shoulde by conceyvynge of Godes mercy, and belevyng of his providence, have helpe of the moste and onely perfect and effectuallye working medicine.

But in heavye case is he, that beynge [A4v] afflicted with that daungerous disease of the felyng of Gods wrath kindled against him, hath not the conserve of belefe of Gods providence remainyng with him, or beyng ministred to him either for feblenesse of stomack can not receive and brooke it, or his oppressed appetite beyng overwhelmed with grosse faithlesse and papisticall humors can not abide the tast of it. Wo is (I say) to them: for theyr disease is daungerous and hard to be cured. For when the wretched man findyng all helpe of man not able to uphold him from perishing, being striken with the mightie hande of God, feleth him selfe unable to stande, no soundnes in his bodye, no strength in his limmes, no helpe of nature to resist the violence of that disease that Gods displeasure hath laide upon him, seeth no signe of Gods grace in his soule, but the depe woundes that Gods anger hath left in his conscience, perceiveth no token to argue him th'elect of God and partaker of the death of his Saviour, hearyng pronounced that the soule which sinneth shall die, knowyng him selfe to have sinned, and felyng him selfe dying: alas what helpe remaineth in this extremitie? If we thinke the helpe of papistes, to begge and borrowe others [A5r] Virgins oyle that have none to spare, to bye the superfluous workes of those men that say they have done more than suffiseth to satisfie Gods lawe and to deserve theyr owne salvation, to appease God with suche extraordinarie devised service as he never commaunded, and such like unholsome stuffe as papisticall soulesleaers have ministred to Christian patientes: If (I say) we thinke these good and sufficient medicines: alas, we do nothinge therby, but plant untrew securitie, promise health, and performe death: the panges wherof when the deceived sick man feleth, he to late espieth the falshod of the murtherous Physician. The pore damned soule in Hell tourmented with the lamentable peines that turmoile him, from whome God the onely author of joy and comfort is absent, perceiveth to late howe wandring the wrong way from heaven, he is fallen into Hell. That selly wretche flamyng in the infernall fire feleth, alas, to late that thei which gave him mans medicines to drincke, have slayne his soule: they which taught him to trust of salvation by mans devises have set his burnyng hert in that place of flames, where th'everlasting Chaos suffreth no droppe of Godes mercye to descende: they [A5v] which taught him to seeke health any other where than in the determined purpose of God, that hath sent his own sonne for our redemption, have spoiled him of all benefit of redemption. He feleth at length all to late howe by faulte of ill diet and throughe poisonous potions which his ignoraunt corrupted and traiterous Physicion suffered him to use, and bad him to take, he lieth dead eternally.

But on th'other side, when the belevynge Christian falleth (as God hathe made none to stande wherby they should not nede his mercye to raise them when they are fallen) he knoweth whither to reache his hande to be raised up againe: beyng stong with the stinge of the scorpion he knoweth howe with oyle of the same scorpion to be healed agayne: beyng wounded with the justice of God that hateth sinne, he knoweth howe with the mercy of the same God that pardoneth sinne to have hys peine asswaged and hurt amended. He knoweth that whome God hath from eternitie appointed to live, shal never die, howsoever sicknesse threaten: no misery, no tentation, no perill shall availe to his everlasting overthrowe. He knoweth that his safetie is much more [A6r] surely reposed in Gods moste stedfast and unchangeable purpose, and in the most strong and almightye hande of the alknowynge and alworking God, than in the wavering will and feble weaknes of man. This healeth the Christians sicknes, this preserveth him from death, this maketh him to live for ever. This medicine is in this litle boke brought from the plentifull shop and storehouse of Gods holye testament, where Gods everabiding purpose from beyond beginning is set fourth, to the everlasting salvation of some, and eternall confusion of other. Beside that, this boke hath not only the medicine, but also an example of the nature of the disease, and the meane how to use and apply the medicine to them that be so diseased. For when a man languishing in corporall sicknes, heareth his neighboure reporte unto him, or himselfe hathe before time sene in an other the same cause of sicknes, the same maner of fits, passions, alterations, and in every point the same qualities of sicknes, and the same disposition of body that he knoweth and feleth in him self: it geveth him assurance, and maketh him to know that he is sick of the same disease that th'other was: wherby knowing howe th'other was healed, what diet [A6v] he kept, what Physicke he toke, he doeth with the greater boldnes, confidence of mynde, and desire, call for, taste, and gredely receyve that healthfull and lifefull medicine wherby he saw and knew his neighbour healed, and with the greater care kepeth the same diet wherewith he saw and knew th'other preserved. So here this good soules Physician hath brought you where you maye se lyinge before youre face the good king Ezechias, somtime chillinge and chattering with colde, somtime languishing and meltyng away with heate, nowe fresing, now fryeng, nowe spechelesse, nowe crying out, with other suche piteous panges and passions wrought in his tender afflicted spirit, by giltie conscience of his owne fault, by terrible consideration of Gods justice, by cruell assaultes of the tyrannous enemie of mans salvation, vexynge hym in muche more lamentable wise than any bodely fever can worke, or bodyly fleshe can suffer. On th'other side for his helpe, you se him sometyme throwe up his gastly eyen, starynge wyth horrour, and scant discernynge for peine and for want of the lyvely moisture to fede the brightnes of theyr sight. You se him sometyme yeldyngly stretch oute, sometyme struglinglye [A7r] throwe his weakned legges not able to sustein his feble body:

sometime he casteth abrode, or holdeth up his white and blodles hand toward the place whether his soule longeth: sometyme with fallyng chappes, he breatheth out unperfect soundes, gasping rather than calling for mercy and helpe. These thinges being here laid open to sight and remainyng in remembraunce, (as the horrour and piteous spectacle can not suffre it to fall out of a Christian tender minde) if we feele oure selves in like anguishe, we finde that the disease is the same that Ezechias had, and so by convenience of reason muste by the same meane be healed. Then behoveth us to remember or to be infourmed by oure diligent Physitian or charitable neighbour, howe we sawe Ezechias healed, whome we imagine in this Boke to see, both dying, revived, and walking after health recovered. There we se the heavenly Physician anoynt him with the merciful Samaritans oyle, purge the oppressing humors with true repentaunce, strengthen his stomack with the holsome conserve of Gods eternall decree, and expell his disease, and set hym on foote with assured faith of Gods mercy, and staieng his yet unstedy pace and foltring legges [A7v] with the swete promyses of Gods almyghtye goodnes. So learne we what Physicians helpe we shall use: and this medicine beyng offered us, we are bolde to take it, bycause we knowe it wyll heale us. And beyng healed, knowyng and hearyng it confessed, that sinne was the cause and nourishement of Ezechias disease, we learne a newe diet, and to fede as Ezechias his Physician and oures apointeth, absteinyng from thinges hurtfull taking things healthfull as he prescribeth. So doth the Christian atteine his health, so beynge atteined he preserveth it for ever. And as it is true that seconde and returned sicknesses by surfit or misdemenour are most cruell and daungerous, so holdeth he yet this also for trueth, that to this Physician with this medicine, no disease never so long rooted, never so oft retourned, is uncurable. Beyng then thus muche beholden to this Physician we must nedes confesse that we owe unto him our life and health, and all that we be or have. And for his faithful minister master Calvine, I beseche your grace wyth me, to wishe hym Gods benefit of eternall happie life for his rewarde, even as I wishe your grace continuall health of life and soule for your preservation, [A8r] not onely for this newe yeare, but also for the tyme that shall excede all extent of yeares, besechinge you to accepte bothe my worke and prayer.

Concernyng my translation of this boke, it may please you to understand that I have rendred it so nere as I possibly might, to the very wordes of his text, and that in so plaine Englishe as I could expresse: Suche as it is, I beseche your grace to take it good parte.

Your graces humble
A. L.

The writinge of Ezechia kinge of Juda, when he had bene sicke, and was recovered of his sicknes. I said in the cuttyng shorte of my daies, I shall go downe to the gates of the grave. I have sought the residue of my yeares, I sayd I shall not see the Lorde, the Lorde in the land of the living. I shall not beholde man any more, nor those that dwell in the world. My life is withdrawen, and is chaunged like a shepeherdes lodge.

AS the name of God is immortall, and we oughte to travaill that they which come after us, do cal upon it, and that it be honored and glorified in all times: So is it not enoughe, that during oure lyfe, we endevor oure selves to honor God: but as I have said before, our care should extende it selfe to the time to come, to the end we may have in store some continuyng seede of religion, in suche sort as the trueth of God may never be abolished. But specially they whom God hath ordeined in anye estate to guide other, ought therfore so much the more[1] to applie them selves unto it. As also we se that S. Peter declaryng his ende to be nere, and that he should depart out of this worlde: addeth [B1v 2] that somuch as he possibly may, he woulde make the doctrine whiche he preached, to remayne alwayes in force and memory, that men might take profit after his death. Behold now wherfore Ezechias was not contented to make this protestation whiche we reade here, with his mouth, but wold also wryte it, that to the ende of the worlde men might knowe how he had ben vexed in hys affliction, and that the same myght serve for doctrine to all the worlde: so as at this day we may take profyt thereof.

He saythe expressely that this wrytinge was made after he was recovered. For oftentimes when we ar touched eyther with sicknes or anye other rod of God, we make protestations enow, but we do nothing els but shake our eares (as the proverbe is) when we ar escaped, and we by and by forget al those thinges which we made a shew as if we knewe. But here it is shewed us that the kinge Ezechias beinge recovered, forgat not the correction whiche he had received at the hand of god, nether the anguishes which he felt, but minded to make a memoriall of the whole, that those which come after might be enstructed therby.

But it appereth at the first shew that this writing serveth not for any instruction of them that shold rede it, but shold rather be an offense. For we see the outragious passions of a man as it were ravished in minde which so abhorreth death, that he thought all to be lost when god shold

[1] *2. Pet. 5.*

take him out of the worlde, and in this we see nothing but the sinne of infidelitie. He tormenteth and rageth with him self (as it semeth) with a rebelling, [B2r 3] uncomely for a servant of god: to be short it appeareth that we can gather nothing of this song, but that al the faithe whiche Ezechias had was only in hys prosperitie and quiet, and also that he gave the bridle to much unto him selfe in his heavinesse, in so muche that he complayned of god, as we see that he compared him to a Lyon. But when all shal be wel considered, we shal see that there is no instruction better or more profitable for us than this. For when we shal have well examined al that is in us, then we shall knowe that the same is also propre unto our selves.

But first let us note how the good king Ezechias did not here set fourthe his owne vertues to be praised of the world, for he might have kept in silence that which he hath declared of his owne waywardnesse, and in place therof he mought have spoken of hys request made to God, and the constance of his faythe: So then he sayth not that he was of valiant courage, that he overcame al tentations without any stoppe or strife, he sayth not that he had a faith so stedfaste that it nothing trobled him to be corrected of the hand of god: nothing of al thys. What then? we see a poore man tormented even to the extremitye, and so striken downe, that he wiste not what myghte become of hym. We se a man astonished with feare of the wrath of God, lokyng on nothyng but his own affliction. Then seyng Ezechias doeth discover him selfe, and sticketh not to confesse his owne faultes, in this we perceive that he was not led of ambition, nether of any vaine glory to be praised of men, or to get reputation, but he rather was willing him self to be confounded with shame, that god might be glorified. [B2v 4] What is then his purpose? It is in one parte to make us know howe he had bene afflicted then, when he thought that God was against him: and moreover that therin men might know somuche the more howe great the goodnes of God was, when he received him to mercy, and woulde not forsake him in necessitie.

We have then to beholde here, as in a loking glasse, our owne wekenes, to the ende that every man may prepare himselfe against the time when his faith shalbe proved as the fayth of Ezechias was, and when God shall shew us some tokens of his wrath, so as if then we seme in maner destroyed, yet we cease not therfore to truste that God will geve to us an end of our troubles, as he did to this good king. Next to this, that we may learne to geve al praise of our safetie to the mercy of God, knowledging that so sone as he forsaketh us, we are utterly undone, and that then we become more then miserable.

And nowe we see howe, and wherfore the good king Ezechias was thus tourmented, that is, because he sawe death so nere at hande. It semeth at the first face, that suche passion besemeth not a faithful man. Trew it is that of nature death is dreadfull to us al. For there is no man but (as they saye) desireth to be, and in death we thinke that we perishe, that we be broughte to nought, and cease to be. Thus of nature we flie from and abhorre death,[2] and therfore also S. Paule saith in the v. chapter of the seconde epistle to the Corinthians. that we do not desire to be unclothed of this body for it is impossible for man to desire to change his [B3r 5] estate, I meane as concernynge thys lyfe. And those that do kyll them selves have no natural affection, but the Devil so carrieth them away that they are altogether blinded. And suche are to be rekened as unnaturall monsters, in whom al the order of nature is changed. To be short it is most assured that death shalbe alwaye to us terrible, and not onely because we are enclined to desire to lyve, but also for so muche as God hath lefte a certeine marke, in suche sorte that the Heathen them selves and the unfaithfull are constrained to fele that death is a curse of God, which was pronunced upon Adam, and al his linage. For asmuch then, as death is come upon the world by sinne, and that it is a witnes of the wrath of God, that by it we are as it were cast of from him, banished from his kingdome (which is the kingdome of life) it must nedes be, although we have no light of faith neyther ever had any one word of doctrine, that this be imprinted in our mindes, that it is naturallye unpleasant unto us. Behold then by what meanes we are brought to flie death, and to withdrawe our selves from it so muche as we possibly maye. Fyrst bicause we are desirous to be: secondly for that we conceyve death to be a certeine signe of Gods wrath: yea althoughe we harde thereof no certaine instruction, yet God hath printed a certaine naturall instinction and feling therof within oure hertes. Yet notwithstandynge it is also trew that the faithfull do overcome those feares, and do prepare them selves to die when it pleaseth God, but not (as the place speaketh whiche we have alledged out of S. Paule) in suche sort that [B3v 6] thei simply and without other consideration desire to die, for that wer the doing of men in desperation, but thei prepare them selves, forasmuch as thei know, that after they have bene unclothed they shalbe clothed againe, that this body which is but a ruinous lodgyng, is nothing but rottennes, and that they shalbe restored to the kingdom of god. For asmuch as then we behold this hope that is geven us, thus we overcome the feares of deth. Besid this on the other side, we know that our lord Jesus Christ hath repared this desolation and ruine that fel upon us by the sinne of our father Adam. So bycause we take hold of life in the middest of deth, that maketh us that we are not afraid to withdraw our selves

---

[2] *2. Cor. 5*

hence when god calleth us to him, for we know that death is but a passage to life. Moreover we know what is our true being: It is not to dwel in this world, for this is but a thorow fare, and we must alwai have in remembrance, that which is spoken that god placeth men here onely to mannage them, and to make them to fetch their compasses (as thei say) and sodenly to turne againe. Then when we are taught that our life is nothing els but a course, and the world is but a shadow, which passeth and vanisheth awai: we know that our true beyng, and our permanent estate is in heven, and not here by low. Thus se we how we ought not to flie deth: but (the more is) we have occasion to desire it, bicause on the one side we ar fraile, and being holden under the bondage of sin, we se so mani corruptions in our selves that it is wofull, and when we desire to serve God we draw up our legs, and when we lift up one fote thinking to set forward one step, we slip backward, and oft it commeth to passe that we stumble or fall. Se now how just a cause we have to lament our life, not in way of despeir, but bicause we ought to hate and [B4r 7] abhorre sin. We ought also to desire god to draw us out of this so miserable captiuitie wherin we ar, as[3] s. Paul sheweth us example. He confesseth him self to be unhappy, bicause he dwelleth in his bodi as a prison. He asketh howe he shalbe delivered. On[4] the other side, we know that we ought to desire death the more that we might come nere to our God. For (as it is saide in this place that we have alledged) while we live by faith we are as it were absent from God. Then, where is our felicitie and perfect joye? but in this that we cleave to oure God in perfection. Far asmuch then, as by death we come nere to him, it is a thing to us happy, and whiche ought to make us joyfull. And therfore he saieth in[5] the first chap. to the Philip. that as touchinge him self, it should be more avauntage to him to die then to live, and although his life was profitable to the church, yet in having no other regard, but to his own person, he was desirous to be drawen away from this place by low: mark then what ought to be the affection of the faithful. Now let us come to king Ezechias. It semeth that he had lost al maner tast of the goodnes of God, that he knew nothing of the resurrection, that he was ignorant that he shold be restored by meane of the redemer, he conceived nothing but the wrath and curse of God: wher is his faith? where is his obeidience? wher is this consolation of the holy Gost, and this joy inestimable, whiche we ought to receive when God certifieth us of the love which he beareth us? In dede if he had had this perswasion deply roted in him, that he was

[3] *Rom. 7.*
[4] *2. Cor. 5.*
[5] *Philip. 1.*

one of the children of god: doth not the adoption bring the inheritance? to what end hath god chosen us for his children, but that we shold be partakers of the hevenly life wherunto he guideth us? but we se none of al this in Ezec. [B4v 8] It semeth then that he was altogether distraught from sense and reason, that he hath forgotten God: that all the good doctrine that ever he heard before is utterly blotted oute, and that he thinketh no more of it. These thinges at the firste shew, seme very straunge. Trew it is that at that time he had no suche revelation of the heavenly life, as we have at this day by the gospel. But yet Ezechias and all the other holy kinges and Prophetes, and all the rest of the faithfull dyd well conceive that God had not chosen them in vaine. For though[6] this sentence of our lord Jesus Christ was not pronounced, yet was it engraved in the herts of all the faithfull that God is not the God of the dead. All they then that are comprised in the number of his people have bene assured to have an abidyng life, and that shall endure for ever. And on the other side it is said that God calleth him selfe the God of Abraham, of Isaac and of Jacob long after their death. It must nedes be then that they then lyved. So therefore the faithfull have this assuraunce that God did not nourishe them in this world as brute beastes, but he gave them a certeine taste of hys goodnes, untyll suche time as they myghte have full enjoyinge thereof after their[7] death. Even Balaam himselfe whiche never knew any thing of the lawe, yet he failed not to say: I wishe my soule to dye the death of the righteous, and my end to be such as theirs shalbe. He desireth to joyne him selfe with the race of Abraham, and yet he was a wicked and refused man. And who maketh him to speake thus? even this, that he is there as upon the racke, and God [B5r 9] wringeth out of him this confession. Now if Balaam which was possessed of the Devill, and gave oute his tonge to hyre, to curse the people of God, hath bene constreined to say thus, what shall we think of them that had trewlye profyted in the lawe of God? But howsoever it be, trew it is that thold fathers had not so cleare and manifest knowledge of the heavenlye life as we have at this daye in the Gospell, and in dede the same was reserved untill the comming of our Lorde Jesus Christ. And with good reason: for we have a good gage of our life in our saviour Jesus Christ, in that he is risen againe, and that it was not for him selfe alone but for all his body. This is the full assuraunce that God hath geven in the parson of our Lorde Jesus Christ, that we passe through this world to come to the life that lasteth ever. The auncient fathers came not to suche degree, they were not so avaunsed. But howesoever it were it is so that the tast which they had of the heavenlye

---

[6] *Math. 22*
[7] *Num. 23*

life so suffised them, that they rendred them selves peaseably to God. And we reade not that they were greatly tourmented in theyr death, as whan Abraham departed, he made not lamentations, wayling and complaintes, as the king Ezechias did: but he was fylled and satisfyed wyth lyfe,[8] saieth the scripture. In like maner was it of Isaac and Jacob, who rendring the laste groane saith: I wyll put my truste in thy salvation, my God. Thoughe Jesus Christ had not yet appered unto the world, yet Jacob had in him selfe a stedfast and undoubted hope, and made him selfe as sure of his salvation, as if he held it in his hand. [B5v 10] So then we see that the holy fathers were not in doubt or suche mistrust, that they did not alwaye aspire unto the heavenly life, but that it was their chiefe desire to atteine thereunto.

Now let us retourne to the king Ezechias. We must conclude that he had some speciall reason in him selfe, why he so complayned of death, which[9] we shall better see in the person of David. David is sometimes in suche anguyshes that he crieth,[10] alas my God, who is he that shal acknowledge thee in death? And when I shalbe a poore rotten carion, what profite shalt thou have? when thou shalt have brought me into ashes, what is it that[11] thou shalt have gained? He made there hys complaints,[12] nevertheles in the end he dyed peaseably. For no man saw that he was so passioned in his departyng, but that he rendred him self mildly into the handes of God. Howe came it then to passe that he wrote thus? It is bicause he conceived the wrath of God, whether it were in sickenes, or in any other affliction, and that is asmuch as if the very hels were presently set before him. The affliction then that he conceyved, was not of symple death, but that God gave him some signe that he punished him bicause of his sinnes. Now seyng that we se this same disputation in the parson of David, it shalbe easy for us to conclud touching the king Ezechias that he was also grevously vexed in his death, but that was not for that he was loth to depart out of this worlde, neither that he was tourmented as the poore Infidels whiche aspire not to a better life, which are also as it wer drowned in theyr delites, and bringe them selves on slepe in such sort that they set nothynge by the [B6r 11] heavenly life. We see that Ezechias was not so striken downe, and yet he thought that God was against him, as we shall se yet more largely. And in dede it was not without cause that the Prophet Esay was sente unto him, for he was as a Her-

8 *Gene. 25.35.49.*

9 *Psalm. 6.*

10 *Psalm. 30.*

11 *1. Reg. 2*

12 *1. Par. 29.*

alde of armes, to make him defiaunce, and to declare unto him: Beholde God is thine enemy: thou muste susteine his extreme rigour, for thou haste offended him. When Ezechias heard that, he had no regard to the simple death, by the which he muste of necessitie passe, but he hathe an other ende of consideration, that he should be cut of from the worlde as an accursed creature, as one unworthy, whom the earth should beare. And when God stroke him, that gave a token to him that the land should be made desolate, for he knewe what should be the estate of the people: he sawe that all should be destroyed after his death, yf God dyd not remedi it by miracles. And he thought thus: My death shall not be onely to sende me into the throte of hell, but it shall be to brynge a generall overflowyng over all, so that in all the land there shalbe nothing but desolation. Shall the service of God then be throwen dowen, and shall al this be cast upon my neck bicause I have offended my God? Alas, and what shall this be? Let us not nowe thinke it straunge if Ezechias speake thus as we heare, but let us hold this alway that it is not the simple death whiche dyd affraye him so. What then? the wrath of God, when he behelde his sinnes, and that God toke away from him all savor of his goodnes, and turned his back unto him as if he had sene him armed against him, and lifted up his arme, as if he would bring him to nought.

[B6v 12] When Ezechias sawe that, he was so confounded that his mouth was stopped, and not without cause.

Nowe this is right worthy to be noted, for there are many blockish persons (and the mooste part) which feare death, but it is not because they fele the curse of God appeare to them. It is true as we have saide before, that God leaveth alway this point in the conscience of man, but they have not all alike consideration therof. Wherfore is it then that death is dreadfull unto them? bycause every one will say, I desire to be. Truely when they speake in this maner it is as much as if they said I would be a calfe, or an asse, or a dogge, for the beyng of brute beastes is in this world, and the beynge of men where is it, but in this that they are joyned to theyr God? But now we are as it were in prison, for in steade that this world shold have bene unto us as an earthlye paradise (if we had continued in the obeidience of God) now we are as in a straunge countrey, wherein we be as lockt up and banished. It is trew that yet we se many times some, yea many trackes of the goodnes of God, but how so ever it be, yet we do but languish here. But there are but few that know this. So much the more then ought we to note wel this doctrine, which I have here before touched, that is to wit, that both in death, and in all other afflictions we are more accombred and troubled with the wrath of God than with the evyll that we can fele. If one be afflicted with povertie, so that he hath hunger and thirst, an other be stricken with sicknes and suffer great tourmentes,

[B7r 13] another be persecuted of men so as he hathe no time of rest, and more if in the end death come before oure eyes, we oughte to knowe that there is nothing so muche to be feared as the wrathe and vengeaunce of God. But men do cleane contrary. And this marke, why I have sayde that we must note this doctrine the better: because a man may se that the pore sicke persones, and they that are afflicted, in what sort soever it be, wyll crye Alas, one wyll cry the armes, another wyll crye the legges, the one here, the other there: but yet they come never to the grounde of the evill. And that procedeth of the leprosie that is in us. For we are so dull witted that we can not atteine to know the judgement of God. So much the more ought we to lerne when we shalbe beaten with such roddes as I have sayd to make us loke upon the cause whence this evill procedeth: which is, that God will have us to fele our sinnes, and that he sommoneth us to the ende that we shoulde there come as it were before oure judge, and that we should not come there with sleyghtes and meanes of excuse, but with franke and free confession, and that the same be not only made wyth mouth, or assent by writyng, but that we be wounded even to the bottome of the herte, felynge what it is to have done agaynst the will of oure God, to have styrred him up against us, and to have made warre against his justice. This is it that we have to holde in minde when we see that the kyng Ezechias was in such extremitie of anguish, bycause God dyd punishe him for his sinnes.

Yea and this we ought to marke well, that [B7v 14] though before he have protested that he had walked in puritie and uprightnesse of lyfe, and that he had studied all hys lyfe long to obey and please God, neverthelesse he resteth not his mind upon his vertues, nor hys owne merites, he entreth not into plea wyth God, for he seeth well that all that coulde nothynge profite him nor brynge hym any relefe. Therfore he setteth not fourthe what his lyfe hathe ben, but he knowlegeth that rightfullye he is afflicted.

So then we learne, when it shall please God to correcte with his roddes, not to grudge at it, as if he did us wronge, as if he had no regarde to oure merites, or as yf he used greater sharpnes wyth us than we had deserved. Let al such blasphemies be beaten down, and let us confesse that he hath just cause to punishe us, yea not only to expulse us out of the worlde, but also to throwe us downe into the gulfe of hell. See then howe we deserve to bee ordred yf wee looke upon all our owne lyfe.

Moreover let us not thynke it straunge that god sendeth us afflictions whiche seme grevous and sharpe unto us, seing wee see that Ezechias hathe walked before us to shewe us the waye. Men when they have had any good affection and desyre to serve god, do muche marvell yf god punishe them more then the wicked, and they suppose that they have lost theyr labour. This tentacion is to common, as we see, that even David was also tormented with it when he saith: what meaneth this? for I see the despisers of God prosper and[13] be in jolitie, and make theyr triumphes, and in the meane time I do nothinge but sup up the [B8r 15] drynke of sorrow, from the evening to the morrow I have no reste. It semeth then that it is tyme lost to serve God: Behold how at the extremitie he is beaten down, yf God by his wonderfull vertue had not upholden him. And because the lyke maye come unto us, let us make us a buckler of the example that is here set before us of the kinge Ezechias: for wee have seen here before howe he had framed all hys lyfe to the law of God: he had a zele which is not to be founde in manye people, to purge al hys land of all superstitions and ydolatries: many alarumes were stirred up agaynst hym, to make him somwhat to revolte: but that nothyng stayed hym but that he set up the trewe and pure religyon, and in his private lyfe he sought nothing but that god might be gloryfyed in, and through all: and yet loke how God commeth to assayle him: yea, and that of a straunge fashion, for he is as a lyon that breaketh his bones: So when we see that Ezechias, is thus handled, ought not we to learne to beare pacientlye the corrections that God shall sende us. Loe this is it that wee have to conceive of this place.

Now to the rest of the passions that Ezechias endureth, and although he slipt here of the henges yet stil in the middest therof he declareth the love that he had to God, and that he desyred not thys present life after the maner of them that art herein become brutish, and whiche seke for nothynge but to eate and drynke, and know not for what ende they are created, but onlye to pastime here for a whyle. But Ezechias sheweth well that hee was guyded by an other spirite. He sayeth: [B8v 16] *I have sayd in the cutting short of my dayes. I shall go down to the gates of the grave, I shall not se anye more the Lorde: even the Lorde.* He speaketh here of his lyfe, that it shalbe cut of in the middes of his course: But yet he sheweth that he desireth not here to live to be at his ease. He was a kinge, and might have fared well, he moughte have had greate store of delicates, and pleasures in this world, shortly he myghte have made him selfe dronk with al sortes of thinges of delite. He mourneth not for want of all these: but he saieth, that he shall no more see the Lorde, and he is not contented to have pronounced this word once, but he repeteth it againe to expresse a greater vehemencie: The Lord, even the Lord, saith he: By this he sheweth that he desireth not so much his life, as to exercise him selfe here beneth to knowe that God was his father, and to confirme him selfe more and more in that faith.

---

[13] *Psalm. 73.*

Let us then marke well wherunto oure lyfe is to be directed, that is, that we should perceive that God already in part sheweth him selfe a father toward us. I graunt it trewe (as I have already said) that we ar absent from him, for our salvation lieth in faithe and hope, it is hydden and we see it not with naturall sense. Yet in the meane while God faileth not to send down certein beames hither by lowe to lighten us so, as we be guided to the hope of the life everlasting and perceive that God is not so farre estraunged from us, but that yet he stretcheth fourth his hand hether by lowe to have care of us, and to shewe us by [C1r 17] experience that he hath us in his safekeping. For when the sunne riseth in the mornynge, se we not what a fatherly care God hath for us? After when it goeth downe at evenyng, see we not that God hath an eye to our wekenes, that we maye have rest, and be somewhat releved? Doth not God then in so hydyng the sunne in the nyghte tyme, shew him selfe our father? Further, when we se the earth bring forth her frutes for our nourishement: when we se the raynes and all the chaunges, and alterations that are in nature: in all this perceive we not that God hath his hand stretched out to draw us alway unto him, and howe he already sheweth him self a liberall father unto us, and that we enjoy the temporall benefites which he doth for us, to the ende that by this meane we may be drawen up hyer, that is to say, to knowe that he hath adopted and made us his chyldren, that we may come to the fulnes of joye and of all felicitie, when we shalbe fully joyned with hym? Beholde nowe wherunto we ought to applie all our life, if we wyll not that the same be accursed, and that as many yeares, monthes, dayes, houres, and minutes as we have lyved here by low, all the same be put together in accompte, for ever to encrese, and enflame the vengeance of God upon us. And therfore let us know that we ought here to study upon the workes of God. For even therfore also are we set in this worlde, and therefore[14] in the v. chapter, when the Prophete mynded to rebuke the Jewes of a certeine vile brutishnes. They have not (saieth he) beholden the workes of God. He speaketh of theyr dronkennesse, of theyr gluttony, and of theyr dissolute [C1v 18] lives, but the lump that maketh up the heape of evell is this, that they have not beholden the workes of God. So nowe the good kyng Ezechias sheweth us, that it were better for us all to have died before we had bene borne, and that the earth should have gaped whan we came out of our mothers wombe, to swallow us, than to live here by lowe, if it were not for thys, that we do here alreadie see oure God: not that we have a perfecte sighte. But first he sheweth himselfe unto us by his worde, which is the trew lokyng glasse. And next, we have above and beneath so

[14] *Esay. 5.*

manye signes of his presence, and of the fatherly care whiche he hath for us, that if we be not to much dulwitted, and altogether unfornisshed of understandynge and reason, we must nedes see hym. For all the world is as a lively image, wherein God setteth fourth unto us his vertue and highnes.

Moreover, this that we are governed under his hand, is a more familiar witnes of his justice, of his grace and of his mercy. Let us then learne to lyve to this ende, to practise our selves to worship God as him that hath created and fashioned us. Next, that we beare to him honor and reverence as to our father, and that in the tastinge of good things (which he nowe dealeth among us) we maye be confyrmed in the fayth of the Heavenly lyfe. And further, for asmuch as he vouchsafeth to extende his providence even hyther by low, for this entent to governe us in this transitory and fraile life, that we doubt not, when we shal come unto him, that then we shal beholde face to face that, whiche we nowe see darkely and in [C2^{r} 19] a small portion.

And so the kynge Ezechias remitteth all to God, as if he shold say: Alas it is true that I am here, as to beholde clearly the graces of God. But nowe I see that all this is as it were plucked from me: For it semeth that God is mynded to spoile me of all that he hath geven me before: and now there resteth no more for me but to despayre, for as muche as he hathe geven over and forsaken me. He hath sent his prophete with this message, that I am undone. Alas, and when I perceive no more signe of the goodnes of my god, neyther that he extendeth this strength to comfort me in my afflictions: no not when I am in the anguishes of death: Lo is not this a wofull thing that our Lorde hath forsaken me there, and that I am cut of from him? Nowe of this we have to gather, that be it in life, be it in death, this grace onely shoulde alwaye suffice us: that is to say, that God geveth us the felynge of his goodnes. And when he sheweth us that he is favourable unto us, let us go on boldely, and if we languish in this life, let us leave it patiently. Trewe it is that we may well grone and sigh that we are captives, in this prison of sin: and besid that we may also bewaile seing these afflictions that God doth send them upon us. And yet oughte we not to cease alwayes to blesse the name of God, and to rejoyse in the myddest of all our sorowes. When we shal fele that he wyll be oure father, and that he wyll knowe us for his children, in death we shall beholde everlastyng lyfe, whiche shall make us forget all lamentations, so as we shall no more say: Alas what shall I do?

[C2^{v} 20] Howe shall I behave my selfe? Whither shal I go? We shal cut of all these thinges, and we shall saye no more: Shall I drinke no more? shall I eate no more? For such is the maner of brut beastes. But now I se that my God draweth neare unto me, I go nowe to throwe my selfe downe before him, I go to yeld my self into his handes, and to joyne my self with him, as with mine own father. When (I saye) we shalbe thus disposed,[15] we may say with David. Lord I commende my[16] spirite unto thee. David sayd this during his life, but our Lord Jesus Christ sheweth us that we must so say when God draweth us out of this world. And last of all, when we thinke upon all the benefites of god, let us learne to glorifie him, as these be thynges inseparable. Accordynge then as God maketh us partakers of his graces and that already in part he sheweth us that al our felicitie is to be of the company of his children, so ought every one of us to endevor to honor him as oure father.[17] This was the cause why Jonas beynge drawen out of the whales throte, saieth: I shall blesse my God. He saith not, I shall lyve to eate and drinke: But I shall come to the temple the sanctuarie of my God, and there I wyll geve him prayse for thys redemption, that is to wytte, for that he hath plucked me back from the deth. Beholde now what it is that we have to do.

Nowe concernynge that whiche Ezechias speaketh[18] of the cuttynge shorte of his dayes, he speaketh as having respect to the naturall course of mans life wherof is made mention in the song of Moyses, for he began to reigne at the age of xxv. yeares. In the xiiii. yere of his raigne, [C3r 21] Hierusalem was beseged, and then he fell into thys sicknes, as we se. Thus was he xxxix. yeres old. Nowe he saieth that his life is cut short, bicause he is not come to old age. Trew it is that Moyses speaketh of the frailtie of men, and saith: What are men? After that God hathe let them walcke here their dayes, then they are gone againe. And in dede when man commeth to lx. yeares, he is al decaied, and if ye adde x. yeares more, there is nothing but lothsomnes and werines, he is nothing but a burden unprofitable, and life it selfe is combersom unto him. He sheweth then that this lif beyng short and fraile, ought not to holde us. But howsoever it were, this kyng Ezechias was as in the flowre of hys age, he was not yet come to the age of xl. yeares. And in this respect he saith that God hath cut shorte his dayes, not that we have any tyme determined. For do not children die sometimes before they come into this world, and so sone as they be come, doth not death already besege them? But he was not yet come to that old age, which is according to the ordinary course of mans life. Ezechias than beholdeth this: and above all thinges hath his eies fastened upon this message of the Prophet Esay, that is, that God hath punished him bicause of

---

[15] *Psalm. 31.*

[16] *Luke. 23.*

[17] *Jonas. 2.*

[18] *Psalm. 90*

his sinnes. And it is asmuch as if he should say talking to him selfe. I see well that God wyll not leave thee in thys world, for the assault is very violent. And wherof commeth that, but of thy offences and sinnes: as we shall see that he addeth afterwarde. It is true that he attributeth al unto God as unto his judge, but he toke the faulte upon his owne parson, confessyng him selfe onely to be culpable. Loe [C3v 22] howe he understandeth that his dayes were cut short.

When he saith *that he shall come to the gates of the grave, that he shall se no more the lyving:*

That was bicause he shoulde be conversant no more amonge men, to exercise him selfe in the service of God. But nowe this is not without cause that in it also he conceyved the wrathe of God. Althoughe he were subjecte to dwell as it were confusely myngled amonge manye rascalles, as in dede there were many Hypocrits in Juda, and many wicked and dissolute persons mockers of God, and of his law. And among the Heathen there was nothing els but ungodlines, and rebellion. Now when Ezechias saw that, I knowe nowe (sayeth he) that I am unworthye to dwell upon the earth, because these tarry styll in the world, and God hath cut me of, yea with a strong hand, as if he would come armed to make open warre against me as my enemye.

Then when Ezechias had suche imaginations, it is not to be marveyled thoughe he made suche complaintes. But howsoever it were, all commeth to this end that God did persecute him. This same was to him a burden so heavy that he as it were foltred under it. So muche the better oughte we to note thys doctrine, that if God at any tyme shall afflict us, more hardelye than we woulde that he should, we shoulde not cease for all that heare to acknowledge that he loveth us, and that this perswasion which we shall have of [C4r 23] his goodnes should make us to overcome al temtations which otherwyse myght overthrow us.

Furthermore, if he reprove us, and cause us to feele our synnes: that we runne unto hym, and take the condemnation upon us: For we shall gayne nothynge by all oure startynge hoales: yf we wyll pleade, of necessitie the case muste passe wyth hym. Then when we see that God is juste in punisshynge us for oure synnes, let us come wyth head bowed downe, that we maye be releved by hys mercye: and let us have no other confidence, nor truste of salvation, but in thys that it pleaseth him in the name of oure savioure Jesus Christ, to receave us to mercye, for as muche as in us there is nothyng but cursednes.

Nowe let us throwe oure selves downe before the majestie of our good God, in the acknowledgynge of oure synnes, besechynge hym, that more and more, he wyll make us to feele them, and that he wyll in suche sorte cleanse us from all oure fylthynesse, that we beynge perfectly awaked from oure dull drowsinesse, maye grone and sobbe: not onelye for the miseryes that we see in the world throughe our synnes: but also bycause we cease not so muche as in us lyeth, more and more to augement the same.

And yet alwaye lette us runne to oure God, and although it semeth that he persecuteth us, and that hys hande be verye roughe and dreadfull unto us, yet let us not cease to approche unto hym, and magnifie hys goodnesse: beynge verye well assured that it shall farre, surmonte and exceade all oure faultes and offences. [C4v 24] And though we fele no rigour in him, yet nevertheles let us acknowledge that it is much better for us to draw home to his house, and under his safegarde, than to runne away from hym as wretched despering persons, and let us beseche him to geve, not only unto us this grace, but also to all peoples. &c.

THE SECONDE sermon.

My lyfe is withdrawen, it is chaunged as a shepeherds lodge. I have cut of my dayes as a weaver, he hathe oppressed me with sicknes. From mornyng untill night thou shalt consume me. I made rekenyng to go untill morning, but he hath brused my bones as a Lion. Thou shalt destroy me from morning to night, and shalt make an ende of me. I chattered like a Crane, and swalow, and mourned like a Dove, my eyes wer lift up on high, and they failed me. Trouble oppresseth me, Lord refresch me. What shall I say, it is he that hath spoken it, and it is he also who hath done it.

EZechias continuynge the matter whiche yesterdaye was entreated of, sayeth here that hys lyfe was changed as a shepherdes lodge. By this similitude he sheweth that there is no reste in the life of man, which he had proved in him selfe, for as much as he was as it were at rest, and in one moment God toke him oute of this worlde. When we make a comparison of our bodies with our houses where we are lodged, it is likely that the bodye of man which is more than the house, shoulde have some rest: For what is the house, but a place for the [C5v 26] bodye[1] to resort unto? For they are builded for the use of men. He then whiche dwelleth in any buildynge, ought to be preferred to the house, as the bodye to the gowne, and other garmentes. But Ezechias saith here, that he dwelt in thys world as a shepeherd: who hath his litle cottage which he draweth and carieth hyther, and thether. He speaketh after the custome of that countrey, bycause men there kepe theyr foldes, and a shepeharde wyll cary hys lodgyng as easely as a man would cary any lyght thyng: he sheweth them in summe, that his life was none other thing then a wanderyng, and that God chaunged him by and by. He speaketh after the opinion whiche he had conceaved: for he was as it wer upon the brinke of the pit. And in dede it was necessarye, that he should dispose him selfe to die seyng God had sent him suche a message as is saide. To be shorte he speaketh as if the thing wer already come. Now afterwarde he commeth to the cause of his sicknes, and confesseth that he is culpable. He saieth that he him selfe had cut of his daies: even as a weaver havyng a pece of clothe upon his Loome should cut it all of. I may not then (sayeth Ezechias) accuse any parson: for this evyll oughte to be imputed to me onely: for I have provoked the wrath of God, and have deprived my selfe of hys blessyng, therfore muste I nowe blame my selfe of all this.

---

[1] *Math. 6.*

Nowe thoughe he do speake here but of one man alone, yet we have thereby a good admonition of the shortnesse of oure owne lyfe also. Trueth it is, that it is a thynge well ynoughe [C6^{r} 27] knowen unto us, and yet we do verye seldome thyncke of it. For althoughe we do confesse thys present lyfe to be nothyng els but a shadowe: yet are we so wrapped therein that no man thinketh upon any other thinge, but to make provision for a hundreth yeres. And to be short, it semeth that we should never depart from this world, we are so occupied on things of the world. So much the more then ought we to call that to mynde which the scripture sheweth us of the frailtie of our life, as s. Paule also saith that now we are lodged in a cabine:[2] the body of a man is not a house worthy to be called a goodly dwellyng, or buyldyng: for in it is nothing but transitory, wherfore let us mourne wayting tyll we may be fully restored, and let us not be tyed so to this world but that alwaies we may be goyng forward. For the unfaithful how so ever it be, they shall come to theyr ende: but by no meanes come they neare unto God, but rather they are settled in this worlde, and in the steade of goynge forewarde, they do drowne them selves more depelye in it. Let us then learne to goe forwarde, that is to saye, let us learne to be so dysposed to folowe God when he calleth us, that death maye never come to us before his time.

Touchyng this that Ezechias saieth, that he was cause of his owne evil, let us also practise well this doctrine. So ofte, and when soever it shall please God to afflicte us, we se that we are gyven to murmurynges: and although it be so that wee bee founde gyltye of oure [C6^{v} 28] faultes, yet cease we not to vexe our selves, as yf God passed measure. So then, that we may confesse with a true humilitie that God doth punish us justly in all thafflictions which he sendeth us, let us saye after the maner of Ezechias: it is I that am cause of this evill.

It is true that by and by he attributeth that to God: but they both agre very wel, to wyt, that man be authour of al the miseries that he endureth, and that God nevertheles worketh as a Judge. For when an evil doer shalbe punished, he ought not to complaine of his Judge: but rather for as muche as he seeth him selfe to have offended the lawes he should condempne him selfe, and also he should know that God by thauctoritie of justice brought him to that just punishment, even so must we do: that is to say, that fyrste we acknowledge that if God do afflicte us, it is not bycause he taketh pleasure in tourmenting us: but that he must rewarde us as we have deserved, thoughe yet he hath not altogether regarde to our

---

[2] *2. Corin. 5.*

offences: For what a thinge shoulde that be? we shoulde be an hundred thousand times overwhelmed if he wold use rigour towardes us: but accordynge to that, which he knoweth to be good for us, he chasteneth us, although we have our mouth alwayes closed, and that no murmuryng escape thereout.

And nowe to the rest, whan we shall knowe that we have provoked his angre, let us understande that we may not go fourther than our selves, to say who is the cause of this? but let us simplie accuse our selves. Lo now in summe what we have to learne of this matter. Now it foloweth, *From the morninge to the nyghte, thou shalte* [C7r 29] *bringe me to naught.*

In which wordes Ezechias sheweth howe horrible the displeasure of God is, for he meaneth that god nede not devise this policie, or that, when he would be revenged on men: but if he speake the worde, the thinge shall forthwith be done. To be short he sheweth here what the power of God is, on the one side, and what the frailtie of man is on the other side. And that is to pull out of us al the folish imaginations that we conceive, in making our selves beleve that we may escape his handes. And we se howe men drawe backe alwaies: and although God handle them streightly, they think they may finde some way howe to flee from hym. To be shorte, we thrust out time with oure sholders (as the proverbe is) and promise our selves, leysure enoughe, and thoughe the corde be straite, yet we conceive still some vaine hope. And what is the cause therof? that we have not respect to our frailtie: for there is no minut of tyme, when deth threateneth us not: And if we are now standing upright, at the turning of a hande, behold we are fallen. On the other side we are ignoraunt of the infinite power of God: For if he do but once laye his hande upon us, he nede not do it the seconde time, it shall suffice that he onely blow on us, and loe, we shall be broughte to nothinge. It is not without a cause that Ezechias sayeth here, that *from morning tyll night, he shalbe brought to naught.*

For we heare also that we are not sustained, but[3] in this that God geveth us strength: but if he withdraw his spirite, it must nedes come to passe that we beyng troubled, must immediatly fayle. [C7v 30] But if he shewe him selfe to be againste us, and that he persecuteth us, then must we be yet more striken downe.

Folowynge then the admonition of Ezechias, let us after consider howe feble we are, and let us acknowledge what we be of oure selves: To witte, that every minute God sustaineth us: but that death nevertheles besegeth us, and that it neede not make any great assaute to overthrow us: for one

---

[3] *Psal. 104.*

blast onely were ynoughe. And loe streight[4] waies we shold be withered like grasse: as we shall se in the fourtie Chapter of Esay.

Moreover let us acknowledge what the wrathe of God is when it is armed agaynst us. For God is not lyke unto creatures, so that he shoulde nede to arme him selfe, and to make great preparation, for so sone as he speketh the word, we shall fourthwyth be destroied by his only word. Seynge it is so then, let us learne to walcke in carefulnesse, commyttynge oure lyves into hys handes, and let us knowe that we are nothynge at all, but in so muche as we have oure beynge in him: And so muche rest as it pleased hym to geve us, let us attribute it whollye to his grace, and so when he prolongeth our life: for we should be as men without strength, yf he would shewe but one onely droppe of his power agaynste us.

Note then what we have to marke upon thys place, where he sayeth: *From mornynge untyll nyght.*

Now he addeth that *he chattered as a Crane or as a swallowe, and that he mourned like a Dove.*

[C8^r 31] Wherin he meaneth that anguishe helde him in locked in suche sorte, that he had not so muche as a word fre to expresse hys passyons. If a man crye and lament, and make hys complaintes, and declare hys evyll, it is then to be sayde that he is sore troubled: but when a man is so striken down that he can not declare what he ayleth, when he stammereth so in him selfe, that he can not draw forth one onely worde to declare howe vehement hys passyon is: when he nowe sygheth, nowe bryngeth forth halfe a worde, and the rest kepte in, as if one had his throte locked up: thys is a greate extremitie. Ezechias then sayeth that he was so. Now there is no doubt, but that he had hys respecte unto God cheifely: As if he shoulde saye, that menne perceaved well ynoughe the heavynesse that he was in: But whan that he woulde frame anye request unto God, he was as it were dombe, and that on the one syde the sicknesse troubled hym, and yet he coulde not plainelye expresse what he ayled: so that he was in two extremities. Thone, that he was in such sort locked up within, that with great payne could he fetch out any complaint. The other that he was oppressed with so vehement passyons, that he wyste no wheare to begynne to make his Prayer. But thys maye be thoughte very straunge, that Ezechias who before had in him selfe so greate strength, shoulde now be so faint harted yea, as it were brought to naught: but that was because he had a spirituall conflict, felynge his sinnes, and knowynge that God was his judge: for (as we touched yesterday) this trouble surmounteth all the other.

---

[4] *Esay. 40.*

[C8v 32] It is very likely that Ezechias had an extreme paine, wherwith he was throughly striken down: And also it may be conjectured that it was some burnyng pestilence. Beholde then that his paine was great in it selfe: but that was nothing in comparison of the conceiving of Gods wrath, when he behelde his sinnes, and knewe God to be armed against him as his adversary, and that it was he that persecuted him. This was it that in suche sorte affraied him: And in dede, whan a man is brought to that point, all his courage and jolytie must of necessitie faile: for what is the constancie of a man to stande against the wrath of God? It must nedes be more then a frensie and mad rage, when a man wyll thinke to do so. It is true that a man may be constant to indure afflictions when God shall sende them: but how? so farre forth as he shall be strengthened of God. Agayne if men trouble or molest one, he will consider that he hath to do with creatures: if he suffer any trouble, well, he biteth on the bridle: but when God summoneth us to appeare, and maketh us to fele that we are giltie before him, and that presently we must render an accompt, that our sinnes threaten us, and that in the meane time we perceive eternal death to abide us: there (as I have saide) can we not thinke that we have any strength to make oure partye good, except we were more then in a mad rage. Let us not then think straunge if Ezechias be so stricken downe, for he hathe not to do wyth resistyng sorowe, neyther with withstandyng injuries done unto him on mens behalfe: neyther bowyng down his sholders to endure any affliction, but he hath to fight agaynst God.

[D1r 33] And howe could he perfourme that? than must he nedes be as a water that is powred out and spilt. See nowe what is the cause that he could frame no maner of complaint to expresse his griefe, and yet could he never kepe silence. Se also why David sayde that sumtymes he helde his peace, and by[5] and by after he set on crying and roring out, and yet felt no release. We se that the passions of David were like to these of the good king Ezechias: as in deede he also addeth that his synnes troubled hym, and that he was affrayed of the wrath of God, he kept not then any certain rule or measure, but sumtyme he caste out sighes, he lyfte up him selfe, and anone after he was so caste downe that he could not recover his breath, and yet styll the[6] payne continewed. And in an other place he saith that he held his peace as if he had bene bridled, and had concluded in hym self to utter not one word more: no (saith he) I wyll be as a dome creature, I wyll not speake, I wyll not brynge forthe one sillable: yet notwithstanding (saith he) I felt the griefe increase, and kindle more and

[5] *Psal. 23.*
[6] *Psal. 39.*

more, even as a fyre that is long kept very close, if it be opened then the strength encreaseth and sheweth greater force, and breaketh out in a flame, so David protesteth that in his anguishe, when he had determined to kepe silence and to say never a word, even then was he deceaved, and shewed all that was hyden in his harte, although it were not by wordes well ordred and placed. And to be short, they that knowe in deede what the wrathe of God is, wyll speake and crye, and yet they know not on whiche side to begin: and again when they holde their peace they wote not why they doe it: [D1v 34] but they ar alway in anguish. And we se a notable example of al these things in the good king Ezechias.

It is trew that God doth not examine al men a lyke with suche extremitie: for if he exercise us it shalbe according to our weaknes: he seeth that we shall not be able to endure suche tormoiles and assualtes. He spareth us them: but when it shall please him to prove us in such sorte as we reade here in the example of kyng Ezechias: We muste then be armed with this doctrine. This it is then that we have to beare away. Now to the rest: let us lerne what is al the constantie of men. They may well shewe some token of valiantnes when God doth not shew forth his force against them, but so sone as he shall call us to accompt, then nedes must all that lustines whiche we thynke that we have within us, droupe and vanishe awaye. This is it that we must practise for our instruction to learne true humilitie, for we know that men do commonly rest in theyr owne presumption and trust in them selves. And what is the cause of that? but for that every man hath an eye to his felow, and therefore think we our selves to be strongly fournished. But we ought to lift up our wit to God, for there shold we finde, that so sone as he setteth upon us we become as nothynge. Let us then learne to knowe what it is to plonge our selves downe to the bottome in one minute, so sone as God maketh us to fele his wrath: Let us also learne that until we be spoiled of all confidence in our selves, we can not be set in the array of right humilitie. For so long as men have any opinion of themselves, and think that they can do this or that, it is certaine that they robbe god of that which belongeth unto him, and so when they lift up themselves without stay to rest upon, it is to breake theyr own neckes. This it is then that we have to hold in [D2r 35] memory, that all the imagination of men when they trust in their own strengthes is nothing but a dreame, bicause they loke not upon God, and do not there stay themselves, that they mighte be spoiled of all vayne overwening of them selves. Nowe when we heare speake of such a chattering, and that Ezechia confesseth that he could not bring forth one word, but that he stammered, not wottyng what to say: let us knowe that when our Lord shal presse us in such sort that we ar not able to frame one request, or to have one formall prayer, the gate yet shall not be locked against us, but that we maye have accesse unto him: Which I speak bicause this tentation is very dangerous. It is true that if we perceive not in oure selves a zele to pray unto God, and also a disposition to way depely the promises whiche he geveth us, to take boldnes to approche unto him, that ought to displease us, and we oughte to thinke that we are farre from him on our behalfe: but yet we must overcome this tentation. Then when a man shall fele himself in suche troble that he can not bring forth one worde to pray to God, that he shalbe there throwen down and that he shal not know at what end to begin, yet must he pray how so ever it be, and in what sort: at the least, let us chatter, that is to say, let us cast forth grones and sighes which may shew some excessive passion, as if we wer even there upon the rack, and God heareth even those groninges: as also we se that s. Paule saith, that the holy gost moveth us to unspekable grones,[7] such as can not be expressed. Therefore if one would make an arte of Rethorick of the praiers of the faithful, it is a great abuse: for our lord humbleth us to this end, that we shold not imagine to obteine any thing at his hands by any fair tale: he had rather that we were so confused, that we had not only one word [D2^{v} 36] a right in oure praiers, but that nowe we shoulde cast out puffynges, and blowinges, and anon that we should abide styll with silence: alas my God, alas what shal I do? and when we shall mourne so, that we should be so wrapped in, and tangled, that there should neither be begynnynge nor ending. Then when we shalbe brought to that point, our lord knoweth this kind of language, although we understande it not, and although our perplexities hinder us, that we can not bringe forthe one perfect sentence, so that men also understande not what we would say: yet God (as we have said before) wyll heare us well ynoughe. Se then what we have to learne at this time: that if troubles oppresse us, so that Sathan by meanes therof go about to exclud us that we shold not pray to God, but that we should be as it were afraied of hym, yet let us not cease to present unto god these gronings, although they be confuse. Now Ezech. after saith: *That he made rekening untill evening, and that God brake all his bones, as yf he were in the throte, and betwene the clawes of a Lyon*. In saying that he made reckening until night, he meaneth that he cast his accompt, well then I will se what will happen betwene this and nyght: but (saith he) the evill encreased: for I knew not yet sufficiently the terrible and dredfull mighte of God, when he setteth him selfe agaynst a pore creature. Now then we have yet to lerne, that by the word of God, we have bene taughte what is his force, and that we have also fealte it by experience, althoughe we conceave thereof but a

---

[7] *Roma. 8.*

portion onely. For God shall exalt him selfe in suche sorte, as we shall perceive that all that we thoughte of hym [D3r 37] before was but a smal shadow. So then let us lerne to consider what is the power of God, and therunto to applie al our wit and studies, and to be desirously minded to walke in his feare, and to dread his majestye, knowing that he doth let us fele but a smal tast of his strength. For if he would lay hard to our charge, we should finde that whiche we before thought was as a farre of, and as it were in a dreame. This was it that the good kyng Ezechias ment to expresse, that we should learne by his example not to recken without our hoste, but that we should know that marveilous are the judgementes of God, and the corrections which he sendeth to punish the sins of men, and that then we should thinke that we have not yet comprehended all, for our capacitie is to sclender. But that we are guided unto it a farre of, that is to saye, that if so be, that when God doth chastise and correct us, we be forthwith taken with feare, and thoughe we be dull witted, yet he maketh us to fele what and how mighty is his majestie, we may imagine that it is a hundred thousand times more than our spirites can conceave, and that therby we may be alway so muche the more styrred up to feare him.

Now as to the similitud of the Lyon, it semeth that Ezechias doth here a wrong to God, for this is not to speake of him with suche reverence as he deserveth to compare hym to a cruell beast, that devoureth,[8] bruseth, destroieth, teareth and breaketh al. And we know that the scripture preacheth unto us of God, cleane contrary thereunto, that is to say, that he is kind, pitiful, pacient, ful of mercy, ful of equitie and mildnes: briefly that he beareth such love to men, that he desireth nothing but to handle them deintely as his owne children. Seyng then it is so that [D3v 38] God declareth himself to be suche a one, it semeth that Ezechias speaketh blasphemy in comparing him to a lion: But the good kinge meant not here to protest against God: but onely he hath declared his passions, and he did it not to preache hys own praises, as we have already sene, but he had rather to receave this shame, even to the ende of the world, that men might know what his frailtie was, and that we should have such instruction thereby as might profit us. And thus Ezechias hath not spared himself, but hath set him self out unto us for an example that we might se how he was taken with feare and therby learne our selves to feare God, and also to arme us with his promises when we shal come in such troubles, to thend that we may continew to cal upon him: and though we faile in al this, and become altogether confused, yet let us still hold this point to offer our selves to god, to send forth unto him our sighes and groninges. And this is it that

[8] *Esay. 103.*

we have hereby to learne. Now is it not without cause that Ezechias compareth God to a lion, for (as we have sene before) al the peines that we shal fele in our bodies, and al the greves that we may conceive are nothing in comparison of this conceving of the wrath of god, and this is the cause that we say that the spirituall battailes are much more hard than al other temtations that we can have. We cal spiritual battails, when god compelleth us to cast an eye unto our sinnes, and on the other sid so awaketh us that he maketh us have in mynd what his wrath is, and to conceve that he is our judg, and that we be summoned to appere before him, to render accompte. This is a battel which we cal spiritual, which is much more heavy, and much more terrible then all the sorrowes, anguishes, feares, torments, doubts and perplexities that we may have as in the world. Nowe when we shalbe come thus farre, we may not marvel if god [D4^{r} 39] be unto us as a lion, as to that we fele of him, for thys word is not here spoken as touchinge the nature of God. And when he hath thus turmented the king Ezechias, it is not for that he hath forgotten his goodnes and mercy, which on thothersid he sheweth unto him. But it was nedefull that Ezechias should first know himself to be in the hands of God, as betwene the pawes, and in the throte of a lion, and so must it be that we come to the same point as I have already saide, for otherwise God can not winne us. There is suche an arrogancye in us that we alwaye think our selves to be strong and mightie, and that we can never be beaten down but with a great thonder and lightening. And forasmuch as we can not magnifie the power of God as it ought to be, we talk of it, and we think somwhat of it, but we do not geve unto it an infinite greatnes so as we be ravished when we think of it, and so as it occupie all our senses in such sort as it ought. It behoveth therfore that our lord do (as a man wold say) transfigure him self, that is to say, make himself terrible more than all the lions in the world, and that he declare himselfe unto us with such a power that we be utterly afraid with all, even as if we espied a hundred deathes. For the wrath of god is not only to make us die: but we se the gulfes of hell open when god sheweth himself as our judge. It is therfore no marvel if we be then so astonished, as if a lion shoulde teare us in peces betwene his pawes, and break our bones with his teth, and if we conceive such horror when god is against us: from hence then procede al these complaints that we see in the Psalmes. They that ar not exercised in these batails and perplexities, think that David meant to make his trouble greater than it was, or they thinke it likely that he was very delycate? but when we come to the profe, we fele that there is not one word to much [D4^{v} 40] for the stormes that the faythfull fele when God searcheth them earnestly and to the quicke, surmount al that may be expressed with mouth. Let us not thinke then that this similitude that is here put forth by the kyng Ezechias is superfluous, for we shall finde the majestie of God a great deale more dreadefull then all the woordes here conteined can expresse, when it shall please hym to call us to accompt, and make us fele that he is a judge: for if the mountayns tremble before him and melt away, howe may we that are nothynge stande before hym? So then let us note wel when somtime god taketh frum us the tast of his goodnes, and we shall thynk our selves to be cut of from his kyngdome, and perceyve nothing but our sinnes whiche are as great heapes of wood to kindle the fire of his wrath, and when we consider only that forasmuche as he is almyghty, it must nedes bee that he stryke us with lyghtning and overwhelme us. When we fele these thynges we must nedes be altogether oppressed untyll he releve us. And in dede in one minute of tyme we shall be plunged even to the depth of hell, were it not that he helde us fast by the hand, and that we were after a secrete maner stayed by hym, although we see not howe. Loe this is a doctrine whiche ought to serve us on the one side to humble us that we may forget all the strengthe whiche men thynke to have in them selves, and reste our selves upon the majestie of God, and that we bee altogether throwen downe under that majestie, and yet neverthelesse that we may knowe the ende and necessitie that we have of hym to upholde us, even after an incomprehensible maner. And when we [D5r 41] shall thinke that he hath altogether forsaken and forgotten us, let us be assured that yet he wyll holde us by the hande, we shall not perceive it, but yet he wyll doe it, and we can never get out of suche a maze unlesse by his infinite mercye he drawe us out: as it is certaine that Ezechias had never bene releved, if God by his holy spirit had not susteined hym within, and enlyghtened hym whyle he was in these great troubles. Now after he hath so sayde, he added. Lorde, the payne vexeth me sore, comfort thou me. But what shall I say? It is he that hath done it even as he hath sayde it. Here Ezechias confesseth in summe that (as touching him self) he is vanquished, and that there is no remedy without God helpe, and set hym selfe as pledge. The word that he useth signifieth some time to answer for, which men terme to be suretie, it may then be thus expressed. Lord be thou my suretie in this extremitie, for I can no more. Thou seest that there is no more power in me, then must thou aunswere as suertie for me in my place. And this worde also is often among the complaintes of Job. But it signifieth also to refreshe, and all come to one point, to wit, as we have touched before, that Ezechias knew that he had no strength and that he muste nedes perishe as touching him selfe: as if a man should declare that he hath nothing to satisfie his creditour that which he oweth, he commeth then to God for refuge. Nowe have we here yet an other good admonition whiche is that we can not call upon god as we ought except we be led to this reason to make our selves as nothing. For while men kepe I wote not what remnant, it is sure that they [D5v 42] shal never cal upon God but by halfes. We must then be so brought in subjection that being altogether stripped naked of our selves, our folly may constrayne us to seke in God that whiche wanteth in our selves. Loe this is one thing to be noted: Yet in the meane time we are advertised not to be discouraged when God shal so have spoyled us that we shalbe voide of all strength. For we may yet move our matter unto hym folowynge the steppes of Ezechias. Lord I can no more, so I beseche thee that thou wylt ease me. Loe this it is that we have to learne of this place. But it is true that we are not alway pressed as Ezechias was, but howe soever it be, though the constraint be not so violent, yet ought we to be spoyled and bolde of all false perswasion of our owne strength that God may be glorified as he is worthy. And in the meane tyme as I have sayde, let us followe with our prayers and requestes unto God, though we be so vanquyshed that we have not one whit of strengthe in us, let us nevertheles have our recourse to our God, and he shall geve us that whiche we want, for asmuche as in hym lieth all the fulnesse of good thynges.

Nowe he further addeth, and what shall I saye? for he that hath spoken hath also done it. Here some thynke that Ezechias woulde nowe rejoyse felyng the delyveraunce whiche God had sent hym that he breaketh all his complayntes whiche he used, and that now he hath his mouth open to confesse the goodnesse of God. But the naturall meanyng of the text beareth it not. Rather Ezechias breaketh his matter to shewe the anguishe whiche suffered hym not to continue as [D6r 43] he would gladly have done. And we see manye suche examples in all the Psalmes where there is some declaration of the chastisementes whiche God sent eyther to David or to his other servauntes. Then when God hath so sharply afflicted his people, ther have bene such like requestes as nowe and then the faythefull enterlace alwayes,[9] I wote not howe, as if they were utterly cast awaye. So doth Ezechias now. And there is an example verye lyke in the nyne and thirtye Psalme, whiche we have already alledged. For there David also acknowlegeth that he had to do with God. It was then muche to knowe that men persecuted hym, but when he sawe the hand of God to be against hym, I maye not (sayd he) come to plede here, nor to pursue actions, there is nothyng better for me than utterly to kepe silence and take the condemnacion upon me. And in Job we see many suche lyke complayntes. Nowe let us come to the meaning of Ezechias. What shal I say? it is he whiche hath sayd and he also hath done it. He lamented not as they whiche founde no hope, for suche people wyll crye alas, but all their sighes vanishe awaye on the ayre. Contrariwyse Ezechias sheweth us here

---

[9] *Psal. 39.*

that if we wyll have God to heare us, we must open all our passions and sorowes before hym, that we may be unburthened, as it is said in the Psalme. Ezechias hetherto hath folowed this order, that is that he hath opened al his perplexities and cares whiche he endured as if he layde them abrode rounde about God. But now he reproveth hym selfe. Alas sayeth he: what shold I doe? for it is God hymselfe whiche hath sayde it and done it. [D6^{v} 44] He hath sent me this message by his Prophet, that there was no hope of life, it is then in vaine that I pray unto hym. What shall I avayle then in all my prayers? what shal I do? And I wote not whether he wil have pitie on me. We se now howe Ezechias outraged against him selfe. It is true that suche disputacion proceded of infidelitie, but it is necessary that there should be infidelitie in us to the ende that our fayth might the better be proved. Yet this is not ment to speake properly that we shoulde be infideles, when we are so tossed with unquietnes, but that we have a feble faith and that our Lorde exercise us in suche maner that we in the meane tyme maye knowe what we are, and that without him we should be a hundred thousand times vanquished every houre. Lo in effect what Ezechias ment to declare here. What shall I say? For I fele not that the prayer and entreating whiche I can make, doth profit me, and why? God afflicteth me and I fele no maner of ease. I am afrayd to present my selfe before him. Yet nevertheles I truste that my request shall not be rejected of hym, although that I knowe for a truthe that when he speaketh by the mouthe of his Prophet, he hathe forthwith stretched out his hande, and I fele by profe that thys message is not as a threateninge of lyttle chyldren, but that God hath published and proclaymed warre against me, whiche he hath done as it were with fyre and bloud, and it appeareth that there is no more remedy.

Nowe have we here a good place to shewe us that we ought to despise Sathan and al unfaithfulnes, when we have to doe with prayinge to [D7^{r} 45] God, so that when we shall have a hundreth thousand disputacions, yet we shall not let to conclude, so it is that I shall overcome all maner of lettes in the strengthe of my God, and I will seke him although he repulse me, and though it appeare that he hath an hundred armies to thruste me far from hym, yet wyll I come unto hym. Thus have I tolde you howe we ought to be armed when we are to praye unto God. For as we have nede in all extremities to runne unto our God, so must we knowe that Sathan applieth all his power to stoppe us that we have no accesse unto God. And there is none of the faythfull whiche doeth not fele this more than he would desire. But in the meane tyme let us lerne to know the sicknes, that in nede we may take such remedy as is here geven us of God. When then the devill shall set before us: What shouldest thou doe to praye to God? And what thinkest thou that in so greate wretchednesse as thou fel-est in thy selfe, he wyll ayde thee? And what thinkest thou myserable creature? to whome preparest thou to go? Is it not God himselfe that doth persecute thee? But let us passe forwarde, this notwithstanding, and force our selves to breake through al stayes, treadyng under foote suche wandryng discourses.

Moreover it chaunceth that being yet in some rest if we lift up our wit to God, by and by this commeth in our fantasie. Alas what are we? shal we dare to approche unto God? Howe ofte have we offended him? And hereupon we sometyme conclude to holde us there still. But yet such disputacions are very ill, and they are even so many blasphemies, if God would lay them to our charge, [D7v 46] as when we make question or doubte whether we be hearde or no, certayne it is that this is a deadly offence, and if God dyd not upholde us in our feblenesse, we coulde not but bee drowned. But howesoever it be, after we have bene condempned, after we have felte that our spirite is wrapped in many dispayres, and that we are in a maze: Yet for all that let us take good courage, and after we have sayde, alas what shall I doe? let us breake that stroke and saye: I muste yet pray and seke for my God. And why? for he hath sayde that he wyll heare them that seeke unto hym, even from the depest bottomes. Now then loe, this is the fit tyme when I must goe to him. This it is that we have to learne of this doctrine of Ezechias, when we see these broken unprofit tales, and that he hath chattred, and we see hys passions so excessive that they torment hym. Let us knowe that it was Gods pleasure to shewe here a mirrour wherein we myght beholde our owne feblenesse and the temtations whereunto we are subject, that we shold fight against them, and styll to followe on tyll we fele the relese that he doth promyse us, even as we shall fele in dede, so that we have a true continuaunce and faile not by our owne slacknesse and slouthfulnesse in the mydwaye.

Nowe let us throwe oure selves downe before the majestie of our good God, acknoweledging our faultes, praying hym, that more and more he wyll make us to fele them, untyll suche tyme as we be utterly spoyled. And though he have alway muche to reprove in us: Yet let us never cesse to hope in his mercy, and that he wyll [D8r 47] make us so to taste the same in the name of oure Lorde Jesus Christe, that it may geve us a true patience in all our afflictions, and that we maye be so holden in his obedience that we desire nothyng but to offre our selves unto hym and by hym to bee throughly sanctified. And that not only he graunt this grace unto us, but also to all peoples and nations. (. · .)

[D8v 48]

THE THIRDE SERmon.

What shall I saye? he who hath sayde it hath also done it. I wyll walke leasurly all the dayes of my lyfe in the bitternes of my soule. Lorde, to all those that shall lyve hereafter, the life of my spirite shall be notable among them, in that thou hast cast me in a slepe, and hast revived me. Behold in my prosperitie the bitternes was bytter unto me: And thou hast loved my soule, to drawe it out of the grave, because thou hast cast my sinnes behynd thy back.

WE have already herebefore declared that the good kyng Ezechias complayning that it is God that persecuteth him, is more confused for that, than if he had all the men in the worlde his ennemies, and if they all had conspired to tormente him, as of truthe it is a case muche harder and that ought to amase us more without comparison if God lyft up him selfe against us, than if all creatures did make warre upon us. Behold then the cause why Ezechias standeth confused and in trouble, because he well feleth that the thinge whiche God declared unto him by his Prophet Esaye, is nowe fulfilled in hym, and this it is that moste toucheth us to the quicke when we make comparison, betwene the worde of God and that [E1r 49] which we fele of his judgements. If God did simply but strike us, we might wel be throwen down wythall: but when he addeth also his word to reprove us, to make us know that it is he that doth chastise us, yea and that for our sinnes, lo this is a cause of muche greater confusion. Expresly then Ezechias saieth: Accordyng as he hath spoken he hath also done it, and therfore he doeth thereupon conclude that he hath nothing to replie agaynst it. For if we had to do with men, we might well make our complaintes againste them, but when we are to accuse God, the case must passe on his side. We may pleade for a tyme, but he shall alway be justified, when we shalbe condemned. Therfore it is lost tyme to thinke to amend our harme when we shall not escape condemnation before God, but when we desire to stande in oure owne defence, and use murmuryng and complaint, all this doth nothing but enforce our evyl, even so farre as to drown us altogether. And therfore let us kepe oure mouthe close as it is sayd in Job: for that is it whiche the good kyng Ezechias meant in this place.

Nowe further he saieth: *That all the tyme of his lyfe he wyll walke in feare, and go on easily or softly as a man whose pride is abated, and draweth his legges after him. Yea in the bitternes of his soule.*

Here Ezechias declareth that God hathe so engraved in hym the felyng of this correction, and hath so printed it in his hert, that the remembrance therof shall never be blotted out. It maye manye tymes come to passe (and we finde it in profe ofter [E1v 50] than we nede) that when God presseth us, we be altogether astonished, and then we grone, and if we be to confesse our faultes with humilitie, it is marvell to here us. Brifly we be not niggardly in wordes, ether to shew the greatnes of our grief, or to declare our faults, or to blesse the name of god. But we do nothing but shake our eares by and by after, and by the next morow after god hath geven us release or rest, we think no more of it. Lo in what sort men be, and howe they seke God (as it is sayd unto the Prophet) while he doth draw them unto him by force, then they cal upon him, and confesse the det as we have said, but so soone as God spareth them, they are as they were before, they lift up theyr heades like stagges, they do nothinge but rejoyse, where before they were so striken down as nothing cold be more, their face was all amazed with feare, shortlye, there was even nowe nothinge but sorrow, and fourthwith they make great chere, they retourne to theyr delites, and (that more is) they fare as if they meant to despise God openlye. We se then this inconstancie, this chaunge, this lightnes in maner in all men. On the contrary side Ezechias saith here that it is not only for the tyme present that he knoweth that God hath chastised him, but for so long as he shal live in this world he shall alwaye have minde of the correction that he hathe receaved, and he shall goe as wyth a tremblynge pace, for the worde whiche he useth, doeth some tyme signifie to go softely, and sometyme to remove. Nowe in effecte, he meaneth to saye that he shall never have stedfast pace, but he shall be so muche enfebled, that he shall be as a man drawen out of the ditch, or as he that hath a long time ben sicke, he doeth with great paine drawe his legges [E2^r 51] after him, and though he shewe him selfe abroade in the stretes yet men see well that, that is all he can do, and when he standeth up he semeth styll readie to rele and stagger. Nowe see we in a summe what Ezechias meant to say. Hereby we are put in remembraunce not to thinke straunge if God somtime afflict us more rigorously than we wold. For we have not sufficiently profited by his roddes untyll we be truely humbled for all oure lyfe after. Who is he that shall find thys in hym self? Let every one nowe looke, if a moneth after that God hath shewed him mercy he hathe reknowleged his faultes and tremble therat. But contrariwise (as I have already saide) we seeke nothinge but to blot out all remembraunce of them, for we thinke it to be matter that moveth melancholie. Sithe then we so easily forget the roddes of God, let us not marvell if after we have bene once chastised he returne againe the seconde time and shew him selfe so sharpe that we shall not knowe where to become. Wherfore behold what we have to do: that is, that during the corrections, and when we be in trouble we beare patiently the rigour of god, knowynge that it is not without cause that he useth so excedyng great sharpenes against us, and that it is bicause he knoweth we have nede of it: take this for one note. And also for another note, that we endevour to awake, bycause of the great slouthfulnesse that is in us, for we are so sluggishe and so coolde, that it is a pitie to see. Let us then durynge the tyme of oure affliction thyncke upon all oure offences, that we may have a felynge and conceavynge thereof engraved even in the bottome of our herts, and when God hath delivered us, [E2v 52] let us styll thinke upon it, and let not the feling of our evill be only for one day or for a small space, but as we praye God to supporte us, and to geve us leisure to blesse his name and to rejoyse in him, let us so do it that he be not compelled continually to stryke us lyke asses, seing our carelesnesse and the slownesse that is in us. Let us prevente the roddes of God unlesse we wyl have them always tyed at our backes. And nowe lette us note that Ezechias trembled in suche sorte, that he cessed not to be holden up by the hande of God, and to seke for comforte in God, knowyng well that he was mercifull unto hym. But these two thinges agree well, that on the one side the faithful are alwayes in care fearing to stomble the seconde and thirde tyme when they have once paste a deadlye fall. And yet neverthelesse they take courage and trust in God to walke frely, for as muche as they knowe that he wyll never fayle them. Loe this it is that we have to practise, on the one side to thinke upon our sinnes and offences, and to be moved with horrour, seing that we have deserved that God should set him selfe against us, and that this do so cut us that it make us to walke tremblyngly, and as scant able to goe. Loe howe we oughte to bee throwen downe and humbled under the hande of God. For there is no question hereof beynge to wylde, but rather we must knowe that the chiefe vertue of the faithfull when God doth afflict and punish them is to be as brought to naught, and yet alwaye drawynge our legges after us to goe on our pace sithe it pleaseth God to shewe us mercy. And that we know, that though we have offended him, yet he will alway continue his goodnes [E3r 53] towarde us, he wil geve us courage, and that therfore on the other side we become fresh agayne. Lo this is the summe that we have here to learne of Ezechias.

After he addeth that the bitternes became to him bitter in his prosperitie. Here he enforceth the evill that he hath felt, because he was sodenly taken with it, when he thought he was at rest and free from affliction. As on the other side we see that the thing whiche is forseen farre of, may be more patiently suffred. For what is the cause that discourageth us when we are in affliction, but that every one during his prosperitie maketh him selfe beleve that all shal go wel. If a man did thinke of the death of his father, or of his wife, or of his children, if he did think that his own life were subject to calamities, it is certain that he woulde be prepared with defense against all temtations, so as he wold not be found so amased when thei come upon him. But because every man deceiveth him self in vaine hope, that is it that troubleth us out of measure, when our Lorde sendeth any adversitie. Nowe Ezechias confesseth that it is so chaunced unto him, and for this cause he sayeth that hys griefe hath bene so much the more bitter for that it happened unto him in his prosperitie. For we have seene here before, howe God afflicted hym even to the extremitie, that is to wete, when he was spoyled of his Realme, and that al his lande was wasted by his ennemies. He was beseged in the town of hierusalem, there he was brought under, there they mocked hym, there they spake of hym all shame and reproche that was possible, yea, even the name of God was vilanouslye [E3^{v} 54] blasphemed. Lo thus was Ezechias all confused. Hereupon God delivered him miraculously, even as if he had come downe from heaven to succour hym. He seing that disconfiture so great whiche was done by the hande of the aungel, rejoysed, and not without good reason, for God gave him cause having declared suche a signe of favour toward him, as if he had reformed all the worlde at his desyre. But there was a fault, wheresoever it was, that is that he thinketh no more of his affliction passed, and resteth him to muche, that is to say, he becometh careles and negligent. Lo herfore now he saith that his sorowe is come upon him in his peace and in his prosperitie. Nowe here we have a very profitable warning, that is to say, when we know the graces of God, we must so rejoyse that yet we forget not the tyme passed, and that for the tyme to come we alwaye have our estate before our eyes, that is to say, that with the turning of a hand our lyfe shalbe turned into death, our light into darkenesse, as we see the dyverse chaunges in thys frayle life. Briefly let us so magnifie the goodnes of God, when he assureth us that he wil maintein us in peace and at rest, that in the meane tyme we still consider what our frailtie is, and let us not be daseled when God shall blesse us and sende us all after our desire, let not that (I saye) make us fal to muche on slepe, but let every man make him selfe ready when it shal please him to sende us any chaunge to receive alwayes in feare, in humilitie, and in all pacience that whiche he wyll sende us. If we doe so, we shall not finde the hand of God so grevous nor so heavy upon us as we are wont to do. But when we ar to sound on slepe, although [E4^{r} 55] we knowe the grace of God, wherof we presently rejoyse, he must awake us, yea and pluck us hard by[1] the eare, yea and laye great strypes upon us. And here we have one example in the kyng Ezechias, as we have also an other in David. For in the. xxx. Psalme he confesseth that he was so dronke that felicitie had made hym to forget hys estate. I have sayde in myne abundance, I shall no more be shaken. And how so? David had had so many prickes to pricke hym forwarde, he had bene exercised so many wayes to have alwaies in mynde what the life of

[1] *Psalm. 30.*

man was, and he did profit right well therin, for he had bene a long tyme as in the shadow of death. He had bene persecuted of the people, being prysoner among his ennemies, and having no minute of rest. Then when God had set hym on the roiall seate, he concluded that he shoulde never stomble, and that he should therein remaine peasable. If David havinge the spirit of God in suche excellence as we know, having had so many profes that he was altogether ravished unto God, yet neverthelesse hath so forgot him self: what shal become of us? After he addeth. It was of thy free goodnesse that I was upholden O Lorde, thou hast establyshed me as on a mountaine, but thou turnedst thy face, and lo I was troubled. Thus sheweth he his unthankfulnes in that. For although he had not altogether forgot the blessing which he had received of the hand of God, yet is it so that he did not thinke upon this, god hath delivered me once that I shold alway have my recourse unto him: knowing that my life hangeth as by a thred except the stay of it be on his goodnesse, and that from minute to minute he worketh [E4v 56] confessing that by and by I should peryshe if he continued not still to ayde me. David thought not upon this and he knewe also that he had fayled, and so he addeth after. Lorde thou hast hyd thy face and behold I was troubled. So is it of Ezechias, he was in peace, and loe sodeinly God wounded hym so that the stripe was deadly, and he coulde not conceive any thing but such an astonishment as if God had striken him with lightning from heaven. Therfore of necessitie must it be that he received a terrible bitternesse.

Nowe let us applie this doctrine to our profit, and let us not stay till God make us with force of strypes to know our infirmitie. But whyle he doth yet spare us and whyle he hathe pitie of our feblenesse, let us not cesse to thynke of hym, and let us feare hym, keping our selves hid as it were under his wynges, knowynge that we can not stand one minute without his ayde. To the rest, if sometime we be overtaken, let us know it was because we were to fast a slepe.

He addeth a lytle after that God hath delivered his soule, but he useth a maner of spech which emporteth more. He sayth thou hast loved my soule, or thou hast had thy good pleasure in it to plucke it back from the grave. By this circumstance he magnifieth the goodnesse of God so much the more for that he is come to seke hym even to the grave. For if God doe holde us styll in our estate, I graunt we therby knowe that we are beholding to him, but therin we knowlege it but very coldly. But if he deliver us from death, then we better perceive howe good he is, for that in suche extremitie he as it were cometh downe unto us. [E5r 57] For it semeth unto us that we are not much bound unto God, if he preserve us in this life, bicause we take that to be but as an order of nature. True it is that the more he spareth us so muche the more we ought to fele his fatherlye goodnes, but we do it not, and so by reason of our dulnes it is become nedefull that God work of another fashion. Now then as I have already sayde, if that God plucke us out of the grave, and that we have bene as forsaken for a time, that it semed we were cut of from al hope, that even men disdaigned to loke upon us as if we were pore rotten carrions, if in this case God have pitie upon us, in this he sheweth us so much greater brightnesse to se his mercye, and so much more we have occasion to acknowledge what and howe infinite his bountye is, in this that god hath so plucked us backe from the death. Lo, this it is that Ezechias meant to say.

Lord (saith he) thou hast loved my soule: And how so? was there any thing in it that might move God to love it. Alas, no: for it was nothinge but shadow, a dead thing. I was (saith he) at the grave, and then thou declaredst thy love towarde me. When then we shalbe altogether disfigured, and that God nevertheles wyll vouchsafe to caste eye upon us, and to have care of us, in this we ought much more to be enflamed to blesse his name, and to geve him such praise as doth here the good king Ezechias. Behold then in a summe what we have to learne of this place: that is, for asmuch as God seeth that we are not touched enoughe with the good thinges that he hathe done for us, nor wyth his graces, and that it is nedefull that we be so striken downe, and in suche extremitie that there [E5v 58] be in us no more hope of life, that when we shalbe as forsaken of him and of men, he maye then take us to mercy. Thus are we earnestly touched and made to geve him thankes, knowyng that he saw nothing in us but miseries when he shewed hys mercy upon us.

Now he saieth also on the other side: Lorde, they that shall lyve after, shall know that the lyfe of my spirite hath bene prolonged. This place bicause of the shortnes therof is darke, for it is not a sentence layd out at length, but they are as it wer broken wordes. He saieth in summe: Lorde they shall live amonges them, and in them all the lyfe of my spirite, thou hast cast me on slepe, and thou hast revived me. Bicause he speaketh not here of the yeres in the beginning of the verse, that is the cause of the shortnes. But when we loke nearer, we shall finde that Ezechias meant to say that the miracle whiche had bene done upon his persone shuld be knowen not only for a dai, but also after his decease. Some men do expound it, that God shall also prolonge the life of other: but that exposition is not to purpose. For Ezechias meant to saye, that this was not a common or ordinary benefit, but rather he hath felt that God hath wrought wyth him after an extraordinary fashion. Hereunto tendeth his porpose, that this miracle of God shal never be put under fote, but thoughe he be dead, yet we shall still talk of it. Before he said I shal remember all the time of my lyfe howe I have bene chastised, and I shall fele the strokes: for I yet go staggering with all. Now he stretcheth forther and largelier that which he saide before, that is to saye, that not onely he him self shalbe humbled before God, [E6r 59] but also all the world shall have occasion to saye: Behold here an act worthy of perpetuall memory that god hath done for a man. For we ought to desire that all the good thinges that God bestoweth upon us, be also knowen of other, that they maye take ensample therof, and that they maye serve for theyr edification. And we se when David wold be heard in his requestes, he addeth commonly this reason, that every man shall thinke of it, that the good shalbe edified, and the wicked confounded. Lord (saith he) when men shal se that thou so assistest thine, al they that call upon thee shall rejoyce, and shalbe so muche more confirmed in waitynge for the like: and also the wicked shalbe confounded and though they now mock at the trust that I have in thee, seyng that thou hast afflicted me, if they knowe that I have not bene disapointed when I have had my recourse unto thee, they shalbe abashed. Thus much then saith Ezechias, now that this miracle of God shall profit not onely him but also other, as a thing knowen and notorious to all. And after he amplifieth it, saying that it shall not be for a smal time, but also after his decease. For asmuch as his lif hath ben so prolonged, it shall be talked of for ever. For (saieth he) thou hast cast me on slepe. This worde to caste on slepe emporteth that he was as it were in the grave, and after was revived. As in dede this miracle is even yet at this day celebrate in the church of god, and shal be to thend of the world. So then we se that it hath not only profited one person alone, but hath bene a confirmation generally to all the faithful, in this that they waite for God, to have pitie upon them in theyr necessitie to succor them, and though he do not prolong theyr life in such sort yet that he shall kepe them [E6v 60] to the ende, and that if he se them striken downe, he shall lift them up againe, he shall geve them some token of his pitie, so that in life and deth they shall fele him alway theyr saviour, and shall know that they have not bene forsaken nor geven over of him. Loe wherunto this song is profitable, and to what intent it was made.

Nowe ought we to have suche like affection, as Ezechias had, to endevour so much as shall lye in us that the graces of God may be knowen of al the world, although they specially perteine to us. For when God doeth good to every one of us, we ought not onely in secrete to thank him, feling our selves bound unto him, but to endevour to publish the same, that other may be confirmed and hope in God, seyng such a profe of his goodnes to them that call upon him: and that praise may be geven hym in common as S. Paule saith, when the faithful shall all together praise God, that he hath bene delivered, and that this gevynge of thanckes shall geve suche a sounde, that this shalbe a cause why God shall alwaye deliver him so muche the more that praises may be given to him by many. I graunt we oft do publish such graces of God as we have felt, but many do it by ambition and hipocrisie, for makynge a shewe to magnifie the name of God, they draw a part of the praise to them selves. Let us beware of that, and let us have an upright and pure affection, so as every one may learne to loke unto God, and to have his hope wholy staied upon him, and let us have this zele and this fervent desire that all creatures beare us company when we are to blesse the name of God.

Moreover when God shall as it were have [E7r 61] striken us dead, and revived us by his grace, let this so much the more move us to praise him. Ther is not so smale a benefit that deserveth not thankes, and when we shall applie all oure wittes to thanke God onely for this that he nourisheth us, yet can we not aquite our selves of the hundreth part of our det. But if God use a more excellent maner to declare his favour toward us, and that the good thinges which he doeth for us, are as it were wonderfull and incomprehensible of men, our bond encreseth so much the more, and we have so much the lesse excuse if we be not then enflamed to praise him with full mouth, and to preache everye where the goodnes that he hathe made us to feele.

After this Ezechias addeth that God hathe cast his sinnes behynd his backe. Here he leadeth us back to that we saw before, that is, that al that he endured was but the payment that was due unto him for his faultes. And that nowe this that god hath bene mercifull unto him, is for that he hathe hidden and buried his offences which brought all the evyll upon him. This sentence is worthye to be well noted. For (as we have before declared) although we knowe well that adversities happen not unto us by chaunce, but that it is the hande of God that stryketh us, yet so it is that we can not come to the true cause as we ought. And that is partly bicause every one doeth flatter him selfe in his owne faultes, and partly also bicause we entre not in judgement or examination of our owne life to knowe whether it hathe bene well ordred: for wyllingly we are very lothe to be disquieted. And yet must we come unto it, for that is the true signe [E7v 62] of repentance when men of them selves search the depth of their sinnes, and tarry not till God force them unto it, but they present them selves unto him they sommon them selves so as they nede neyther sargeant nor officer, but they examine themselves and say: Alas, how have I lyved? how stande I with God? When men of their own mynde enter into this triall, in this thei declare that God hath touched them by his holy spirite. But this is a rare thing as I have sayde, on the one syde hipocrisie stoppeth us that we examine not our owne faultes, and that we discover them not, seking always to flee from the shame and to hide our owne evyl: yea and we say that the evill is wel, and we make our selves beleve that we have not offended God, or at least we make our faultes lesse as if thei wer nothynge, and as if we neded but only wype our mouthes. Loe howe we are caried away by pride and ambition that is roted in our nature when we come not rightly to God in knowledging what we are. On the other part we are desirous to flee from sorowe, as naturally it is a thyng that greveth us. Now there is no sorow so great as when we thinke that God is our judge, and that we ar evill doers before hym, for there we fele that whiche before hath bene sayde, that he breaketh our bones as a Lyon: the wrathe of God is so terrible a thyng that it is no marvell though we flee from it. And yet is this a faulte, for we oughte not to make our selves lyke to them that are so blockish that they wyll in no case thynke upon that which they have deserved of God, that is the punishment wherof they ar worthy. For this cause we ought so muche the more to note thys doctrine where [E8r 63] Ezechias leadeth us by his example to knowe our synnes, so ofte as the Lorde doth rygorouslye handle us, that we may not only knowe that it is his hand which afflicted us, but also that then he serveth his processe upon us, and accuseth us of the synnes that we have committed, and bicause we would not of our owne mynde come to have our cause tryed before hym, and to aske hym pardon that he is dryven to drawe us thereunto by force. This is the firste thynge that we have to learne of this place.

The seconde point is that when God withdraweth his hande which he had hevyly layde upon us, that is a token that he is mercifull unto us, and that he wyll no more laye our synnes unto our charge. True it is that somtime God after that he hath afflicted the wicked and reproved, leaveth them there and they ware lustier than they were before as I have already sayd. But here Ezechias sheweth how we ought to fele the goodnesse of God when he sendeth us any release, when he releveth us of any sicknesse, when he delivereth us from any daunger, when he comforteth us in povertie, when we have bene in trouble and sorrowe and he draweth us out. If then we be sad and sorrowefull, it is not enough for us to fele the evyll, but we oughte to looke unto the principall cause and to come to the originall spring therof. So when a litle babe crieth, so sone as the teate is geven him he is appeased. And why? he sucketh and is content, for he hath no understanding to go further than to his own hunger, he knoweth not whence the meat cometh, he hath no skil to thanke her that gave him his substance, for he hath neither wit nor reson. [E8v 64] But whan a man of the age of discretion shall see his father angry with him, and shall here him say to hym: away villein, get the out of my house: it is certaine that this sorrowe more perceth hym to the quicke to be thus cast of by his father than to endure hunger or thirste, and all the poverties that it is possible to thinke on. But if the father afterwarde doe pardon hym at the request of his frendes, or for that he seeth his sonne to be sory that he hath offended hym, and sayth unto hym, come home againe and dyne with me, if that childe have any reason he wyll not so muche esteme his dyner as that he is returned into the favour and love of his father, so as he had rather to tast and to abide hunger and thirst than ever to geve occasion to his father so to caste hym of agayne, and is a greate deale more glad that his father hath forgeven hym than of eating and drinking his fill.

Nowe let us applie this to our use. The moste part are as litle chyldren: if God be quickely appeased with them and plucke backe his hande, so as they have no more outwarde occasion to be sorowefull, by and by they waxe joyfull, and praysed be God (say they) which hath holpen me out of this sicknes: but in saying praysed be God they thinke not upon hym, they enter not into examination of their sinnes, thei loke not upon the cause why God afflicted them, and so sone as they be comforted they doe not acknowledge that it is because God loveth them and is favourable to them. And yet thereunto ought all their joy to be applied and not to say behold my myrth is returned. He that hath bene in any daunger, if he see himself delivered, he rejoyseth that he is no more in torment as he was, [F1^{r} 50] but in the meane time doth he loke upon the principall benefit and soveraigne felicitie of men, to be reconciled unto God? No, that commeth not in his mynde. So muche the more ought we to take holde of this doctrine, where Ezechias sayth not only, I am nowe up on foote agayne, and it hathe pleased God to releve me, my life is prolonged, as he hath sayde before: but he resteth all upon thys: God hath pardoned me my faultes, he hath taken me to mercie, he layeth not to my charge the offences that I have committed, he hath so forgeven me that nowe he is well pleased with me, he will no more call me to accompt as my judge, for he hath forgotten all my sinnes and hath cast them behind his back. Loe this it is wherunto Ezechias leadeth us by his example.

So, as oft as we shalbe afflicted by the hand of God, let us learne to entre into examination of our owne sinnes: and when we praye God to delyver us, let us not set the cart before the horse, but let us pray him to take us to his mercy. And though we have deserved a thousande moe afflictions than he maketh us to endure, let us praye that yet he cesse not to be mercifull unto us: and when he hath set us up againe, let us geve hym prayses not only for the good that he hath done us touching our bodies, but for that whiche is muche more to bee estemed, that he hath forgotten all our offences and so is agreed agayne with us that he accepteth us as his owne chyldren, because he tourneth his face from our sinnes, for whyle God loketh upon our sinnes he can not loke upon us but with indignation, and he doth but abhorre us.

Then that God may loke upon us with a [F1^{v} 51] mercifull and favourable face, it must firste be that he forget our sinnes, and thinke no more on them. True it is that when we so speake, it is after the maner of men, for we know that all is present before God. But when we say that he muste forget our sinnes and loke no more on them, that is to expresse that he cal us not to accompt, but love us as well as if we never had offended him.

Moreover by this fashion of spech that Ezechias useth, we se what is the remission of our sinnes, that is, that God cast them behind his back, and cast them there in suche sorte that he punishe them no more, nor aske vengeaunce on them. And this is worthy to be noted: For the devill alwaye travaileth to darken this doctrine bicause it is the principall point of oure salvation, and as it is shewed us in holy scripture, there is no other righteousnes nor holynes, but this fre forgevenes of sinnes. Happie is the man (saith David) whose sinnes are pardoned. Saint Paule saieth that hereby we see what is our righteousnes, and that David hath made a briefe summe therof.

For this cause the devill hath alwaye travailed by suttle meanes to tourne men from this that they may not knowe what nede they have of thys forgevenes of sinnes, as in the Popes church we partly see they say it is not but with penance and confession, and beside that, that we muste bringe some recompence, and if God pardon us the fault yet that he reserveth the punishment as a judge. And that this should be a derogation to his majestie, if we should say that he wholly and fully pardoneth, and they saye that he muste nedes shewe alwaye some rigor with his mercy, and that [F2^r^ 52] otherwyse it were to spoyle hym of his nature: Loe howe the Papistes have treated of the remission of sinnes, so that if a man should say unto them that God pardoneth oure sinnes of his mere goodnes, this shold be to them as a blasphemi, for (say they) we must make satisfaction. And what is that? works above measure, which we do more than god commandeth us in his law. It is certain that these are detestable sayings. But howsoever it be the pore world hath ben so made dronk with such sorceries. So much the more then must we note this place wher it is said that God in receivyng us to mercy, will entre no more into accompt with us, as Ezechias saith here. *Thou haste caste my sinnes behinde thy backe.*

It is true that God hath neither backe nor stomack. For we know that his essence is infinite and spirituall: but he useth thys similitude to signifie that he pardoneth our sinnes like as when it is said that he casteth them to the bottom of the sea, that is as much as if he would have no more remembrance of them nor would have them more spoken or made mention of. We see then in summe when God receiveth us in such sort that he is at one with us, that it is not onely to pardon us the fault as the Papistes have imagined and jangled without reason, but it is to thende that we maye fele his favor everye way, and that he wyll persecute us no more. And in stede that we were afflicted of his hande, and in stede of that he gave us by it a testimony of his wrath that contrariwise he maketh us to know that he taketh us for his children, and that he wil use us gentlye shewing the love that he beareth us. Lo here in sum what Ezechias meant to say, using this maner of spech that god had cast al his sinnes behind his back.

[F2v 53] Now true it is that many tymes though God doth pardon us our faultes yet he wyl not cesse to chastise us, as it happened to David: but that shal not be but for our commoditie and profit, to thend that we may walke so muche the more warely in tyme to come. I sayde even nowe that God sendeth his punishement in suche sorte that there remaineth alway some marke to put us in mynde. Then God wyll surely punyshe us although he be mercifull unto us. But these two thynges are not contrariant, that is, to cast our sinnes behynd his back, and to receyve us by and by to mercye and make us prosper by his blessynge, and yet in the meane tyme not to nourishe us in our idlenesse, but to awake us and make us fele some signe of his wrath to prevent us. Yet nevertheles if he meane to declare unto us fully the remission of our synnes, he will geve us oftentymes outwarde signes, that is to saye he wyll geve us suche a tast of his goodnesse that we may perceive assuredly that he hathe shewed mercy unto us, and that it is impossible that he shoulde use us with suche gentlenesse and favour, except he wold examine our sinnes no more, and that he fully and perfectly acquiteth us, and that he requireth nothing but that we should walke with him as being made at one and truly reconciled unto his majestie. Loe thus God declareth unto us the remission of our sinnes not only by his worde or inwardlye by his holy spirit, but also by the frutes, that is to say, when by his blessing he maketh us to prosper, and when he handleth us so favourably that we are compelled to confesse in our own conscience that he useth a fatherly bountie toward us.

[F3r 54] Then when we shall have these signes, let us conclude boldly that God hath pardoned our sinnes and that he hath cast them behinde his back, never to examine or thinke of them any more. So then so ofte as we shalbe afflicted of the hande of God, let us remembre that he hath shewed hym selfe good not only to those whome he hath taken out of this world wher they somtime have endured strong and grevous afflictions, but that he hath also pardoned their sinnes, and let us knowe that he wyll use the same goodnesse toward us. And in doing this let us learne to humble our selves hereafter. Moreover the grace of God shall so muche the more brightlye shyne, as he shall not onlye handle us with all favour touching our bodies, but also in this that he woulde not have respect unto oure sinnes, and wyll shewe us that although we did provoke his wrath and gave him occasion alwaye to forsake us in our myseries, yet he wyl not handle us with rigour but that he wil drawe us unto hym by his infinite mercye and goodnesse.

Now let us throwe our selves downe before the majestie of our good God, acknowledging our faultes, beseching him that more and more he will make us to fele them, and that it may be to humble us in suche sorte that comming unto hym we may bryng only a pure and simple confession of our sinnes, and that in the meane tyme he geve us suche tast of his goodnesse that we maye not cesse to runne unto hym although our consciences doe reprove and condempne us, that we may embrace his grace whiche he hath promysed in the name of our Lord Jesus Christe, and as oft as he [F3v 56] maketh us to fele it by experience that we may learn to turne it to our profite, and that we may be so armed againste all tentations, that we maye never sinke downe under the burden, how heavy or troublesome soever it be. And that he wyll not only graunt unto us that grace, but also to all peoples. &c.

[F4r] THE FOURTH SERmon.

For the grave shall not singe of the, and the dead shall not prayse the, nether shall they that are brought down into the pitte waite for thy truthe. The lyving, the lyving shall sing of the, as I do this day: the father shall make thy truthe knowen to his children. The Lorde it is that saveth me: we wyll sing a song in the temple of the Lorde all the dayes of our lyfe. And Esai, commaunded, that one shold take a cluster of figges, and make a plaister of them to lay upon the sore, and he shoulde be whole. Then sayd Ezechias, what signe shall I have that I shall goe up into the house of the Lorde?

IT is certaine that if our lyfe were ordered as it ought to be, we shoulde alway shoote at this principall marke, to honour God so longe as we be in this worlde. And good reason it is that we applie all our studie therunto seing that without ende and cessing we prove the gracious good dedes that he doth us. For this cause nowe Ezechias after that he hath knowledged that god prolonged his life, and hath geven him a profe to witnesse his singular love toward him, sayth that with so muche more courage he wil magnifie the name of [F4v 57] God to confesse the receit of so great a benefit. And expresly he sayth that this shall not only be whyle he is in the worlde that he will travayle to have the name of God blessed, but he wil endevour also for his successours that it may for ever be knowen howe God hath wrought for him. Finally for conclusion he saith that there is no saviour but God: and if men rest them selves upon hym their salvation shalbe certain and infallible.

But it may seme straunge that he sayeth that the death nor yet the grave shall not be to prayse god, for it semeth that he accompted upon and knoweth no other goodnesse of God but when he preserveth men in this frayle life. In dede if we loke not but here belowe, our faith shalbe but weake. And we knowe that we lyve to no other purpose but to tast in part the goodnesse of God, to the ende we may be drawen up hier and altogether ravished to the heavenly lyfe. It semeth then that Ezechias is to muche geven to the worlde, and that he hath no conceiving of the spirituall kyngdome of God. For in saying that the grave can not praise God, nor they that be dead, it semeth that he hathe no other regarde but to this present lyfe. And we knowe that it is sayde in the first place, that God wil be glorified as wel in our death as in our life. And S. Paul for the same cause sayeth, that he careth not whether he lyve or die, so the glorye of God might be alway avaunced. There appeareth to be great diversitie betwene S. Paul and Ezechias, for the one fleeth and abhorreth death, alleging that those whiche are departed shall not prayse God, the other saith it is to me al one whether I lyve or dye, for God shall alwaye be [F5^{r} 58] glorified in me. If we beholde the estate of those that are departed in that, that they are drawen oute of this world, and that God hath taken them nerer to him, it is likely that they shold be better disposed, and more chearfull to blesse his name. For-thy we be here heavely loden in this prison of oure body, we can not half (as a man may say) open our mouth to praise God, we goe not with a free courage nor with so vehement fervor of zele, as were requisite:[1] now the dead are not so encombred, they are not absent from God as we are (as S. Paule speaketh in the seconde to the Corinthians) they may then so muche the better agree with the angeles of paradise in this melodie. And we knowe what is said of the angels (as it is to be sene in the vi. Cha. of Esay) that without ceasing they cry, blessed be the Lorde of hostes, the holy, the holy, the holy. Then as farre as we may judge, those whom God hathe drawen out of this transitorye life, ought to be more readye to prayse hys name. But let us firste marke that Ezechias here had respect to the cause why God placed us in thys world, and wherfore he kepeth us therin. He asketh not any reward of us. He is not lyke unto a man that setteth servauntes in his house: for that wer to emprow his lands, and make profite therof, nether is he like unto a great prince which requireth to have manye subjectes, for that he is to be maintened and succoured by them when he hathe nede. But God seketh no avauntage by us, as he hathe no nede: Onely he will that we do homage to hym for all the benefites that he geveth us. For all our life ought to be applied to this marke, (as even now we have touched) that we blesse god, [F5^{v} 60] and render witnes that his benefits were not cast away upon us as they should be if we were lyke domme men. Lo this it is that we have to observe, that Ezechias (in sayinge that the lyvynge shall praise God) meant to note, that men pervert the order of nature when they apply not themselves to praise God, and that theyr unthankfulnes is by no meanes excusable, when they bury the graces of God and put them in oblivion. Seyng it is so then that our Lord requireth of us nothyng but that hys name be glorified in the world, it is not to be merveyled that Ezechias saieth: the living, the lyving shall praise God.

We must also note what difference is betwene the state of the living and of the dead. Though the dead praise god, yet we can not judge nor imagine that they assemble after our maner to shewe an agrement of theyr fayth. Eche one of them can right well praise God by him selfe, and yet it meaneth not that they ar gathered together in one body, as we are nowe, for the scripture saieth nothing thereof. And we maye not forge fantasies

---

[1] *2. Cor. 5.*

of oure owne braine as we thinke good. For we know that god reserveth this perfection to the latter day that we should be all united and in suche sort joyned unto our God that his glory should fullye shine in us. For as muche then as they whiche are departed have not suche a manner of exercysinge them selves in the praysynge of God as we, therefore it is said that, that is a thynge properly perteynyng to us that be lyvyng.

But there is yet more. For Ezechias speaketh not here simply of death as we have touched alreadye, but he setteth oute hys death to be suche [F6^{r} 61] as if he had bene cut of from the Churche of God, and from all hope of salvation, when this judgement was come to be executed, or as if he had bene before hys Judge: Then Ezechias prepared not him selfe to dye, as by nature we can not flee thys necessitie: but he had thys testymonye of Godes wrath, wherewith he was so feared as if all were lost to hym. Nowe we knowe that no man can synge the prayses of God excepte he have occasion and matter. For whan oure Lorde sheweth us a terrible countenaunce, oure mouthes are stopped, we are fylled wyth suche anguisshe, that it is impossible for us to blesse hym. Rather contrariwise there shall be nothynge but gnashynge of teethe, when the wrath of God shall so astonishe us. Loe thus stoode Ezechias. On the other syde, when God[2] sheweth hym selfe mercyfull towarde us, and uttereth some signe of hys favor toward us, he[3] openeth oure mouthes, as it is sayde in the li. Psalme. Lorde thou haste opened my mouth: therefore wyll I synge thy songes. And in other places. Lorde thou haste put a newe songe in my mouthe, by thys the Prophete signyfieth when God maketh them joyfull for theyr delyveraunce frome some evyll, that by thys meane, he styreth them up to synge hys songes, and to blesse hys name, and to be myndefull of hys benefytes. So then, when we conceave nothynge but altogether terrour in God, we are in a swounde, and then the gate is shutte so that we can not prayse God. So Ezechias in this place, sayinge that the dead shall not praise god, meaneth not generallye all those that departe oute of this transitorye lyfe, [F6^{v} 61] but those whiche are as it were cut of from God, and are confounded with his wrath, who also tast not his goodnes any maner of way, and are made naked and estranged from all hope of healthe. It is then impossible that such should praise God.

There is yet another point to note. For when the faithfull are holden downe and oppressed wyth any distresse, they se nothing but theyr own grief, and every man hath experience of this in him selfe to much. When any evyll hath cast us downe altogether, we can not applie oure selves

---

[2] *Psal. 51.*
[3] *Psal. 40.*

to anye other thing, for we are there holden fast as in a streight prison. So was Ezechias, as also it is said in the lxxxviii. Psalme. That the state of those that are dead, is a land of forgetfulnes: men knowe not there what God is. This semeth to be a blasphemie. But these maners of spech procede of the unskilfulnes and weakenes of men, that is bicause they can not withdraw them selves to judge with a setled sence, and to have a well framed and ordered knowledge. But the trouble so vexeth and carieth them awaye that they speake as at randon and confusely. Behold, Job saieth that men beyng taken out[4] of this world have no more carefulnesse, but every one is at rest, as if there were a confuse mixture, that the master and the verlet were all one, and that the tyrant shoulde cause no more terror. He speaketh of the state of those that are departed, as if death should destroy all thinges. Yet he had not such opinion, but it was bicause that his sorow suffred him not to speak as a man at rest. For he was tossed with such unquietnes that his words wandred. So may we think of Ezechias. He speaketh not of the estate and condition of those that are [F7r 62] departed as the scripture teacheth us, and why? his heavines, and the horrour whiche he had conceived bare rule over him in suche sorte that he wiste not where he was: it is true that this is not for excuse.

And thus therfore oure Lorde geveth us mirours of our frailenes when we see that the moste holy, and most perfect speak so. Yet in the meane time God supported Ezechias, because the principall thing remained with him styll, as we have already sene, that he tended to this mark to glorifie the name of God, for he had rather die a hundred tymes than to be one minute in this world prophaninge by unthankfulnes the benefites that God hath done for him. Lo than Ezechias kepeth this rule that men ought not to desire to live one daye but to that end that God might be glorified in it. But in the meane time this that he was tossed with so great troubles that he could not orderly speake as he ought, proceded of his weakenes, whiche God holdeth for excused and supporteth. For it is not a disobedience, though we have many ranging wordes in our prayer. It is true that we oughte alway to frame our selfes to his rule, which is geven us, to thend that every man pray to God, not at adventure, and after his own fansie. But how soever it be, we shall have measurable sorowes, and complaintes in us, and it behoveth that god have pitie of us in this behalfe. Loe in a summe what we have to learne, that above all, while we lyve, we alway tend to this ende that God be honored. For therfore it is he that hath set us in this worlde, to that end it is that he hath chosen us to be of

[4] *Job. 3.*

his flok, to wete, that we might be assembled to singe his prayses with one accorde.

[F7^{v} 64] And we see this yet better in the 115. Psalme, where is a lyke sentence. And it is not one man that speaketh, but the whole body of the Churche of the faithfull, which say that one can not prayse God in death, but we that lyve (say they) unto the ende shall confesse that god hathe preserved us. There it is signified unto us that God wil alway kepe his church, and that he will have some people remaining unto the ende of the worlde. Why? bicause he wyll be knowen the father and saviour among men. And although it be not of the greater multitud, yet wil he have some company that shal praise him. So then let us learn to exercise our selves in blessynge the name of God while he kepeth us here below, and while we be nourished by his liberalytie, and while (whiche more is) he calleth us unto him to tend alway to the hope of the eternall heritage. Sithe then it is so, let us applie all our study therunto, yea all the daies of oure lyfe. If we do otherwise, it wer better for us that our mothers had bene delivered of us before our time, or that the earth had gaped to swallow us up, than to be here gluttons, as brute beastes, and to continue unthankfull for so manye benefites as God hath geven us, and that his praise shoulde be buried by us. Take this for a note.

The residue: Let us alwaye be ready folowyng the example of S. Paule, to glorifie God, be it by life, be it by death. If at any tyme we be in trouble as the good kynge Ezechias was, let us know that all our sorowes, complaintes and groninges, oughte to be suspicious unto us, bycause we can not kepe measure by reason of the frailtie [F8^{r} 65] that is in us.

So that this which is sayd here, The dead shall not prayse God, may not be drawen of us for a consequent profe, to pleade wyth God when it shall please him to call us unto him. Let us not make this excuse under pretext of Ezechias, or David who spake so in the vi. Psalme, or of all the people as we shall aledge. For there was excesse, bycause as well David as Ezechias, and generally al the Churche then when a horrible dissipation was neare tempted as if god wold reject them, and utterly disclaime in them, and woulde have no more to do with them. As they then were pulled backe from God, so were they abasshed. And no marvell. Let us not therfore make therof a rule, as if we might do the like: but let it serve to make us knowe our own weakenes. Moreover although God do support us, yet let us not please our selves in suche a vyce. Loe this it is that we have to learne.

Nowe we are taughte for as muche as God hath made us to fele his graces, to have our herts set at large, and our mouthes opened to blesse hys name. And on the other side that we can not pronounce one worde to his prayse, whiche procedeth from a good hartie affection, except we be throughly perswaded in this, that God is mercyfull unto us, and that we use to our profit the benefits which we receave of his hande.

As touchinge the firste pointe, let everye one learne to styrre up him selfe accordynge to that whiche he receyveth of the graces of God, for the number is infinite.

[F8ᵛ 65] There is none of us when he shall duely consider him selfe, but ought to be ravished as it is saide in the xl. Psalme, that if we wyll number the testimonies that God hathe geven us of the fatherlye care which he hath for us, and of his mercye, they are mo than the heares of our head, and we shalbe therat as it were astonyshed. But accordynge as God setteth fourth the richesse of his goodnes toward every one of us, let us be so muche the more moved to blesse his name, and let every one exercise and pricke him selfe forward unto that. Lo this is in summe that whiche we have to marke upon this place.

Now on the other side, let us confesse that our lyfe is cursed if we gluttonously devoure the good thinges that God geveth us and do not therin behold his goodnes. For we unchristianly abuse all that which was apointed for our use and salvation unlesse we be brought to this point that God sheweth him selfe a very father unto us, and that by all meanes of gentlenesse he draweth us unto him, that we should not doubt that he taketh us for his children. And in this also we see how miserable is the state of Papistes, for they will not assure them selves of the goodnes of God, but saye that alwaies we must be in doubt of it. And so all theyr prayeng and thankesgevyng to God, is nothing but Hipocrisie and faining. For we can not call upon the name of God but with affiaunce, we can not praise his name except we know that he is favourable unto us. Then they are altogether excluded. Let us learn then that we can never offer to God a sacrifice of thankesgeving which he estemeth and setteth by, and that we can never attein [G1ʳ 67] to the right scope of oure life, unlesse we be fullye perswaded of his goodnes. And so as ofte as we thinke upon all the graces and benefites of God: let this come into our minde, that God doth confirme and ratifie unto us his adoption to the ende that we maye not doubte that he compteth us as his children, and that we freely call upon him as our father: Lo in a summe what we have to learn of this place.

Nowe we must also note this which Ezechias saieth. The lyving, the lyving shal prayse the? Yea the father shall declare to his children thy vertue. He had said before that the dead shal not wait any more for the truth of God, that is to say, they shall have no hope. And in this we see that which I have touched, that Ezechias speaketh not indifferently of all these whom God hath taken out of this world. For it is certeine that the faithfull do waite upon the truth of God. When Jacob yeldyng up his spirite, saide: I wyll waite for the salvation of the Lorde. He saide not that for one minute, but he declared and protested that he had this assurance imprinted in his hert, which shold never be pulled out, so that though he passed through a hundred deathes yet alway this treasure should remayne with him. Nowe then the saintes and faythful although God called them out of the world ceased not alway to nourishe the hope of the resurrection, and of this felicitie which is promised them. But Ezechias speaketh of the departed, whiche are as it were banished and estraunged altogether from the kyngdome of God whome also he forsaketh. Now, he was even in the same estate in his own conceit until god comforted him by his prophet. [G1ᵛ 68] For the messag which was sent to him, was to shew that God was his enemy, and that he came as his adversary with armed hande against him. Than was Ezechias driven to remayne confounded. Then it is not without a cause that he saide, that those which are departed, waite not for the truth of God, that is to say, that they ar altogether shut out from the promisses, so as they are no more of the number of his children.

But nowe he saieth that the lyvinge whiche tast the goodnes of God, shall cause theyr children to knowledge hys truth. Nowe here we se again how God shalbe duely praised and honored among us, that is, when a man shall knowe that he is faithfull to all his owne, that he never forsaketh them, but that his helpe is ready for them in their necessitie, and that they shall never be disapointed which leane unto him. Lo this is the true substaunce of Gods praise. So in a summe we se that it is nothing but falshede and lies when men shal pray unto God, and shall make as thoughe they gave thankes unto him, and in the meane time they are not instructed of the love that God beareth them nor certified of theyr salvation, and shall knowe of no promise. Then when that wanteth, it is certaine that all theyr prayses of God, whiche maye be sounded in the mouthes of men, are but winde, and smoke. Wyll we then prayse God as it apperteyneth, in suche maner as he alloweth the sacrifices whiche we shall offer unto hym of praise, and thankes gevinge? Let us profit in his word, lette us knowe what it is, to truste in hym, which we canne not doe tyll he declared hys good wyll [G2ʳ 69] towarde us, and have certyfyed us that he hathe receaved us, that we may frely come unto hym, and that we shal never be forsaken, so we fle unto him. If we have not suche an instruction, we can never pronounce one worde of Goddes prayses as we oughte. Loe hereunto it is to be applyed, that Ezechias sayeth here, that the father shall make knowen unto hys chyldren the treweth of God.

Moreover, where as he sayeth, that the dead can not wayte for it, nor leane unto it. Lette us knowe, that for as muche as God declareth hymselfe mercyfull and lyberall unto us, that is alwaye the more to confyrme oure hoope: That we shoulde take so muche the more courage to runne unto hym, and not to doubte that he hathe hys hande alwaye readye to helpe us at neade.

Howe then shall we use the graces of God as we oughte? When we shall be alwaye confyrmed more and more in the faythe, when we canne dyspyse all temptations, when we canne resolve oure selves, that in callynge upon God, we oughte in no wyse to feare the losse of oure laboure, for as muche as oure hope shall never be confounded.

When then we shall be well satisfyed in thys so as we maye fyghte agaynste Sathan, to beate backe all temptations, beholde howe we maye wyselye applye the benefytes of God to oure own use, and howe wee maye take profyte of theym: Loe in a summe what wee have heare to learne.

[G2v 70] Moreover, when he speaketh howe fathers ought to behave them selves towarde theyr chyldren we have to gather in generall (as hath bene said here before) that it is not ynough that we procure that god be glorified during our life, but we ought to desire as his name is immortall so that from age to age it may be honored, and that those which shall come after us, may kepe the pure religion, and that the service of God may never fall in decaye. That it maye be folowed and advaunced alwaye and that the goodnes of God maye be every where magnified. They that have children, let them knowe that God hath committed them incharge to them, and that they must rendre an accompt if they bestow not al travaill to teache them to serve God. For when it is sayd that the father shall shewe to his children the truth of god, we must alwai come to this end. Why? to this ende that the children may trust in him, that they may call upon him, that they maye geve to him the prayse of all good thynges, that they may dedicate and consecrate them selves wholy to him, and to his obedience. Then if fathers wil discharg them selves of theyr duties, let them knowe that this is the principall heritage that they ought to leave to theyr children. But if they heape up goods and yet geve them the bridle when they shall see them dissolute, mischievous, wicked despisers of God. Wo be to them in that they shall take peine to advance them in this world: for they lift them up very hye to make them break theyr neckes, and theyr fal shall be more deadly when they shal have store of goodnes: and yet in the meane tyme they shall despyse God in his doctrine, there confusion shalbe more [G3r 71] horrible, bicause theyr unthankfulnes shalbe lesse excusable. Let the fathers then thinke better of this then they have bene accustomed, that is to say, when God geveth them children, he bindeth them to this charge, that they endevor so much the more, that they may be instructed in his truth, so long as they lyve, as also we se thexample geven us in Abraham, which is the father of the faithful. For when God meant to shewe that Abraham would governe his house, as appertened: Shall I hyde from my servaunt Abraham (saith he) that which I have to do? No. Lo howe God maketh hym selfe familiar with him. For (saieth he) he shal instructe his children in my statutes, in my lawes, and in my ordinances: Lo, this is the marke whereby the faithfull are knowen from the despisers of God. If then we will be numbred in the church, let us folow this zele, and this affection of Abraham, that every one accordynge to the familie that he hath, travaile that God be honoured in it, and that hys truth be alway knowen even to the ende.

Nowe for conclusion Ezechias saieth: The Lorde it is that shall save me. This worde doeth emport that he despiseth and throweth awaye all other safegarde, as if he should saye, there is none but God. He might have said: The Lord hath saved me. He might have said: I hold my life of him and of his mere grace. But he goeth further, as if he meant here to mainteine the honor of God, and to beate down all the affiances that men conceive in theyr fantasie. For we are wonte to make our discourses when we mynde to mainteine oure selves, and when we seke to be assured, we take this meane, and that meane.

[G3^{v} 72] Nowe Ezechias forsaketh all and declareth that there is none but God, and that he it is whom we ought to go unto.

True it is that God suffreth us to use all the meanes that he offreth us, and he hathe ordeyned them for that use, but yet he wyll not that his glorye be darkened, as it is no reason it shoulde be. Nevertheles men be so wicked and froward, that alway they take occasion to minishe the glorye of God under this coloure that he helpeth them by his creatures. If God hath not bene content only to make us fele his owne vertue, but also applieth al his creatures to our use we ought to be so much the more styrred to prayse him. But cleane contrary, we robbe him of his right, we forsake him, and fasten our affiaunce here, and there, and we thinke that oure salvation procedeth from thys thing and from that. Lo how God is defrauded of his ryght. So much the more ought we to marke this that is here sayd by Ezechias. The Lorde it is that saveth us. That is, thoughe the Lorde do stretch his hande unto us, and geveth us wherewith to be mainteined, yet let us confesse that he is the fountain, and let the river that floweth from him unto us, not hinder us to knowe whence the river commeth. Let us then tende alway to thys welspring that God be glorified, and that he kepe his owne wholy: and after, when we are made naked of all other meanes, let us say: the Lord alone shall suffise. And for this cause saith David. The mercye of God is more worth than all lyves, not meanyng that the lyfe of men is not of the mercye of God, but he sheweth that men ought not to be fast bound here beneth, and that they are become brutish [G4^{r} 73] when they thinke to preserve, mainteine, or warrant them selfes by this, or that mercy, and that they ought above all thinges to preferre the only goodnes of God and to rest in the same. So then beholde here a saying of great doctrine, if we can have skil to take profite therof. Let us then folowe the example of Ezechias, and when God hath succored us at our nede: let us geve him the prayse for our life confessinge that there is none but he alone to save us. Herunto he addeth againe. And we wyll singe our songes all the dayes of our life in the house of the Lord. Here he repeteth agayne the saying that he spake before, that is, that he will employe all the residue of the life that god hath geven him to make to God acknowledgement therof, that he might not be found unthankful. For as I have said it were better that we had never bene borne, than to enjoy the good things that God hath done for us, and yet to have oure mouth close and to thinke no more upon him. Let us then note well that thys repetition is not superfluous when Ezechias saieth so manye times that sith his lyfe is prolonged, he wyll be so muche the more styred to prayse God. Take this for one note.

Now, he furder sheweth that this shal not be for a sodein braide, as many can wel praise God with a metely vehement affection, when they have had profe of his goodnes, but that droupeth awaye by and by, and the memory is lost of it, and they thynke that it is enough that at one time they have testified that thei thank God for the good that thei have received. But Ezechias sheweth us that we ought to continue therin with a true perseverance, for we are beholden to god no more for one day of our life than for another. [G4v 74] It must therfore be fully dedicate and avowed unto him. So seyng the slouthfulnes and coldnes that is in us, let us learn to styrre up our selves when we shall fele that oure zele waxeth colde for feare lest it be wholy quenched. Let us awake. How? If I have once or twise reknowledged the grace of God. What is that? must it be now forgotten? And if I blesse the name of God duringe one moneth, a yere, or two, or thre: And now I think no more of it. To what purpose shal that serve me? but to make me so much the more giltie of hipocrisie, and to shew that ther was nothing but a fire of stubble, that there is no constancie nor stedfastnes. If then we beholde well the example of this good kynge, we shall everye one be the more pricked forwarde, to fede our selves no more in this idlenes whiche is naturall unto us, and whereunto we be to muche enclined.

When he sayeth, In the house of the Lorde. He meaneth not that the prayses of God shoulde be enclosed within the temple, for every man in hys owne house maye and ought to praise God. But Ezechias sheweth that it is not ynoughe that he prayseth God in secrete, but that he wyll styrre up other, to have more companye. He speaketh here of a solemne sacrifice of praise which he wil make to God in a great assemblie. And for this same cause our Lorde hathe wylled his to gather together. For he was able ynough to have taught them perticulerly if he would, and to saye: Let every man prayse me in his chamber. But his pleasure is that there be this policie, that we be knit together in one body, that we call upon him with one mouth, and that we make confession of our fayth with one [G5r 75] accord. And why so? True it is, that firste we see that it behoveth that all oure senses be applied to glorifie him, but there is also a seconde point, that every one styrre up other as we have nede, for ther is none of us that feleth him self disposed to praise God, but he hathe yet a pricke forwarde when he shall see the company of the faithfull, and example shewed him. For asmuche therfore as this doeth styrre us up, God willeth that openly and in common we sing his praises. And for this cause Ezechias saieth expresly that he will go to the temple of the Lorde to prayse and blesse his name, as we se[5] also that Jonas dyd the lyke. He speaketh of house of the Lorde, and why? not (as I said) that the praises of the Lorde are there shut up and hidden but for that the people there assemble together, and for that he knew that this should bring more profite because there shoulde be some that shoulde be styrred up by his example. Lo in a sum the songe of Ezechias.

Now in the end it is here recited that the Prophet Esay commaunded to make him a plaster of figges upon his wounde, wherby it is likely that it was a pestilence which he had. And after he by and by addeth that Ezechias also demaundeth a token which is graunted him, as we se when the sonne was drawen back of his course upon the diall of Achas. A man mighte here move a question, whether thys playster were for medicine, or a token that the Prophet gave him. And it semeth that if it had ben for medicine, it should have diminished the glory of God, for it behoved that Ezechias life should be miraculous. Why did he not then heale him without any meane? But when all shalbe [G5v 76] wel considered, the signe or miracle that was geven to Ezechias when the sonne stayed his course, and when the shadowe of the dyall was drawen back so many degrees, was sufficient, and toke awaye all doubt. Moreover although Ezechias used this plaister it is not therfore to be saide that his healyng was naturally wrought, for sith God had chaunged the order of the heaven, and shewed a witnesse so evident that this proceded from his hande, and that it was an extraordinary benefite, we ought to content our selves with that, and we see many times that God is served with his creatures and yet he hath sufficientlye declared that it was his owne power only.

They whiche thinke that Ezechias rather had this plaister as a sacrament to confirme hym, doe thinke that the figges would more have hurt his wounde than helped it. But a man maye make a compound of them to ripe a sore, and that is commonly knowen. True it is that God somtime geveth signes that seme cleane contrary, and that is to drawe us the more

---

[5] *Jonas. 2.*

to him, to make us forsake our owne fantasies and hold us content with that whiche he hath spoken. As how? God promiseth that the worlde shall never be destroyed with water, and what signe geveth he therof? a signe that naturally threateneth us raine. When we see the rainbowe, what token is it? it is such a drawyng together of waters, that maketh seme we shall all be overwhelmed and the earth shal peryshe. And how so? This signe is geven us of God to make us know that therth shal never be destroied with overflowynge of water. Yea but it is to make us learne to stay upon his truthe and to stoppe our [G6r 77] eyes against all the rest, and against al that we conceive in our selves, and that the truthe of God be of so sufficient credit with us, that we receive it without gainsaying. So then God worketh wel in suche sorte: but as to this place, we maye rather judge that the Prophet to asswage the griefe of Ezechias gave hym thys remedye, lyke to a fyre that burneth a man. And so when GOD hadde prolonged the lyfe to this good kynge, he would yet of abundant grace adde this goodnesse also, that the paine should be mitigate. Then the prophet gave him this as it wer an overplus that God had not only prolonged his life, but also wold not have him endure so muche or suffer the tormentes whiche he felt before.

Thus behold howe in all and every waye God hath declareth him selfe pitiful towarde this good king, how he would shewe him selfe pacified altogether after that he had used suche roughnes toward him and had stretched out his arme as if he wold have altogether overwhelmed him. But this meaneth not that God doth the very same to every one of his children, to the ende that we shold not aske that in one minut of time God make us glad after he hath drawen us out of the grave and hath geven us throughlye to content us, but that it maye be his pleasure by litle and lytle to geve us ease of all our greves, in the meane time lette us be content with this.

And in dede we may gather that God hetherto hath wrought by degrees in Ezechias: for this miracle was done since the shadow of the sonne was drawen back, and the message of prolonging his lyfe was geven him by the prophet.

[G6v 78] It semeth then that Ezechias was altogether delivered, and yet this plaister was also requisite. So then when our lord after he hath geven us anye ease in oure trouble shall leave some remnaunt of peine: let not that trouble us, nether let us be wery of bearyng his correction, untill he have healed us altogether.

Nowe we have to declare why Ezechias demaunded a signe, for although it wer of wekenes yet God heard him in suche a request, and herein we se howe lovynge God is towarde us, when he doeth not onely graunt the requestes whiche we make of a pure and right affection: but also though there be some infirmitie mingled withall, and that we bear passions somwhat excessive, yet God hath pitie on us in this point. Certaine it is that Ezechias when he had perfect faith he was content to have heard the word from the mouth of the Prophet. Then when he saieth alas shall I not have some signe: herin he sheweth that he geveth not ful and perfect faith to the word of God. But yet he confesseth his fault, and in confessyng it, he asketh remedy: and of whom? of God him self. Then when we shalbe so encombred, fyrst let us acknowledge our owne povertie, and let us not go aboute to excuse the evell, but let us take upon us the sentence of condemnation willyngly. If then we aske of God to helpe it by his goodnes, he wyll succor us, and heare our requestes.

It is true that it becommeth not us to require a signe or miracle when we thinke good, for as it hath bene declared in that place wher the prophet even nowe made mention of the signe. Ezechias had[6] a speciall motion unto it, as Gedeon also had: [G7^{r} 79] Let us leave that to the good pleasure of God, when we know our infirmitie, and pray him to helpe, and to confirme us to the ende we may be fullye satisfied in his worde. Lo then how we muste go forward, and in this doyng we shall fele that this is not written onely for the parson of the kyng Ezechias, but that God would geve it for a common instruction to all his church, that in oure troubles when we shalbe come to the extremitie: yea, to the bottome of hell, we may yet know that we ought to have our refuge to him that hath called us, and handled us so gently, hopinge that he wyll shewe fourthe his strength towarde us, althoughe for a time it be farre from us, and that we se no signe of it, and so that he will geve us mater to glorifie him, and also we are taughte to applye all oure lyfe to blesse the name of God, and to sing his prayses accordyng as we have experience of his goodnesse towarde us.

Now let us throwe downe our selves before the majestie of our good God, in acknowledgyng of our faultes, praying him, that more and more, he wyll make us to feale them, and that this may be to beate us altogether downe, and humble us before him that we may fight with the vyces which make warre against us, knowyng that our Lord hath ordeyned us to this conflict, till we be fullye renewed and clothed with his justice, and that there may be no stoppe to let us from the obedience of his good will, and that he graunt this grace not onely unto us, but to all peoples and nations. &c.

---

[6] *Judj. 6.*

[Aa1r] A MEDITA
TION OF A PENI-
TENT SINNER: WRIT-
TEN IN MANER OF A
Paraphrase upon the
51. Psalme of David.

¶ I have added this meditation folowyng unto the ende of this boke, not as parcell of maister Calvines worke, but for that it well agreeth with the same argument, and was delivered me by my frend with whom I knew I might be so bolde to use and publishe it as pleased me.

[Aa2r] ¶ The preface, expressing
the passioned minde of
the penitent sinner.

[1]

THe hainous gylt of my forsaken ghost
So threates, alas, unto my febled sprite
Deserved death, and (that me greveth most)
Still stand so fixt before my daseld sight
The lothesome filthe of my disteined life,
The mighty wrath of myne offended Lorde,
My Lord whos wrath is sharper than the knife,
And deper woundes than dobleedged sworde,
That, as the dimmed and fordulled eyen
Full fraught with teares and more and more opprest
With growing streames of the distilled bryne
Sent from the fornace of a grefefull brest,
Can not enjoy the comfort of the light,
Nor finde the waye wherin to walke aright:

[2]

So I blinde wretch, whome Gods enflamed ire
With pearcing stroke hath throwne unto the ground,
Amidde my sinnes still groveling in the myre,
Finde not the way that other oft have found,
Whome cherefull glimse of gods abounding grace
Hath oft releved and oft with shyning light
Hath brought to joy out of the ugglye place,
Where I in darke of everlasting night
Bewayle my woefull and unhappy case,
And fret my dyeng soule with gnawing paine.
Yet blinde, alas, I groape about for grace.

While blinde for grace I groape about in vaine,
My fainting breath I gather up and straine,
Mercie, mercie to crye and crye againe.

[3]

[Aa2v] But mercy while I sound with shreking crye
For graunt of grace and pardon while I pray,
Even then despeir before my ruthefull eye
Spredes forth my sinne and shame, and semes to say:
In vaine thou brayest forth thy bootlesse noyse
To him for mercy, O refused wight,
That heares not the forsaken sinners voice.
Thy reprobate and foreordeined sprite,
For damned vessell of his heavie wrath,
(As selfe witnes of thy beknowyng hart,
And secrete gilt of thine owne conscience saith)
Of his swete promises can claime no part:
But thee, caytif, deserved curse doeth draw
To hell, by justice, for offended law.

[4]

This horror when my trembling soule doth heare,
When markes and tokens of the reprobate,
My growing sinnes, of grace my senslesse cheare,
Enforce the profe of everlastyng hate,
That I conceive the heavens king to beare
Against my sinfull and forsaken ghost:
As in the throte of hell, I quake for feare,
And then in present perill to be lost
(Although by conscience wanteth to replye,
But with remorse enforcing myne offence,
Doth argue vaine my not availyng crye)
With woefull sighes and bitter penitence
To him from whom the endlesse mercy flowes
I cry for mercy to releve my woes.

[5]

And then not daring with presuming eye
Once to beholde the angry heavens face,
From troubled sprite I send confused crye,
To crave the crummes of all sufficing grace.
[Aa3r] With foltring knee I fallyng to the ground,
Bendyng my yelding handes to heavens throne,
Poure forth my piteous plaint with woefull sound,

With smoking sighes, and oft repeted grone,
Before the Lord, the Lord, whom synner I,
I cursed wretch, I have offended so,
That dredyng, in his wrekefull wrath to dye,
And damned downe to depth of hell to go,
Thus tost with panges and passions of despeir,
Thus crave I mercy with repentant chere.

[Aa3v] *A Meditation of a peni-*
tent sinner, upon the 51.
Psalme.

[1]

HAve mercy, God, for thy great mercies sake.
O God: my God, unto my shame I say,
Beynge fled from thee, so as I dred to take
Thy name in wretched mouth, and feare to pray
Or aske the mercy that I have abusde.
But, God of mercy, let me come to thee:
Not for justice, that justly am accusde:
Which selfe word Justice so amaseth me,
That scarce I dare thy mercy sound againe.
But mercie, Lord, yet suffer me to crave.
Mercie is thine: Let me not crye in vaine,
Thy great mercie for my great fault to have.
Have mercie, God, pitie my penitence
With greater mercie than my great offence.

Have mercie upon me (o God) after thy great merci

[2]

My many sinnes in nomber are encreast,
With weight wherof in sea of depe despeire
My sinking soule is now so sore opprest,
That now in peril and in present fere,
I crye: susteine me, Lord, and Lord I pray,
With endlesse nomber of thy mercies take
The endlesse nomber of my sinnes away.
[Aa4r] So by thy mercie, for thy mercies sake,
Rue on me, Lord, releve me with thy grace.
My sinne is cause that I so nede to have
Thy mercies ayde in my so woefull case:
My synne is cause that scarce I dare to crave
Thy mercie manyfolde, whiche onely may
Releve my soule, and take my sinnes away.

And according unto the multitude of thy mercies do away myne offences.

[3]

So foule is sinne and lothesome in thy sighte,
So foule with sinne I see my selfe to be,
That till from sinne I may be washed white,
So foule I dare not, Lord, approche to thee.
Ofte hath thy mercie washed me before,
Thou madest me cleane: but I am foule againe.
Yet washe me Lord againe, and washe me more.
Washe me, O Lord, and do away the staine
Of uggly sinnes that in my soule appere.
Let flow thy plentuous streames of clensing grace.
Washe me againe, yea washe me every where,
Bothe leprous bodie and defiled face.
Yea washe me all, for I am all uncleane,
And from my sin, Lord, cleanse me ones againe.

Wash me yet more from my wickednes, and clense me from my sinne.

[4]

Have mercie, Lord, have mercie: for I know
How muche I nede thy mercie in this case.
The horror of my gilt doth dayly growe,
And growing weares my feble hope of grace.
I fele and suffer in my thralled brest
Secret remorse and gnawing of my hart.
I fele my sinne, my sinne that hath opprest
My soule with sorrow and surmounting smart.
Drawe me to mercie: for so oft as I
[Aa4v] Presume to mercy to direct my sight,
My Chaos and my heape of sinne doth lie,
Betwene me and thy mercies shining light.
What ever way I gaze about for grace,
My filth and fault are ever in my face.

For I knowledge my wickednes, and my sinne is ever before me.

[5]

Graunt thou me mercy, Lord: thee thee alone
I have offended, and offendyng thee,
For mercy loe, how I do lye and grone.
Thou with allpearcing eye beheldest me,
Without regard that sinned in thy sight.
Beholde againe, how now my spirite it rues,
And wailes the tyme, when I with foule delight
Thy swete forbearing mercy did abuse.
My cruell conscience with sharpned knife
Doth splat my ripped hert, and layes abrode
The lothesome secretes of my filthy life,

Againste thee onelye have I sinned, and don evill in thy sight.

And spredes them forth before the face of God.
Whom shame from dede shamelesse cold not restrain,
Shame for my dede is added to my paine.

[6]

But mercy Lord, O Lord some pitie take,
Withdraw my soule from the deserved hell,
O Lord of glory, for thy glories sake:
That I may saved of thy mercy tell,
And shew how thou, which mercy hast behight
To sighyng sinners, that have broke thy lawes,
Performest mercy: so as in the sight
Of them that judge the justice of thy cause
Thou onely just be demed, and no moe,
The worldes unjustice wholy to confound:
That damning me to depth of during woe
Just in thy judgement shouldest thou be found:
And from deserved flames relevyng me
[Aa5r] Just in thy mercy mayst thou also be.

That thou mightest be founde just in thy sayinges, and maiest over come when thou art judged.

[7]

For lo, in sinne, Lord, I begotten was,
With sede and shape my sinne I toke also,
Sinne is my nature and my kinde alas,
In sinne my mother me conceived: Lo
I am but sinne, and sinfull ought to dye,
Dye in his wrath that hath forbydden sinne.
Such bloome and frute loe sinne doth multiplie,
Such was my roote, such is my juyse within.
I plead not this as to excuse my blame,
On kynde or parentes myne owne gilt to lay:
But by disclosing of my sinne, my shame,
And nede of helpe, the plainer to displaye
Thy mightie mercy, if with plenteous grace
My plenteous sinnes it please thee to deface.

For loe, I was shapen in wickednes, and in sinne my mother conceived me.

[8]

Thou lovest simple sooth, not hidden face
With trutheles visour of deceiving showe.
Lo simplie, Lord, I do confesse my case,
And simplie crave thy mercy in my woe.
This secrete wisedom hast thou graunted me,
To se my sinnes, and whence my sinnes do growe:
This hidden knowledge have I learnd of thee,
To fele my sinnes, and howe my sinnes do flowe

But lo, thou haste loved trueth, the hidden and secrete thinges of thy wisedome thou haste opened unto me.

With such excesse, that with unfained hert,
Dreding to drowne, my Lorde, lo howe I flee,
Simply with teares bewailyng my desert,
Releved simply by thy hand to be.
Thou lovest truth, thou taughtest me the same.
Helpe, Lord of truth, for glory of thy name.

[9]

With swete Hysope besprinkle thou my sprite:
Not such hysope, nor so besprinkle me,
[Aa5v] As law unperfect shade of perfect lyght
Did use as an apointed signe to be
Foreshewing figure of thy grace behight.
With death and bloodshed of thine only sonne,
The swete hysope, cleanse me defyled wyght.
Sprinkle my soule. And when thou so haste done,
Bedeawd with droppes of mercy and of grace,
I shalbe cleane as cleansed of my synne.
Ah wash me, Lord: for I am foule alas:
That only canst, Lord, wash me well within.
Wash me, O Lord: when I am washed soe,
I shalbe whiter than the whitest snowe.

Sprinkle me, Lorde, with hisope and I shalbe cleane: washe me and I shalbe whiter then snow.

[10]

Long have I heard, and yet I heare the soundes
Of dredfull threates and thonders of the law,
Which Eccho of my gylty minde resoundes,
And with redoubled horror doth so draw
My listening soule from mercies gentle voice,
That louder, Lorde, I am constraynde to call:
Lorde, pearce myne eares, and make me to rejoyse,
When I shall heare, and when thy mercy shall
Sounde in my hart the gospell of thy grace.
Then shalt thou geve my hearing joy againe,
The joy that onely may releve my case.
And then my broosed bones, that thou with paine
Hast made to weake my febled corps to beare,
Shall leape for joy, to shewe myne inward chere.

Thou shalt make me heare joye and gladnesse, and the bones which thou hast broken shal rejoyse.

[11]

Loke on me, Lord: though trembling I beknowe,
That sight of sinne so sore offendeth thee,
That seing sinne, how it doth overflowe
My whelmed soule, thou canst not loke on me,
But with disdaine, with horror and despite.

Turne away thy face from my sinnes, and do away all my misdedes.

Loke on me, Lord: but loke not on my sinne.
[Aa6r] Not that I hope to hyde it from thy sight,
Which seest me all without and eke within.
But so remove it from thy wrathfull eye,
And from the justice of thyne angry face,
That thou impute it not. Looke not how I
Am foule by sinne: but make me by thy grace
Pure in thy mercies sight, and, Lord, I pray,
That hatest sinne, wipe all my sinnes away.

[12]

Sinne and despeir have so possest my hart,
And hold my captive soule in such restraint,
As of thy mercies I can fele no part,
But still in languor do I lye and faint.
Create a new pure hart within my brest:
Myne old can hold no liquour of thy grace.
My feble faith with heavy lode opprest
Staggring doth scarcely creepe a reeling pace,
And fallen it is to faint to rise againe.
Renew, O Lord, in me a constant sprite,
That stayde with mercy may my soule susteine,
A sprite so setled and so firmely pight
Within my bowells, that it never move,
But still uphold thassurance of thy love.

Create a cleane hart within me, O God: and renew a stedfast spirit within my bowels.

[13]

Loe prostrate, Lorde, before thy face I lye,
With sighes depe drawne depe sorow to expresse.
O Lord of mercie, mercie do I crye:
Dryve me not from thy face in my distresse,
Thy face of mercie and of swete relefe,
The face that fedes angels with onely sight,
The face of comfort in extremest grefe.
Take not away the succour of thy sprite,
Thy holy sprite, which is myne onely stay,
The stay that when despeir assaileth me,
[Aa6v] In faintest hope yet moveth me to pray,
To pray for mercy, and to pray to thee.
Lord, cast me not from presence of thy face,
Nor take from me the spirite of thy grace.

Cast me not away from thy face, and take not thy holy spirit from me.

[14]

But render me my wonted joyes againe,
Which sinne hath reft, and planted in theyr place
Doubt of thy mercy ground of all my paine.
The tast, that thy love whilome did embrace
My chearfull soule, the signes that dyd assure
My felyng ghost of favor in thy sight,
Are fled from me, and wretched I endure
Senslesse of grace the absence of thy sprite.
Restore my joyes, and make me fele againe
The swete retorne of grace that I have lost,
That I may hope I pray not all in vayne.
With thy free sprite confirme my feble ghost,
To hold my faith from ruine and decay
With fast affiance and assured stay.

Restore to me the comforte of thy saving helpe, and stablishe me with thy free spirit.

[15]

Lord, of thy mercy if thou me withdraw
From gaping throte of depe devouring hell,
Loe, I shall preach the justice of thy law:
By mercy saved, thy mercy shall I tell.
The wicked I wyll teache thyne only way,
Thy wayes to take, and mans devise to flee,
And suche as lewd delight hath ledde astray,
To rue theyr errour and returne to thee.
So shall the profe of myne example preache
The bitter frute of lust and foule delight:
So shall my pardon by thy mercy teache
The way to finde swete mercy in thy sight.
Have mercy, Lorde, in me example make
Of lawe and mercy, for thy mercies sake.

I shal teach thy waies unto the wicked, and sinners shall be tourned unto thee.

[16]

[Aa7r] O God, God of my health, my saving God,
Have mercy Lord, and shew thy might to save.
Assoile me, God, from gilt of giltlesse blod,
And eke from sinne that I ingrowyng have
By fleshe and bloud and by corrupted kinde.
Upon my bloud and soule extende not, Lorde,
Vengeance for bloud, but mercy let me finde,
And strike me not with thy revengyng sworde.
So, Lord, my joying tong shall talke thy praise,
Thy name my mouth shall utter in delight,
My voice shall sounde thy justice, and thy waies,

Deliver me from bloud o God, God of my helth and my tong shall joyfullye talke of thy justice.

Thy waies to justifie thy sinfull wight.
God of my health, from bloud I saved so
Shall spred thy prayse for all the world to know.

[17]

Lo straining crampe of colde despeir againe
In feble brest doth pinche my pinyng hart,
So as in greatest nede to cry and plaine
My speache doth faile to utter thee my smart.
Refreshe my yeldyng hert, with warming grace,
And loose my speche, and make me call to thee.
Lord open thou my lippes to shewe my case,
My Lord, for mercy Loe to thee I flee.
I can not pray without thy movyng ayde,
Ne can I ryse, ne can I stande alone.
Lord, make me pray, and graunt when I have praide.
Lord loose my lippes, I may expresse my mone,
And findyng grace with open mouth I may
Thy mercies praise, and holy name display.

Lord, open thou my lippes, and my mouth shal shewe thy praise.

[18]

Thy mercies praise, instede of sacrifice,
With thankfull minde so shall I yeld to thee.
For if it were delitefull in thine eyes,
Or hereby mought thy wrath appeased be,
[Aa7v] Of cattell slayne and burnt with sacred flame
Up to the heaven the vaprie smoke to send:
Of gyltlesse beastes, to purge my gilt and blame,
On altars broylde the savour shold ascend,
To pease thy wrath. But thy swete sonne alone,
With one sufficing sacrifice for all
Appeaseth thee, and maketh the at one
With sinfull man, and hath repaird our fall.
That sacred hoste is ever in thine eyes.
The praise of that I yeld for sacrifice.

If thou haddest desired sacrifice, I wold have geven thou delytest not in burnt offringes.

[19]

I yeld my self, I offer up my ghoste,
My slayne delightes, my dyeng hart to thee.
To God a trobled sprite is pleasing hoste.
My trobled sprite doth drede like him to be,
In whome tastlesse languor with lingring paine
Hath febled so the starved appetite,
That foode to late is offred all in vaine,

The sacrifice to God is a trobled spirit: a broken and an humbled hart, o god, thou wilt not despise.

To holde in fainting corps the fleing sprite.
My pining soule for famine of thy grace
So feares alas the faintnesse of my faithe.
I offre up my trobled sprite: alas,
My trobled sprite refuse not in thy wrathe.
Such offring likes thee, ne wilt thou despise
The broken humbled hart in angry wise.

[20]

Shew mercie, Lord, not unto me alone:
But stretch thy favor and thy pleased will,
To sprede thy bountie and thy grace upon
Sion, for Sion is thy holly hyll:
That thy Hierusalem with mighty wall
May be enclosed under thy defense,
And bylded so that it may never fall
By myning fraude or mighty violence.
[Aa8r] Defend thy chirch, Lord, and advaunce it soe,
So in despite of tyrannie to stand,
That trembling at thy power the world may know
It is upholden by thy mighty hand:
That Sion and Hierusalem may be
A safe abode for them that honor thee.

Shew favour, o lord in thy good will unto Sion, that the walles of Hierusalem may be bylded.

[21]

Then on thy hill, and in thy walled towne,
Thou shalt receave the pleasing sacrifice,
The brute shall of thy praised name resoune
In thankfull mouthes, and then with gentle eyes
Thou shalt behold upon thine altar lye
Many a yelden host of humbled hart,
And round about then shall thy people crye:
We praise thee, God our God: thou onely art
The God of might, of mercie, and of grace.
That I then, Lorde, may also honor thee,
Releve my sorow, and my sinnes deface:
Be, Lord of mercie, mercifull to me:
Restore my feling of thy grace againe:
Assure my soule, I crave it not in vaine.

Then shalt thou accept the sacrifice of righteousnesse, burnt offringes and oblations. Then shall they offre yonge bullockes upon thine altare.

FINIS.

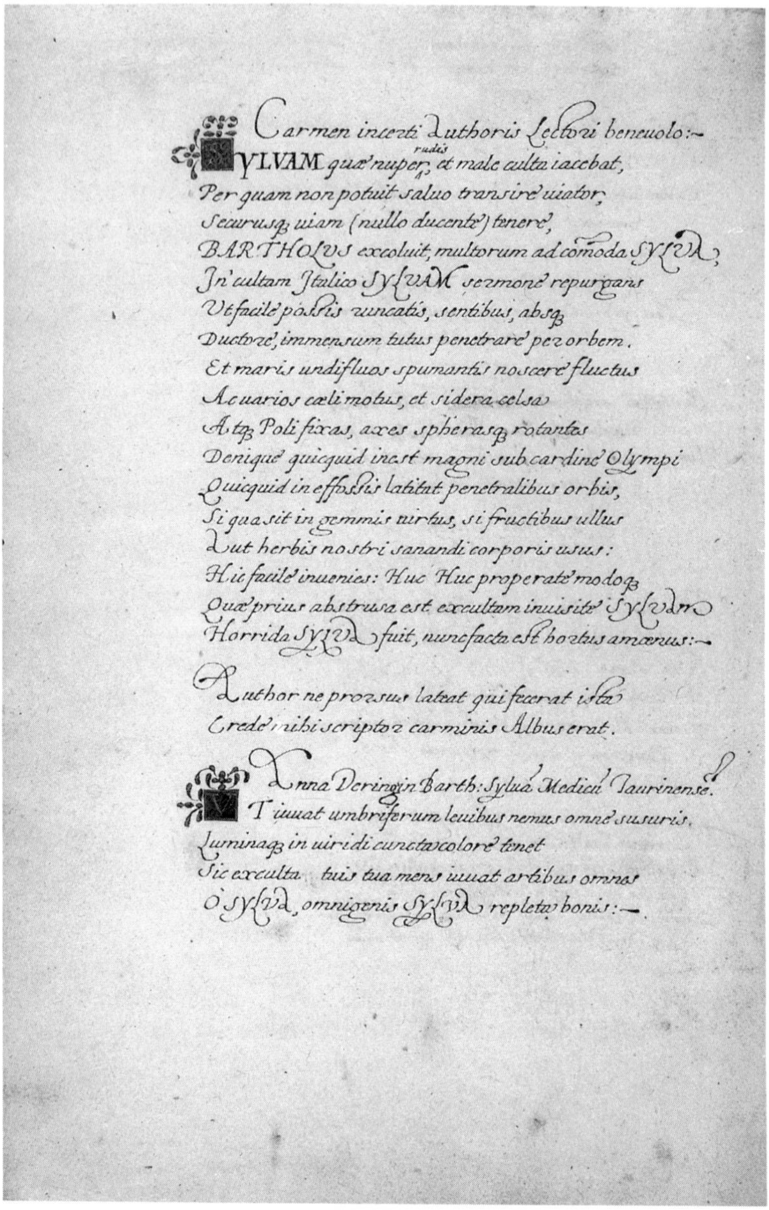
Carmen incerti Authoris Lectori beneuolo:–
SYLVAM quæ nuper rudis et male culta iacebat,
Per quam non potuit saluo transire uiator,
Securusq; uiam (nullo ducente) tenere,
BARTHOLVS excoluit, multorum ad comoda SYLVA;
In cultam Italico SYLVAM sermone repurgans
Ut facile possis runcatis, sentibus, absq;
Ductore, immensum tutus penetrare per orbem.
Et maris undifluos spumantis noscere fluctus
Ac uarios cæli motus, et sidera celsa
Atq; Poli fixas, axes spherasq; rotantes
Denique quicquid inest magni sub cardine Olympi
Quicquid in effossis latitat penetralibus orbis,
Si qua sit in gemmis uirtus, si fructibus ullus
Aut herbis nostri sanandi corporis usus:
Hic facile inuenies: Huc Huc properate modoq;
Quæ prius abstrusa est, excultam inuisite SYLVAM
Horrida SYLVA fuit, nunc facta est hortus amœnus:–

Author ne prorsus lateat qui fecerat ista
Crede mihi scriptor carminis Albus erat.

Anna Deringin Barth: Sylua Medici Taurinensis.
UT iuuat umbriferum leuibus nemus omne susuris,
Luminaq; in uiridi cuncta colore tenet
Sic exculta tuis tua mens iuuat artibus omnes
O SYLVA, omnigenis SYLVA repleta bonis:–

Figure 6. Latin poems from the
Giardino cosmografico coltivato (1572), fol. 5v.

Cambridge University Library MS Ii.5.37

[fol. 5^{v}] Anna Dering in Barth: Sylvam Medicum Taurinensem.
Ut iuvat umbriferum levibus nemus omnem susuris
Luminaque in viridi cuncta colore tenet
Sic exculta tuis tua mens iuvat artibus omnes
Ò SYLVA, omnigenis SYLVA repleta bonis:

Anna Dering on Bartholo Sylva, a doctor from Turin.
As a shadowy grove delights everyone with its light whispers
And holds all shades of light in its green hue,
So, too, your cultivated mind delights all (people) with your skills
O Sylva, Sylva endowed with manifold virtues.
[English translation by Kenneth D. Bratt]

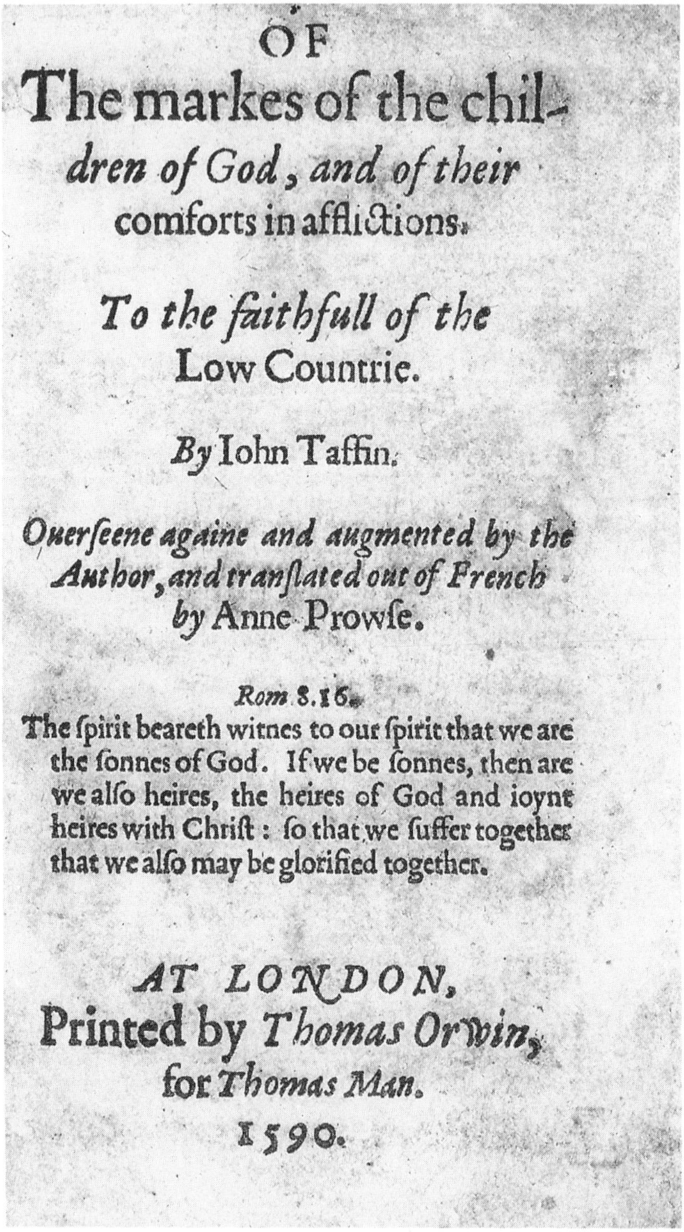

OF
The markes of the children of God, and of their comforts in afflictions.

To the faithfull of the Low Countrie.

By Iohn Taffin.

Ouerseene againe and augmented by the Author, and translated out of French by Anne Prowse.

Rom. 8.16.
The spirit beareth witnes to our spirit that we are the sonnes of God. If we be sonnes, then are we also heires, the heires of God and ioynt heires with Christ: so that we suffer together that we also may be glorified together.

AT LONDON,
Printed by *Thomas Orwin*, for *Thomas Man.*
1590.

Figure 7. Title page from *Of the Markes* (1590).

OF

The markes of the chil-
dren of God, and of their
comforts in afflictions.

To the faithfull of the
Low Countrie.

By John Taffin.

Overseene againe and augmented by the
Author, and translated out of French
by Anne Prowse.

Rom. 8.16.
The spirit beareth witnes to our spirit that we are
the sonnes of God. If we be sonnes, then are
we also heires, the heires of God and joynt
heires with Christ: so that we suffer together
that we also may be glorified together.

AT LONDON,
Printed by *Thomas Orwin*,
for *Thomas Man*.
1590.

[A2r]

To the right Honorable *and vertuous Ladie, The* Countesse of War-*wicke.*

FOrasmuch as it hath pleased almightie God of his infinite goodnesse, to give unto the glorious Gospell of his eternall sonne, so long and prosperous successe in this our Countrie; it is now time (right Honorable and my verie good Ladie) for everie one that is a true professor of the same, all carnall perswasions of humane reason deluding the soule being set aside, to prepare our selves to the day of trial. For although it pleaseth God sometimes, for the gathering of his Church, to give unto it as it were *Halcyon* daies: yet common it is not, that it should any long time continue in rest and pleasure. Nay, by the word of GOD wee [A2v] know, and by experience sometimes of our selves (her Majesties royall person not excepted) and now of our neighbours round about us we see, that the Church of God in this world, as it ever hath bin, so must it ever be under the crosse. And therefore if wee will bee compted of the Church indeede, and glorie in that excellent name of a Christian, let us knowe assuredlie, that unto us, even unto us (that have so long lived in rest and pleasure, if wee be the children of God) in some sort and measure a triall must come. For, if God chastise everie sonne whom he receiveth, and every member of Christes body must be fashioned like unto the head, if the afflictions of this world are manifest tokens to the children of God, of his favour and love towards them, and sure pledges of their adoption: how can we looke, or how can we desire to bee [A3r] exempted from this common condition of God his owne children and household? To this end therefore (right Honorable Ladie) I have translated this little booke, first to admonish some (who for lacke of experience, never feeling other daies than these full of peace and quietnes) that they learne to applie unto themselves whatsoever they heare or reade of the triall of GOD his children, least falselie imagining it to appertaine either to the times that are past, or to other Nations, it fall sodainlie upon them as a theefe in the night, and they be destitute of all hope and comfort. Secondlie, to awake others abounding both in knowledge and other graces, whom notwithstanding, satan (by the deceaveable lusts and vaine pleasures of this wicked world) hath so rockt a sleepe, that they seeme almost, as they that are diseased with the Lethargie, to have forgotten both [A3v] themselves, their holie calling and profession. Last of all, to comfort an other sort, whome it hath pleased GOD so to presse downe with sorrowes, and to exercise with the continuall afflictions and calamities of this mortall life, as no times seeming favourable unto them, they can scarse receive the words of any comfort. And because your

Honor hath been of long time, not onlie a professour, but also a lover of the trueth, whom the Lord (exalting to an higher place of dignitie than many other) hath set up, as it were a light upon an high candlesticke, to give light unto manie, I have especiallie dedicated unto your Honour this my poore travaile, humblie beseeching the Lord to make it no lesse comfortable to your Honour, and to those that shall reade it, than it hath been unto me who have translated it. Everie one in his calling is bound to doo [A4r] somewhat to the furtherance of the holie building; but because great things by reason of my sex, I may not doo, and that which I may, I ought to doo, I have according to my duetie, brought my poore basket of stones to the strengthning of the walles of that Jerusalem, whereof (by grace) wee are all both Citizens and members. And now to returne to those whom experience hath not yet taught, and whom prosperitie will not suffer to awake: I earnestlie beseech them both in the Lord, no longer to deceive themselves with vaine imaginations, neither to suffer their hearts so to be tied to earthlie vanities, that they should despise or neglect those things that can truely make them happie indeed. When it shall please GOD to open their eyes to discerne betweene heavenlie and earthly, betweene things transitorie, and things everlasting, I know they [A4v] will of themselves bee ashamed of this their negligence. For what are all the pleasant things of this world, which most bewitch the minds of men, if they be compared with heavenlie and eternall things? If statelie and sumptuous buildings do delight; what building is so statelie and glorious as newe Jerusalem? If riches; what so rich as that, whose pavement is of pure gold, whose foundations and walls of precious stones, and gates of orient pearles? If friends, kinsfolke and neighbours; what Citie so replenished as this, where God himselfe in his Majestie, Jesus Christ the head of the Church in his glorie, and all the holie Angels, Patriarchs, Prophets, Apostles and Martirs do dwel together in happinesse for ever? If honor; what honor comparable to this, to be the servant and child of so mightie a King, and heire of so glorious a kingdome; where neither [A5r] time doth consume, nor envie deprive of honour, nor power of adversarie spoyle of glorie, that is endles and incomprehensible? If then there be no comparison betweene things heavenlie and things that are earthlie, and no man can attaine to the things that are heavenlie, but by the same way that Christ himselfe attained unto them; which was by the crosse: why (casting off all impediments that presseth downe) doo we not runne on our course with cherefulnes and hope, having Christ so mightie a King, for our Captaine and guide, who (as the Apostle saith) for the glorie that was set before him, indured the crosse, and despising the shame, sitteth now at the right hand of the throne of God? How slowe and dull of heart are wee, if as *Esau,* (who for a messe of pottage sold his birthright) wee are contented for a small and short pleasure in this [A5v] wicked world, to leese that incomparable and everlasting glorie, which Christ the sonne of GOD with so great a price hath purchased for us. The Lord give us wisedome to understand, and grace to heare his voice while it is saide to day, that when daies and nights and times shall cease, wee may (without time) enter into his joye and rest which never shall have end. The Lord ever preserve your Honor; and adde unto a multitude of happie yeares spent in his feare, a continuall increase of al spiritual graces to his glorie, and your endles comfort.

Your Honors in the Lord

most humble *A. P.*

[A6r] *To the faithfull of the*
Low Countrie.

I*T is not without reason (right deare and worshipfull bretheren) that the Church of Christ is called militant upon earth: and compared as well to a woman in travaile of child from the beginning of the world, as to a ship upon the sea tossed with tempests, and to a field tilled, upon which the plowe is drawne to cut it. The present estate of the Church exercised by so manie dissipations, assailed so mightelie by continuall warres (the mother and nurse of all calamities) and afflicted by revolts, by Libertines, by people prophane, and by so many heretiques, is to us a livelie mirrour, a manifest seale, and an example good to be marked. Now, as the infirmitie of the flesh which dieth not in the verie children of God, but at their death, taketh from thence, and from other matter, occasion of temptations most dangerous, and many assaults: so the bounden* [A6v] *duetie and affection which I beare towards you, driveth me to testifie unto you the fervent desire which I feele continuallie in my heart, of your comfort, constancie and perseverance in the way of salvation. For this cause it is that in my voiage from* Germanie *I made this little treatise* Of the markes of the children of God, and of their consolations in their afflictions: *the which (being G O D be thanked returned) I was willing, with the advise of my brethren and fellowes in the holie Ministerie, to put to light and dedicate unto you, to the end that reading it you might knowe and feele more and more the incomprehensible grace of G O D towards you, by the testimonies of your adoption, and the full assurance of the certaintie of it: and that in the middest of your so long and heavie afflictions, you might bee partakers of the unspeakable comforts which G O D setteth forth to his children in his word: whereby also you feeling your selves truelie happie, you maie constantlie persever in his holie trueth and obedience of his will, aspiring with contentment and joy of the holie Ghost to the injoying of that kingdome of glorie, the right* [A7r] *and possession whereof is purchased for you, and kept in your head Jesus Christ. Finallie, I pray God with all my heart to shewe me this favour, that this my little labour may bee acceptable unto you, and that it will please him to blesse it, by the efficacie of his holie spirit, to your comfort and salvation, and to the advancement of the Kingdome of our Lord Jesus Christ:* Harlem *15. September 1586.*

Your humble brother and
servant in Christ:
John Taffin Minister of the
holie Gospell in the French
Church at *Harlem*.

[A8r] The matters that are handled *in this Treatise.*

[B1r 1]

Of the markes of the children of God, and of their *consolations in their afflictions.*

To the faithfull of the Low Countrie.

Of the great and incomprehensible felicitie of the everlasting life promised to the children of God.

CAP. I.

SAint *Paul* hath verie aptlie set forth unto us the incomprehensible excellencie of the felicitie of the children of GOD, saying, *That*[1] *the eye hath not seene, the eare hath not heard, neither hath it entred into the heart of man, what things God hath prepared for those that love him.* According to this sentence, Saint *Augustine,* tending to the same butt, saith of the [B1v] goodnes[2] of grace: *Let your hearts goe beyond all that you are able to comprehend, and stay not your selves at the greatnes and excellencie of it which you imagine: but say, yet this is not it; for if it were it, it could not enter into thy thought and heart.* This happines then cannot bee comprehended by us according to the greatnes and excellencie of it, so[3] long as wee dwell in these earthlie mansions,[4] where we knowe God but in part and darkly. Notwithstanding, seeing the same Apostle addeth, that the holie Ghost who searcheth the most[5] deep things of God, hath given us[6] some revelation: Seeing also he praied to God for the *Ephesians*; That he[7] would open the eyes of their understanding, that they might knowe, what is the hope of their vocation, and what are the riches of the glorie of his inheritance among the Saints: we should be too unthankful to God, and enemies of our owne comfort, if wee should make curtesie or refuse to understand that, which it pleaseth him to reveale unto us by his word. Now, [B2r 2] in it this felicitie is oftentimes signified by the promise of life everlasting, and not without reason. For in our felicitie,[8] two poynts may and ought

---

[1] 1. Cor. 2.9.

[2] Aug. Enarrat. 2. Psal. 26. Tom. 8.

[3] 2. Cor. 5.1.

[4] 1. Cor. 13.9

[5] 1. Cor. 13.12.

[6] 1. Cor 2.10.

[7] Ephe. 1.18.

[8] Life everlasting comprehendeth the felicitie of the children of God.

speciallie to bee considered: first, the greatnes and excellencie of the good thing: secondlie, the long continuance and surenes of it. Now, both the one and the other is noted by these words, *life everlasting:* For by life is signified the greatnes of the felicitie, and by everlasting, the infinite length of it. As touching life, wee may consider[9] three degrees as wel in the bodie, as speciallie in the soule. The first degree of life as touching the soule, is ment by this peace of conscience, and joy[10] of the holie Ghost which wee receive and feele, being reconciled to God[11] in Jesus Christ. And this peace and beginning of life, surmounteth al understanding,[12] as Saint *Paule* doth witnes, and God his children doo feele. And indeed it is a thing ravishing our soules with joye unspeakable, when GOD maketh the brightnes of his face to shine upon us: As also *David* [B2ᵛ] sheweth,[13] when he asketh so oft of God this grace, for a full measure of all felicitie. As touching the bodie, the first degree of life lieth in this, that the afflictions of it be not onlie mitigated, and made light by this life of the soule reconciled to God, and feeling joye through[14] the brightnes of his countenance,[15] but also are converted (being the fruits of the love of God towards us) into salvation and glorie. The second[16] degree of life may bee considered in the seperation of the soule and the bodie, the which improperlie (as touching the faithful) is called death. For even as touching our bodies, although they goe to rot in the earth, yet being then delivered, and free from all sicknes, from hunger, thirst, heate, cold, and from a thousand other torments, which of their nature are a kind of death, they goe to rest in their[17] beds, as *Esai* saith; and being delivered from their labours and travailes,[18] they are blessed, as Saint *John* saith. And this rest proceeding from the favour of God, cannot properlie [B3ʳ 3] be called death, but is to them a kind of life. But speciallie the soule then entreth into the possession of the second degree of life. For being delivered from the bodie, she is carried up by[19] the Angels into the bosome of *Abraham*,[20] and into

9 Three degrees of life to the body and to the soule.
10 The first degree of life.
11 Rom. 5.1.
12 Philip. 4.7.
13 Psalm. 80.
14 Rom. 8.27.
15 Heb. 12.6.
16 The second degree of life.
17 Esay. 57.1.
18 Apoca. 14.13.
19 Luk. 16.22
20 Luk. 23.43

Paradise with Jesus Christ, exempted then from ignorance, from incredulitie, from mistrust, from covetousnes, ambition, envie, hatred, feare, terrour, lustes, and from all other passions, vices and corruptions which are deadlie in them, which also bring forth the fruites of death. And contrariwise, is then fully sanctified, victorious, and assured against Satan, Hell, sinne and all other enemies: waiting after that, with great joye, for the accomplishment of her glorie in the resurrection of her bodie.[21] The third degre, shall bee at the glorious comming of Jesus Christ, when our bodies being awaked out of their sleepe, they shall rise againe all[22] renued, bodies incorruptible, spirituall and immortall, yea fashioned like[23] to the image of the glorious [B3^{v}] bodie of Jesus Christ: And so being joyned[24] together againe to their soules, they shall be together caught up into the[25] clowdes before our Lord Jesus Christ[26] in the ayre, and exalted above all the heavens, into the house of God our[27] father. Then also shall be the accomplishment of the life of our soules reunited to their bodies, being together where Jesus Christ is, and with him, as members of his bodie, his brethren, and his spouse, united to him, and by him, to God the fountaine of life. And by this union injoying a communitie in all his goods, and of this[28] incorruptible inheritance, which can neither faile nor fade away, reserved[29] for us in heaven. Then shall God wipe all teares from our eyes, and death shall be no more, neither shal there be any sorrow, crie or travaile any more. All these old things shall be gone away: God shall make all things new. Then[30] shall we be before the throne of God, and shall serve him night and day in his Temple, and shall be led by the Lambe to the living fountaines [B4^{r} 4] of[31] waters. Then shall be the day of our mariage with the Lambe, when being clothed with pure and bright raiments, wee shall sit at his mariage banquet. Then shal we be like unto the Angels. If[32] our bodies shall shine then as the Sunne, what shall

[21] The third degree of life.
[22] 1. Cor. 15.42.
[23] Philip. 3.21
[24] 1. Thess. 4.17.
[25] Ephe. 4.10. Joh. 14.2.
[26] Joh. 17.24.
[27] 1. Thess. 4.17.
[28] 1. Pet. 1.4.
[29] Reve. 21.4.
[30] Reve. 7.14.
[31] Reve. 19.7.
[32] Matth. 22.30.

the brightnes of our[33] soules be? Then our pilgrimage being finished, we shall be indeed the citizens[34] of this heavenlie and holie Jerusalem, which shall bee all of pure gold[35] like unto the cleere glasse: having the foundations of the wall garnished with pretious stones: whereof also the twelve gates, are twelve pearles: which hath no need of the Sunne, nor of the Moone to shine in it, because the brightnes of God shall be the light of it, and the Lambe him selfe shall be the candle of it. O how happie shall the citizens be, that shall live in such a Citie? See then what good things are signified by life everlasting, and the three degrees of it. But Saint *Paul* lifteth us up yet higher into the contemplation of this life which wee shall injoy after the [B4v] resurrection.[36] Then, saith Saint *Paule*, Jesus Christ shall give up his kingdome unto God his father, as if he should say: Father, behold those whom thou hast given to me before the foundation of the world: they were lost, and thou diddest send me to save them: I have redeemed them with my bloud; thou hast appoynted me King over them: they are my kingdome which I have gotten, and which I have so guided and governed, that having sanctified and delivered them from all their enemies, I have brought, given and presented them unto thee, that having as touching my selfe, accomplished the worke and charge which thou haddest enjoyned me, from this time forth, thou maiest be king raigning immediatlie in them, and filling them with all happines and glorie. Then shall there be no creature either in heaven or in earth, that shall have any domination or Lordship. There shall bee neither[37] King nor Prince, neither Master nor Lord. There shall bee neither father, mother, husband nor wife. [B5r 5] There shall be neither Prophet, Doctor, Minister nor Pastour. There shall be neither riches, nor estates. All the enemies also of Jesus Christ shall bee destroyed for evermore, death being swallowed up into victorie, and Satan with his angels, and all the reprobate being cast into the bottomlesse pit. Contrariwise, the Elect being fullie sanctified, shall bee lifted up both in bodie and soule above all the heavens. The worke of Christ shall be finished. And[38] all being done. The verie same offices which Christ hath received, and shall exercise for the accomplishment of our salvation, to be a King, a Priest, and a Prophet, and to sit at the right hand of God, shall cease, but so, as the fruites and the incomprehensible benefits gotten by them unto the church, shal ever abide to his

33 Matth. 13.43.

34 Bern. meditation. 9.

35 Reve 21.18.

36 1. Cor. 15.24.

37 1. Cor. 15.28.

38 Reve. 21.6.

everlasting glorie. But what shall that be then? God the Father, the Sonne, and the Holie ghost, one onlie God shall be immediatlie all thinges, both in this man Christ, and in all us the members of his bodie. The Godhead (I say) shall [B5ᵛ] be in the man Jesus Christ and in us, King, Prince, father, riches, life and glorie. To be short, all things, and such a heape of happines and felicitie, that as sundrie vessels cast into the sea are full of water, so as they can neither want, nor have more: So this sea of Divinitie being all things in us al, we shall be filled and satisfied with life and glorie, so as we can neither want, nor receive more. Then shall we not onlie tast[39] how sweete our God shall be, but we shall be filled and throughlie satisfied with his sweetnes most wonderfull.[40] Then shall the sonne himselfe be subject to the father, to wit, as touching[41] his humanitie: but that shall be for the increase of his glorie, and our felicitie. For the sonne of man abiding[42] still united to the sonne of God, and then ceasing the governement which he shall have untill the resurrection, God shall in such sort be in this sonne of man, and in us, that the majestie and brightnes of the divinitie then raigning immediatlie, shall cause the difference between the [B6ʳ 6] divinitie[43] of Christ, and his humane nature subject unto it to appeare. But as[44] the principall glorie of the sonne of man, is to be united unto the sonne of God in one person, and that this his divinitie shall be for the most part as it were, hid until that day, and that then it shall bee fullie revealed: how much more the divine majestie of the sonne of God, shall cause the subjection of the sonne of man to appeare, so much the greater shall appeare the glorie of this sonne of man united in one person to the Godhead then raigning in his full majestie and glorie. As (if a man may find any thing never so little to represent this high mysterie) wee may consider, that the felicitie[45] and glorie of the brethren of *Joseph* was so much the greater, that by the greatnes of *Joseph*, exalted to the government of *Ægypt*, they were subject unto him, and there appeared a great difference between *Joseph* and his brethren, not by the diminishing of them, but by the increasing of *Joseph*, his brethren having this [B6ᵛ] happines and honor, to be the brethren of *Joseph*, so much more great and honorable, by how much, the greatnes of the majestie and glorie of *Joseph*, made their subjection more to appeare. And this is it that may in some sort be noted in the church. For although that now, her subjection and the difference appeare

---

[39] Psal. 34.9.
[40] *Cipri. de ascen. Christi*
[41] 1. Cor. 15.18.
[42] *August. lib.* 80. *quæst.* 69. *and lib. de trinit.* 1. *cap.* 8.
[43] Jhe. 17.22.
[44] Phil. 2.7.
[45] Gen. 47.

betweene her, gathered and composed of sinfull men, having their sanctification and their life of their head Jesus Christ: and betweene him verie G O D, and perfect man sitting at the right hand of God the father almightie: yet as then, the more great the glorie of Christ shall appeare, shewing himselfe immediatlie with his divine majestie in his brightnes: so much the more clearelie shall the subjection and difference of the Church appeare, not by diminishing the happines and glorie of it, but by the increase of the glory of her head, brother and bridegrome: The Church having this happines and honor, to be, and stil to abide united unto Christ, making with her this new [B7r 7] man,[46] whereof Saint *Paule* speaketh, yea so much the more happie and glorious, by how much the excellencie of the majestie and glorie of Christ, the sonne of man with us, shall exceed in greatnes, being united to the sonne of God, shining then with the Father and the Holie ghost, one onlie G O D in his divine majestie. Hereof also it followeth, that our chiefe felicitie shalbe to behold this glorie of Christ. And indeed this is that benefite and happines which he asked for us of God[47] his father, saying: Father, my desire for those whome thou hast given me, is, that they bee where I am, and that they may see my glorie. And what[48] glorie? That we should see him, as he shall bee in majestie incomprehensible as touching his Godhead, and consequentlie in soveraigne glorie as touching his humanitie united to this divine majestie. Behold also how this shall be accomplished which is[49] written, that wee shall see God face to face for the accomplishment of our felicitie. Which that we may the [B7v] better[50] comprehend, we must finallie conclude,[51] that the fruit thereof, shall bee this,[52] joy full and perfect, which Christ hath promised us, promising further, to make us enter into the joye of our Lord.[53] Saint *Augustine* in a certaine meditation (which is inded both holie and heavenlie) sheweth verie excellentlie, how great this our joy shall be, and that joy of our Lord which we shall enter into. Having discoursed of the everlasting felicitie of the children of God, thus he saith. O heart humane, poore and needy, O hart exercised with miseries, and almost consumed of them, what should thy joy be, if thou haddest the full injoying of the aboundance of these good things? Aske of thy soule if thou were capable of the joy, which thou shouldest feele of one such felicitie.

[46] Ephe. 2.15.
[47] Joh. 17.24.
[48] 1. Joh. 3.2.
[49] 1. Cor. 13.12.
[50] Joh. 15.11.
[51] Joh. 16.24.
[52] Matth. 25.21.
[53] *Aug. in manuel. cap.* 35.

But if besides, any other whom thou lovest as thy selfe, should injoye the same happines with thee, surelie this superabounding joy which thou shouldest feele of thine own happines, should it not be twise doubled, for the glorie and the joy of him whom thou [B8r 8] lovest as thy self, and for whose happines, thou shouldest bee as joyfull as for thine owne happines? Now, if there were two, three, yea a great number injoying the same happines with thee, whom also thou lovedst as thy selfe, thou shouldest feele as much joy for the happines of each of them, as for thine owne happines. What then shall be in this perfect charitie, when wee shall love all the blessed angels, and all the elect, loving everie each one of them even as our selves, and being no lesse joyfull of the felicitie of each of them, than of our owne? Surelie if never a one of the elect shall be capable of his owne joy for the greatnes of it, how shall he bee capable of so manie joyes for the happines of so manie of the elect, for whom he shall feele as much joy, as for his owne? Loe what it is Saint *Augustine* saith. But yet how much shall this joy be augmented for the happines, felicitie and glorie of this elect of God, in whome wee our selves have been elected, who having died for the elect, shall sanctifie, [B8v] preserve and lift them up into heaven to the injoying of this felicitie? who is not onlie man holie and just, but also true God, especiallie beholding him in his glorie, to bee united in one person to the Godhead then shining in his Majestie. Surelie if wee, loving other elect as our selves, should have as much joy of the happines of each of them, as of our own, what shall be the joy that we shall receive of the happines and glorie of this soveraigne Elect Jesus Christ, whom by good right we should love more than our selves? See then more than a sea of joy proceeding from the happines of the servants of God. Let us now understand the great deapth of joy which we shall feele, entering into the joye of our Lord. The cause why wee should love God[54] (saith Saint *Bernard*) is God him selfe. And the measure which wee ought to keepe in this love, is to love him without measure, and so, infinitlie. But according to that wee knowe him,[55] we love him. But now we knowe him, but in part, and as it were in [C1r 9] darknes; even so very little and obscure is the love which we beare him. But when wee shall knowe him as he is, wee shall love him according as he is. What shall our love bee towards him[56] then, when Jesus Christ having given over his kingdome to God his Father, God the Father, the Sonne, and[57]

[54] *Bernard in tract. de diligendo deo.*

[55] 1. Cor. 13.12.

[56] 1. Cor. 15.24.

[57] 1. Cor. 15.28.

the Holie ghost one onlie God, shall bee all things, in this man Jesus Christ, and in us? and when wee shall knowe him as hee is, beholding the brightnes of his face, and his Godhead then raigning immediatly in us, and filling us with all happines? Without doubt this contemplation of the glory of the divine majestie shal bring forth in us an infinite love towards God. Now (to returne to the meditation of Saint *Augustine*) if according to that we love each one, wee should rejoyce of his happines. Then as in this blessed felicitie each one of us shall love God without comparison, more than himselfe, and more than all the Angels and elect with us: so shall we feele more joy without [C1^{v}] comparison of the blessednes and glorie of God, than of our owne, or of al the Angels and the elect with us. And if then wee shall love God with all our heart, with all our soule, with all our understanding: yet so as al our hart, al our understanding, and all our soule shall not be capable of the excellencie of this love: Surelie wee shall so feele joy with all our heart, with all our understanding, and with all our soule, as yet all our heart, al our understanding and all our soule shall not bee able to comprehend the fulnes of this joye. Howsoever it bee then, that this full joy, yea more than full, through the greatnes of it (whereof all our heart, all our understanding, and all our soule shall not be capable) cannot enter into us: It shall remaine that we, (filled with the sea of joye of the felicitie of the Angels, and of all the elect) shall enter into this great deapth of joye proceeding from the contemplation of the glorie of our God. And this shalbe the joy of the Lord, into which all[58] his faithfull servants shall enter. [C2^{r} 10] Now, when this felicitie so great, and joy incomprehensible, shall indure so manie yeares as there bee drops of water[59] in the sea, or graines of sand in the whole earth, yet should not this be a perfect happines. For howsoever the continuance shall seeme to us infinite, yet the end will once come. And indeed the drops of water, and the graines of the sand are numbred before God. But this our felicitie and joy shal last without end. Such shall bee the life everlasting: As also[60] Saint *John* saith, we shall raigne in heaven[61] world without end. We shall bee the kingdome of that immortall king[62] whom *Esai* calleth the father of eternitie, who hath promised life and immortalitie[63] to those that shall beleeve the Gospell. Also death shall then bee swallowed up into victorie.

[58] Matth. 25.21.

[59] Of the eternitie of the life to come

[60] Apoc. 22.5.

[61] 1. Tim. 1.17.

[62] Esai. 9.6.

[63] 2. Tim. 1.10.

The[64] author and prince of life, having vanquished[65] the divell, who had the rule over death, shall make us partakers of the life that is everlasting. And as[66] we shall be united to the fountaine of[67] life, so shall it run in us eternallie. [C2^{v}] For as the fountain of this life which we shall injoy, hath no beginning, so the life that procedeth from it, shall have no end. The mercie of G O D (saith S. *Bernard*) is from eternitie to eternitie uppon those that feare him; from eternitie, because of the predestination; to eternitie, because of the glorification: The one hath no beginning, the other hath no ending. This therefore shall be a happines incomprehensible for the greatnes, and infinite for the eternitie of it. Behold also[68] how we shall then injoy a ful and perfect joy, which shal never be taken away from us. Now, this life is promised and assured to all the children of God, in as much as they are heires of God[69] the fountaine of life, and coheires and[70] members of Jesus Christ, who is the[71] way, the trueth, and the life: who also hath so often protested, that whosoever[72] beleeveth in him, he hath life everlasting. Let us conclude then, that the children of God are truelie and onlie blessed, being assured to injoye this great and incomprehensible [C3^{r} 11] happines of life everlasting, which is purchased, promised, and kept for them in Jesus Christ our Lord.

---

64 1. Cor. 15.45.
65 Act. 3.15.
66 Heb. 2.14.
67 Apoc. 21.6
68 Joh. 16.22.
69 Rom. 8.17.
70 Psal. 36.10.
71 Joh. 14.6. Joh. 3.15.
72 Joh. 6.

How we shall knowe that we are the children of God.

Cap. 2.

OF this conclusion it followeth, that there is no greater joy or contentment in this present life, or any thing more sure or more necessarie for the happie overcomming the difficulties of it, than to knowe and feele that wee are the children of God. For this foundation being laid, wee ought to bee assured that whatsoever shall happen unto us, can bee none other than the blessing of a father, and so consequentlie a meane, aide, and way disposed by his providence, either to leade us unto life everlasting, or to increase our glorie in it. True it is, that GOD onelie knoweth[1] his owne, whom hee hath [C3^{v}] chosen before the foundation of the world to bee his children. Yet there are[2] two principall meanes by which he giveth us to understand who are his children: the one is outward, by markes visible unto men: the other is inward by testimonies, which he that is the child of GOD feeleth in himselfe. The outward marke lieth in this,[3] that we be members of the church of Christ. Now, wee call that the church of Christ, in which the word of God is trulie preached, the Sacraments are purelie ministred, and one onelie God is called upon in the name of his onelie[4] sonne Jesus Christ. First, this Church is often called the kingdome of heaven, because that by it, wee enter in thether; so that it is (as it were) the suburbs or the gate of it. Whereof it followeth, that being the true members of the Church, we are in the way and forwardnes to enter, and make our[5] abode in heaven. It is also called the house of God, to give us to understand, that those that abide there, are by[6] good right accompted the children [C4^{r} 12] and household of God. Furthermore, when after wee have protested in our Creede, that wee beleeve the holie Church universall, we adde the communion of Saints, the forgivenes of sinnes, the rising againe of the bodie, and the life everlasting: is not this to assure us that those that are the members of the Church, have a communitie in all these treasures and goods of it, and consequently that they are the children of God, and inheritours of everlasting life? According unto this S.[7] *Luke* also saith resolutlie, that God joyned unto the Church those that should be saved. The

---

[1] 2. Tim. 2.19.

[2] 2. markes of our adoption.

[3] Of the outward mark

[4] Matth. 13.

[5] Mat. 21.13.

[6] Ephe. 2.19.

[7] Act. 2.47.

which is confirmed[8] by the Prophet *Joel* saying, that there shall be salvation in Sion. And S.[9] *Paule* himselfe sticketh not at all, to call those that are the members of the Church, the elect of God. But yet so much the more to resolve us, let us consider the marks of the true church touched here before. The first is, the pure preaching of the word of God. Now, Jesus Christ saith, my sheepe heare[10] my voyce, and they follow me: [C4v] shewing thereby very manifestly, that this[11] is one marke to bee the child of God, to heare the voyce of his sonne Jesus Christ: As also he saith in another[12] place, that he that is of God, heareth[13] the voyce of God. And indeed, seeing[14] that the preaching of the Gospell[15] is called the ministerie of reconciliation,[16] the Gospell of peace, the word[17] of grace, of salvation and of life, (as without doubt, God by the ministerie of his word, presenteth Reconciliation, peace, grace, salvation and life): So they that are the members of the Church, heare and receive the word, shew therein, that they are partakers of all these benefites, and consequentlie, the children of God. The second mark of the Church consisteth in the Sacraments of Baptisme and of the Lords supper. As touching Baptisme, it is a seale and sure warrant that the[18] sinnes of those that receive it are washed[19] away by the bloud of Christ: that[20] they are ingrafted and incorporate into his death and resurrection: that they are regenerate, and that they [C5r 13] have put on Jesus Christ. Whereof it followeth,[21] as S. *Paule* affirmeth, that they are the children of God. The like assurance of our adoption is given us in the Lords supper. For if the bread[22] and the cup, which are given to the members of the Church, are the communion of the bodie and of the bloud of Jesus Christ: it followeth that in this communion of Christ, they have the foode and life of their soules. And that consequentlie, as the children of GOD, they shall obtaine life everlast-

[8] Joel. 2.32.
[9] 1. Thes. 1.4
[10] Joh. 10.27.
[11] Joh. 8.47.
[12] 2. Cor. 5.18
[13] Ephe. 6.15.
[14] Act. 14.3. Act 20.32.
[15] Act. 13.26.
[16] Act 5.20.
[17] Phil. 2.15.
[18] Act. 22.5.
[19] Rom. 6.4.
[20] Tit. 3.5. Gal. 3.27.
[21] Gal. 3.26.
[22] 1. Cor. 10.16.

ing, according to the protestation of Christ. He that eateth my[23] flesh, and drinketh my bloud, he hath everlasting life. The third marke of the Church of God, is the invocation of the name of God, in the name of that onlie one Jesus Christ. Now, as[24] all the service of God is oftentimes signified[25] by this invocation: So Saint *Luke*[26] noteth the faithful and children of God by this description, that they call upon the name of the Lord. As on[27] the contrarie side, it is said of the reprobate, that they do not call upon [C5ᵛ] the name of God. And indeede when the members of the Church joyne together and lift up their praiers unto God,[28] saying: Our Father which art in heaven: and so calling him father, by the commandement of Christ, they may well assure themselves that God doth acknowledge them for his children, and that he wil make them feele the fruit of their praiers, according to the promise of Christ, that whatsoever[29] they shall with one consent aske of G O D, it shall bee given them. By this that is above said, it manifestlie appeareth, how everie member of the Church may and ought to assure him selfe to be the child of God, and to acknowledge all other members of the Church with him in like manner to be the children of God. If any alledge that we may thus accompt such a one for the child of God, who possiblie is an hypocrite, and may after shewe himselfe a reprobate, we answere, that such discourses are contrarie to charitie, so much recommended unto us by[30] Saint *Paule,* noting amongst other [C6ʳ 14] properties of charitie, that she thinketh not evill, or is not suspitious, but that she beleeveth all things, and hopeth all things. Wee ought then to hold the members of the Church, for the children of G O D, untill that departing from it, or discovering their hypocrisie, they shewe themselves reprobates. Furthermore, as G O D would that al those to whom he vouchsafeth to bee father, should acknowledge the Church for their mother: so let us not doubt, but being borne againe, and nourished in the Church our mother, we may call God our father, and abiding united to the familie of the mother, let us not doubt but that wee bee the heires of the father. Thus much for the outward markes.

Now let us come to the inwarde markes. As to the blind and deaffe the opening of their eyes and eares is needfull, clearelie to see and heare

---

[23] Joh. 6.54.
[24] Psal. 14.4.
[25] Gen. 12.7.
[26] Act. 2.21. Act. 9.14.
[27] Psal. 14.4.
[28] Matth. 6.9.
[29] Mat. 18.19.
[30] 1. Cor. 13.

the voyce of him that speaketh: So being of[31] our owne nature both blind and deaffe as touching understanding, the holie spirit is hee, that openeth our [C6v] eyes and eares, to comprehend the revelation of our adoption, and to feele in our harts the assurance of it, ingendring in us faith, which is as it were the hand, by which wee apprehend this great benefite: whereof also the fruites and effects as well of the holie ghost dwelling in us, as of the faith that is in us, are the principall and most assured markes, to give us knowledge of our adoption. According whereunto,[32] Saint *Paule* saith, that the Holie ghost giveth testimonie to our spirits that we are the children of God, so as having received this spirit of adoption, wee crie with all assurance, Abba father.[33] This is it also which S. *John* teacheth us, saying: we know that he abideth in us, by the spirit which he hath given[34] us. Also, By this we knowe that we dwell in him, and he in us, because he hath given of his spirit unto us. In like manner the Apostle S. *Paule* affirmeth,[35] that by the peace and quietnes which we feele in our consciences before GOD in the free forgivenes of our sinnes by the bloud of Jesus [C7r 15] Christ, we shewe and proove that wee are justified by faith, and so the children of God. Wherein to confirme us, he saith in another place, that after wee have beleeved, wee are sealed by the holie spirit of promise, which is the[36] earnest penie of our inheritance, untill the redemption of the possession purchased to the praise of his glorie. First he sheweth there, that faith is as it were the seale whereby the Holie ghost imprinteth in our hearts for our assurance, that wee are the children of God. Furthermore, as in a thing that is bought there is somtimes given an earnest penie, to wit, some part of the monie agreed on, as well for the beginning of the paiment, as by consequent, for the assurance that the bargaine shall be held firme: so the holie ghost, who by faith ingendreth peace and joye in the hearts of the faithfull, is the earnest penie, assuring us, by this beginning, of the spirituall blessings which God promiseth to his children, that he holdeth us for his possession, purchased to the praise [C7v] of his glorie, and that at the length he will gather us into the full injoying of the inheritance of heaven. Hereunto it is also, that that goodly gradation leadeth us, which is proposed of the same Apostle,[37] saying: Those whom God hath before knowne, those hee hath also predestinate to be made like

---

[31] Of the inward marks of our adoption.
[32] Rom. 8.16.
[33] 1. Joh. 3.24
[34] 1. Joh. 4.13
[35] Rom. 5.1.
[36] Ephe. 1.13.
[37] Rom. 8.28.

unto the image of Jesus Christ: and those whom he hath predestinate, he hath also called, and those whom he hath called, he hath also justified: and those whom he hath justified, those he hath also glorified. For all will confesse, that those that are elected and predestinated to be made like unto the image of Jesus Christ, are the children of God, as also they, who in his eternall counsel and decree are glorified. Now they, who being lightened with the knowledge of the Gospell, beleeve that their sinnes are washed away by the bloud of Jesus Christ through his satisfaction, and so are called and justified, are elected and glorified before God, as S. *Paule* teacheth here: it followeth then, that they are the [C8^{r} 16] children of God. And this is so certaine, that the Apostle, opposing the will and power of GOD, against all impediments,[38] addeth: If GOD bee on our side,[39] who shall bee against us? S. *Bernard* teacheth the selfe same thing verie aptlie, saying: we are certain of the power of God to save us: but what shall we say of his will? who is he that knoweth whether he bee worthie of hate or of love? who is he that hath knowne the will of the Lord? or who hath bin his counseller? It behoveth that herein faith helpe us, and that trueth succour us. That that, which is hid concerning us in the heart of the father, may bee revealed unto us by the spirit, and his spirit testifying unto us, may perswade us that wee are the children of God; that he perswade it us, I say, in calling and justifying us freelie by faith, which is as it were a meane or passage from the predestination of GOD to the glorie of the life everlasting. The same thing is it which[40] S. *Augustine* meaneth, saying: Wee are come into the way of faith, [C8^{v}] let us hold it constantlie, it shall leade us from degree to degree even unto the chamber of the heavenlie King, where all the treasures of knowledge and wisedome beeing hid, wee may learne and behold the revelation of our election. From hence proceedeth yet another fruite serving us for a marke to assure us more and more that we are the children of God, when we love God, and our neighbours for his sake: whereof also followeth the hatred of evill, and an earnest desire to render obedience to God. For if it be[41] so as Saint *John* saith, that our love to God commeth of this, that he hath first loved us: The love that we beare unto him, is a testimonie that he loveth us. As also Jesus Christ maintaineth and sheweth, that by the signes of[42] love, which the sinful woman gave him, God loved her greatly, and had forgiven her manie sinnes. So the brightnes of the Moone is a certaine argument that the

---

[38] Rom 8.30.

[39] *Bern. ser.* 5. *in dedica. templi.*

[40] *Aug. Hom. in Joan.* 35.

[41] 1. Joh. 4.19

[42] Luk. 7.47.

Sunne ministreth whollie to her, for otherwise she hath no brightnes at all. And in sommer, [D1r 17] the heate that is felt in the stones set against the Sunne, is a signe that the Sunne shineth uppon them. Of our owne nature and first generation we are unprofitable to all goodnes, and inclined[43] to al evill, as Saint *Paule* very largelie setteth forth unto us writing to the *Romanes.* If then on the contrarie wee walke in the feare of God, giving our selves to his service, and occupying our selves in all good works: is not such a chaunge a testimonie of our regeneration, and consequentlie of[44] our adoption? The tree is knowne by his fruit, saith Jesus Christ: If then wee beare the fruit of justice, holines and of charitie, wee are trees planted in the garden of God by his holie spirit, and so consequentlie the children of[45] God. Charitie, saith Saint *John*, is of God, and he that loveth, is borne of God, and knoweth God. As then the heate and light of a coale is a signe that it hath fire: and as the mooving and actions of the bodie are certaine signes, that it liveth, and that the soule is within it: so the testimonie of the [D1v] holie ghost in our hearts, the peace and quietnes of our consciences before G O D, feeling our selves justified by faith; this love towards God and our neighbour, this chaunge of our life, and desire to walke in the feare and obedience of God, are assured tokens of our adoption: as also this, that we are members of the Church of Christ hearing his word, participating with the holie Sacraments, and calling uppon God in the name of Jesus Christ, are testimonies that wee are the children and houshold servants of God, and heires of eternall life.

---

[43] Rom. 3.10.
[44] Matt 7.17.
[45] 1. Joh. 4.7.

How everie member of the Church ought to applie unto himselfe the tokens of it, to assure himselfe of his adoption and salvation.

CAP. 3.

NOw, although the tokens before mentioned are certaine to assure us that wee are the children of God: yet there are two [D2r 18] sorts of temptations, which above all other tend to shake us. The one proceedeth of our selves, either for lacke of applying to our selves the testimonies, which God giveth to the members of his Church to assure them of their salvation: or through the feeling of a want (as wee thinke) but rather, of the smalnes or weaknes of those tokens of adoption here above alledged. The other temptation commeth unto us from some other where, and consisteth speciallie in two points. To wit, in the revolt of some having made profession of the true religion: and in the grievous and long afflictions which are ordinarie to those that followe the doctrine of the Gospell. Now, as there is nothing of greater importance than the salvation of the soule: so there is nothing that doth more grievouslie afflict and trouble the tender consciences desirous of eternall life, than the doubts and feares not to be the child of God, getting to themselves hereby such sorowes and anguishes, as none are able to [D2v] comprehend, but those that have themselves felt and tried them. To helpe then, to the consolation of the soules so daungerouslie, and so mightelie afflicted: first it is to be noted, that this disease commeth to many of this, that they pretend to resolve themselves of their salvation, examining themselves whether they be worthie to be the children of God or no. And as there is none that is, or can bee worthie, so this is at the last to turne doubts into despaire. Other discourse, whether they bee of the number of the elect, and whether their names bee written in the booke of life, to wit, if God love them, and hold them for his children. But it is not so high, that we must mount, but in the doctrine of the Gospell it is, where we should search the revelation hereof, and resolve our selves if God hath loved us, if he doo love us, and will hold us for his children in Jesus Christ. For as a man if he be of credite, maketh the hid thoughts of his heart to bee knowne by speaking: even so [D3r 19] God, who is the trueth it selfe, revealeth unto us, by the preaching of the Gospell, his counsell, and his will touching our adoption and salvation: and confirmeth this revelation by the use of the holie Sacraments. But we must note, that this revelation of the will of God in the Gospel comprehendeth first two poynts: to wit, that there is perfect and entire salvation in one only Jesus Christ, and that the meane to obtaine it, is to beleeve in him. Moreover, when this Gospell is preached unto us, GOD revealeth unto us yet two poynts more: first, that he will make us partakers of this salvation in Christ. Secondlie, that he will have us to beleeve the testimonie that he hath given us of this his will, to the end that we might bee saved. Now, the difficultie of beleeving lieth in the perswasion of these two last points, which notwithstanding are certaine and true. Behold, saith S. *John*, the testimonie[1] of God, which he hath given us of everlasting life, and this life is in his sonne, he saith not onelie that [D3v] the life is in his sonne, but saith further, that he giveth us this life, and that the Gospell is the witnes. And having protested a little before, that he which[2] beleeveth not this testimonie of God, maketh him a lier: he sheweth sufficientlie that he will that wee should beleeve it. The Apostle to the *Hebrues* passeth further, and saith; that God,[3] willing to shew the immutable stablenes of his counsell to the heires of the promise, interposeth himselfe by an oth, that by two things immutable in which it is impossible that God should lie, wee might have firme consolation, wee, I say, who have our refuge to the hope that is set before us, the which we hold as the ancker of the soule sure and stable, pearcing even into the sanctuarie of heaven, where Jesus Christ our forerunner is entered for us. By this he teacheth us first, that when we heare the Gospell, wee ought to hold for certaine, that the counsell of God which was hid in his heart, touching his will to save us, and to take us for his children, is there [D4r 20] made manifest unto us. Secondly, that he will that wee beleeve it, seeing he confirmeth it by two things immutable, in which he cannot lie, to wit, his word and his oth, to the end that wee might have firme consolation, which cannot bee in us, if we beleeve not. Moreover, he calleth the revelation of his counsell, the hope set before us. Speaking then to us, he would that we should have hope: yea and he will that this revealing of his counsell should be unto us a sure anchor of the soule, to shewe, that as a ship is held fast by the anchor, that it might not be carried away of the wind: so God would that this revealing of his counsell by the doctrine of the Gospell should hold us fast, and assure us against all doubts of our adoption, yea and to pearce even into the verie heavens with assurance, whereof our forerunner Jesus Christ hath taken possession both for himselfe, and for us. See then one place shewing very expreslie, that when thou hearest the Gospell, God declareth and revealeth unto thee, [D4v] that it is his will to save thee by his sonne Jesus Christ. And to this end he will further, that thou beleeve it. And indeed[4] when S. *Paule* saith, that faith commeth by hearing the Gospell, he sheweth that thou canst not beleeve, except that

[1] 1. Joh. 5.11
[2] 1. Joh. 5.10
[3] Heb. 6.17.
[4] Ro. 10.17.

thou heare. Now, faith is a knowledge and certaintie, that it is the will of God to save thee, and to take thee for his welbeloved child in Jesus Christ. Then it followeth, that the Gospell which is preached unto thee, and which thou hearest, conteineth the revealing and testimonie: first, that it is the will of God to save thee by Christ: secondlie, that thou shouldest beleeve this testimonie which he giveth thee, that thou maiest have everlasting life. Who now is he, that ought or can doubt? Seeing also he is not content to say in generall, he that[5] beleeveth hath everlasting life: but he commandeth thee to beleeve. Beleeve[6] (saith he) the Gospell. Also, This is his commandement, saith S. *John*,[7] that wee beleeve in the name of his sonne Jesus Christ. Now, to [D5r 21] beleeve the Gospell, or in the name of Jesus Christ, is not onelie to beleeve that there is salvation in Christ, and that he that beleeveth in him hath life everlasting. For the divell himselfe beleeveth that, and yet he beleeveth not the Gospell, neither in the name of Jesus Christ. But this is to beleeve, that he hath salvation in Christ[8] for thee, as *Esai* saith: A child is borne to us, a sonne is given to us. And so speaketh the Angell to the shepheards.[9] This day is borne unto you a saviour. Also, that it is the will of God that thou shouldest be his child, and thou shouldest beleeve it so. The which thing the divell cannot beleeve for himselfe: neither is the Gospell offered unto him. Now, when GOD revealeth unto thee his good will and love towards thee, wherefore doubtest thou? He is true, he neither will, nor can either lie or deceive. And when he commaundeth thee to beleeve it, must thou examine thy selfe whether thou bee worthie or no? Thou art bound to obey, and so to beleeve, that [D5v] he doth love thee, and that thou art his child by Christ. Call to mind that which is written, whosoever beleeveth (what[10] manner a one, or whosoever it be) he hath life everlasting. Neither is it presumption so to beleeve, and that constantly, but it is to him obedience most acceptable. And indeed it is an honour that he requireth of thee to beleeve his word, and so to put to thy seale that he is true. It is verie true that in preaching the Gospell, hee saith,[11] not, I am come to save Simon Peter, Cornelius the Centurion, Marie Magdalen, and so of others. He nameth no man by his name that was given him by men, either at their circumcision, or at their baptisme, or otherwise: for so might we yet

[5] Joh. 3.36.
[6] Mar. 1.15.
[7] 1. Joh. 3.23
[8] Esay. 9.5.
[9] Luk. 2.11.
[10] Joh. 3.16.
[11] Joh. 3.39.

doubt of our salvation, thinking that it might be spoken not of us, but of some other that should have the same name. But when thou hearest that Jesus Christ is come[12] to save sinners: either renounce the[13] name of a sinner, or confesse that hee speaketh to thee, and that hee is come to save thee. Make then boldly [D6^{r} 22] this conclusion: Jesus Christ is come to save sinners, I acknowledge my owne name, for I am a sinner: therefore he is come to save me. And also when he saith: Come unto me all ye that[14] travaile and are heavilie laden, and I will refresh you: Thou must marke well these words, all ye; for seeing he saith, all ye, he speaketh to all those that travaile and feele the heavy burthen of their sinnes. Wherfore shouldest thou doubt then, whether hee speake to thee? Conclude rather on this manner, seeing he saith, all ye, he speaketh then also to me, promising to comfort me. And to this purpose saith[15] S. *Paule*, that there is no difference of men before G O D, but the same who is Lord over all, is rich towards all those that call uppon him: Have thou then recourse unto him, and beleeve in him, and thou art assured that he will also be rich in mercie even unto thee. If there were two or three hundred inhabitants of some towne banished for some offence, and after a generall pardon should be published, [D6^{v}] that all the banished of such a towne should have free libertie to returne thether, with all assurance to enter againe uppon all their goods and honors: suppose that thou wert one of those banished, and that he that hath given the pardon were a faithfull and true Prince: wouldest not thou beleeve, that thou wert comprehended in the pardon, although thy name were no more expressed, than the names of the other banished, and that returning to the towne thou shouldest againe bee placed in thy goods? Now, we have bin banished from the kingdome[16] of heaven by the transgression of Adam. Jesus Christ dying for these banished persons, causeth a generall pardon to bee published by the preaching of the Gospell, with permission, yea with commandement to returne into heaven. He is a true King, yea the trueth it selfe: and the abolishing of this banishment, and the reentrie into heaven hath cost him verie deere, even the shedding of his most[17] precious bloud. What occasion [D7^{r} 23] then hast thou to doubt of thy pardon, and returne into heaven? For, although thy Christian name bee not expressed; yet if thou be of the number of the banished, he speaketh to thee, behold thy name, thou art

[12] Matt. 9.13.
[13] 1. Timo. 1.15.
[14] Math. 11.28.
[15] Rom. 10.12.
[16] Gen. 3.24.
[17] 1. Pet. 1.19.

there comprehended. Beleeve that he speaketh in trueth, and that his wil is such towards thee, as he declareth to thee by his word. But let us passe further to the Sacraments, which serve greatlie to resolve us to beleeve that wee are the children of God. The Sacraments[18] are (as it were) a visible word, representing the grace of the Gospel. But more then that, they are communicated to thee, and thou receivest them. Is not this to put thee, as it were, into reall possession of thine adoption, and to give thee assurance of everlasting life? The Pastour preacheth unto all, the grace of the Gospell in the name of Christ. But in thy Baptisme he directeth his speach to thee by name, to assure thee of the forgivenes of thy sinnes, and of thine adoption, as S. *Paule* saith, that those [D7v] that[19] are baptised have put on Christ, and that so they are the children of God. And it is as if a Prince having called backe againe all the banished, amongst whom thou shouldest be one, calling unto thee by name, amongst the other banished, by a letter sealed of thy pardon, and of reestablishing thee in thy goods. Should not this be to assure thee? As touching the holy supper, Jesus Christ, having published by his Minister, that his flesh is meate indeed and his bloud drinke, addeth, that[20] whosoever eateth his flesh and drinketh his bloud, he hath life everlasting: He calleth thee among others to his table, and giveth thee of the bread and wine, namelie, to assure thy person, that he died for thee, and that he giveth thee his bodie and his bloud, yea himselfe all whole, and all his benefites, that thou shouldest bee with him, the child of God, and an inheritour of life everlasting. If the divell or thy conscience trouble thee, to doubt of thine adoption, assure thy soule against such a temptation, by the [D8r 24] communication of the holie supper. Say boldlie, Satan, canst thou denie that I have been at the holie supper, and that I have received bread and wine? I have seen, touched and tasted it, thou canst not denie it. Further, canst thou denie that this bread and wine were given me for seales and sure pledges of my communicating with the body and bloud of Christ? Saint *Paule* saith plainlie,[21] that the bread which I have received, is the communion of the bodie of Jesus Christ. Seeing then thou canst not denie, but that I have received the bread and wine: and that the bread and wine are the communion of the body and of the bloud of Christ, I have then communion with the bodie and bloud of Jesus Christ, and thou canst not denie it. True it is that there are some, who being out-

[18] *August. in Joan. hom.* 89.
[19] Gal. 3.27.26.
[20] Joh. 6.55.56.
[21] 1. Cor. 10.16.

ward members of the church, baptised in it, hearing the word, and communicating at the holie supper, shewe themselves after hypocrites, declaring that they were never indeede the children of God. But wee cannot say therefore, [D8^{v}] that the revelation and testimonie of the will of God contained in his word, and sealed by the Sacraments, are doubtfull or uncertaine. For G O D, who offereth his grace in his word, and hath sealed it by the Sacraments, is faithful and speaketh truelie, revealing unto us and assuring us that he will take us for his welbeloved children in Jesus Christ. And he can neither lie nor deceave, as is alreadie said. But these are unfaithfull men, who rejecting the testimonies of the will of GOD towards them, deprive themselves by their incredulitie of the[22] grace which was offered unto them, doing this dishonor to Christ, to compt him a lier. As the Sunne then ceaseth not to give light and brightnes, although some man shutteth his eyes that he may not see it, nor bee lightened: and as meate ceaseth not to bee good and nourishing, although it be received without profite of a stomack evill disposed: So, if manie unwilling to beleeve that the will of G O D is such, as he hath declared by his word, [E1^{r} 25] rejecting (by their incredulitie) the grace which G O D offereth them; should their incredulitie make thee call in doubt the trueth of God, and the testimonie of his good will towards thee? If some few among these banished, not trusting the pardon published by a true and faithfull Prince, doo him this dishonor to compt him as a deceiver or lier: acknowledge thou that justlie and by good right they remaine banished. But thou, seeing that faithfull Prince Jesus Christ hath sent to pronounce unto thee a generall pardon, and namelie, hath given thee his letters sealed by the Sacraments, commaunding thee to beleeve, and promising thee, that it shall bee unto thee according to thy faith:[23] Assure thy selfe, that his will is that thou shouldest be his child, and heire of everlasting life. See how everie one should assure himselfe, by the preaching of the Gospell, and the use of the Sacraments, the true markes of the Church: that (being a member of it) he is the child of God: and [E1^{v}] consequentlie, an inheritour of his everlasting kingdome. True it is, that faith is the gift of G O D, yea proceeding from the operation of the mightie power[24] of his strength, as S. *Paule* speaketh.[25] And this is it which he maketh us to feele in this difficultie of apprehending (by an assured faith) so manie, so cleare and so certaine

---

[22] 1. Joh. 5.10

[23] Matt. 9.29.

[24] Phili. 1.29.

[25] Ephe. 1.19.

testimonies of his good will towards us, touching our adoption. It is therefore needfull that he worke farther with us by his holie spirit, which (without ceasing) asking of him in the name of Jesus Christ, we are assured by his promise, that he will give us, and that, so joyning with the power and efficacie of his spirit, the preaching of his Gospell, and the use of the Sacraments, he will give us grace to applie unto our selves (by a true and livelie faith) the testimonies which he hath given us of our adoption, to our salvation and everlasting life.

[E2r 26] *How although the markes of our adoption bee in us but small and feeble, yet wee ought, and may assure our selves that we are the children of God.*

CAP. 4.

I See well (will some say) that I have just matter to beleeve it: and therefore am I the more sory that I feele not faith in my self, to assure me without doubt that I am the child of GOD, which thing troubleth mee greatly, so as I feare least by this mine incredulitie, I reject the grace of God. But understand I pray thee for thy comfort, that there is great difference betweene unfaithfulnes and weaknes of faith. The unfaithfull man or infidell[1] careth not for his salvation: or, rejecting the salvation which is in Jesus Christ alone, seeketh salvation other where. Contrariwise, the faithful desire salvation: he knoweth that [E2v] his salvation is in Jesus Christ alone: he seeketh it in him, and feeleth a desire to increase in assurance, that he hath salvation in Jesus Christ, though he doo not yet feele this peace and joy in the holie Ghost so manifestlie as faith bringeth it forth at the last. Also it is not written, he that feeleth, but hee[2] that beleeveth hath everlasting life.[3] And indeed, as faith is of things that[4] are not seene, so the understanding of it consisteth more in certaintie, than in apprehension. In this complaint of *David,* yea and of Christ himselfe: My God my God, why hast thou[5] forsaken me. We heare the testimonie[6] of faith by these wordes: my God my God, but without apprehension or feeling of favour or joy, as this complaint, why hast thou forsaken me, sheweth. Also our faith may bee so small and weake, as it doth not yet bring forth fruites that may be livelie felt of us. But if such as feele themselves in such estate, desire to have these feelings: if they aske them of God by praier. This desire and praier [E3r 27] are testimonies that the spirit of God is in them, and that they have faith alreadie. For, is such a desire a fruite of the flesh, or of the spirit? It is of the holie spirit, who bringeth it forth onlie in such, as he dwelleth in. He dwelleth then in them. In like manner, is not this praier the worke of the holy ghost in them? For it is the holy ghost (saith[7] S. *Paule*) which praieth for us, and in us, with

---

[1] The first temptation proceeding of the small feeling of our faith.

[2] Jho. 3.36.

[3] Heb. 11.1.

[4] Rom. 8.23.

[5] Psal. 22.1.

[6] Mat. 27.46.

[7] Rom. 8.25.

grones that cannot be expressed. Againe, none can come to God by praiers, if he have no trust in him. Then these holie desires and praiers, being the motions of the holie ghost in us, are testimonies of our faith, although they seeme to us small and weake. As the woman that feeleth the mooving of a child in her wombe, though verie weake, beleeveth and assureth her selfe that she is with child, and that she goeth with a live child: so if we have these motions, these holie affections and desires before mentioned, let us not doubt, but that wee have the holie ghost (who is the author of them) dwelling in us, [E3^{v}] and consequentlie that wee have also faith. And we must understand, that the faith of the children of God ceaseth not to bee a true faith, although they feele doubts, feares, and mistrusts. For if they delight not in such infirmities,[8] to nourish them; but are sorrowfull and resist them, with desire to feele their salvation in Jesus Christ, behold a battaile in them: and betweene whom? Betweene the spirit and the flesh: betweene faith and mistrust. There is then in them faith assailed with doubts, and the spirit fighting against mistrust, and labouring to overcome it. These doubts, mistrustings, and incredulities are the fierie darts which Satan throweth against our faith, the which bearing the blowes, as a buckler, as S. *Paule* saith: thrusteth them back and quencheth[9] them, so as they pearce not to the heart. What devises or assaults soever the divel make against us, saith S. *Augustine,* so he occupie not the place of the heart where faith dwelleth, he is driven backe. Incredulitie [E4^{r} 28] then assaulteth us without, but woundeth us not deadlie: It troubleth onlie, or so woundeth, as the stroake is yet curable. And such temptations and assaults are common to the most faithfull and excellent servants of God. If wee consider the continuall course of the life of *David*, there is no mirrour of faith better to bee noted than in him. And yet was not he assaulted with great feares and doubts? What complaint maketh he in the 77. Psalm? Hath the Lord forsaken me for ever? will he[10] no more shewe me favour? Is his mercie cleane gone for ever? Is his promise come to an ende for evermore? Hath God forgotten to bee gracious? Hath he shut up his loving kindnes in displeasure? And to conclude, he holdeth such a course, as a man desperate, saying: This is my death. Where was then in *David*, the feeling of his faith? For al this he had not lost it. And indeed all these words were but representations of feare and dispaire assailing the faith that was in him, and fighting against it: As hee [E4^{v}] sheweth in other places verie plainly,

---

[8] Rom. 7.

[9] Eph. 6.16.

[10] Psal. 77.8,9 10,11,vers.

saying:[11] My soule, why art thou cast downe,[12] why art thou so heavie within me? Put thy trust in God, for I will yet give him thanks, for as much as he is my manifest deliverance (as it were before my face) and my God. If these testimonies of faith before mentioned seeme small: how small and dark was the faith of the Apostles before the resurrection of Jesus Christ? They beleeve that Christ is the sonne of God,[13] the saviour of the world: but yet[14] they understand not that he must die,[15] and rise againe: wherein notwithstanding[16] lieth the principall rest of our faith.[17] Yea, and after his resurrection they (acknowledge him for a King) imagined rather a carnall, than a spirituall kingdome. If their faith was darke in their understanding: it was also small in their hearts, when they were offended at Christ, and all forsooke[18] him: and Peter himselfe renounced[19] him. And yet we cannot say, that they[20] were without faith, though it were[21] then verie weake and small. And [E5^{r} 29] also[22] when the ship being covered with flouds[23] they cried to Jesus Christ: saying, save us, we perish: he calleth them not infidels, but men of little faith, and fearefull: shewing that they had some faith in them, though verie small, and assailed with feare, wherein notwithstanding having recourse unto him, they were heard, and delivered out of daunger. For he came not to breake the brused reede, nor to quench the smoaking[24] flax: As *Esay* foretold, shewing[25] therby, that there are some of the children of God, weake as a brused reede, and having as little strength of faith, as in steed of flaming, it smoaketh onlie. This smalnes and beginning of faith is verie aptlie noted by S.[26] *Paule*, saying: that the righteousnes of GOD is revealed by the Gospell from faith to faith. He sheweth that there are degrees in faith, and that it happeneth to us in the revealing of the righteousnes of GOD, by which we are justified, as when we see one so

[11] Psal 42.12.
[12] Psal. 43.5.
[13] Mat 16.16 John 6.69.
[14] Mat. 17.23
[15] Luke 9.45.
[16] Luk 24.11
[17] Act. 1.6.
[18] Mat. 26 31
[19] Mar. 14.27.
[20] Mar. 14.50.
[21] Mat. 26.70 Mar. 14.68
[22] Luk. 22.32
[23] Matt. 8.25.
[24] Esa. 42 3.
[25] Matt. 12.18
[26] Rom. 1.17.

farre off, as with much a do wee know him: but the neerer we approach, the [E5v] more cleerelie we discerne him. Manie of the children of God are like to that blind man, whose eyes Christ opened,[27] but so at the beginning, as he sawe men like trees, forthwith he recovered his sight, but yet troubled at the beginning, but afterward cleared. To bee short, he who in the person of his Apostles hath taught us to pray unto[28] God to increase our faith, sheweth that he hath children in whom it is weake, and hath neede of increase. Also the chiefe wisedome of the most perfect is to profite. And to this purpose wee must remember, that in all spirituall graces, there is nothing but beginnings and imperfections, in the most perfect, and most highlie exalted in this life. But that the perfection (to the which notwithstanding wee must alwaies tend) and the accomplishment shall be in heaven. To conclude, there are two effects or fruits of faith, to wete, the rest and peace of the conscience before God: and sanctification, which consisteth in the mortification of the workes of the flesh, [E6r 30] and newnes of life. Now, as the rest and peace of conscience proceeding from faith, is a testimonie that it is in us, so is also sanctification, and the desire to walke in the feare and obedience of God. And indeed, faith is the fountaine of good workes. If then, one of these fruites be languishing, the other sufficeth to assure us that wee have faith. As it is knowne that there is true and naturall fire, by the flame and the heate, which are two effects and operations of fire: but if the flame shall become weake, the heate shall suffice to assure us, that it is naturall, and not a painted fire. In like manner, if this fruit of thy faith be weake, to feele peace and rest in thy conscience, and yet thou feelest the other effect of faith, to wete, a desire to the workes of the spirit, love towards God, and desire to walke in his obedience: This fruit of thy faith is to thee a sure testimonie that it is in thee, though but smal and weake. But thou wilt say: what comfort or assurance of salvation can a faith so weak [E6v] and little give me: I answere; It can assure thee of thine adoption. For so thou have but one spark of true faith, thou art the child of God. Faith is of such a force, that (following the promise[29] of God) one onelie graine of it, though never so little, laieth hold on Jesus Christ to salvation. Againe, it is properlie Jesus Christ which saveth us, and not our faith: saving in so much as it is the instrument, and as it were the hand by which wee take hold on Jesus Christ. Now, faith how little soever it bee taketh hold on Christ and receiveth him, not by halfes, but all whole: as an infant taketh and holdeth with his little hand a whole

---

[27] Mar. 8.29.
[28] Luk. 17.5.
[29] Mat. 17.20

apple, though he doth it not so stronglie or surelie as a man. By the apple of our eye, though merveilous little, we see verie great mountaines, and the verie bodie of the Sunne, much greater than the whole earth: so our faith, though verie little, taketh and receiveth all whole Jesus Christ the sunne of righteousnes. He who (being in a darke tower) seeth not the light of [E7r 31] the Sunne, but by a verie little hole, may notwithstanding assure himselfe, that the Sunne shineth uppon the tower, as well as he that seeth it by an open windowe, knoweth that it shineth upon his house. Even so although we are hindered by the cloudes of mistrust, that we cannot see the Sunne of righteousnes to shine upon our soules in his brightnes: yet so that wee see but a little beame, wee know that the sunne of life shineth uppon us, which assureth us that we are the children of God. Also whosoever in this life shall have the least faith among all the elect, shall yet injoye Jesus Christ all whole, and not a little or halfe salvation, but the full accomplished salvation of eternall life. For whosoever beleeveth in Jesus Christ, saith Saint *John*,[30] shall not perish, but have life everlasting. Now, as this ought greatlie to comfort us in the weakenes of our faith, so ought it to bee a sharpe spurre to inforce us to growe in faith, that feeling so much the more clearelie and livelie the peace and joye of [E7v] our consciences, by the assurance that we are the children of God, wee may the more stronglie resist all temptations, and glorifie our God. There are[31] others, who call their faith and adoption in doubt, saying: That true faith cannot be without good works. Now, I feele my selfe so miserable a sinner,[32] that it maketh me to doubt of mine adoption. Indeed this is a thing greatlie to be lamented, that we render no better obedience unto God, that there is in us no greater zeale of his glorie, nor more fervent charitie towards our neighbours: and to be short, no better amendement of life. But if thou hast begun to hate and flee sinne, if thou feelest that thou art displeased at thy infirmities and corruptions: If having offended God, thou feele a sorrowe and griefe for it: if thou desire to abstaine: if thou avoidest the occasions: if thou travailest to doo thine indevour: if thou praiest to God to give thee grace: All these holie affections proceeding from no other than from the Holie ghost, [E8r 32] ought to be unto thee so manie pledges and testimonies, that he is in thee: As[33] also Saint *Paule* teacheth us, saying: that as those that delight in the workes of the flesh, are of the flesh. So on the other side, those that delight in the workes of

---

[30] Jho. 3.16

[31] 2. Temptation throgh the smalnes of our sanctification.

[32] Ja. 2.17.20.

[33] Rom. 8.5

the spirit, are of the spirit. These holie desires then to the workes of the spirit, are testimonies of the spirit dwelling in thee. So as being thus led by the spirit of God, thou art[34] the child of God, saith Saint *Paul:* And[35] indeed seeing the children of *Adam* are naturallie inclined to all vices and corruptions, it is a marke of regeneration, and so of being the child of God, when contrarie to nature we are displeased with our infirmities, and fighting against them, wee desire and indevour to fashion our selves according to the will of our GOD. God[36] hath commaunded us to love him with all our heart, with all our understanding, and with al our soule. Now, as we cannot know God in this life, but in part, and darklie, so we can [E8v] not[37] love him but in part, yea verie little. The perfection is reserved for heaven[38] as also S. *Augustine* saith: All the faithfull ought earnestlie to aspire to this, that they may once appeare before God pure and without spot. But for as much as the best and most perfect estate that we can attaine unto in this present life, is no other thing, than to profite from day to day: then shall we come to this marke, when, after putting off this sinfull flesh, wee shall cleave fullie to our God. Therefore also, as the same author saith, when men speake of the perfection of the children of God in this life: to this perfection is required the acknowledging of their imperfection. It is as well in trueth, as in humilitie that the Saincts acknowledge how imperfect they are. God deferreth the accomplishment of our holines and charitie untill the life to come, to the end that this pride (which taketh force through the increase of vertue) should not overthrowe us, but that walking in humilitie, God might [F1r 33] accomplish[39] his mercie in pardoning us, his power in sustaining us, and his truth in saving us. And indeede there is nothing more weake, saith S. *Augustine,* than the proude, nor more strong than the humble: For as the proude, trusting in himselfe, who is nothing but vanitie, hath God his adversarie, who resisteth the[40] proude; so the humble mistrusting himselfe, hath God for his strength and salvation. God indeede in his lawe requireth a perfect obedience. But that which he looketh for of us his children in this life, consisteth more in the desire to[41] obey, than in the obedience it selfe. According whereunto hee

---

[34] Rom. 8.14
[35] Rom. 3.10
[36] Mat. 22.37.
[37] 1. Cor. 13.9.12.
[38] *Aug. ad Bonif. lib.* 3. *ca.* 7.
[39] 2. Cor. 12.9
[40] 1. Pet. 5.5. Jam. 4.6.
[41] Rom. 8.5

saieth by his Prophet[42] *Malachi*, I will spare them, as a father dooth his owne sonne that serveth him. If a child take paine to write well, or to do as he should do anie other service that his father hath commaunded him, although there be great want both in the writing, and in the other service; yet in bearing with him hee praiseth him, and saieth, that hee hath written well, hee had doone his duetie. Godlines, the love towardes God, and [F1v] the obedience that we owe unto him, is often signified by the feare of God, the which[43] also *David* calleth the beginning of Wisedome. And those that have this feare of God, are acknowledged and called the children of God. Then if thou feel such love and reverence toward God, that thou feare to offend him, thou art the[44] child of God. But then thou fearest to offend God, when thou shunnest the occasions and inticements to sinne, and when having offended, thorough ignorance, oversight, or other infirmitie, thou feelest sorrow and displeasure, to raise thee up againe, being resolved to sin no more, and praying to God that he will conduct thee by his holy spirit, that thou maist walke constantly according to his worde.[45] S. *Jhon* saith, that the children of God sinne not: not that they offend not God every day, or that they commit not sometimes most greevous offences, as[46] *David* and Saint *Peter:* And as dailie[47] experience dooth too much convict everie one of us. But he saith, that they sinne not, because they love God, and are afraide to offend him, and doe not [F2r 34] willingly give themselves to doo evill: but have sinne in such detestation, that they feele in themselves that conflict, which[48] Saint *Paule* setteth foorth unto us in his owne person, in as much as they woulde doo the good which they cannot doo, and doo unwillingly the evil which displeaseth them: whereof it followeth, as the Apostle concludeth, that if they doo that which they would not doo, it is no more they which do it, but sinne which dwelleth in them: which on the one side ought to give them occasion to mourne and to crie wyth the Apostle, Alas wretch that I am, who shall deliver mee from the bodie of this death? But on the other side they ought to feele the comforte which hee addeth, saying, I thanke my God through[49] Jesu Christ. And wherefore? Because there is no condemnation to those, who thus fighting against the flesh, walke after the spirit, and consequently are in Jesus Christ.

---

[42] Mal. 3.17.
[43] Psa. 111.10
[44] Psa. 112.1
[45] 1. John 3.9
[46] 2. Sam. 11
[47] Mat. 26.74
[48] Rom. 7
[49] Rom. 8.1

For the rest, when thou feelest a doubt of thine adoption through the want of rendering to God such obedience as thou oughtst, [F2v] knowe, that Satan is at hand with thee falsifying the gospel in persuading thee, that thou shouldest bee saved by thy workes; or willing to make thee blaspheme Jesus Christ, in making thee beleeve, that thou mayest and oughtest to be (at the least) in some part, a Saviour of thy selfe, and so a companion of Jesus Christ. Answere to this temptation, that[50] thou arte a poore sinner, but that Christ came to save sinners, and that there[51] is salvation in none but in hym. Furthermore,[52] if thou feel a desire to the works[53] of the Spirit, thou art of the Spirit, and there is no condemnation to thee, as is saide. If thou delight, as touching the inward man, in the obedience of the commaundements of GOD, hee accepteth thee for holie and just, receiving this desire to obey him, for an obedience acceptable unto him. He accepteth his owne worke in thee, and pardoneth thee thine. Continue in this holie desire, fighting against the flesh and the world, strengthening thy self by fervent praier to the Lord. And behold the certaine testimonies of thine adoption.

[F3r 35] But[54] thou wilt say, I have of long time asked of God, and do daylie aske his holie Spirite, the encrease of faith and grace to be obedient unto him; yet I feele no manner of fruite of my prayers. If G O D loved me, and accounted mee for his childe, woulde hee not heare mee? It is the same complaint, that in old time past *David* made, saying:[55] I am wearie of crying, my throat is hoarse, mine eies are failed, while I wait on[56] my God. And in another place, My God, I crie by day, and thou answerest not, and by night, and I have no rest. Now in saying he had no rest, he sheweth that he did continue in prayer. Also Jesus Christ exhorteth us to this diligence, by the example or similitude of the[57] importunate widdow, crying still upon the wicked Judge to do hir right, and at the last obtaining by her importunacie. And besides that, hee waketh us up, saying: Heare what the wicked Judge saieth: Because shee troubleth mee, I will doe her justice. And God which is your Father and Saviour, who is[58] just and lov-

[50] 1. Tim. 1.15

[51] Matt. 9.13. Rom. 8.5.

[52] Rom. 8.1.

[53] Rom. 7.22

[54] 3. Temptation, because the feeling of the fruit of our prayers is so long deferred, and because of the weakenesse of them.

[55] Psa. 69.4.

[56] Psa, 22 2

[57] Luke. 18.1

[58] Psal. 11.7

eth righteousnesse, shall [F3v] not hee heare the crie of his children crying unto him night and day? Verely I saie unto you, that hee will doe it, and[59] that quickely. Hee that went by night to his neighbor to borow bread, continuing still his request, though the other alleadged many excuses, yet at the length he obtained what he would. Continue then in praying to G O D, without discouragement. This perseverance in prayer, is an evident and vehement testimonie of thy faith. For that is not founde but in the children of God, guided by his Spirite: especially seeing[60] thou askest the holie Ghost, whom Jesus Christ promised thee, thou askest that, which by his promise is due unto thee, without doubt he will give it thee. And seeing thou askest the increase of faith, and grace to obey him, thou askest that which he commandeth thee to have, and so that which he liketh and is pleased withall. Be then assured that thou shalt be heard. Beholde, sayth[61] Saint *John,* the confidence that wee have with G O D, that if wee aske anie thing according unto his wil, [F4r 36] he heareth us. And if wee know that he heareth us, whatsoever we aske, wee knowe wee shall obtaine the requests that we have asked. His promises can not faile nor deceive. Yea, bee thou certaine, that before thou hast ended thy prayer, hee hath heard thee, as *Esay* saith,[62] For our God is a God that heareth[63] prayers, sayth *David.* But thou owest him this honour to submit thy selfe to his wisedome as touching the time of feeling or receiving the fruite of thy prayers. If Jesus Christ had healed[64] the daughter of the Cananite at the first petition, her Faith had not beene so kindled in her, nor so commended in the Church unto the ende of the worlde. The fruites of all trees are not ripe in one daie. In some they doe ripen sooner, and men waite patiently for the other, which ripen in the latter[65] season: *Zacharie* and *Elizabeth* thought that they had prayed in vaine, asking of G O D posteritie in their youth. And when they were olde, and without all hope for to obtaine it, the Angell of the Lorde saide unto [F4v] *Zacharie,* Thy prayer is heard: not that prayer which hee made then, for he thought not nowe to have issue, but the prayer which hee made long time before. That which is more, doe wee not aske of G O D manie graces, the which wee knowe well that wee obtaine, either in part, or in hope onelie? the enjoying or full accomplishment whereof is deferred either untill death, or even

---

59 Luke 11.5.
60 Luk. 11.13
61 John 5.14.
62 Esa, 65.24
63 Psal. 65.3
64 Mat. 15.22.
65 Luke 1.13

untill the day of the resurrection. In the Prayer of all Prayers taught by Jesus Christ, wee do aske of G O D[66] that his name may be sanctified, his Kingdome may come, his will may bee doone in Earth, as it is in Heaven. And when shall wee see the full accomplished effect of this prayer, but in Heaven, when Christ having given up his kingdome to G O D his father, wee shall love him perfectlie, and praise him everlastinglie? Furthermore, he oftentimes heareth us, so as Saint *Augustine* saith: not according unto our will, but as is most for our profite, giving us better thinges than those that wee expresselie aske. The [F5^r 37] *Jewes* desired the comming of the *Messias*, and asked it of God. He deferred it of long time: at the last hee sent him, but not such a one, as al (as it were) and[67] the Apostles themselves looked for: to wete, victorious in battaile as *David,* to deliver them from the yoake of the *Romans*, triumphing in riches and worldlie glorie, as *Salomon*; but such a *Messias*, as obtaining victorie against the divell, death, and sinne, hath established a spirituall kingdome in everlasting life and glorie. Jesus Christ feeling and apprehending the terrible gulphes of the fearful wrath of God upon him for our sinnes,[68] prayed with strong cries and teares to God his Father that he might not enter into the deepe pit of death. The Apostle[69] to the *Hebrewes* saith, that he was heard: and yet notwithstanding he entred, and dranke the Cup of the wrath, and of death which the Father had given him. But he was heard, saith the same Apostle, as touching that which (in making his praier) he fered: to wit, from being swallowed of death. In like manner, S. *Paul*[70] praieth to God oftentimes that he [F5^v] would deliver him from the Angell of Sathan that buffeted him, but G O D much better (as he himselfe confesseth) gave him to understand, that the power of God was made perfect in his infirmity: so as he protesteth, as it were enjoying the frute of his praiers, thogh otherwise than he thoght, that from that time forth he would rejoice in his infirmities, and woulde take delight in them, forasmuch as being weake in himselfe, he was strong in God. So wee will demaund manie times commodities concerning this life, as health, goods, parents, friends, or our country: and God depriving us of them, giveth us spirituall graces, patience, faith, contentment in God, and other like: yea, and our prayer tending onely unto the preservation, and enjoying such commodities appertaining unto this life alone: G O D contrariwise depriveth us of them, to keepe them for us in heaven, and to give us everlasting enjoying of them, as when wee are deprived of them, being persecuted

---

[66] Matth. 6.9
[67] Act. 4.6.
[68] Mat. 26.39
[69] Heb. 5 7.
[70] 2. Cor. 12.

for his name. And that which more is, when wee [F6r 38] feele weakenes in faith, negligence to heare the worde of G O D, coldnesse in charitie, impatience in our afflictions, and we having asked of God graces contrarie unto these, feele no amendment: his wil is to make us feele that these graces are the gifts of God, seeing we have them not when we will, and that he wil keepe us in humilitie by the feeling of our infirmities, and trie our patience and faith, in waighting patiently untill hee make us feele the fruite of our praiers. I thinke well (wilt thou say) that those that pray unto God ferventlie and continue constantlie in such praiers, have therin testimonies that they are the children of God, and are assured to be heard. But what comfort may I take therein, seeing my praiers are so colde, and with so litle feeling of zeale and faith required in them? But is it not in the name of Jesus Christ that thou prayest? And it is for[71] the love of his welbeloved Sonne, our advocate and mediatour, that God heareth[72] us, and not for the excellencie of our praiers. It is, as it were, by the mouth of Jesus Christ that we present [F6v] our praiers to God, to be sanctified by him, and acceptable to God for his sake, in[73] whom he hath delight. Satan, the enemie of our praiers, by the feeling of this infirmitie, would make thee leave praying to thy God. Resist then this temptation. Thinke that it is not a thing indifferent, or left in thy liberty, to pray to God[74] or not. God hath commanded thee to pray;[75] thou owest him obedience; it is an honour he requireth of thee; thou canst not[76] denie it him. God commandeth thee to love him with al thy hart. Wilt thou say, I will not love God at all, because I love him so coldly: I will help the poore no more, because I can not doo it with a fervent charitie. To conclude, what infirmitie or coldnes soever thou feelest, thou art bound to pray, and to continue in[77] thy dutie. In the mean time, acknowledge thy infirmitie, and in thy prayers aske double pardon, first of thy sinnes which thou hast committed before, secondly for this sinne, that thou prayest to God so negligently. See how G O D (supporting the infirmitie of thy prayers) will smell a sweete savour of them, [F7r 39] as[78] incense offered by our high Priest Jesus Christ, and shall make thee at last feele the fruite of thy praiers. Manie complaine of another infirmitie, that hardly they begin

---

[71] Joh. 16.23.
[72] Exo. 28.38.
[73] Mar. 17.5.
[74] Mat. 6.9.
[75] 1. Th. 5.17.
[76] Mat. 22.37
[77] Ro. 12.12.
[78] Psal. 141.2.

their praiers, but instead of thinking of God, and of that which they aske of him, their minde is wandring other where. And for this they are vexed and troubled: and in truth it is a great infirmitie, for the which we ought gretly to be displeased with our selves. Notwithstanding it is common to all the children of God in general. *Chrisostome* reprooving those of his time for this infirmitie, sheweth quickly the first originall,[79] and after the remedie. Whence commeth this (saith he) that if we talke of[80] warre, of merchandize, or of other things of the world, wee can discourse a great while without thinking of anie other thing, and so soone as wee set our selves to praye unto God, our mindes wander? It is because the Divel knoweth well, that in speaking of things of this world, thou doost him no hurt, and therefore he suffereth thee to talk at thy pleasure: but when he seeth, that thou [F7v] settest thy selfe upon thy knees to pray to God, he knoweth that thou goest to procure that, which is against his heart, and to the ruine of his kingdome. Therfore he thrusts himself in by and by, trobling and drawing thy thoughts hither and thither, to hinder the fruite of thy praiers. Say then to satan, who is hard by thee, and fighteth against thee; go behind me satan, for I must pray to my God. And if hee bee importunate, yet must thou pray to god to drive him away from thee. So thinking to whom thou speakest, to wete, to the Majestie of God; and how great things thou askest of him: be displeased with thy infirmity, fight against it, and lifting up thy hands to heaven continue in praier; and doo it so much the more couragiouslie and constantlie, for that satan feareth nothing more than the praiers of the children of God; and showeth sufficiently in going about to troble and turn away their mindes to other things, that he feeleth himselfe hindred by their praiers, and that hee feareth the fruite of them. On the other side, if it happen that by affliction either of body [F8r 40] or of spirite, thou art so cast downe, that thou canst not make a framed praier unto God; bee not discouraged for that, for at the least thou canst desire thine owne health and salvation. There is neither sicknes nor yet tyrant that can let thee to desire: now, desire is praier before God, saith Saint *Augustine;* according whereunto *David* saith, that God heareth[81] the desire of the humble. Say thou then with *David;* Lord, all my desire[82] is before thee, and the sighs of my thoughts are not hid from thee. *Ezechias*[83] King of *Juda* in his affliction, could not distinctly pray unto God, but chattered as a Crane or a Swallowe, and mourned

[79] Chrisost. Homil. of the Canaanit.

[80] Mat. 15

[81] Psal. 10.17.

[82] Psa. 38,10.

[83] Esai. 38.14.

as the Dove; yet so lifting up his eyes on high, hee was heard. What prayer maketh the little Infant to his mother? Hee weepeth and cryeth, not beeing able to expresse what hee lacketh. The Mother offereth him the breast, or giveth him some other thing, such as shee thinketh his necessitie requireth. Much more then the heavenly father heedeth the sighes, the groanes, the desires and [F8v] teares of his children: and dooing the office of a Father, he heareth them, and provideth for them. There are some also[84] that doubt of their adoption and salvation, because they feele not anie comfort or increase of the graces of GOD, neither by reading or hearing the word, neither by communicating at the holie Supper[85] of the Lord. Now, if thou feele thy selfe afflicted and troubled in this respect; understand, that when thou goest to employ thy selfe in these spirituall exercises, satan followeth thee, to make it unsaverie to thee, yea and to take out of thy minde the word of GOD that thou hast heard. Pray then to GOD, that he drive him away from thee. Secondlie this commeth, forasmuch as thou art not yet much accustomed to the language of the holie Ghost, so as it is to thee as if thou didst heare an excellent sermon, but of one whose language thou didst scarce understand, whereby thou canst neither feele taste nor pleasure, and so thou canst receive but small profit. Then thou must continue, and also accustome thy selfe to read and heare the [G1r 41] word of God, thinking alwaies that God speaketh to thee for the salvation of thy soule, praying him that he will give thee grace by his holie spirit to profite to his glorie and thy salvation. And thou shalt feele at the last that which is said to sicke men that have lost their tast, that thy appetite will come to thee by eating: And that the word of God, and the participating of the bread and wine in the holie[86] supper shall be to thee more sweet, than[87] honie to the mouth, as *David* saith. Manie sicke persons having neither taste nor appetite, eate notwithstanding and receive noriture. So, though in reading and hearing the word of God, and communicating at the Lords supper, thou feelest not any tast or appetite: yet in continuing, thou shalt receive some noriture for thy soule. And if it seemeth to thee that thou forgettest by and by, that which thou hast read or heard, practise for thy soule that which thou dooest for thy bodie: because the meates digest and abide not in the [G1v] bodie, thou returnest to eate meat again everie day: So be thou so much more diligent to heare and reade the word, and to communicate at the holie supper without leesing

---

[84] The 4. temtation, because of the little increas of grace by the exercises of religion.

[85] Mat. 13.19.

[86] Psalm. 119.103.

[87] Psal. 19.11.

anie one meale for thy soule, when GOD offereth it thee. And as the corporall meate though it passe away: yet there remaineth alwaies some noriture for the bodie: so shall this spiritual meate be to thy soule. Yea it may be that at one sermon thou shalt heare and remember one sentence, which shall serve thee, as it were, for a passeport, a ladder or wings at thy neede to conduct thee by, and by comforting and strengthening thee, to lift thee up into heaven. If then, when thou goest to reade or heare the word of God, or to communicate at the Lords supper, thou praiest to God (as thou oughtest daylie to do) that he will give thee his spirit, that thou maiest profite: and so doest continue constantlie in these spirituall exercises. This disposition, this holy affection and obedience shal serve thee for sure testimonies of thine [G2^r 42] adoption, and thou shalt without doubt, feele increase of the graces of God.

Finally, there are some, who having had[88] lively feelings of their faith with comfort and joy in their consciences, walking besides in the feare of God, are afterwards greatlie troubled, when these graces seem to be dead in them, falling into doubt and mistrust of their salvation, or into crimes and sinnes too unworthie the children of God. For satan hereby indevoureth to perswade them, either that they never had the true faith, or that God hath cast them off, taking from them the gifts and graces of his holie spirit: but both the one and the other conclusion is as false, as the author of them is a great lier. And indeede, if the trees which have flourished and borne their fruite in sommer, are in winter without fruite, without leaves, yea and without apparance of life: dooth it followe therefore either that they had not life in sommer, or that they are dead in the winter. When men go to bed, they rake up the fire which did [G2^v] burne: if thou marke it verie neere, there is no apparance either of heate, nor of brightnes: dooth it followe therfore, that there had been no fire, or that it is then quenched or dead. Contrariwise, having been covered over night, men kindle againe in the morning the same fire that was hid and covered: and the trees that seemed to be dead in the winter, flourish and beare fruite a while after. If thou seest a drunken man, not having for a time the use of reason, nor anie feeling of it, wilt thou say therefore, that he never had a reasonable soule, or that having had it, it is now dead? Abide a fewe houres and thou shalt be convict of the contrarie. And so of that, that thou hast not presentlie the feeling or effects and fruites of faith, can it followe that thou never hast had them, or that having had them, thou hast lost[89] them? When S. *Peter* renounced Jesus Christ three times, cursing himselfe, was his faith quenched? On the contrarie,

---

[88] The fift temptation by the interruption of the graces of God.
[89] Matt. 26.74

Jesus Christ having praied to[90] God that his faith should not faile, [G3r 43] and being without doubt heard, faith remained in him, but verie weake and sore beaten, but not destroyed nor quenched.[91] *David* having committed adulterie and murther, acknowledged his sinnes and offences, praying to God that he would not take his holie spirit from him. Then he had not lost it, rather it abode in him but as a fire covered with ashes so as it is said; without having anie feeling of it to keepe him from such a headlong fall. Faith then may bee in a man without kindling: and being kindled, it is not out, although it be not perceived for a time. Yea, but (wilt thou say) the Apostle to the *Hebrues* sheweth that there[92] be some, who having been lightened, having tasted the heavenlie gift, having been partakers of the holie ghost, and tasted the good word of God, and the power of the world to come, fall backe and leese these graces, yea without hope ever to recover them againe. What assurance then can I have that faith abideth in me, and that GOD will yet make me to [G3v] feele it hereafter? For as he hath shewed mercie unto *David*, and to Saint *Peter*; so dooth hee exercise his just judgements upon other, as upon those of whome the Apostle spake before. Wee denie not but that there bee reprobates that are greatlie lightened in the knowledge of the mysteries of salvation (which the Apostle termeth here to bee partakers of the holie ghost) and yet that such apprehensions, tastings and feelings as he proposeth followe not thereof. For, reading or hearing the testimonies and representations of the mercies of God toward his Church, of the love of Jesus Christ towards his elect, and of the excellencie and felicitie of eternall life, they conceave these things in their understanding, and for the greatnes of them, they are after a sort moved: and when they talke of them, they seeme to be partakers of them. But the difference that there is betweene them and the children of God, lieth chieflie in this, that the apprehensions and feelings of the reprobat [G4r 44] are such, as a man may have in the reading or telling of an historie, which toucheth us nothing at all: but the feelings of the children of God are as of a matter that toucheth themselves.

Let us consider for example the historie of *Joseph*. Who is hee that reading attentivelie, how *Joseph* was sold[93] of his brethren, carried into *Ægypt,* put in prison: and the sorrowe that[94] *Jacob* had, understanding that he was devoured of a wilde beast, that would not bee mooved with

---

[90] Luk. 22.31
[91] Psal. 51.
[92] Heb. 6 4,5,6.
[93] Gen. 37.
[94] Gen. 39.

compassion towardes *Joseph* and *Jacob*? Who is hee that reading how *Joseph* beeing[95] able to containe himselfe no longer, made himselfe knowne to his brethren, and how weeping and crying out hee saide unto them: I am *Joseph*, is my father yet alive, and causing them to come neere unto him, said, I am *Joseph* your brother whom ye sold, but be not sorie. Shew to my father al my glorie: Then throwing himselfe upon the neck of *Benjamin* his brother, he wept, and in like manner *Benjamin* [G4v] wept upon his necke: after kissing all his brethren hee wept uppon them. Who is he, I say, which is not touched and weepeth not with them? But because this is a historie of the fact of an other, these motions and feelings soon passe away, so as having turned the leafe or talked of another matter, all these feelings are vanished and gone. So is the feeling of the reprobate, hearing or reading the testimonies of so great a mercie of God towards men, and of the greatnes of the happines of the kingdome of heaven: The understanding and apprehension of these things, causeth some motions or feelings in them, as the Apostle saith. But for as much as these good things appertaine not unto them, neither do the feelings that they have, take anie seate or roote in their hearts, but are easilie quenched and vanish away. On the contrary, the feeling that the children of God have, is, as of the good things that appertaine unto them, and therefore it may well bee colde and drowsie, but not die. As also the [G5r 45] feelings that *Joseph* and his brethren had were such, as although they had them not when they slept, yet when they awaked they returned againe. And although that by the death of their father, they were (as it were) interrupted: yet the benefite and the comfort abode by them still. Following this that is above said, we say boldlie, that what feelings, what illuminations or apprehensions so ever the reprobate have: so it is that they never feele the holie ghost in them, giving them testimonie that they are the children of God. For according to this testimonie, they should be, and should abide the children of God: seeing the holie ghost can neither deceive nor lie. As also after that God hath made us once feele by the testimonie of his holie spirit that wee are his children, wee are certaine that wee cannot perish, but that wee are indeed, and shall continue the children of God. For it is the testimonie and revelation of the spirit of trueth. Also he that giveth[96] faith, doth not change: and [G5v] therefore[97] his gifts are without repentance. The[98] second difference may bee taken from this word, tast, which the Apostle useth: To

[95] Gen. 45.
[96] Mal. 3.6.
[97] Ro. 11.29.
[98] Heb. 6.4.

wete, that the reprobate are like to him who having tasted a good peece of wine, making shewe as if he would buy it, understanding the price, and not willing to give so much, leaveth it there, without buying or drinking of it any more. So the reprobate having tasted the heavenlie good things, finding them good, and praising them exceedingly, after they understand the price, that is, that they must renounce themselves, and beare the crosse of Christ, to goe to take possession of the kingdome of heaven, which he hath purchased for them with his precious bloud. They will none of it at this price, and so renounce these good things without drinking or injoying them. But the children of God on the other side, having never so little a taste of these heavenlie treasures, desire in such sort to have the enjoying of them, that they make resolution to forsake all, to injoye it. [G6^{r} 46] We will adde this third reason: That as those that have their stomackes charged with evill humours, cease not to eate sometimes for all that, yea and to find tast in some good meates, but are constrained after (through the evill disposition of their stomacke) to cast it up againe and to vomit: So some reprobates having within them an evill conscience, may well taste the good heavenlie gifts, but this evil conscience, not being able to agree with the true and sure faith of the hart, stoppeth, that these gifts take no root to fructifie to salvation, so that finallie they cast it off, or let it wither and come to nothing. And this reason with those before, are the principall causes, for the which many, that seemed to bee the children of God, do revolt, as we will shew hereafter more at large. On the contrarie, those who have faith, are assured, that though the graces of the holy ghost are often weak in them, and like fire covered with ashes, and trees in the winter, yet it can never come to nought or die: rather they recover strength [G6^{v}] at the last, whereby they are certaine to be, and to continue the children of GOD, and heires of everlasting life. Furthermore, let us remember that these foule and grosse faults of *David* and of S. *Peter*, and of others are set before us, first that they should bee to us as a mirrour of the fragilitie of man, to acknowledge, that if we be exempted, it is by the grace of our God. Secondlie, that wee should so much the more stand uppon our garde. As if in walking thou shouldest see him fall that goeth before thee, thou goest not to fall with him, but thou art to be so much the more circumspect that thou fall not, as he did. Thirdlie, that understanding that faith abideth in them (although very weake and feeble) thou maiest take courage, beleeving certainlie that faith which was once given thee, cannot bee quenched nor die. And therefore continue in assurance that thou art the child of God, raising up thy selfe by their example, and resolving with thy selfe to walke constantlie as the child of God in true [G7r 47] holines[99] and righteousnes before him all the daies of thy life. See how wee ought to bee resolved, that although the markes, feelings and testimonies of our adoption set forth here above, be in us but small and weake, and accompanied with great infirmities and conflicts: yet wee may and ought to assure our selves that these marks are truelie in us, and that therefore wee are certainlie the children of God, and inheritours of everlasting life.

[99] Luke 1.75.

That the Apostacie and revolt of some having made profession of the true religion, ought not to make us call in doubt neither our religion nor our adoption.

CAP. 5.

WE have understood here before how we may and ought to resist the doubts of our adoption, proceeding from our selves. Now, we must shewe how wee may overcome the temptations which come from others. There are two things [G7v] principallie, which trouble the consciences of many, to make them doubt whether they be the children of God, and in the way of salvation and of eternall life, or no. First, the horrible offence or stumbling blocke of those which abandon this church, renouncing the doctrine of it, and returning to the puddle of idolatrie: and speciallie when any persons having sometimes held any honorable place in the Church do revolt, and become persecutors of the doctrine which they have before taught and maintained. For thereof the divell gathereth two consequences, no lesse daungerous than false: either that our Church is not the true Church, and so that we are not the children of God: or that there is no assurance of perseverance in the faith, and consequently no certaintie of being the children of God, which have had and borne in aparance the markes of adoption. The other offence consisteth in the grievous and long afflictions which we indure: for the prosperitie of the wicked, deriding our miseries, and the apprehension of our own [G8r 48] troubles, give occasion to doubt whether God care for us, or whither he love us or no. And this ordinarie condition to those that make profession of our religion, causeth many to condemne it, and have it in detestation, as the mother and nurse of al calamities. As touching the I.[1] point, concerning those that revolt, it is a small stumbling block to trouble us: for this was foretold us, and it is a disease wherwith the church hath alwaies bin afflicted. Many shall be called, saith Jesus Christ, but few chosen. And[2] the parable of the seed falling in divers sorts of earth sheweth, that with much a doo the 4. part of those that shal[3] heare and professe the Gospel, shall continue to the end. S. *Paule* hath foretold[4] expreslie, that in the latter times many shal fall from the faith. And he advertiseth[5] the *Ephe.* that even from among themselves there should rise up men that should teach

---

[1] Of the certaintie of the doctrine notwithstanding the revolts.

[2] Matt. 20.16

[3] Matth. 13.

[4] 1. Tim. 4.1.

[5] Act. 20.30.

perverse things. And[6] the *Cor.* that there shall be in the church not only divisions, but also heresies.[7] Saint *Peter* speaketh yet more largelie: As there hath been (saith he) false prophets among the people [G8v] of Israel, so shal there be false teachers amongst you, which shall secretlie bring in damnable errours, and manie shal follow their damnable waies, by whom the way of trueth shall bee blasphemed. Now, we must thinke the accomplishing of such prophecies so much the lesse strange, because such hath bin the condition of the church of[8] God at all times. What revolt was there in the house of God before the flood, eight persons onlie being found saved in the Arke, and yet amongst them one hypocrite, who after was cast[9] off and accursed. Now, the church of God being inlarged in the posteritie of *Sem*, againe there was seene such a revolt, that the church of God was[10] onlie found in the familie of *Abraham,* himselfe being pulled out of idolatrie. In the time of *Elias* the revolt[11] was so great in *Israel*, that hee thought he had bin left alone. At the comming of our Lord Jesus Christ, the Apostacie was so generall, that almost all the Church, at the least the principal members of it, lift up [H1r 49] themselves against the Sonne of G O D, and crucified him. When Jesus Christ had gathered manie Disciples, he was forsaken[12] of the most part of them: yea, *Judas* also the Apostle fell from him, sold him,[13] and betraied him. Jesus Christ being[14] taken prisoner by his enemies, all his[15] Apostles fled away and forsooke him. Saint *Peter* himselfe denied him thrice. Saint *Paule* complaineth, that all they[16] of *Asia* had revolted, And saieth in an other place, that all had forsaken him. He noteth *Alexander* the Copper Smith, *Hymenæus* and others, who having[17] beene the chiefe members of the Church, were become heretikes, and enemies of the truth. Now it is the same Church, and we must no more be astonished at such revolts, than at a man having rheums all his life (whereby hee casteth out of his bodie aboundance of humours) that shoulde continue in the same disease still even in his olde age:

---

[6] 1. Cor. 11.19.
[7] 2. Pet. 2.1.
[8] Gen. 6.
[9] Gen. 9.25.
[10] Gen. 12.
[11] 1. Reg. 19.10.
[12] John. 6.66
[13] Mat. 26.14 Mat. 26.65
[14] Mat. 26.69
[15] 2. Tim. 1.15
[16] 2. Tim. 4.16
[17] 2. Tim 4.14

Herein rather we ought to acknowlege the holines of God, wherewith also he would his Church should be adorned. For he purgeth his Church, not being [H1v] able to indure that hipocrits should any long time keepe the place and title of his children aproching to his Majestie. And hereunto we may aplie that which *Moses* saith, when he saw the fire had devoured[18] *Nadab* and *Abihu* the sonnes of *Aaron*, for offering before the Lorde strange fire: This is it which the Lorde hath spoken, saying; I will be sanctified in those that approch unto me, and will bee glorified in the presence of all the people: shewing therby, that the nearer men approch unto him by honorable offices in his church, and profession of his worde, so much the lesse will hee suffer their corruptions, but punisheth them more sharply, to the end, that as the nearer the peece of wax approcheth to the fire, so much the more the heat of it appeareth in melting it. In like maner the holines of God may better be knowne in the revolt of hypocrites approching unto him, and so he may be the more glorified of the people in such judgements. This is also the cause why manie, who before they had the knowledge of the gospell, seemed in outward apparance [H2r 50] very good people. Afterward being joined to the church, become wicked and dissolute in their lives, and very persecutors. It is the vengeance of god that pursueth them, punishing their ingratitude, their love of the world and of the flesh, which they brought and nourished in the church, and the contempt of the honor that God did them, when he made them aproch unto him, receiving them into his house, speaking to them by the preaching of his word, and presenting unto them upon his holy Table, his own Sonne Jesus Christ for the foode of their soules. So farre off is it then, that we should be troubled for such revolts, that on the contrary, seeing that they are the vengeances of GOD, wee ought so much the more to feare, and to continue the more constantly and holily in the church of GOD. And indeede if wee did at this[19] day see *David* execute that protestation which hee did make of purging his house from vicious and wicked persons, would we (thinke you) depart from it, doubting of the holinesse of it? Shall we not rather be confirmed to [H2v] tarrie there stil, desiring to live holilie? But more, what damage receiveth the Church in such revolts? The glorie of it before God consisteth not properlie in the greatnesse of the number, but in the holinesse of them. The health of a man consisteth not in the abundance of humors, which will cause some deadlie disease at the last: for even they that are laden with them, take medicines to purge them,

---

[18] Levit. 10.3

[19] Psal. 101.

that they might bee the more[20] whole. This is it which God, having spoken of his Church of *Israel*, that her silver was turned into drosse, and her wine mingled with water, added for a great benefit, that he would take cleane away al her scomme, and remove al her lead from her: and that having restored the Judges and Counsellers, so as they had bene at the beginning, it shoulde be called the righteous and faithful Citie. Experience sheweth, that in the prosperitie and peace of the church many thrust in themselves, ful of avarice, ambition, pride, and of other corruptions and vanities; to be short it hapneth even as in a sweet and rainie season, that many weeds [H3r 51] come up amongest the good hearbes, which should bee choaked of them, if the Gardeiner pulled them not out. Then, when such people departe from the Church, returning to their vomit, it is as if God gave a purgation to it, to make it more holy, and more acceptable to her bridegrome. Let us further consider the causes of revoltes. If this hapned then when the Church was in peace and prosperitie, it shold seeme there were more occasion to call into dout our doctrine: But it is in the time of persecution, that these revolts are seen; and so, it is feare to leese their goods, their dignities, their parents, their country, their lives, that causeth them to revolt. It is then the flesh, it is the world, it is the mistrust of God, and not the allowing of the Papisticall doctrine, that maketh them to change[21] their religion. As also S. *Paule* saith, that *Demas* had forsaken him, having loved this present worlde. And indeed did this miserable *John Haren* revolt during the prosperous estate of the towne of *Bruges*, wherein he was minister? By no meanes. But perceiving the [H3v] danger, although he might yet have exercised his ministerie, he began to seeke the meanes as a hireling, to forsake his flocke. He knoweth what letters I writ unto him, reproving his slothfulnes, his crafts and evill conscience in the reasons which he put forth, to have some colour to withdraw himself. He knoweth also what reproofes he had receyved by the letters of others, that he should not defile his ministerie in intermedling so ernestly in the matters of war and of policie. After the Towne of *Bruges* was rendred to the enemy, he withdrew him self into *Zeland* and *Holand*. Where perceiving that hee began (as good reason was) for many considerations to bee suspected in our churches, and in no reputation, he gote him out of the countrie. So feeling in his conscience small apparance to be established in his Ministery againe, having no hope of preferment in any other vocation, and being pursued by the just judgement of God falling upon evil consciences; he revolted, thinking happilie that hee should receive some re-

---

[20] Esay. 1.22

[21] 2. Tim. 4.10

compence for the offence that [H4r 52] he had offered against the holie Ministerie, and at the least to enter againe into the possession of his goods. This then is not the chaunging of doctrine, which mooved him, but (as wee have saide) it is the flesh, and the world: it is envie that maketh the Monke. It is ambition the mother of heresie, as saint *Augustine* sayth: It is an evill conscience, the rocke that maketh the shippewracke[22] of Faith, as Saint *Paule* sayth, which hath made him to chaunge his profession. To be short, G O D could no longer suffer such an hypocrite in his church, nor such a filth in his holie temple: hee woulde bee sanctified in taking vengeance upon him, who so inordinately approched unto him. Hee hath set him foorth for an example of his judgements, that those that make profession of Religion, and chieflie the Ministers of the worde, may study more and more to walke with a good conscience to keepe themselves in their vocation, to renounce the passions of the flesh, and the illusions of the world, and so with fervent praiers to continue [H4v] constantly in the grace of the Lorde. Furthermore, let him make as manie shewes as he wil, let him sweare, let him lift up his hands, and his eies to heaven, let him weare a great paire of beads, let him goe oft and devoutlie to the masse; yet shall hee not easily make the Jesuites (who are cunninger than he) to beleve, that hee dooth it indeede and from his heart. For those who among them have any little more wit than the common sort, understand well enough if they wold confesse it, that the change of the holy Supper into the Masse, the worshipping of bread in it, the fiery purgatory after death, the opinion of meriting paradise by workes, specially those of supererogation; the setting foorth of God the father, who is an invisible and eternal spirit, under the figure of an old man: the worshipping of images, the invocation of Saints departed, candles lighted at noone dayes, and borne in procession, the great beads hanging at their neckes, and other such idolatries and superstitions, are either so abhominable or so manifestly contrary to the word of [H5r 53] God, yea, or so absurd, that he that hath once knowne them by the light of the gospell can never allow them in his heart. But be it, that by the inchantment of satan, and judgement of God, he were indeed become a Papist, and that S. *Paule* himself shuld revolt, preaching another gospell; we ought, as he himselfe protesteth,[23] to holde him accursed, and not to be mooved to doubt of our faith. For our religion and faith is not founded upon the constancie or stedfastnesse of men, but upon the truth of our God, and uppon the testimonie of the holy Ghost in our hearts. If men be unfaithfull, saith S.[24]

[22] 1. Tim. 1.19
[23] Gal. 1.
[24] 2. Ti. 2.13.

Paule, he remaineth notwithstanding faithfull, and can not denie himselfe. When Jesus Christ forsaken of his Disciples, should aske us, if wee also would leave him: we are taught to answer with the[25] Apostles; Lord, whether shall wee goe, thou hast the words of eternall life. The faithfull Pastor must (without being astonished at the revolt of manie) say[26] with *Esai,* Behold I and my children which god hath given me, are for signes and wonders. The horrible and fearfull [H5v] vengeance, which waighteth on, and followeth these cursed apostates at the verie heeles, should make us to tremble, and to resolve to renounce all that is uppon the earth, that we may get and hold fast all that is in heaven: and so leaving these poore revolters to the judgement of God, to cast our eyes uppon those, who even in our time have indured so constantlie the losse of their goods, reproaches, prisons: to be short, who chearfullie have entered into the flaming fire, and by cruell death mounted into the kingdome of heaven; to the ende that such autentique seales of the heavenlie doctrine, may confirme our hearts to continue constantlie, and chearfullie to follow their steps, and so be their companions in[27] glorie. We ought not to be troubled at these revoltes, as if we were not assured to continue in the faith, whereby also it shall come to passe, that wee shall be in doubt whether we are, or shal continue the Children of G O D. For as the markes of our adoption set foorth here before are of two sorts: the one inward before God, and the other outward [H6r 54] before men: they which have the inward markes, which consist in the testimonie of the holy Ghost in our hearts, in the peace of our consciences, and in the holy desire of our soules, feele these graces, which assureth them that they are the children of G O D, chosen to eternal life: yea more certainly than we are assured by the light of the Sunne that we see, and by the heat that we feele, that the Sun shineth. And in deed they have the white stone, whereof mention is made[28] in the revelation, and in that stone a new name of the childe of god written, which none can know but he that receiveth it. *The world,* saith Christ, *cannot receive the spirit of truth, because it hath not seen*[29] *him, neither hath known him: but ye know him,* saith hee to his Apostles, *for hee abideth with you, and shall be in you.* As touching the outwarde marke of beeing a member of the visible Church, it is also verie certaine in respect of God, inasmuch as speaking to us, and sealing his words by the sacraments, he neither wil, nor can deceive or lie. But if men hearing his word, and com-

---

[25] Joh. 6.67.

[26] Esai. 8.18.

[27] Of the assurance of our adoption, notwithstanding the revolts.

[28] Reve. 2.17.

[29] Joh. 14.17.

municating [H6v] at the Sacraments, reject in their hearts the spirituall graces which are offered unto them, and so abide unfaithfull, and wicked within (when notwithstanding they are helde for faithfull and the children of god, because of the outward profession:) it is no mervaile if God at the last do discover them, and cast them off: shewing therin, that they wer never his. And[30] this is it that S. *John* saith of such; They went out from amongst us, but they were not of us; for if they had bin of us, they would have tarried with us. But this is, that it might appeare that all are not of us. They that are once grafted in Christ, can not perish: for the giftes of God[31] are without repentance. But everie[32] plant, saith Jesus Christ, which my father hath not planted, shall bee pulled up.[33] The parable of the seede falling into divers sortes of earth, teacheth us two points to this purpose. First, that manie shal heare the gospel, but without frute. Secondlie, that it shall be their own falt. For if entring into the Church, they bring their cares and love to the world, without having will to forsake them, so [H7r 55] as it like thornes, choake the good seede of[34] the word. And so having no moisture of the grace of God, they wither at the first sunne of persecution; a man may see the cause of their revolte, to wete, because they were not the children of God. Saint *Paule* having said, that God knoweth who are his, addeth: and whosoever calleth upon the name of Christ, let him depart from all iniquitie: shewing thereby, that if there bee anie which joyne themselves to the Church, calling upon the name of Christ, and doo not depart from iniquity; they discover thereby that God never tooke them for his. Which thing is good to be noted. For manie thinke, that to be of our Church nedeth nothing, but to change the masse to the preaching, and to the communicating at the Lords supper. And when they understand, that to be the childe of God, is required to renounce themselves to leave covetousnes, ambition, drunkennesse, the world, and all pompes: to be short, that they must put off the olde man, and be a new creature: not beeing disposed to do this, they leave the [H7v] preaching, and returne to the Masse. Now be these the children of God that revolt, that they should make those that are in deed and continue to doubt? Nay, rather they are the children of the world, who having brought the world in with them, have also carried the world away with them. They therefore that have once beleeved, who also beleeving, feele a desire to live according unto god, are assured that they cannot perish. He

[30] 1. Joh. 2.19

[31] Ro. 11.29.

[32] Matt. 15.13

[33] Matt. 13.

[34] 2. Tim. 2.19.

that beginneth[35] this good work in them, wil accomplish it, even unto the day of christ. And[36] to this purpose saith S. *Augustine* verie wel, He which made us good, maketh us also to persever in goodnes: but they that fal and perish, were not of the number of the predestinate. It remaineth, that considering in the fall of hipocrites, the double mercie of god toward us. First, that he hath received us into the number of his children. Secondly, that he will continue this grace towards us even to the ende: there remaineth, I say, that we feele our selves double bound to practise the exhortation of S. *Paule*, beseeching us by the mercies of God, to [H8^r 56] offer[37] our selves a living sacrifice, holy and pleasing to God, and not to be fashioned like this wicked world: but rather endevouring to this, that being transformed by the renuing of our understanding, we may approove and follow, the good and perfect will of God. And let us remember[38] that which S. *John* saith, That they that have hope to live with Jesus Christ, and to see him as hee is, do purifie themselves as he is pure.

[35] Phil. 1.6.
[36] Aug. de correct. and gra. ca. 12. to. 7.
[37] Rom. 12.1.
[38] 1. John 3.3.

That afflictions ought not to make us to doubt of our adoption, but rather confirme us.

CHAP. 6.

LET us now come to that stumbling blocke and trouble, that proceedeth from our afflictions. What apparaunce is there (saieth the flesh) that wee are the Children of GOD? Our goods are violently taken from us, our possessions are confiscate, and our Offices and Estates are taken away. [H8v] We are driven out of our Countrey, yea from Countrey to Countrey like vagabonds: wee are hated of father and mother, and of our other kinsfolk and frends: we are drawen and kept in prison: wee are derided and brought into extreame calamities and miseries: we are as sheepe of the shambles, apointed to the sword, to the gallowes and to the fire: To bee short, wee see nothing but the signes of the wrath and the curse of God upon us. And that which more is, the Church which wee have said was the kingdome of Christ, and the house of God, how is it assailed by the mightie men of this world? whome also we see to come to the end of their enterprises, to oppresse, tread under foote, rent and scatter this Church, exercising al crueltie against it, as hungrie wolves upon a flock of sheep, forsaken of their shepheard. They triumph in their victories, and wee hang down the head and weep, bowing down our necks under the yoke of afflictions. They increase in riches, and we consume in povertie: they are advaunced to honours and dignities, and we are despised [I1r 57] as rebels, and wicked and seditious people. See what the flesh saith: and yet these are but discourses and complaints of great ignoraunce or infirmitie. For what is that which troubleth and offendeth us in this condition and estate. Even that whereby wee ought rather to be confirmed, in the assuraunce that wee are the children of GOD, and indeede happie. First, if GOD had promised to entreate his Children in this worlde delicatelie, and to set them up in riches and high estate, wee might have some occasion to doubt whether wee were the Children of GOD, all calamities and afflictions quite contrarie falling upon us. But seeing it is so, that the Holie Ghost hath foretolde us both often and manifestlie, that the children of GOD shoulde bee afflicted, and that those that woulde live faithfullie in the feare of GOD in Christ, shall suffer persecution;[1] this persecution and affliction ought rather to serve us for a signe that wee are the children of GOD.

Moreover, if the most excellent [I1v] servants and children of GOD have alwayes beene most afflicted. Afflictions ought not to make us doubt

---

[1] 2. Tim. 3 12

of our adoption and salvation, except wee will call in doubt the salvation and felicitie of those, whom wee confesse to bee the verie blessed children of G O D: Especiallie, if afflictions do serve greatlie to pull our hearts from the Earth, and to lift them up into Heaven, to purifie our faith as golde in the fire, and to fashion us into a true obedience of God. Then the utility and profite which commeth unto us thereby, ought to serve us for a sufficient proofe, that in afflictions G O D sheweth himselfe to be our father, having care of our welfare and salvation. And yet more, seeing the taking awaie of our goods temporall, shall bring us foorth an eternall treasure in Heaven, the mockeries and reproches shall bee turned unto glorie before G O D, the teares into joy, our sufferings into comfortes: Who is hee that will not confesse, that such afflictions proceede from the verie love of G O D towards [I2r 58] us? To be short, seeing that G O D, strengthening us in the middest of the fires of tribulations, sheweth in our infirmitie his might and bountie, and seeing (when wee suffer for his name) hee maketh us witnesses of his trueth: our afflictions are (as it were) stages from whence he maketh his own glory to shine, and giveth increase unto ours. So farre off is it then, that beeing afflicted, wee shoulde bee troubled or offended, that contrariwise those troubles ought to serve us for an assurance, that we are the children of G O D: whereof that wee may bee the better resolved, we wil treate of these points more at large.

[I2v] *That the afflictions that happen unto us, have beene foretolde, and therefore they ought to confirme us in the assurance of our adoption.*

CAP. 7.

THE holie Ghost hath at all times foretold and testified by sundry and manifest sentences, that the children of God shoulde be persecuted and afflicted in this life, yea, in such sort, as the first afflictions shoulde bee but the beginnings of greater; and that passing one evill, they shoulde prepare themselves to indure others that should followe as the waves in[1] the Sea. GOD from the beginning[2] of the worlde, having pronounced, that hee woulde put enmitie betweene the seede of the woman and the seede of the Serpent, hath advertised us, that as long as there shalbe devils in the world, and children of God, they must understand, that such enemies will [I3r 59] imploy all their strength and means to persecute them: As this also is represented in the[3] *Revelation* in that which is said by S. *John*, that the olde serpent not being able to devoure the Sonne of GOD, nor the body of the church, was very angry, and went to make war with the rest of her seede which kept the commaundements of God, and which had the testimonie of Jesus Christ. Likewise God having promised seede unto *Abraham*, and added, that it shoulde bee as the Starres[4] of the Heaven. He tolde him by and by, that it shoulde bee afflicted, saying: Knowe thou for a certayne, that thy seede shall dwell and serve in a Land that is not their owne, and shal be afflicted foure hundred yeeres. And that which is more, hee confirmeth this advertisement by a vision or notable signe, commaunding him to divide in peeces an heifar, a ramme, a hee goate, a turtle, and a pigeon; and sending a flight of Birdes upon the dead carcases cut in peeces: he shewed him, that his seede (by the greatnesse of afflictions) should be like unto dead [I3v] carcases cut in peeces, and exposed for a pray unto the Birdes. *David* in a few wordes sheweth this condition to be common to all the children of GOD, saying,[5] that the afflictions of the righteous are manie. And in howe manie sortes, and in how many places have the Prophetes foretolde of the afflictions that came upon the tenne tribes of *Israel* carried after captives into *Assyria*? In like manner of the kingdome of *Juda*, the destruction of the Temple, the sacking of the Citie, the massacre

---

[1] Gen. 3.15

[2] Prophecies of the olde testament.

[3] Reve. 12

[4] Gen. 15.13

[5] Psal. 34.20

of a great part of the people, and the captivitie of the rest, by the space of[6] seaventie yeares in *Babylon*. Above all, Jesus Christ, who is the wisedome of[7] G O D, how often hath hee foretolde the afflictions of his faithfull servants and members of his body? Beholde (saith he) to his Apostles, I send you as Sheepe amongest Wolves. Yee shall bee delivered unto the Consistories, and whipped in the Synagogues. Yee shall bee hated of all men for my names sake. If they have called the Master of the house Beelzebub, how [I4r 60] much more his servauntes. I am not come to bring peace upon the Earth, but[8] a Sworde. If anie will followe mee, let him renounce him selfe, and take up his Crosse and followe mee. They shall deliver you to bee punished, and[9] shall slay you. If they have Persecuted mee, they will also persecute you.[10] Againe, Verelie, verelie I saie unto you, that yee shall weepe and lament, and the worlde shall rejoyce. Yea, hee compareth the faithfull unto[11] a Woman which travaileth of childe. True it is, that the wicked are also tormented in their course. But[12] Judgement sayeth Saint *Peter*, must beginne at the house of G O D. And of this judgement it is that Saint *Paule*[13] dooth speake, saying: That wee are ordayned to bee afflicted, which hee dooth confirme by a Sentence[14] full of comforte, saying: That by manie tribulations wee must enter into the Kingdome of Heaven. Agayne,[15] all they that will live godlie in Christ, must suffer persecution. But above al, that is to be noted that hee [I4v] saide[16] in an other place: I rejoyce, and fill up in my selfe that which wanted of the sufferings of Christ: meaning by Christ, all the faithfull, with their head, and shewing, that GOD hath ordained a certain measure of passions for this Christ, and consequently to every one of his members his portion, which hee must suffer, to accomplish the passions of Christ. Now this is not without great reason, that the Holie Ghost hath so carefully, and in so many sortes and manners foretolde, that the children of G O D shoulde bee afflicted. It is to this ende, as Jesus Christ[17] him selfe teacheth his Apostles, that we

---

[6] Prophecies of the newe testament.
[7] Mat. 10.16
[8] Mat. 16.24
[9] Mat. 24.9
[10] Jhon 16.2
[11] Jho. 16.21
[12] 1. Pet. 4.17
[13] 2. Thes. 3.7
[14] Act. 14 22
[15] 2. Tim. 3.12
[16] Col. 1.24.
[17] Jhon 16.1.

...en we see the faithful to be spoiled,
...d murthered, that then we should re-
...nd that it commeth not to passe by
...ute will of men that we are afflicted.
...father, and that this is the entertain-
...servants and children. [I5r 61] But our
...behalfe. For as the *Jewes* in olde time,
...n the world, were offended at his hu-
...e crosse of Jesus Christ, and therefore
... even so our flesh at this day doth still
...ble to their desires, and a kingdome of
...e now why it is troubled and offended,
...ornes, bearing his crosse uppon his shoul-
...hat will be the children of God with him.
...that which *Esai* foretold of the *Messias*,
...e out of a drie ground, That he shuld have
...e to be desired, That he should be despised
...licted and accustomed to sorowes, that men
...so much should he be contemned; That hee
...rie, afflicted, and led to the slaughter as a
...e shuld be numbred among the transgressors.
...Behold thy king commeth to[19] thee humble,
...which *Daniel* saieth, That the Christ[20] should
... If, I say, the Jewes had well weighed these
...e these, touching the abasement and afflictions
...hey would have rejected him, that on the con-
...en by the accomplishment of those thinges that
... was indeede the *Messias* promised. In like man-
...editate on that which the holie Ghost hath fore
...nd that wee must[21] be conformable unto the
...ie with him: the tribulations which accompanie
..., shoulde bee unto us signes and testimonies, that
...Children of God.
...ewed unto the Shepards the nativitie of Jesus
...ewe unto you great joy, that this day is borne to
...of *David*, which is Christ the Lord: Hee addeth,

...rapped in swaddeling
...rds (beeing come to
...ble pallaice, and the
...had just occasion to
...eing with the signe
...re estate in a maun-
... to beleeve, that it

...word, that hee hath
...by the testimonie
...g also given us the
...of his Church: hee
...our adoption, that
...d did make much
...dout of the word
...e accomplishment
...ch the more con-
...but appertaine to
...stles, saying;[23] If
...but nowe because
...u. If we aske the
...of the right way)
...we wil leave the
...d finding in that
... for a signe, wee
...e right way.
...thorough manie
...n,[25] and that the
...e finde the way
...dge that we are
...ght therfore to
...re the Children

you shall have these signes, yee shall finde the childe w cloathes, and laid in a maunger. Now, if these shephea *Bethlehem,)* had found the holie Virgine in an honoura Childe in a magnificall and royall cradle, had they not doubt of the tidings of the Angell, this estate not agr that hee had given? But having found the Childe in po ger, as the Angell had foretolde, they were confirme was the *Messias*.

Even so, G O D having revealed unto us by his W chosen us to be his Children, having sealed it in us and effects of the unction of the holie Ghost: and havi markes in this, that he hath made us the members [I6v] hath foretolde, and hath also given one signe more of we shall be reproached and persecuted. If then the wor of us, loved and honoured us, we might after some sort of God, and of our election and adoption. But seeing th of that, that was foretolde us, we ought to bee so mu firmed in this assurance, that we are not of the world, our God. And this is it that Jesus Christ tolde his Ap yee were of the world, the world would love his owne: I have chosen you out of the world, the world hateth y way to goe to anie place, and that one tell us (for a signe that it is at the beginning durty and afterward full of hils, other waies which seeme straight, drie, faire and easie: an way which wee take, durte and hills foretold and given u will bee so much the more confirmed, that wee are in t

[I7r 63] So[24] the holie Ghost having foretolde, that tribulations wee must enter into the Kingdome of heave waye leading to eternall life is narrow and difficult: If w of the Gospell narrow and full of troubles, let us acknowl in the right way to the kingdom of heaven, and that we o bee so much the more confirmed in assuraunce that wee a of God.

---

[23] Joh. 15.19.
[24] Act. 14.22.
[25] Matt. 7.13.

That the Children of God have alwaies been afflicted, and yet still beloved of God.

CHAP. 8.

THis that the Holie Ghost hath fore spoken, that the condition of the Children of GOD is to bee afflicted, hath by experience been found to bee true in all ages, whether we consider the people and Church of GOD in the whole bodie, or speake of it [I7v] particularly[1] in the members of it. How long and greevously was the people of *Israel* afflicted in *Ægipt? Moses* reciteth, that their life was vexed bitterly, thorough grievous servitude, and that all the service wherein they served was tyrannous, *Pharaoh* intending to destroy them,[2] and to roote them out by travaile and excessive labour. And not so being able to come to his purpose, neither yet by the commaundement made to the midwives,[3] to slay secretly all the male children which should be borne: at the last[4] he appointed certeine of the *Ægiptians* his subjects to bee their hangmen openly. Whereby also when *Moses* was borne, his parents having hid him some time with great feare, they were at the last constrained (for the avoiding of the furie of these hangmen) to put him out into the brinke of the river, as abandoning him unto death. Could there be anie more barbarous crueltie used to anie people? And yet, did they still continue to bee grievouslie afflicted foure score yeares after the birth of Moses. So that it is not without a cause that the [I8r 64] Lord[5] called *Ægipt* the house of bondage,[6] and an iron fornace. The which also he confirmeth, appearing to *Moses* in the[7] middest of a burning bush, saying, I have seene the affliction of my people. They were not so soone in the way to depart[8] out of *Ægipt*, but they wer pursued by the Armie of *Pharaoh,* having the sea before them, and the mountaines on their sides, and so seeing present death before their eyes. Did they escape the hands of *Pharaoh* in passing over the sea on drie foote? Then they entred into the horrible and fearefull Deserts, and going three dayes through the Desertes, they found no water, the first that[9] they founde was so bit-

---

[1] Examples of the afflictions of the Church during the time of the olde testament.

[2] Exo. 1.14.

[3] Exo. 1.18

[4] Exo. 1.22.

[5] Exo. 20.2.

[6] Deut. 4.20.

[7] Exo. 3.2.

[8] Exod. 14.9.

[9] Exo. 15.22.

ter, that they coulde not drinke it; They were assayled of enemies, vexed with fierie Serpents, and inflammations unaccustomed, and wandred up and downe fortie[10] yeares in those Deserts, living by Manna and water.

In the time of the Judges, how ofte was the people of god broght under the cruell tyranie of divers enemies? Under [I8v] the raigne of *Manasses* King of *Juda*, there[11] was such persecution against the faithfull, that *Jerusalem* was filled with bloud from the one ende to the other. But above all, it was unkindlie handled both before and during the Captivitie of[12] *Babylon*. The Citie of *Jerusalem* was taken and sacked, the Temple of God spoyled,[13] burnt and destroyed. Hee that escaped the pestilence, famine, and the sword, was transported into *Babylon* among the Idolatours their Enemies, and plunged into all miseries and calamities, and that by the space of threescore[14] and tenne yeares, as it was foretolde. The Prophet *Esai* doth sufficientlie set before us their miserable estate,[15] calling the Jewes persons despised, an abhominable people, servaunts to Lordes, wormes of Jacob, the dead men[16] of Israel, people afflicted, overwhelmed[17] with tempests, without anie comfort. Are they returned out of this captivitie into *Judea*? There they were vext of their enemies: and above al, how many horrible cruelties did thei indure by *Antiochus, Herod*, and other tyrants.

[K1r 65] Let us also see what complaints the people of God make of the calamities that befell them by the *Assirians*, or (as other thinke) by this *Antiochus*, saying:[18] O God the heathen have entred into thine inheritance, they have polluted thy holie temple, and have brought Jerusalem to a heape of stones. They have given the dead bodies of thy servants for meat to the foules of the ayre, and the flesh of thy Saints to the beastes of the earth: they have shed their bloud like water on everie side of Jerusalem, and there was none to burie them. We have been a reproach to our neighbours, and a mockerie, and a derision to those that are about us.[19] Againe, Thou hast put us (O Lord) farre from thee as sheepe to be eaten, and thou hast scattered us among the heathen. Thou hast sold thy people without gaine, and doest not increase their price. Thou hast smitten

---

[10] Num. 21.6.
[11] 2. King. 21.16.
[12] 2. King. 25
[13] Jer. 39. and 52.
[14] Jer. 25.12.
[15] Esa. 46.7.
[16] Esa. 41.14.
[17] Esa. 54.11.
[18] Psalm. 79.
[19] Psalm. 44.

us downe into the place of dragons, and hast covered us with the shadowe of death. Also[20] comparing the church to a vine: wherefore (saith he) hast thou broken [K1v] downe her hedges, that all they that go by pluck of her grapes? The boare out of the wood hath destroyed it, and the wild beasts of the field have eaten it up. It is burnt with fire and cut down. To be short, we may behold the estate of the Church in these words: Let Israel[21] now say, They have often times afflicted me from my youth, they have often times vexed me. The plowers have plowed upon my backe, and made long furrowes. In like manner, after the ascension of Jesus Christ into heaven,[22] hath not the Church been, and that continuallie, persecuted, and extreamelie afflicted: as may appeare by the booke of the Acts of the Apostles, and by the Ecclesiasticall histories, in the verie which, a man may note ten general persecutions, which were kindled in al the quarters of the earth, by the publike decrees of the Emperours, besides those that were particular, which were made in divers places by the Governors, or seditions of the people. It is a horrible thing to thinke, and almost incredible, of the [K2r 66] bloud which was then shed, and of the desolations of Cities, yea and of some whole Provinces. For as the Church was then spred over all the world, so in all the kingdomes of the earth this furie of persecution was kindled. It was enough for any to confesse that they were Christians, and they should be slaine by thousands. Among other persecutions made by *Hadrian* Emperour of *Rome* in the *9.* yeare of his Empire,[23] he caused ten thousand Christians to be crucified in *Armenia. Dioclesian* and *Maximinian* having enterprised to constraine the Christians, by al[24] manner of torments and cruelties, to renounce their religion, and to sacrifice[25] to the Idols, they forced them after a fashion so furious, that in the space of 17. daies there were 30000. put to death, and as manie or more chained and carried to the mettalls, a torment resembling after a sort, the punishment of the gallies at this day. In[26] those daies such crueltie was exercised at *Trenios* uppon the river *Mosel*, that the river was red with [K2v] the bloud of the Christians beeing slaine. The booke intituled *Fasciculus temporum,* witnesseth that the Christians that were in *England*, were all put[27] to death. To bee short, whole townes were burned with their in-

---

[20] Psalm. 80.

[21] Psal. 129.

[22] Examples of the afflictions of the Church since the time of the newe testament.

[23] *Henrie of Erford.*

[24] *Oros. lib.* 7. *chap.* 25.

[25] *Ursperg.*

[26] *Vincent. in his mirrour lib.* 12. *chap.* 136.

[27] *Euse. lib.* 8. *chap.* 11.

habitants, for the hatred of Christian religion. As touching the varietie of the sorts of tormens and cruelties, the divell surmounted himselfe in devising them: Some were cut in peeces: Some were tormented with stripes of rods even to the bones: Some were cast to the Lions, to the Beares, and to the Tygers to bee devoured: Some were covered with beasts skins to be torne in peeces of wolves and doggs: Some were burned quicke: Some were broyled upon gridirons: Some were crucified: Some had their bodies dropped on with burning pitch and boyling lead: Some were drawne upon the pavement of the streetes: Some were dashed against the stones: Some were tumbled downe headlong from high places, and into rivers: Some they smothered with smoake [K3r 67] proceeding from a small fire: Some had their intrailes pearced with sharpe stakes: Some were throwne into the Lime kils: Some were slaine with the stripes of staves and lead: Some had sharpe reedes thrust betweene their nailes and their flesh: Some had red burning plates put under their armepits: Some were scorched quicke, and then sprinckled with vineger, or powdred with salt: Some were set up quicke uppon forks, and suffered to die of hunger or thirst. And those that could escape into the deserts and mountaines, either they died of hunger, or of thirst or of cold: or they were devoured of wild beasts, or slaine of theeves, or caried away slaves to the *Barbarians*. Now, although these examples ought to suffice to make us understand what the condition of the Church hath alwaies been, and so consequentlie of the children of God: we will yet notwithstanding, set forth some particular examples of those that have been the most excellent servants and children of God. *Abel* having offered [K3v] unto[28] GOD a more excellent sacrifice than *Cain*, and so receiving the testimonie that he was just, was mischievouslie and traiterouslie murthered by his brother. Among the Patriarches, let us consider the afflictions of *Jacob* beloved of GOD: After he had been long[29] time in feare of the threatnings[30] of his brother *Esau*, at the last he[31] was constrained to forsake his fathers house: Being with *Laban* his unckle,[32] he served him the space of 20. yeares, feeding his flockes, induring the cold of the night, and the heate of the day: In the meane time he received so manie injuries at the hands of his unckle, that he resolved with his wives the daughters of *Laban*, to steale away from him, and to depart without bidding him farewell. He being thus (as it were) fled, he was pursued of *Laban* provoked to anger, and determining to use him violentlie, if God (as himselfe

[28] Examples of particular members of the Church afflicted in the time of the old testament·

[29] Gen. 4.

[30] Mal. 1.2.

[31] Gen. 28.

[32] Gen. 31.

confesseth) had not forbidden him. Having escaped his hand, he fell into a newe and horrible feare,[33] for the comming and meeting [K4r 68] of his brother *Esau*, fearing (as he sheweth by the praier which he made to GOD) least he would slay both him, with[34] his wives and children. His eldest sonne committed adulterie, and that not with a straunge woman, but with his fathers owne concubine. His daughter[35] is ravished and defiled. His children prophane circumcision the sacred seale of the covenant of God, making it to serve to murther, as they did,[36] al the inhabitants of *Sichem*, who asked nothing of them but friendship. By this crueltie more than barbarous, they exposed their father, themselves, and all their house, to manifest daunger of utter rooting out by their neighbours, if GOD had not held them backe. His owne children having sold their brother *Joseph*, they made[37] their father beleeve that he was devoured of wild beasts. Being pressed with famine, he sent his sonnes into *Ægypt* to get corne: whereby *Simeon*[38] being kept prisoner, he understood that there was no hope of his deliverie, but in sending his yongest [K4v] sonne *Benjamin:* which was, as it were, to take away his soule. What manner of life then is this of the good Patriarch, but continuall anguishes and afflictions, as himselfe confesseth, saying[39] unto *Pharao*, that the daies of his pilgrimage were fewe and evill? Among the Prophets let us take *Moses*, to whome GOD shewed himselfe more familiarlie. When he was yet a little infant, he was put foorth and abandoned[40] unto death: beeing after come to the age of fortie yeares, and feeling that God had ordained him to[41] deliver his people *Israel*, he began to exercise his vocation in slaying the *Ægyptian*: whereupon he was constrained to forsake the Court of *Pharao*, and to flie. And withdrawing him selfe into the land of *Madian*, he served *Jethro*, feeding his sheepe the space of fortie yeares: He, I say, that was taken for the sonne of *Pharaos* daughter, that might have enjoyed the riches and pleasures of *Ægypt*. Being after returned into *Ægypt* by the commandement of GOD, to deliver the [K5r 69] people of *Israel*, incontinently so soon as he began to exercise his charge in speaking to *Pharao*, the *Israelites* being more afflicted than before, tooke occasion to murmur against him. Having[42] conducted the people to the

---

[33] Gen. 32.
[34] Gen. 35.22.
[35] Gen. 34.
[36] Gen. 35.
[37] Gen. 37.
[38] Gen. 42.
[39] Gen. 47.9.
[40] Exod. 2.
[41] Act. 7.25. Exod. 2.
[42] Exod. 14.1

red sea, againe they rose against him with dangerous complaints. And finallie, having retired themselves into the desert, he was in continuall trouble, anguish and torment, for the plaints and murmuring of the people, for the envie of his owne brother and sister: but[43] above all, for the vengeances that God executed upon his people, and speciallie for their sinnes, as when they made[44] the golden Calfe: And this having continued the space of 40. yeres, at[45] the last he died in the desert without entring into the land of promise. Wee may to this purpose set downe many other notable examples, as of *Job, David*, and others. But as everie one may note their great and sundrie afflictions by the reading of the sacred Histories, so it shall suffice to set foorth this which the Apostle writeth [K5v] to[46] the *Hebrues*, speaking of divers of the faithfull, and servants of GOD: Some (saith he) were racked, and would not be delivered, to the end that they might obtaine a better resurrection. Other were tried with mockings and stripes: yea and by bands and imprisonment. They were stoned, they were hewen asunder, they were tempted, they were slaine with the sword, they wandered up and downe in sheepe skinnes and in goates skinnes, being destitute, afflicted and tormented, of whome the world was not worthie, wandering in deserts and in mountaines, and in deepe pits and caves of the earth. As touching the examples of[47] the children and servants of God, which have been since the comming of Christ in the flesh, he alone maie and ought to suffice, for as much as wee must bee fashioned like to his image, and followe his steps. Now, this Prince of glorie making his entrance into this world, created and maintained by him, found no place in the Inne, it pleased him to bee borne [K6r 70] in[48] a stable, and to be laid in a manger in stead of a cradle. By and by after *Herode*[49] sought to slay him: for the which cause he was carried into *Ægypt* by *Joseph* and *Marie*. And what povertie (trow ye) indured he there? Is[50] he returned into *Judea?* there he passed his life untill he was 30. yeares old, in the abject and base estate of a Carpenter:[51] Did he begin his charge? after hee had fasted fortie daies and fortie nights, he was hungrie, and had not whereof to eate

---

[43] Num. 12.1.

[44] Exo. 32.19.

[45] Deut. 34.

[46] Heb. 11.35.

[47] Examples of the children and servants of God afflicted under the newe Testament.

[48] Luk. 2.

[49] Matth. 2.

[50] Mark. 6.3.

[51] Matth. 4.

in the desert. During these fortie daies and fortie nights, he was assailed of Satan and tempted, and finallie indured those three mightie assaults recited of the Evangelists.[52] Hee suffered povertie, not having one pillowe to rest his head on, and lived by almes.

Hee[53] was violently pressed with injuries, being called glutton, drunkard, deceiver, and one possessed with[54] divells. He was carried violentlie to the top of a mountain to throw him[55] downe headlong. Hee was betraied of one of his owne Apostles: [K6ᵛ] He[56] was taken prisoner, spet on, buffeted,[57] beaten, mocked, scourged, crowned[58] with thornes. He was condemned to die, and hanged upon a crosse betweene two theeves. And besides these persecutions and outward torments, what anguishes did he feele, when he swet bloud and water for distresse and feare? When hee cast his face upon the earth, and when he cried on the crosse, My God, my God why hast thou forsaken me? let us adde to this[59] example, that of S. *Paule*, that vessell of election. When he was converted, Jesus Christ said unto him, that he would shewe him what he should suffer for his name. And so it came to passe, as he himselfe doth brieflie recite, making comparison of his owne person, with some of the false Apostles:[60] Are they the ministers of Christ? I am above them, in travailes more aboundant, in stripes more than they, in prisons more, in deaths often. Of the Jewes I have received (saith he) five times fortie stripes saving one. I have been three times beaten with [K7ʳ 71] rods, once I was stoned, three times I suffered shipwracke: night and day have I bin in the deepe sea, in jornies often, in perills of floods, in perills of theeves, in perills of mine owne nation, in perills of the Gentiles, in perills in the Citie, in perills in the deserts, in perills in the sea, in perills among false brethren, in labour and travaile, in watching often, in hunger and in thirst, in fasting often, in cold and in nakednes: besides the things that happen to me without, there is that which combereth me everie day, even the care that I have of all the Churches. Now, let us applie these examples to[61] our purpose. When the Church is persecuted, and the members thereof afflicted, the flesh calleth

---

[52] Luk. 9.58.
[53] Luk. 8.3.
[54] Mat. 11.19
[55] Mat. 27.63.
[56] Joh. 7.20.
[57] Luk. 4.29.
[58] Matth. 26. and. 27.
[59] Act. 9.16.
[60] 2. Cor. 11.23.
[61] The use of the afflictions of the church, and of the members thereof.

in doubt, whether we bee the true Church and children of God, or no. But what afflictions indure we, that the most excellent servants and children of God have not suffered before us, as it appeareth by the examples here before alledged. And where is it that we find, that troubles and the crosse are markes [K7ᵛ] of the false Church, and of the children of the world, and not rather the contrarie, as it hath been shewed above? The people of *Israel* beeing so grievouslie afflicted in the captivitie of *Babilon*, and that for their sinnes, God by *Esay* calleth them, his welbeloved[62] one, and his elect: and protesteth that hee can lesse forget them, than the mother her child. And that he had them graven in his hands, having them alwaies before his eyes. And speaking of them to *Ezechiel,* he[63] saith: Thy brethren, thy brethren, the men of thy kindred. He contenteth not himselfe to call them once his brethren, but doubleth the word, saying: Thy brethren, thy brethren, and addeth, men of thy kindred, that he should not thinke, because they were in this miserable condition, that they were cast off of GOD, but that he should acknowledge them for his brethren. In like manner, the Holie ghost speaking of those that were murthered and cast to wild beastes, calleth[64] them the servants of God and [K8ʳ 72] his faithfull ones. The Apostle to the Hebrues speaking of the faithfull which were tormented and afflicted after sundrie manners, and cruellie put[65] to death, saith: That the world was not worthie of them. It is as if he should say, that they being the welbeloved children of God, and brethren of Jesus Christ, the world full of abominable people, was not worthie that they should be conversant and be any more among them. And so farre off was it that S. *Paule* entred into doubt of himselfe for his troubles, that contrariwise he alledged them to proove that[66] he was a more excellent servant of Christ than the others, having indured more than they al. And if this sentence pronounced by the father touching Jesus[67] Christ: This is my welbeloved sonne in whom I am well pleased, bee true, even then when he swet bloud and water for distresse, and then when he thought[68] he was forsaken of GOD, so as being in this hell, he continued still the dearelie beloved sonne of GOD: what occasion have we then, when wee are afflicted with our head, [K8ᵛ] to doubt of our adoption? Let us set before us the great number of faithfull which were before the throne and in the presence of the Lambe,

---

62 Esay. 41.8. and 49.15.

63 Ezec. 11.15

64 Psalm. 79.2

65 Heb. 11.38.

66 2. Cor. 11.23.

67 Mat. 17.5.

68 Luk. 9.31.

clothed with long white robes, holding palmes of victorie in their hands: and let us understand by the testimonie of the holie[69] Ghost, who they be. These are they (saith he) which are come from great tribulation, and have washed their long robes, and have made them white in the bloud of the Lambe. Therfore are they before the throne of God, and serve him day and night in his temple. And he which sitteth uppon the throne will over shadowe them: they shall neither have thirst nor hunger, and the Sunne shall beate upon them no more, neither any heate: for the Lambe which is in the midst of the throne shall governe them, and leade them to the fountains of living waters, and God shall wipe away all teares from their eyes. When S. *Peter* exhorted his disciples to constancie, saying:[70] That they knew well, that the same afflictions were accomplished in [L1r 73] the companie of their brethren which were in the worlde. And when Jesus Christ[71] said to his Apostles: ye are happie when you suffer injuries and reproches, for so have they persecuted the Prophets which were before you. The intention neither of Christ nor of Saint *Peter* was to set before them the comfort of miserable persons, as it is saide, to have companions in their miseries, but rather to shew them, that the afflictions which they indured were proper to the servants and children of G O D, and that therefore they ought to comfort themselves, beeing honoured with the liverie of their other brethren and members of Christ, yea, the most excellent servaunts of God, as the Prophets[72] were. And indeede seeing those whom God had foreknowne, those hee hath predestinate to be fashioned like unto the Image of Christ. Let us not doubt (for so Saint *Paule* saith) that it is[73] a true saying, that if we die with him, we shall live also with him, and if wee suffer with him, wee shall also raigne with him. Let us remember the [L1v] saying[74] of Christ to his Apostles: The servant is not above his Master, If they have persecuted mee, they will also persecute you, if the world hate you, know that they have hated mee before you. And this should be a thing monstrous to[75] see, under a head crowned with thornes, members handled delicatelie. Shall wee doubt then of our adoption, beeing called unto the same condition which the welbeloved Sonne of G O D tooke upon him going to the injoying of his glorie? Will wee refuse to follow him, ascending up by the crosse into his Kingdome?

---

[69] Reve. 7.9.
[70] 1. Pet. 5.9.
[71] Mat. 5.12
[72] Rom. 8.28
[73] 2. Tim. 2.11
[74] Jho. 15.20
[75] Jho. 15.18

Hee hath suffered (sayth Saint[76] *Peter*) Leaving us an example that wee should followe his steps. Let us not then thinke it strange, as he saith in[77] an other place, when wee are as in a fornace, for our triall, as if an unwonted thing had come unto us. But rather in as much as wee communicate with the afflictions of Christ; Let us rejoyce, that when his glorie shall appeare wee also may rejoyce with gladnes. Now let us understand how he addeth, that suffering injurie for Christes sake, wee are [L2r 74] happy, forasmuch as the spirit of God, which is the spirit of glory resteth in us, and the feeling which we have, causeth us to glorifie him, though of the blinde worlde he is evill spoken of. Seeing then the heavenly father hath vouchsafed us such[78] love, that wee are called the sons of God, although the world persecute us, because it knoweth neither the Father, nor us: Let us saie boldlie with S. *Jhon*, We are now the children of God: And although it dooth not yet appeare what we shal be, yet we knowe (as hee also addeth) that when Christ shall appeare we shall be like unto him, for we shall[79] see him as hee is. Let us be contented to be dead in this worlde, and to have our life hid with Christ in God, beeing assured, that when Christ our life shall appeare, we shall also appeare in glorie. If the Divell will gather of our afflictions, that we are not the children of GOD; let us say boldlie that he is a lyar, or let him first plucke out of the ranke of God his children, the Martyres, the Apostles, the Prophets, and other of the best and most [L2v] approoved children and servants of GOD, which have beene afflicted as well as wee, and more than wee: Even the holie Virgine and Christ himselfe. But rather seeing that wee beare their liverie, let us acknowledge our selves the children of GOD with them, and let us say (with a holie resolution) with Saint[80] *Paule*, that there is neyther death, nor life, nor Angells, nor principalities, nor powers, nor thinges present, nor thinges to come, nor heigth, nor depth, nor anie other creature which can separate us from the love of GOD, which he beareth us in Jesus Christ our Lorde.

---

76 1. Pet. 2.21.
77 1. Pet. 4.12.
78 1. Jhon. 3.1
79 Col. 3.3.
80 Rom. 8.38.

[L3^r 75] *That the faithfull have the common afflictions of the children of Adam, because of the excellent fruites of them, testimonies of their adoption, and of the love of God toward them.*

CAP. 9.

TO bee yet better confirmed in this trueth, let us now consider how the afflictions themselves, even those that are common to the children of *Adam* serve for our profite[1] and salvation. First, for as much as the reliques of sinne abide still, even in the most perfect in this life, which maketh them hardened in their faults, and inclined to offend God: We have neede of helpes, to be waked, to be humbled, and drawen from our sinnes, to keep us in the time to come, and so to dispose us to a perfect obedience, holie, and acceptable unto God. And to this ende tend the afflictions of the children of God, which for this cause are called [L3^v] chastisements, corrections, and medicines of our soules. The children of *Jacob* having committed a detestable crime in[2] selling their brother *Joseph*, but they never thought of it, untill that beeing in *Ægypt* pressed with reproches and imprisonment, they called to minde their sinne, saying one to the other, surely we have sinned against our brother: for we saw the anguish of his soule, when hee besought us, and wee woulde not heare him, and therefore is this trouble hapned unto us. *Manasses* King of *Juda* having set up Idolatrie againe, persecuted those that woulde purelie serve the[3] Lorde, so as *Jerusalem* was full of blood, and having shut his eares to the admonitions of the Lorde, at the last was taken by the army of the king of the *Assyrians*, bound with manacles, fettered in chaines, and carried prisoner into *Babylon*. Then, being in affliction, he was exceedingly humbled before God, hee prayed to the Lord, and was heard, and caried backe unto *Jerusalem*. Then hee pulled downe all Idolatrie, reformed the service of God, and [L4^r 76] commanded *Juda* to serve the Lorde the God of *Israell*. Yea, the poore pagane marriners, of whom the historie of *Jonas* maketh mention, seeing the continuaunce of the tempest, concluded to cast lots to know who was the cause of that affliction; and God making it to appeare that[4] it was the sinne of *Jonas*; thereof is come a common Proverb in a daungerous tempest; that there is some *Jonas* in the ship. And this proceedeth of a feeling and apprehension of the providence and justice of GOD: this little sparke yet still remaining in man of

---

[1] 1. Fruit to awake us out of our sinnes.

[2] Gen. 42.21

[3] 2. Chro. 33

[4] Jon. 1.7

the image of God, whereby we thinke, that it is hee that afflicteth, that he is just, and doth nothing but justlie, and so, that afflictions are corrections of our sinnes. Therefore *Jeremie* justly reproveth the blockishnesse of the people of *Israel* in this,[5] that being afflicted, no man saide what have I done? See now why God, to make us more livelie feele his judgements, and to the intent to wake us up, and to convert us unto him, sendeth us oftentimes afflictions, which after a sort answere, and have some conformitie to our [L4^v] sins. As for example, *Ezechias* king of *Juda* sinned by ambition or vain confidence, in shewing all his treasures to the Embassadors of the king of *Babel:* and GOD tolde him by the Prophet *Esay*, that[6] all his treasures should be transported into *Babel*. *David* offended God in[7] committing adultery, and in putting to death *Uriah*, and GOD chastised him[8] in this, that *Amnon* his sonne defiled his sister *Thamar*; and that *Amnon* was slaine by his brother *Absolom*, that[9] *Absolom* laie publikely with his fathers Concubines, according to that which[10] God had saide unto him: Thou hast done it in secrete, and I will doo it in the sight of all the people. The child borne[11] in adultry died, and he was threatned, that the Sword should not depart from his house. Now as the afflictions bring[12] us to the feeling of our sinnes, to wake us up, and to humble us; so therof riseth the resolutions and protestations to fall into them no more, but to amend them. And this is it that is seene in those that by tempest of sea, or some grievous disease, are in manifest danger [L5^r 77] of death. They examine their conscience, their sinnes and infirmities then come before them: they aske pardon, and make protestations to live better in time to come. The same also we see in children that are beaten of their fathers. This is it which the Apostle to the *Hebrewes* teacheth[13] us saying, That no chastisement for the time seemeth pleasant, but grievous: but after it bringeth the peaceable fruites of righteousnes. And before he had said, That God chastiseth us for our profite, that we might be partakers of his holinesse. The goodnesse of God[14] (saith S. *Augustine)* is angrie with his children in this world, that hee may not bee angrie with them in the life to come: and by his mercie he useth some temporal severi-

[5] Jerem. 8.6
[6] Esa. 39
[7] 2. Sam. 11
[8] 2. Sam. 13
[9] 2. Sam. 16.22
[10] 2. Sam. 12 11
[11] 2. Sam. 12 10
[12] 2. Fruit, amendment of life, and first in workes.
[13] Heb. 12.11.
[14] *Prosper in sen. ex. Aug.* 5.

tie, to exempt them from everlasting vengeance. According unto this, S. *Bernard* made this praier unto God; Lord burne and cut in this temporall life, that thou maist be mercifull to me in the life that is everlasting. And it is the same that S. *Paule* teacheth saying;[15] When we are judged and afflicted, we are nurtured of the Lord, that wee [L5v] might not be condemned with the world. And to this purpose *David* protesteth, that[16] before hee was afflicted hee went wrong: but now (saith he) I keepe thy commandements. Againe, It was good for[17] me that I was afflicted, that I might keepe thy statutes. Medicines are given either to heale diseases, or to prevent them, and therefore are verie requisite for the health and life of man. Nowe what bee these afflictions, but medicines of our soules? as also S. *Augustine* saith, This which thou so lamentest, is thy medicine, and not thy punishment. As in a house where there are manie children, the rod is necessarie: and as in a Citie subject to divers diseases, and where there is an evill aire, Phisitions are needfull: so in the house of god, where ther are manie children inclined to evill, the rod is many times more necessarie than bread: and in such an hospitall full of diseases and sores, as the Church is (for out of it they are dead) it is a great fault if there be not Phisitions and Surgeons to heale the corruptions of our soules, and to keep us from offending God, and from falling into death. Many accustomd to delicate [L6r 78] meats, have their mouths out of tast, and after falling sick, they take bitter drinks to recover againe the health of their bodies: let us chearfully doo the same for the health of our soules. And indeede, behold the difference betweene a madd man, and one that is sicke of a corporall disease; The mad man is angry with the Phisition, chaseth him away, and throweth awaye the medicine: but the other sendeth for a Phisition, taketh drinke at his hand, thanketh him, yea and giveth him a reward: So when God the soveraigne Phisition of our soules, visiteth us and giveth us wholsome medicines, let us not be like mad men rejecting the hand of God, but receiving the medicine,[18] let us give him thankes and blesse him, after the example of *Job*. Furthermore, howsoever the goods and other commodities of this life ought to bee helpes to lift up our hearts to the spring from whence they come, that is to the goodnesse and power of God, to prayse him: our corruption and affection to the world dooth turne them quite contrarie to thornes and hinderances, so as God oftentimes cutteth them off, or [L6v] taketh them away, or mingleth them with afflictions, to

---

[15] 1. Cor. 12.32.
[16] Psa. 119.67
[17] Psa. 119 71
[18] 2. In words and affection of heart.

turn us from evill, to draw us unto him, and the better to dispose us to his service. Experience sheweth, that in bankets and feasts men talke of the world: but where sicknesse, death and burials are, they talk of everlasting life. It is also seene that riches lift us up in pride and insolencie, and that povertie bringeth us downe and humbleth us: that in prosperity we triumph, and feele not the force of the spirituall instructions and teachings: but being afflicted with sicknesse or anie other way, then we are godly people, wee confesse that all flesh is but grasse, and that we have here no abiding Citie. To be short, our infirmities tending unto death, make us to lift up our understanding and affections to a better life. Then God, who is good, and dooing well unto men, who taketh not pleasure in our evills, afflicteth us not, but to wake us the better, and to sanctifie us in his obedience, purifying our affections, and by the sorrowes of troubles maketh us to abhorre our corruptions, the verie cause of them. He [L7r 79] doth[19] as the good keeper of a vine, who cutteth his vine, that it may beare more and better fruite, not suffring it to grow wilde, in leaving too manie boughes on it. And as we cut the winges of hennes and other birdes, that they should not flie away and be lost: so God cutteth off from us the commodities of the flesh to keepe us downe, that we lift not up and destroy our selves with vain confidence and pride. We see also that the corne shut within the chaffe commeth not foorth, if the eare be not beaten: and that it tarieth stil in the chaffe if it be not fanned. The like hapneth to the children of god if they be not beaten and fanned by tribulations, to be seperated from the chaffe of the world, and the pleasures and impediments that be in it. The Prophet *Oseas*[20] when he would shew how God wold turne away his people from following idolatrie. I will hedge (saith he) thy way with thornes: wherein hee giveth us to understand, that as the beasts that go by the way, and see on the side of them faire fields, assaying to goe to them, and running upon the hedges of thornes, if they feele [L7v] the sharpe prickes, they goe backe and return into the way: So, when the children of God goe out of the right waye to heaven, to goe to the fieldes of this world and of the flesh, God maketh them to come upon the thornes of afflictions, to the ende that by their prickings they may turne backe againe. When a Mother willing to weane her childe shal say unto him night and day, My childe, it is time to weane thee, thou art growen great inough, and I am with childe, my milke is corrupt, it will make thee sick; yet he is so fond of the breast that he cannot forsake it: but if the Mother put wormwood or mustard upon the breast, the childe sucking it

---

[19] John 15.
[20] Hose. 2.6.

and feeling the bitternesse, hee quite forsaketh it without sucking anie more. Even so, though the preachers preach unto us, and exhort us to forsake the corrupt milk of the world and of the flesh, yet we seeme deafe still and are alwaies backward, untill God put uppon these cursed teates the mustard and wormwood of afflictions to weane us.

We have also of our owne nature too [L8^r 80] much[21] confidence in our selves, and in humane meanes, so as we know not what it is to hope in God against hope, and to trust to him without gage in the hand. So the riches, estates, traffiques, the leaning upon men, on the husband to the wife, on the father to the children, on the good Prince to the Subjects, are unto us as vayles, that keepe downe our sight uppon the earth, and as staves for us to leane upon. Now, our God takeing away these vayles and carnall leaning stocks, maketh us to feele the weaknesse of our faith to humble us, and to constraine us to looke unto him with a pure eye, to cleave unto him alone, and wholly to depende uppon him. According to that Saint *Paule* saith, That[22] hee had received the sentence of death in himself, that he might have no confidence in the flesh, but in him that raiseth up againe the dead.

This is it also which Saint *Peter* teacheth by the similitude which hee proposeth in the first chapter of his first Epistle and the seaventh verse, comparing the afflictions to fire, and faith to the [L8^v] golde, for as golde is put into the fining pot and furnace, not to consume it, but to trie and purifie it: so our faith is tried and purified in the fire of tribulations. For as it hapneth to him that is quiet and at his ease, that he falleth soone asleepe, and having an apple or anie other thing in his hand, it falleth, or is easely taken from him: so the ease of the flesh bringeth us a sleep in the world, and causeth us to leese the spiritual good things and to suffer them to fall to the ground. On the contrarie side, the more one forceth to take away a staffe which I holde in my hand while I am awake: so much the faster I shut it in, and hold it the harder, that it may not be taken away from me. Even so the more the divell indevoureth to take faith from us by tribulations, so much the more doo wee meditate on the promises of God to holde it fast: and the more he thrusteth at us to overturn us, so much the more strongly we leane upon the staffe of faith, to overcome[23] his assaults. From hence also proceedeth this excellent fruite of invocation of the name of God. [M1^r 81] And surelie in the time of prosperitie, when we are at our ease wee pray not ordinarilie, but of custome and for fash-

[21] 3. In confidence.

[22] 2. Cor. 1.9.

[23] 4. In Invocation and praiers.

ion, but being pressed with necessitie, being assailed on all sides, finding no comfort in the earth, and feeling that we perish if God doo not strengthen, aide and deliver us: Then it is, that with all our hearts, wee crie unto the Lord, that wee protest that he is our father and saviour, and that our trust is in him: as the feeling of our diseases is it that maketh us runne to the Phisition. The historie of the booke of Judges sheweth by manie examples that the people of Israel being in peace grewe corrupt, but after beeing afflicted they had recourse to G O D, asking of him deliverance. When[24] God slewe them (saith *David*) then they sought him, and turned them selves, and rose earlie in the morning to seeke after God, and then they remembred that God was their rocke, and that the high and mightie G O D was their redeemer. I will goe (saith the[25] Lord by his Prophet *Osee*) and [M1ᵛ] returne to my place, untill they confesse their fault, and seeke my face: They shal seeke me diligentlie in their trouble, saying: Come, let us returne unto the Lord, for it is he that hath spoiled us, and he wil heale us, he hath striken us, and he will cure us. So long as the prodigall[26] sonne had meanes, he continued in his disorders: but beeing brought to extreame povertie, he remembred his fathers house, and returned unto him. Furthermore, our patience[27] is prooved and augmented by troubles, as S. *Paule* teacheth: and by[28] the experience of G O D his assistance, our hope groweth, in so much as making us (in the time of need) to feele his goodnes, his power, and his trueth, in strengthning and sustaining us in assaults and conflicts, and in delivering us out of our afflictions: he sealeth in us the assurance of this his promise,[29] that whosoever calleth upon him shall be saved. And he that shall put his trust in him, shall never be confounded.[30] For this cause S. *Paule* teacheth us to rejoyce in our tribulations: [M2ʳ 82] adding,[31] that tribulation bringeth patience,[32] and patience experience, and experience[33] hope. And S. *James* exhorteth us to compt temptations for matter of great joy, forasmuch as the triall of our faith ingendreth patience. By the same meanes he trieth our obedience and fashioneth us. For

---

[24] Psal. 78.34.
[25] Ose. 5.15. and 7.1.
[26] Luk. 15.11.
[27] 5. In patience and hope.
[28] Rom. 5.3.
[29] Joel. 2.32.
[30] Ro. 10.13.
[31] Ro. 10.11.
[32] Rom. 5.3.
[33] Jam. 1.2.

when God[34] intertaineth us in prosperitie according to the flesh, it is easie to submit our selves to so sweete handling, and to frame our selves according to his will, with acknowledging of his goodnes and love towards us. But when he afflicteth us with sicknes, povertie, reproach and other calamities. Then to feele that he loveth us, to like this handling, to subject our selves to[35] this his will: herein consisteth true obedience. Then, he afflicteth us to trie us and to fashion us in this obedience, in as much as working in us his children by his spirit, he maketh us to commit our selves to his government, to depend upon him, and to suffer our selves to be guided by his hand, offring our selves as a living sacrifice, [M2v] holy and acceptable unto God, considering that it is reasonable, that wee being his, by right of creation and redemption, he may dispose of us as it pleaseth him. And herein there are two things to be considered. First, in as much as hee is our creatour, wee ought to practise that which *David* saith:[36] Lord I have held my peace, and have not opened my mouth, because it is thou that hast done it: shewing thereby, that whether he tie us to our bed by sicknes, or bring us to povertie, or driving us from place to place, he bring us to many discommodities, or even make us to languish in prison, or passe through the sword or fire, we must thinke and say, Lord I hold my peace and will not murmure against thee: but render thee obedience, because it is thou that hast done it: for thou hast all authoritie over me, in as much as I am thy creature. And indeed if after the similitude of a potter, who is able to make of the selfe same lumpe of earth, some vessells of honor, and others of dishonor, Saint [M3r 83] *Paule*[37] sheweth, that God hath authoritie to chuse some to salvation, and to reject others, so as they that are rejected to be damned eternallie, have no cause to replie or murmur: how much more ought wee to hold our peace and obey, when he disposeth that we shall be afflicted but for a little time, and that in the bodie onelie? But that in this[38] obedience wee may feele indeed that we are happie, we must marke an other poynt: that he which doth afflict us, is not onelie our creatour, but also our redeemer: not only God, but also our G O D and father. And that same assureth us, that according to the love that he beareth us, and according to his infinite wisedome, hee will dispose nothing of us, which shall not be to his glorie, and to our benefite and salvation. It is well knowne that fathers and mothers take no pleasure to afflict their children, and to make them to weepe. And although they have power to beate

[34] 6. In obedience, because he that afflicteth us, is first our creatour.

[35] Rom. 12.1.

[36] Psal. 39.10.

[37] Rom. 9.20.

[38] 2. Because he is our father and redeemer.

them, to appoynt them their diet, and to put them abroad, either to schoole, or to [M3v] serve some other, yet when they doo this, men doo not onlie confesse that they have authoritie so to do: but also everie one beleeveth, that it is for the benefite of the children, whose duetie also it is to like well of it, and to render unto them willing obedience. Now, properlie God onlie is our father,[39] as Jesus Christ saith: Call ye no man father uppon the earth: ye have but one father, which is in heaven. What injurie then doo we to this onlie true father, that we being afflicted by his hand, after what manner soever, doo not sanctifie his name, conforming our selves to his will, thinking and confessing, that all proceedeth from his goodnes and love, to his glorie, and our benefite and salvation? See how, in the schoole of affliction, we learne what it is properlie to obey God: and that is verie necessarie[40] for us. For, if Jesus Christ being the sonne, notwithstanding learned obedience, by the things which he suffered: how much more had wee neede to learne to submit our hearts [M4r 84] and our neckes by afflictions, to the guiding of our God, as children yeelding themselves peaceablie to the government of their father, saying with[41] *Job:* The Lord hath given, the Lord hath taken, his name be blessed: And with *David* persecuted of *Absalom:*[42] If God say to me, thou pleasest me not, behold I am here, let him do unto me whatsoever pleaseth him. And beeing readie to sacrifice our owne children with our owne hands unto God, when he shall commaund us, as *Abraham*[43] did in olde time. To bee short in following GOD, as the old proverbe is, in what condition or estate[44] soever it shall please him to call us. If then afflictions serve, to awake us out of sinne, to humble us, to correct the infinite corruptions that are in us, to pull us from the world, to cleave unto God, and to draw our harts from the earth, to lift them up to heaven, to fashion us in the obedience of GOD, to give us increase in patience and faith. To be short, to make us so much the more fervently to pray [M4v] unto God; it resteth that wee conclude, that indeede they proceed from the love of God toward us, and of the care that he hath of our salvation, and so, that in afflicting us, he sheweth himselfe indeed our father: as the Apostle to the *Hebrues* doth also teach us, saying:[45] That God chastiseth those whom he loveth, and correcteth every child whom he receiveth: If you indure (saith he) chas-

---

[39] Mat. 23.9.

[40] Heb. 5.8.

[41] Job· 1.21.

[42] 2. Sam. 15.16.

[43] Gen. 22.

[44] *Sen. de vita beata. cap.* 15.

[45] Heb. 12.6.

tisement, God offereth himselfe unto you, as unto his children. For what child is it whom the father doth not chastise? Then, if ye be not under chastisement, whereof all are partakers, yee are bastards and not sonnes. Rods then are testimonies, that he accompteth us his lawfull children, and not bastards. And nature it selfe teacheth it us. For, if wee see two children strive together, and a man comming by, taketh the one of them and beateth him, leaving the other, we will judge by and by that this man is the father of him that he did beate, and that the other appertained not unto him. And this is it that S. *Peter* [M5ʳ 85] meaneth,[46] saying: that judgement beginneth at the house of God: shewing that they are his children and household servants, which are afflicted in this life. The which thing a good auncient father did thinke and well expresse, calling his afflictions, bitter[47] arrowes shot from a sweet and amiable hand. Therefore as, when we see the Carpenters strike with their hatchets upon pieces of wood to pare it, or plane it: and Masons to polish stones with the strokes of an hammer; wee gather that these are stones and timber, which the master would imploy to some building: Even so let us conclude of our selves, that if God lift up upon us the hatchets and hammers of afflictions to polish us: It is a manifest and sure testimonie, that he hath chosen us to put in the building of his temple. And that so, we are his children both welbeloved and happie. But let us passe to another consideration of singular comfort.

---

[46] 1. Pet. 4.17.

[47] *Grego. Nazian.*

[M5v] *Of the afflictions for the name of Christ, and of their fruites.*

Chap. 10.

TRue it is that God being just, doth never afflict us unjustlie, which thing we ought alwais to think and confesse, to humble our selves, and to give glorie unto God. Neverthelesse, GOD doth not alwaies take occasion of our sinnes to punish us, but often times hee sheweth this favour to his children to dispose that the cause and title of their afflictions should bee honorable, calling them persecutions[1] and sufferings for righteousnes[2] sake, for the Gospell, for the Church,[3] for the name of our Lord Jesus[4] Christ, and for the love of GOD. And[5] this commeth when we are persecuted of men, because wee will not approve iniquitie, or false doctrine, nor defile our selves with idolatries [M6r 86] and superstitions, but serve God purelie and holilie according to his word. To be short, when we will live in the feare of God in Jesus Christ, as Saint *Paule*[6] speaketh, who speaking of these afflictions saith: To you it is given of God[7] not onlie to beleeve, but also to suffer[8] for his name: wherein he sheweth, that such afflictions are the gifts of GOD proceeding from good will and love towards us: And see why Jesus Christ said, Blessed are they which are[9] persecuted for righteousnes sake: Also, Blessed are you when men shall revile you, and persecute you, and speak all[10] manner of evill against you, lying of you for my sake: rejoyce ye, and be glad.[11] Whereunto Saint *Peter* agreeth, saying: If ye suffer wrong for the name of Jesus Christ, ye are happie.

Now, if we have no other foundation than the onelie testimonie of Jesus Christ to assure us, that being persecuted for his name, God loveth us, and will make us blessed, were it not an untollerable impudencie for the divell, and an incredulitie [M6v] inexcusable for us, to call that in doubt, which he, who is the trueth it selfe, doth affirme? Notwithstanding, to the end that we may the more livelie feele this felicitie than when wee are persecuted

---

[1] Matt. 5.10.
[2] Mar. 10.29.
[3] Col. 1.24. Matth. 5.11
[4] Rom. 8.35.
[5] What are the afflictions for Christ.
[6] 2. Tim. 3.12.
[7] Phil. 1.29.
[8] They that suffer for Christ are happie.
[9] 1 By the testimonie of the word of God.
[10] Mat. 5.10.
[11] 1. Pet. 4.14.

for his name: let us consider the reasons which the holie ghost giveth us. First, when Jesus Christ had said: blessed are they which suffer for righteousnes sake, he addeth as a reason:[12] For theirs is the kingdome of heaven. They that through zeale and charitie[13] imploye themselves to maintaine the innocencie and right of an other,[14] and above all the trueth of God, incurre ordinarilie the hatred of the world, lifting up it selfe against them, to bring them to ruine. But let them comfort themselves: for what can they leese, seeing the kingdome of heaven is theirs, and cannot bee taken from them? Yea farther, seeing these persecutions assure them, and prepare them to come thether, Jesus Christ addeth that wee are blessed,[15] and that wee ought to skip for joye when anie injurie is offered us, [M7ʳ 87] either[16] in word or deed, lying on us for his names sake. For your reward (saith he) is great in heaven. Note that he saith in heaven: for it shall be speciallie in the life to come, that we shall receive it. Yet notwithstanding, in an other place he promiseth recompence in[17] this present life. For marke what he[18] speaketh to his Apostles: Verelie I say unto you, that there is none that shall forsake house, or brethren, or sisters, fathers, mothers, or wife, or children, or lands, for the love of me, and of the Gospell, which shall not now in this world receive an hundred folde as much, houses, brethren, sisters, fathers, mothers, children and lands with persecution, and in the world to come life everlasting. Now, the purpose of Jesus Christ is to teach us, that when by persecution it shall happen that wee shall be constrained to forsake father, mother, brothers, sisters, and lands, he will give unto us, in that poore, vile and base estate caused through persecution, more joye, contentment and happines, than if [M7ᵛ] wee had recovered an hundred fathers for one, and an hundred times as much lands and possessions, as was taken from us. And experience maketh the faithfull to feele the trueth of this promise. And we should feele it much more aboundantlie, if the mouth of our faith were greater. But yet in this weakenes of faith, doo not we knowe, that the wicked in their aboundance are poore, and wee in our povertie are rich. Their covetousnes is insatiable, and like unto fire, which, the more wood you put on, the greater it is. As for us, wee finde contentment and rest in the providence of GOD, which never forsooke those that put their trust in him. In the time of[19] *Eliah*, manie had greater store of foode than the wid-

---

[12] 2. For the promises.
[13] 1. Of the kingdome of heaven.
[14] Mat. 5.10.
[15] Mat. 5.12.
[16] 2. For the reward:
[17] 1. In this life.
[18] Mar. 10.29.
[19] 1. King. 17.

dowe of *Sarepta*, unto whom he was sent: but she having this blessing of the Lord, that the oyle failed not in the cruse, nor the flowre in the barrell, she had more than the richest in the countrie: As he that hath a spring of running water in his house, may say, that hee is [M8^{r} 88] more assured, and hath more plentie of water, than he that hath it in a cesterne, and that all broken. Besides, this great happines that we feele our selves to be the children of God, that being pilgrimes in this world, the end of our voyage is to come to heaven, which also wee see open, and Jesus Christ reaching out his hands unto us to gather us into his glorie, giveth us more contentment without comparison, in eating of bread, and drinking of water, than the unfaithfull have in all delicates, having nothing in their hearts but the world and the earth; and living, or rather languishing in continuall feare to be sodainlie deprived of all that, wherein they set their whole felicitie.

This[20] is it which *David* noteth, saying: A little that the righteous hath is more worth, than the great aboundance of the wicked. Yea, the verie ordinary experience teacheth us, that GOD provideth for our necessities both more aboundantlie than ever we looked for, and also by such meanes [M8^{v}] as we never thought, accomplishing in his children persecuted, that which Saint *Paule* saith: That godlines hath the[21] promise of this present life, and of the life to come. If then (as it is said) the contented bee rich, and that it is not the aboundance which giveth this contentment, but the feeling that wee are the children of a father that is almightie, which loveth us with a love incomprehensible, in his beloved sonne, who hath taken upon him to make us happie. It must needes followe, that even in this life we recover an hundred times as much, as we have lost through persecution. And who is he that can doubt if he carefullie meditate this sentence of Saint[22] *Paule*? He that hath loved us so much, as he gave his owne and onlie sonne unto the death for us, much more shall he give us all other things with him. And indeede, seeing wee are the members and brethren of him, whom God hath appoynted the universall heire of all things: let us not doubt but that all things are ours. [N1^{r} 89] As also the goods of the house appertaineth to the pupils, although the Tutor governe it, and giveth it them by portion: and that which is more, hee shall sometimes appoint to every one his diet, according to that which by the counsell of the Phisition shall bee thought fit.[23] And indeede if wee seeke first the kingdom of God and his righteousnes, Let us not doubt, following the promise of Jesus Christ, but that

[20] Psal. 37.16.
[21] 1. Tim. 4.8.
[22] Rom. 8.31.
[23] Mat. 6.33

all other things shall be added. In the meane time we must especially lift up our understanding to the reward promised in the life everlasting. For true it is, that besides this contentment whereof wee have spoken: God (to shew that it hapneth not for lacke of power to enrich his children, that povertie and other afflictions do often follow and accompanie the profession of the Gospell) dooth oftentimes dispose, that they which have forsaken father, mother, and their worldly goods for the name of Jesus Christ, finde afterwardes many, which serve them for fathers and mothers, and obtaine after greater [N1^{v}] possessions in following the Gospell, than they had before. Alwayes this is not the purpose of Christ to have us to rest upon so bare recompence, as to give us goods which are common to the wicked and the infidels. Saint *Paule* proposeth to the bondslaves of men, for recompence[24] of their faithfull service, the inheritance of Heaven. The children then of the house of God, shold do themselves great wrong, to looke for at the hands of a Father, so mightie, so rich, and so liberall, earthlie and transitorie riches, and other commodities of the flesh. Hee esteemeth it not agreeable to his greatnes, nor to the anguishes and travailes of those which have forsaken father, mother, their goods and their life for his service, to give them things so vaine: to the ende, that they should not set their mindes thereon, thinking that their felicitie lay in them. The Master of a house, who keepeth his inheritance for his Sonne, doth not thinke that he doth any thing for him, to clothe him with the liverie of his servants: as also when any one shall be received for a [N2^{r} 90] Prince into any countrie, he may well cast some peeces of golde or silver, amongst the people, to shew his liberality, but the honors and dignities are distributed among his favourits. GOD wil not feast our bodies with the service of our soules. He is liberall and just, and therefore will recompence Spirituall conflicts with Spirituall Crownes, and accept our labors, not according to the vilenes of our harts, but according to the dignity of his greatnes: seeing also, that[25] he crowneth not in us, our workes, but properly his owne. Of one and the selfe same service, there is one recompence of a King, and an other of a Merchant; so as when we would content our selves with earthly goods, God might answere with better reason than (in old time) *Alexander* the great, that it were enough in regarde of us that shoulde receive it, but not in regard of him that should give it us. They that knowe the vanity of worldly thinges, have no contentation but in heavenly things,[26] yea, and will say with Saint *Augustine*; Lorde, if thou

---

[24] Col. 3.24

[25] *August.*

[26] *Manuel. Aug. cha.* 3

shouldest give [N2v] mee all that thou hast created in the world, that shoulde not suffice thy servant, except thou gave mee thy selfe. As also he saith in another place, All aboundance, which is not my God, is to me[27] scarcitie. Wee must then set before us the reward promised in the eternall life, wherwith (without al doubt) *Moses* was lively touched in his hart, when he refused to be called the son of Pharaohs daughter, choosing rather to bee afflicted with the people of G O D, than to enjoy for a small season, the pleasures of sin, esteeming the reproch of Christ greater riches than al the treasures of *Ægypt*. For (saith the apostle) he had respect to the reward, which also he received, not in this present life, wherin he was afflicted until his death; but in heaven, whither hee lifting up his eies, feared not the furie of the King, but held fast, as if hee sawe him, that is invisible. The same Apostle writing to the *Hebrewes* that beleeved, sheweth very well, that they also did understand this reward. For he beareth them witnesse,[28] that they had taken joyfullie [N3r 91] the spoyling of their goods, knowing, that they had a better riches in heaven, which abideth for ever. Wherein also he confirmeth them, adding this exhortation:[29] Then cast not off your confidence, which hath great reward. Now although, as touching our selves, we can not comprehend what this reward shall be, yet ought we certainly to beleeve it, that it is most certaine, because Jesus Christ[30] hath promised it; and most excellent: seeing that Saint *Paule* affirmeth, that the suffrings of this present life are not woorthie of the glorie to come, which shall be revealed in us. As also he sayth[31] in an other place: That our transitorie afflictions which indure but a small time, and are gone in a moment, shal bring forth in us an eternal waight of glorie marvelous excellent. And to give some taste in waighting for the ful revelation, and injoying of it, let us note in this last sentence of Saint *Paule*, the comparison that hee maketh of our afflictions that are swift, and passing in a moment, and the eternall waight of glorie marvellous excellent, which [N3v] they bring foorth. For true it is, that our outward man decayeth, as hee said, meaning thereby the losse of health, of riches, honours, friendships, aliances, and other such aides and commodities of this life, and the life it selfe: but in the meane time the inward man is renued every day, by an happy and excellent chaunge, in goods and honours that are spirituall, heavenly, and eternall. And indeede what is all that which we suffer and lose here for Jesus Christ, in respect of the infinite and incomprehensible good

[27] 2. In the life to come
[28] Heb. 10.34
[29] The fruite in the life to come incomprehensible: first, for the greatnesse.
[30] Rom. 8.18
[31] 2. Cor. 4.17

things, which we shall recover in heaven, whereof also we have a feeling in this present life? Are we constrained to forsake a fleshlie father? Beholde the heavenly father which offereth himselfe at hand, who alone properly is our Father,[32] as is saide before. What lost the man borne blinde beeing cast out of the Synagogue, and refused of the Scribes and Pharisies, when Jesus Christ met hym and receyved hym? If any spoyle our worldly goods, God offereth us the Kingdome of heaven. If the earth will not beare us, the heavens open to [N4r 92] receive us. If the people of the worlde drive us away, the Angells offer their presence, acknowledging us their companions in glory: If men curse us, those wordes are but winde; and God in the meane time doth blesse us, and turneth even the curses of our enemies into blessings[33] as *David* speaketh. If we be thrust out of our offices or dignities, Jesus Christ giveth us things more excellent, making[34] us kings and priests to God his father: If our parents disdaine us, and wil not know us, Christ is not ashamed to avow[35] us, and call us his brethren. If we be deprived of the succession and inheritance of our parents, Christ acknowledgeth us the heires of God his father, and fellow heirs with him. Do any make us weep for sorow? Christ presenteth him selfe to wipe away our tears, and to turne our sorows into perfect joy. Are we not received into any town to be an inhabitant there? God giveth us freedome in heaven, to dwel in that heavenly *Jerusalem*, the streets whereof are paved with fine gold, the wals are made of pretious stones, the gates are pearls, whereof the [N4v] son of god is the temple and the sun. Are we put to death? it is to enter into a better life, ful of joy and glorie. And indeed let us consider here the wonderful goodnes of God. As he knoweth that we are too much tied to goods, dignities, and other commodities of the flesh, that in stede of willingly laying up our tresure in heaven, we lay it up in earth: he so disposeth that we shalbe persecuted for his name, and doth therin, as a good and faithful Tutor, who takyng the mony of his pupill, putteth it out to profit, or buieth for him good rents with it. And hereunto[36] tendeth that which *David* sayeth: Thou hast numbred my fleetings, do then put my tears in thy bottle, are they not noted in thy register? This beeing true, how much more wil he put the drops of blood which we shed for his name into his barell, and in his Register the reproches, the flittings, the losses of father, mother, lands and other goods, the imprisonments, the other afflictions; and above all, the deaths which we indure for his service and glorie? As also it is written,[37]

---

[32] John 9.
[33] 2. Sam. 16 12
[34] Reve. 1.6
[35] Heb. 2.12
[36] Psal. 56.9
[37] Psa. 116.15

Right deare in the sight of God [N5r 93] is the death of his Saints. And to what ende serve these registers? They shalbe laid before, not onely the persecutours, to make them feele so much the more horrible judgement and vengeance: but especially before us, to make us feele an incomprehensible increase of glorie and of joy, in shewing us what we have suffered for his name, and in accepting us before his Angels. But let us now consider[38] how our afflictions are of small continuance, and passing away as in a moment, in respect of the weight of the eternall glorie which they bring. And first let us say boldly, that our troubles are short, because our daies are short; and that the glorie is of long continuaunce, because there shall be no ende of it. But for the better understanding of the shortnes of our afflictions, we must consider according to the instruction of S. *Paul,* the[39] things invisible, that are eternal. For in respect of them, wee shall finde, that the visible things which concerne this life, are temporall, that is to say, during a little time. The Patriarch *Jacob* being demaunded of *Pharao* of his age, he [N5v] answered,[40] that the yeres of his pilgrimage had been few and evill. And how were they few, seeing he had lived 130. yeres? surely in comparison of 8. or 900. yeres which his forefathers had lived, as also he addeth, that his yeres had not attained to the yeres of his fathers. How then are not our daies short, not comming at the most but to 70. or 80. yeres, and that in those that have the strongest or mightiest[41] bodies, as the song of Moses importeth. God speaking of the captivitie of *Babylon* which continued 70. yeres, saith thus:[42] I have for a little while as in a moment of mine indignation hid my face from thee. How? 70. yeares, are they a little time, is that but a moment of indignation? yea, in respect of the comforts and everlasting happinesse, which he would communicate to his people: as he addeth, That he would have compassion on them with everlasting mercie. This also is the cause why S. *John* calleth the time folowing Christs comming[43] in the flesh, the last houre: as if he wold divide the continuance of the world into 3. or 4. hours, wherof the last shuld be after this comming of Jesus Christ [N6r 94] until the end of the world: so this last hour should now have continued 1587. yeres, and these 1587. yeres should not be yet a whole houre finished. This seemeth strange to us. But let us set before us 2. eternities of times: that which was before the foundation of the world, and that is an infinite time (if a man may cal

[38] 2. Because of the eternitie.
[39] 2. Co. 4.18.
[40] Gen. 47.9.
[41] Psa. 90.10.
[42] Esai. 54.8.
[43] 1. Joh. 2.18

that time) and a swalowing up of the understanding of man: and the eternitie of time which shal be after the ende of the world, and behold againe an incomprehensible infinitenes of time. Now let us consider the continuance of the world betweene these two eternities. When it shall continue 7. 8. or 9000. yeares, this should not be, in respect of these 2. eternities, 2. or 3. houres, no not one houre: it should bee yet lesse than one graine in respect of all the sand in the world: for, as touching the sand the number is finite, but in eternitie there is no end. And here unto tendeth that which S. *Peter* sayth, That[44] before God, 1000. yeres are but as one day, and a day as 1000. yeres, forasmuch as before the eternitie of G O D, there is no numbring of time; for there is no time at all. According unto this, [N6v] *Moses*[45] saith, that 1000. yeres before god are as a day that is past. If then 1000. yeres are but as a day past, or an houre, 60. or 80. yeres are but as one minute of time: so the longest continuance of our afflictions should be but one minute; and yet there are some that accomplish not that. And when doo we begin this minute of tribulations? seeing that a great part of our life passeth before we suffer anie thing for the name of Christ; and yet there is some intermission in them, if it were but in sleeping. Then, we doo now see how true it is, that S. *Paule* saith, that our afflictions passe in a moment. And what is that which this moment of afflictions bringeth us? An eternal waight (saith he) of glorie, as wee have largely shewed[46] here before. And in deede there shall be no ende saith the Angell, of the kingdome[47] of Christ. And wee are the house of *Jacob*, over whom he shal raign for[48] evermore. And S. *Paul* saith, that being risen againe, and ascended into heaven, we shalbe with Jesus Christ everlastingly.[49] For whosoever beleeveth in him hath everlasting life. If God for the [N7r 95] full[50] measure of our felicitie shalbe all in al, when we have him in us, who is eternall and immortal, we shall enjoy a glorious immortalitie: as also S. *Paul* saith, That hee hath brought to light, life and immortalitie by the gospel. To be short, S. *Matthew* having set forth unto us the last[51] judgement, saith, That the sheepe that shall bee at the right hand of Jesus Christ, shall goe into everlasting life. Even[52] so, when he promiseth us a perfect joy, he addeth, that it shal never be taken from us.

---

[44] 1. Pet. 3.8.
[45] Psal. 90.4.
[46] In the first chapter.
[47] Luk. 1.33.
[48] 1. The 4.17
[49] Joh. 3. and 6.
[50] 1. Co. 15.28
[51] Mat. 25.46.
[52] Joh. 16.22.

Now, what comparison is there betweene one moment of affliction, and a glorie, a life, and a joy, that shal last eternallie and without end? Then when we thinke that our crosse is long and heavie to beare, let us set before us the excellencie and the eternitie of the incomprehensible glorie, wherunto we ascend by it, whereof also wee feele the earnest pennie and beginnings in our hearts, waiting for the full feeling, and thorow enjoying of this felicitie, when we shall be lifted up, and put in possession of the kingdome of heaven. Now this reward is certaine and assured to al those which [N7v] shall suffer for the name of Jesus Christ. Such afflictions then are seales of the love of God towards us, and testimonies that he taketh us into the number of his best beloved children, and that he will make us indeed and everlastingly happie.

Other fruites of the afflictions for the name of Jesus Christ.

CHAP. 11.

BEsides these, both excelent and eternal[1] good things, which the sufferings for the name of Jesus Christ doth bring us, there is yet the honor that he doth us, to bring us foorth to be witnesses of his truth. In regard whereof, although all they that preach the Gospell are called witnesses of Jesus Christ, yet this title of Martyr or witnes, is after a more particular maner, and by excellencie attributed unto such, as to maintaine the truth of the doctrine of the Gospell, suffer constantlie persecution, and especially unto death. So[2] we read that S. *Paule* gave to S. *Stephen* this title of honor, calling him the [N8r 96] Martyr of Jesus Christ. And S. *John* maketh[3] mention of *Antipas,* whome hee calleth a faithful Martyr of Christ. And in the same booke of the Revelation, he saith,[4] that he saw the great whore drunk with the bloud of the Saints, and with the bloud of the Martyrs of Jesus. In like manner the apostle to the *Hebrues,* having[5] recited how many faithful had bin mocked, scourged, cut in peeces, stoned, and otherwise persecuted, he addeth, that in them wee have as it were a cloude of martyrs or witnesses compassing us round about, and exhorting us to follow constantly their example. The Apostles did well understand and confesse this honor, who after they had been publikelie whipped for the name of Jesus Christ, they[6] went before the councel, rejoycing that they had this honour to suffer reproach for his name. And indeed when we indure persecution, to maintaine the glorie, the authoritie, and the truth of Christ, against Antichrist and his supposts, it is as if Jesus Christ shuld borrowe our goods, our renowme, our bloud, our life, to serve for autenticall [N8v] seales, and most sure witnesses that cannot faile, of the right and the glorie that appertaineth unto him. And what are we poore wormes of the earth, that the eternall Sonne of GOD, the King of Kings, and Lord of Lords, shall doo us this honor, to put his glorie (as it were) into our handes, to bee the keepers and defenders of it, against those that would spoile him of it? And heere let us consider the incomprehensible wisedome and goodnes of God towards us. The most perfect offend God daylie, and one onely sinne, be it never so little to our judgement, deserveth death, and everlasting condemnation, then it is yet

---

[1] 1. Fruit, honor to be a Martyr of Christ.

[2] Act. 22.20

[3] Rev. 2.13.

[4] Rev. 17.6.

[5] Heb. 11. and 12.

[6] Act. 5.40.

more than the losse of our goods, and the corporall life. Now in stead of exercising his just judgements upon us, hee doth us this honour, that it which wee endure (which is not the thousand part of that wee have deserved) chaungeth the nature, and instead of beeing the punishment of sinne, God imputeth it, as a most excelent service for the maintenance[7] of his glorie. But yet there is more. For what are wee to suffer [O1r 97] willingly? The love of riches, ambition, the pleasure of fleshly commodities, the affection toward father, mother, wife, children, and above al to this life, is so strong and vehement in us, that in stead of renouncing them for Christ, we renounce Christ, and his Kingdome to entertaine us. And experience sheweth this too much. We are also so very impatient and daintie when there is any question of suffering, that if we should but onely snuffe a candle with our fingers, we wet them with our spittle, that wee might not feele the fire of that small snuffe, which yet we throw from our fingers in al haste: and how then should we abandon our bodies to the death, entring quicke into the fire to be there consumed, if God did not strengthen us supernaturally? Howe shoulde wee maintaine his trueth against the supposts[8] of Antichrist, if the spirit of his father, the which he promised us, did not worke mightily in us? Then when we see these vessells so fraile and weake, to surmount the threatnings of kings, the apprehension of fire, the assaults of [O1v] Antichrists supposts, and the temptations proceeding from father, mother, wife, and children; are not these so many testimonies of a wonderfull and mighty grace and power of God, which fortifieth them, and maketh them victorious against Sathan, the worlde and the flesh? I can doo all things (sayth Saint *Paule*) through Christ who strengthheneth[9] me. And in an other place, I rejoyce[10] (sayth he) in infirmities, in injuries, in necessities, in persecutions, in anguishes for christ. For when I am weake, then am I strong, even thorough the might and power of Christ, which shewed it selfe, and was made perfect thorough his weaknesse, as hee had saide before. So then this constancie, this faith, this zeale, and other vertues which God communicateth (by his free goodnes) to his elect, are manifest by persecutions, which otherwise shoulde bee hid. As in running the course, the agility or swiftnes of the horse is known, the strength of a man in the combat, the savour of many drugges, in rubbing, or brusing of them, or casting them into [O2r 98] the fire, as we see in the incense. The

[7] 2. Frute, the glorie of God, declaring and accomplishing his power in our infirmitie, and shewing his goodnes, and the trueth of his promises: first toward every faithfull.

[8] Mat. 10.19 20

[9] Phil. 4.13

[10] 2. Cor. 12 10

Starres[11] (saith Saint *Bernard*) which appeare not by day, shine in the night, so the vertue that is hid in prosperitie, sheweth[12] it selfe in adversitie. Now, this which wee have saide of the power of GOD, shewing it selfe in the infirmitie of his children to his glorie, is seene also in the bodie of the Church, which ordinarily is so poore, so weake, so little holpen, at the handes of men, that if GOD did not sustaine it, it shoulde quickly be swallowed up. Then when we see it so mightelie assailed, by the potentates of this worlde, conspiring her ruine, by so many forces and slights, and by so many heretiks, doth not God in the guiding, delivering and preserving of it, shewe that it is hee himselfe, and he alone, which maintaineth and defendeth it? And that his power and wisedome is woonderfull, in preserving it against so many enemies, and that his truth is certaine, in accomplishing that, which he hath promised us, of being with his Church untill the end of the world? And that it is he which is [O2ᵛ] the[13] stone cut out without hand, which hath[14] broken, and dooth still breake the great image representing the empires, and kingdomes of the worlde: Which to shew unto us more lively, oftentimes he so disposeth, that leaning upon the strength of men, she hath beene throwen downe, and being throwen downe, God hath lift her up againe without meanes, and beyond all hope of man, that all men may know, that the preservation of the Church is not the worke of Man, but indeede the very worke of God. As also the Lord declareth to *Gedeon*[15] this his intent, commaunding him to abate his army. There is too many people with thee (sayth the Lord) that I shoulde give *Madian* into their handes, least peradventure *Israel* would glory in themselves against mee, saying:[16] My hand hath delivered me. See also howe it commeth to passe, that when the Devill thinketh quite to overthrowe the Church by persecution, God, quite contrary, hath advanced and increased it: Saint *Luke* having recited that the high Priestes and the chiefe [O3ʳ 99] rulers[17] of the Temple, and the Sadduces laying hands upon the Apostles, put them into prison, he addeth by and by, that many of those that heard the word, beleeved, and the number was about five thousand[18] persons. When Saint *Stephan* was put to death, the Church at *Jerusalem* was quite dispersed: but by the faithfull dispersed, there were as many more newe Churches set up. And it is as if GOD tooke,

---

[11] *Bernar. in Can.*

[12] 2. Toward the body of the church.

[13] Mat. 28.29

[14] Dan. 2.34

[15] Judg. 7.2

[16] 3. Fruit, the advancement of the church.

[17] Act. 4

[18] Act. 8. and 11 19

at the handes of his enemies, corne into his Garner to sowe, whereof should follow a goodlie and plentifull harvest. It is a fruit that Saint *Paule* noteth in his afflictions, saying,[19] Brethren, I woulde have you to understand, that the things which hapned to mee, came to the advauncement of the Gospell: so as my bandes were made famous in Christ, through all the Judgement hall, and in all other places: And many of the brethren (made bolde by my bandes) durst speake of the worde more freely. *Justine* in his communication with *Triphon* writeth that the same thing hapned in his time. It may appeare (sayth hee) every day, [O3^{v}] that wee which beleeve in Christ, cannot be astonished nor daunted of any, if they cut off our heades, if they crucifie us, if they cast us unto wilde beasts, or into fires, or unto any other torment; the more they torment us, so much the more increaseth the number of the christians, neyther more nor lesse, than as men cut their Vines, to make them the more fruitfull. So the Divell is greatly beguiled. For in persecuting those which professe the Gospell, hee thinketh to stoppe men from beleeving in Jesus Christ, to be saved. But it falleth out quite contrarie. For the poore ignoraunt men seeing the constancie of the Martyres: gather twoo pointes, first, that there is no hypocrisie in them, nor any fleshlie passion which maketh them to followe this doctrine, which to maintaine they utterly abandon all the commodities of the flesh, the honours of the world, and life it selfe. Next, they are induced to thinke, that the doctrine for which they suffer, is of GOD, seeing it is by no humane, but by very [O4^{r} 100] divine power, that they suffer constantly and willingly so many reproches, discommodities and cruelties. And so is this Sentence so famous verified: That the blood of the Martyres is the seede of the Church. In like manner those that have alreadie the knowledge of the doctrine, are confirmed as wel to persevere in it, as to take corage and strength to suffer in like manner for the maintenance of it. For, seeing that GOD forsaketh not his servants in the conflict, but is with them, and in them, making them victorious: we take thereof assuraunce, that GOD will also overcome in us all temptations, threatnings and torments: And beholding them, thorough death to enter into life, and by the Crosse to ascend into the Kingdome of Heaven, wee feele our selves inflamed with desire to be their companions both in the troubles, and in the triumph of glorie. The which thing maketh us to persevere constantly in the trueth of the doctrine, which setteth (as it were) before our eyes this soveraigne felicitie, [O4^{v}] even the heavens open, and Jesus Christ stretching out his hand, to drawe us up into the fellowshippe of his joye, and glorie incomprehensible and eternall.

The people of the world cannot understand these so excellent fruites of the afflictions for the name of Christ, which we have set downe heere

[19] Phil. 1.12

above, being therein like to the Philistins the companions of *Sampson*, which coulde not comprehend this proposition that hee[20] made them; Out of the eater came meate, and out of the fierce came sweetnesse: But wee, that are taught in the Schoole of Christ by his Spirite, wee understand and beleeve that as *Sampson* having vanquished the Lion, found in the bodie of it honnie, so we having constantly overcome all the persecutions and troubles of this life, which are like unto fierce and cruell Lions, readie to devoure us, wee shall finde this honnie so excellent of the fruites of the crosse of Christ, which shall make us blessed for evermore. Seeing then, that the persecutions and afflictions that we [O5ʳ 101] suffer, serve so abundantly and so manie waies and manners to the glorie of god, and the edification of our neighbors, and doo also turne to so great good and honour unto us: let us conclude boldlie, that we beeing so afflicted for the name of Jesus Christ, ought to bee confirmed in the assurance that wee are the members of the true Church, and that God compteth us for his welbeloved Children.

[20] Judg. 14.14

An exhortation to persevere constantly in the truth of the Gospell in the time of persecution, not to feare death, to keepe us from apostacie and dissimulation, to use the holy Ministerie, to walke in the feare of God, and to pray to him.

CHAP. 12.

BY this that is said above, it appeareth that it is so far off, that we have anie matter to complaine or to be offended at our afflictions, that rather wee have [O5v] just[1] argument to rejoyce, and to comfort our[2] selves. And indeed, behold the counsel of God, who hath ordained that such should be the way which leadeth us to glorie. When anie runne in a race, all runne, but hee onely beareth away the prize, which shal runne best. They then runne uncertainly, but wee runne with assurance to obtaine the prize, although other runne better than we: onelie let us runne constantly unto the ende. Likewise we strive, not in doubt as those that beate[3] the aire, but it is with the good fight[4] of faith, assured of the victorie, and by the victory of a crowne, not of leaves that fade in three daies, but incorruptible for ever. And we be not as they that are mad or superstitious, suffering at all adventure without knowing wherfore. Wee knowe that it is for the truth, wee know that this truth appertaineth unto us, we know that God hath created and lightened us, to maintaine this truth and grace of God to his glorie. How manie Martyrs hath there been in olde times past, that had not so much knowledge as wee. If wee goe backe, they shall be [O6r 102] our Judges: their zeale and constancie shall condemne our careles knowledge, and unthankfulnesse unto God. God hath not called us to fight and to suffer, leaving us wandring without a captain: Jesus Christ himselfe is our head, Captaine and guide, bearing his crosse before us and crying, He that loveth me, let him followe me. Himselfe hath not refused this condition, but hath beaten and made the way, to draw and lift up his owne into his kingdome. All the Prophets, Apostles, Martyrs, and blessed servaunts and children of GOD are gone thether before us. The worke it selfe of our salvation calleth us thether, and the glorie of God requireth it. Ought we to dispute, whether we ought to obey? Shuld we doubt whether we will be fashioned like his Image, and weare the liverie of the children of God? Let us boldly enter into this streight waye, at the ende whereof

---

[1] 1. *Cor.* 9.

[2] To persever constantly in the doctrine of the truth, with constancie and hope under the crosse, for the assurance of the felicitie and honour of it.

[3] 1. *Tim.* 6.12

[4] 1. *Cor.* 9.

we shall finde the gate of heaven. Let us give our neckes to Jesus Christ to receive his yoake, and the honour of his order.

How manie great Lords of the world [O6v] travaile all their life to come to this honour, to be Knights of the Order of any Prince? And having attained to it, they accompt themselves happie men. And what bee the ensignes of such Orders? The one shall have a Fleece, the other a Garter: and the ensigne of the Order of Christ, is prison, bannishment, losse of goods, reproaches, beatings, death. This is the Order that Saint Paule received, and whereof he gloried, saying, I beare in[5] my bodie the markes of Jesus Christ. Now although that a Fleece and a Garter, are in themselfes vile or base things, yet are they honorable and to be desired in the world, because princes take them for the ensigne of their Order, acknowledging and calling them brethren that weare them. The ensigne then that Christ the King of kings hath taken for his order, shall not it be honourable? Shal we not accompt our selves happie to attain unto it. Let us folow cheerfully this glorious troupe marching before us with triumph; honoured with this Order of the Prince of Glorie, JESUS Christ.

[O7r 103] Let us suffer our selves to be guided by him, who is infinitely wiser than we, and loveth us better than wee love our selves. And let us receive this favour of GOD, that so serving his glorie, our glorie may also be advaunced. Let us not be troubled nor shaken with feare, when we see the persecutors come to the ende of their enterprises, and the children of GOD afflicted. That is to[6] them (sayth Saint *Paule*) a manifest token of destruction, and to us of salvation. There is no greater curse (sayth Saint *Augustine*) than the prosperitie and felicitie of the wicked, because it is as a strong wine to make them drunke in their iniquities, and to make a heape and tresure (as it were) of the wrath of GOD upon them. It seemeth to us that the worlde goeth to confusion and disorder, when the wicked triumph, and the children of God weepe. But on the contrarie, that is to us a manifest token of the just judgement of GOD, as Saint *Paule* sayth, That[7] wee are also made worthy of the kingdome of GOD, for which also wee [O7v] suffer. For it is a just thing (saith hee) with God, to render affliction to those that afflict us, and to us that are afflicted, deliveraunce; then, when the Lord Jesus shall shewe himselfe from heaven with the Angels of his power, and with the flame of fire to doo vengeance upon those that did not know God, and obeyed not the Gospell of our Lord Jesus Christ, the which shal be punished with an everlasting punishment from the face of the Lord, and from the glorie of his power, when he shall come to be glorified in

[5] *Gal.* 6.17.
[6] *Philip.* 1.28
[7] 2. *Thess.* 1.5

his Saints, and to be made wonderfull among all the faithfull. Wee are so impatient, so hot, or so foolish, that wee consider nothing but the beginning of the workes of our God: but wee must joyne them together, and consider the accomplishment of them, as S. *James* teacheth us, Ye have heard the patience of *Job*,[8] and have seene the ende which the Lord made, and that the Lord is verie mercifull and full of pitie. He that shall set himself to consider in his minde how poore *Joseph* was handled, and sold of his brethren, and how (refusing to consent to [O8r 104] the[9] shamefull and detestable request of his Mistres) he was cast into prison, and kept there 2. yeres, surelie a man would take pitie on him, as on a miserable person: but let us see the accomplishment of the worke of God: let us consider him (by this meanes) exalted to the government of al the Kingdome of *Ægipt*, and then we shall count him happie. Above all, if we behold Jesus Christ, mocked, scourged, crowned with thornes, crucified between 2. theeves, who would not be offended, that the Prince of glorie and Savior of the world shuld so be handled? But let us behold him risen againe, ascended into heaven, and sitting at the right hand of God, above al principalities and power, injoying a glory incomprehensible, and we will admire and praise the worke of God. So if we behold his members persecuted, banisht, mocked, spoiled, imprisoned, entering into the fire: what (will we say) is this a father, which handleth his children in this sort? But if we joyne to the crosse the glorie, and the resurrection to the death: to bee short, if wee beholde them in that estate, [O8v] wherein we shall be, when Jesus Christ meeting us in his majestie and glory shal lift us up above al the heavens, into the house of GOD his father, to live with him everlastingly, and that the Crosse shall be to us as a ladder to go up upon, to the injoying of such a glory. Who is he then among us that would not shout out for joy, seing this wonderful worke of God? Who is he that wold not count himself happie? Who is he that would have bin more daintily handled? Who is he that would not be ravished with the bounty, wisedome and love of God towards his children? He that never saw a harvest, seeing the plowman taking so much paine to till the earth, to spread it with dung, and after to cast faire wheat into the field so tilled, he would thinke that this man were mad, and that a childe were to be whipt that should do such a thing: but seeing after the harvest that should come of it, he woulde chaunge his minde, and acknowledge, that the husbandman had doone an excellent worke. Now, this is the time to til, to dung and to sowe, the harvest shal folow. [P1r 105] Let not us change the course of the seasons: neither yet let us seperate them the one

---

[8] *Ja.* 5.11.

[9] *Gen.* 37.39.

from the other, but let us joyne the time of the death with the day of the resurrection: and let us assure our selves, as it is written in the Psalmes,[10] that having sowed with teares, wee shall reape with joye. He that in old time had seene poore *Lazarus*[11] full of sores at the gate of the rich man, and the rich man at the table in all delights and pleasure, he would not have chosen to bee *Lazarus*, but the rich man. But if tarrying a while, he sawe the soule of *Lazarus* carried straight, by the Angels, into heaven, and the rich mans soule goe to the fire of hell, he would change his mind and would desire to be *Lazarus*. Let us then detest the glistering state of cursed riches, and let us compt, the poore and afflicted condition of the Lazarusses of our time, waighting to be carried up into everlasting glorie, happie. The wicked have nothing in heaven, nor we in the world. Blessed is[12] the man (saith *David*) whom the [P1^{v}] Lord instructeth by the power of his spirit, and by the doctrine of his lawe, to have contentment and rest in the time of adversitie, while the grave is digged for the ungodlie, for an end of his felicitie. Yea, if we were called to suffer death for the name of Jesus Christ.[13] What other thing is this death, but (after a long conflict) the day of victorie, the birth of a blessed soule after a great travaile, the haven desired after so furious tempests, the end of a dangerous and troublesome voyage, the healing of all wounds and sicknes, the deliverance from all feare and terrour, the accomplishment of our sanctification, the gate of heaven, the entrance into paradise, the taking possession of the inheritance of the father, the day of our mariage with the Lambe, the injoying of our desires? Who is it then among us, who feeling with S. *Paule* the bondage of sinne, would not crie out with him: Alas[14] wretched man that I am, who shall deliver me from this bodie of death? And feeling the good that [P2^{r} 106] death bringeth unto us, will not also say[15] with him, I desire to be dissolved, and to be with Christ. If death wherewith God threatned our first parents is[16] a feeling of the wrath of God in the soule, and in the body because of sinne. Wee may well say that death and life are two twinnes united and knit together, untill the separation of the soule and the bodie: and this separation, which is commonlie called death, is rather the deadlie stroke of death, the bodie beeing then exempt from paine, and the soule from vice and corruption, waighting untill the rest of death bee swallowed up in victorie at the day

---

[10] Psal. 126 6
[11] Luk. 16.19
[12] Psal. 94.12.
[13] 2. Not to feare death.
[14] Rom. 7.24.
[15] Phil. 1.23.
[16] Gen. 2.17.

of the resurrection. It is then an abuse to call life a continual death, and to call that, death, which is the end of a thousand deaths, and the beginning of the true life. It is then also against reason, that wee have horrour of that which we ought to desire, and desire the continuance of that, the onlie end whereof bringeth us to eternall felicitie. And to this end Saint *Chrisostome* saith verie well, that it, [P2v] which is called life and death, have deceaveable visours. Life deformed, and accompanied with manie miseries and calamities, hath a faire pleasant visour which maketh it to bee desired: and Death, so faire, happie, and to be desired, hath one deformed and fearefull. Let us put off then, saith he, these visours, and we will change our minds, when wee shall finde under the faire visour of life, nothing but matter of heavines and displeasure, and under the foule and hideous visour of death, such a beautie and felicitie, as we shall incontinently be taken with her love. So long as we live we have cruell enemies, which never cease making warre with us, whome wee can never vanquish, but by death. And indeed wee cannot make the world to die in us except we die our selves. Sinne which is in us, liveth in us, and fighteth against us, untill wee, dying, it also die with us. And by death alone, the deadlie assaults of Satan our chiefe enemie, die foorthwith. But yet why should we feare it, which cannot come [P3r 107] unto us, but by the will of him who is our heavenlie father, yea and at such a time as he appoynteth? As *David* said:[17] Lord my times, that is to say, all the minutes of my life are in thy hands. There is no creature more enemie to man, nor more able to hurt, than the divell. And indeed he is called,[18] the enemie, the murtherer, and the[19] roaring Lyon seeking whome he may[20] devour. But the historie of *Job* sheweth plainlie, that GOD holdeth him brideled, so as hee can attempt nothing, nor goe either forward or backward, more than GOD will permit him. And this which is more, he hath[21] not power to enter so much as into the swine, without the leave of Christ. What is this then that wee should feare men? Are not they also under the providence, power and government of our GOD? It is GOD, saith[22] *Hannah* the mother of *Samuel*, who weigheth their enterprises, so as they cannot passe one ounce of the waight ordained of GOD. It is he [P3v] that[23] slaieth and maketh alive againe: which bringeth downe to the pit, and lifteth up againe: he maketh poore, and maketh rich:

---

[17] Psal. 31.16
[18] Mat. 13.39 Jho. 8.44.
[19] 1. Pet. 5.8.
[20] Job 1. and 2.
[21] Luk. 8.32
[22] 1. Sam. 2.3
[23] 1. Sam. 2.6.

he abaseth and exalteth. To bee short, It is he alone, as *David*[24] saith, which doth whatsoever he will. Now, wee doubt not, but he will do that which he hath promised us, and wee knowe that he hath promised us, yea and that he hath taken upon him to make us happie. If then, the doctrine of the providence of God importeth, that he hath not onlie ordained in his eternall counsell the end and issue of his worke (which is his glorie, and the salvation of his elect) but also the fit meanes, according to his infinite wisedome, and requisite for the execution and accomplishment of it: let us be assured that there is no creature that can let or alter his wil, as Saint *Paule* saith: If God be for us, who shall bee against us. Let us[25] also bee assured, that whatsoever happen unto us, is the way whereby he hath ordained to leade us to life [P4r 108] and everlasting glorie. Saint *Paule,* speaking[26] of Jesus Christ, saith, that all creatures are of him, stand by him, and are for him. As also he saith in an other place, that of him, and by him, and for him all things are. Wherefore[27] then doo wee feare our enemies, seeing even this, that they are, is by the power and will of him, who is our head and saviour; for asmuch as they can neither enterprise, nor consult, neither yet bee alive one moment without the will of Christ? And besides this, seeing their life and being, is for him, and for his service, that they might be to his members, as fire to purifie them, a rod to correct them, medicines to heale them, a bridge for them to passe upon over the desert of this world, into the land of promise, ladders to helpe them to ascend into heaven, instruments to glorifie them, and as a knife that cutteth the cords by which we are held in the earth, and hindered to go unto God, and to be where Jesus Christ our head is? Also, what threatning can the most mightie [P4v] of the world threaten us with more horrible, to make us turne from the service of God, than those wherewith God threatneth all those that turne away[28] from him? Feare not, saith Jesus[29] Christ, those that can kill the bodie (and yet so, and when GOD will, and the bodie, which within a verie little after must needes die) and can doo nothing more: but feare him, who after hee hath killed the bodie, hath power to throwe both soule and bodie into everlasting hell fire: him I say unto you, feare indeede. In like maner, what promises can the world make us greater, or more certaine, to draw us unto it, than those which our God hath made us, to keepe us in his service, and in his house, promising us everlasting life? Now, the Church is his house,

[24] Psal. 115.3.
[25] Rom. 8.30.
[26] Col. 1.16.
[27] Ro. 12.36.
[28] Mat. 10.28
[29] Luk. 12.24

and this good GOD hath called you (my brethren) thither, and hath received you. He hath nourished you in it sometime. He hath there given you the seale of your adoption. He hath begun to clothe you with the liverie of his children, and hath [P5r 109] fashioned you like to the image of Jesus Christ. A great part of your way is past. In this your travaile of childhood you have passed manie torments. If the greatest torments come, the happie deliverance approacheth. He[30] that shall continue unto the end, shall be saved. They that are revolted, and doo revolt, make you to feele in their unhappines, how happie you are, to be the children of God elected to[31] eternall life. For it is upon this election, and so, uppon the good pleasure of God, that your perseverance doth depend. Acknowledge in it both his infinite mercie, supporting you, and pardoning you daylie so manie faults and sinnes, and also his incomprehensible goodnes leading you, as it were by the hand, to the injoying of eternall life. Abhorre you and detest that miserable, yea cursed and unhappie state of these Apostates, that ye may also hate and detest the ambition and the pride, the evill conscience, the despising and abuse of the gifts of GOD, the love of the world [P5v] and those other vices, which threwe them headlong into ruine. And on the contrarie, love, search and follow all that which God hath ordained to nourish godlines, faith, charitie, humilitie in us, and other gifts and graces which proceed from the election, and are meanes ordained by the providence of GOD, to guide us to the happines promised to those which shall continue unto the end. Keepe your selves hereafter from these false *Nicodemites*, who to avoid the crosse, will abandon (by a sacrilege untollerable) their bodies to idolatrie, and so consequentlie to the divell, in reserving, as they say, their hearts unto God. Will the most careles husband among them, content himselfe, if his wife, giving over her bodie to whoredome, should say unto him, that she keepeth neverthelesse her heart unto him?[32] Ye are not your owne, saith S. *Paule*, yee are bought with a price: Then glorifie God in your body and in your spirit, which both appertaine unto[33] God. Againe, Clense your selves [P6r 110] from all filthines both of bodie and spirit, finishing your sanctification in the[34] feare of God. Persever constantlie in the Church, which is your mother, that you may bee the heires of the father. It sufficeth not to keepe your soules from poyson, ye must nourish them, that they may live. Rather than we will suffer our bodies to die of hunger, wee will sell all to get bread: and wee would runne through the fire in such a case to save it. At the least, let us

---

[30] Mat. 14.13

[31] 3. To keep our selves from apostacie and dissimulation.

[32] 1. Cor. 6.19

[33] 2. Cor. 7.1

[34] 4. To use the holie ministerie.

followe those that in the time of famine, forsake their Countries to finde foode. The soule is more precious[35] than the bodie. And therefore must wee labour more to have the bread abiding unto eternall life, than for it that perisheth. Alwaies thinke with your selves our soules must live, and it is to tempt GOD to desire to live without foode. Therefore wee must seeke foode, that wee maye live.

Now, true it is, that to reade and meditate the worde of GOD in the house, and to keepe there the familie, [P6ᵛ] is a holie exercise, and very profitable for[36] the noriture of the soule. It is commaunded[37] of GOD, and such as are negligent[38] in this duetie, shewe that they[39] have no care of the life of their soules:[40] yet this doth not suffice. Wee must confesse the name of God, and call upon him in the assemblie: Wee must heare the sermons, and communicate[41] at the holie Sacraments: wee must joyne and keepe our selves united with the Church, which is the piller and sure ground of trueth, and the mother of the children of God. This onelie[42] title of mother given to the Church, teacheth us, that there is no entrance into the life that lasteth ever, except wee bee conceived in the wombe of this mother, that she beare us, and bring us forth, and give us sucke of her breastes: finallie, except shee hold and keepe us under her conduct and government, untill (being unclothed of this mortall flesh) we be made like unto the Angels. In ancient time the[43] faithfull were called disciples. For the Church is also called the schoole [P7ʳ 111] of Christians, wherein (according to the infirmitie that is in us) we must be the disciples of Christ all the daies of our life. This Church is also often signified by a Temple: and the holie ministerie is ordained of GOD to build it.[44] Therefore whosoever despiseth it, cannot be builded in this Temple to be[45] there a living stone. This Church is[46] the house of God: the faithfull, his household[47] servants and

[35] Joh. 6.27.
[36] Col. 3.16
[37] Psa. 1.2.
[38] Act. 17.11 Deut. 6
[39] Psa. 119
[40] Act. 2.42
[41] 1. Tim. 3.15
[42] Gal. 4.26
[43] Act. 11.26
[44] 2. Cor. 3.6
[45] 1. Tim. 3 15
[46] Heb. 3.6
[47] Ephe. 2.19

children. Therfore[48] whosoever doth not enter, and abide in the Church, cannot call himselfe the child or household servant of God. The preaching of the Gospel is the ministerie of the holie ghost, of life and of glory: whosoever refuseth to heare it, hath not the spirit of Christ, and[49] consequentlie pertaineth not unto him, and so abideth in death and everlasting shame. See how ye must thinke in your selves of the benefite, utilitie, yea and the necessitie of the holie[50] ministerie, to say with *David:* O Lord of hosts how amiable are thy tabernacles? My soule desireth greatly, yea and longeth after the courts of [P7^{v}] the Lord. My heart and my flesh rejoyce in the living God. Blessed are they which dwell in thy house, and praise thee continuallie. Let the tast and need of this spirituall food cause those that are now deprived of it, to say with *David:* Like as the Hart desireth the water brookes, so longeth my soule after thee O God: My soule is[51] a thirst for God, yea even for the living God, saying: Alas when shall I come to appeare before the presence of God? When we shalbe deprived of our countrie, wife, husband, traffick, goods, dignities, and other thinges pleasant to the flesh: let all these bee nothing to us: but let us say with *David*, I have asked one thing of the Lord, which I will still require, that I may[52] dwell in the house of the Lord all the daies of my life, to behold the faire beautie of the Lord, and carefullie to visite his temple. If *David*, a man excellent in faith and all vertue, a prophet, and as an Angell amongst men, confesseth so roundlie, and so often, the neede that himselfe had to bee in [P8^{r} 112] the Temple of the Lord, feeling himselfe as it were ravished with a most fervent desire of this benefite, what ought wee to feele in our selves, who are yet so ignorant, so weake, so corrupt, in the middest of so manie dangers? Say then from the heart with the[53] same *David*: O Lord I love the habitation of thy house, and the place where thine honour dwelleth: And that good God and almightie father, who hath care to nourish our bodies, yea and provideth for the nourishment of the little birds, will without doubt heare your desire, and wil provide for the nourishment of your soules.

Moreover, (accomplishing his promise[54] made by *Esay*, of powring out of waters upon the drie ground) hee will make you to growe as the grasse, and as the willowes by the river sides, for the joye and comfort wherof, one shall say, I am the Lords, another shall call himselfe by the name of *Jacob*, an other

---

48 2. Cor. 3.8
49 Rom. 8.9
50 Psal. 84.2
51 Psal. 42.1.
52 Psal. 27.
53 Psal. 26.8.
54 Esay. 44.

shall subscribe with his hande, I am the [P8v] Lords, and shall call himselfe by the name[55] of Israel. But understand farther, that the Gospel wherof ye make profession, is a doctrine not to flie about in the understanding, but to take seate in the hart; not in the tongue to talk onlie, but in the life and holie works. Then be ye doers of the word, and not onlie hearers deceaving your selves. God[56] hath adopted you for his children, but on this condition, that the image of Christ may shine in you. God hath chosen and called you to be his Temples, and to dwell in you by his holie[57] spirit: Remember yee that the temple of God is holie, and that it is not lawfull to defile it, nor to put holie things to prophane uses. God hath created you for his glorie, and Christ hath redeemed you, that ye might be his: Remember then that you must bee consecrated and dedicated unto God, neither to thinke, say nor doo anie[58] thing but to his glorie. Ye are dead to sinne, but living to GOD by Jesus Christ: Applie not then your members to bee instruments of [Q1r 113] iniquitie to sinne, but applie you unto God, as being of dead, made alive, and your members to be instruments of righteousnesse[59] to God. Yee are made free from sinne by Christ, but it is to bee servants to righteousnes. Remember that which S. *Paul* saith, that if ye live according[60] to the flesh ye shal dy: but if by the spirit ye mortefie the deeds of the flesh, ye[61] shal live: they that are of christ, have crucified the flesh with the concupiscences of it. If ye live in the spirit, walke also[62] in the spirite. As out of fire proceedeth inseperablie heate and brightnes: in like manner if ye have received Christ for justification, ye must have him also for[63] sanctification. If yee have hope to see Christ as hee is, purifie your selves as he[64] is pure, following peace with al men, and[65] holinesse, without which none shall see God. Remember what the faithful soule[66] saith, I have washed my feete, how shall I file them againe.

The band betweene GOD and us is holinesse, inasmuch as it appertaineth to his glorie, that hee which is holie, have no acquaintance with [Q1v]

---

55 5. To walk in the feare of God.
56 Jam. 1.22
57 1. Cor. 6.19 1. Cor. 3.16
58 Rom. 6
59 Rom. 6.18
60 Rom. 8.13.
61 Gal. 5.24
62 Gal. 5.25
63 1. Cor. 1.30
64 1. Jho. 3.2 3
65 Heb. 12.14
66 Can. 5.3

iniquitie[67] and uncleannes. Be ye then holie,[68] for I am holie saith the Lord. What participation is there, saith Saint *Paule*, of righteousnesse with unrighteousnes? what fellowship hath light with darkenesse? what agreement hath Christ with *Belial*, or what part hath the beleeving with the infidel? or what agreement hath the Temple of GOD with Idolls? For yee are the Temple of the living God; wherefore depart from amongst them, and separate your selves, sayth the Lorde, and touch not anie uncleane thing. The ende of our regeneration is, that there may appeare in our life, an holy melodie and consent betweene the righteousnesse of GOD and our obedience. Yee have understoode here before, that the desire of the heart to consecrate your selves to God, is a marke of your election and adoption. But see yee that this desire may shew it selfe by the workes of godlines and charitie. If you make profession[69] that ye know Christ: know ye according to the doctrine of S. *Paul*, that yee have not knowne him as ye ought, if ye [Q2r 114] mortifie[70] not the olde man, and put on the newe, walking in righteousnesse and true holinesse. God hath drawne you out of the power of darkenesse, and hath transported you into the kingdom of his beloved Sonne. Walke ye then, as the children of light: Renounce this cursed bondage of Sathan: Shew that ye are faithfull and not traytours to Jesus[71] Christ: Be ye without reproch and single harted. The children, I say, of God unreproveable in the midst of this crooked and perverse nation. Among whom ye shine as lightes in the worlde, which beare before you the worde of life.[72] Shew your selves to feele the wholsome grace of God, which teacheth you to renounce all infidelitie and worldlie lusts, to live soberly, justly, and godly. Thinke in your selves, that the friendship of the world is enmity to God. And that[73] ye cannot be friendes to the world, but that yee must needes be enemies to God.[74] Have no fellowship with the unfruitful works of darknes, but rather reprove them, so as your holy conversation may serve for a reproofe and checke [Q2v] to[75] such as walk disorderly. Remember what[76] God said to man, The feare of the Lord is true wisdom, and to depart from evil is understanding. Let the favour of God be our treasure: walke, as it were,

---

[67] 1. Pet. 1.15
[68] 2. Cor. 6
[69] Ephe. 4.20
[70] Col. 2.13
[71] Phil. 2.15
[72] Tit. 2.11
[73] Jam. 4.4
[74] Eph. 5.11
[75] Job. 28.28.
[76] Esay. 33.6

before[77] him, as he commanded *Abraham*. Think that ye are not your own, to live for your selves according to your owne wisdome and pleasure, but that ye appertaine unto God, that ye might live unto him, and according to his wisdome and will revealed unto us in his word. That man hath much profited, who knowing that he is not his owne, hath taken away from himselfe, and his owne reason all lordship and dominion, to resigne it to God, and to suffer himselfe quietlie to be guided according to his pleasure. There is no vice more common, more pernicious, or more hard to cure than the love of our selves: and therefore there is no lesson more necessary than it, which Jesus Christ taught his apostles: That to be[78] of the number of his disciples, we must renounce our selves. Renouncing then your selves, hate ye that which is evill, and cleave unto that which is good, [Q3r 115] inclined by brotherly charity to love one another.[79] Procure things that are good, not onely before God, but also before men. If it be possible, so much as in you lieth, have peace with al men. Be yee as the elect of God, holy and beloved, clad with the bowells of compassion, of kindnes, of humility, of meeknes, of longsuffering, forbearing one another: and forgiving one another, if any man have a quarel with another, even as Christ hath forgiven[80] you. Love one another, as God hath loved you. For herein is the difference betwene the children of God, and the children of the devil, and wherein ye may be knowne to be the true disciples of[81] Christ. Ye are al members of one body, let there be no division or parts-taking[82] among you, but feele the afflictions of those that weepe, to weepe with them, and to comfort them, and rejoyce with those that rejoyce, to praise God with them. If yee be the Citizens of the City *Jerusalem*, and wil have a sure dwelling[83] in it, walke in integritie, labour to deale justly, speake the truth from your harts, keepe you from slandering, covetousnes, and all other corruption. [Q3v] Acknowledge in al men the image of God, whereunto you owe honor and love: and in your brethren acknowledge the renuing[84] of this image, and the brotherly conjunction in Christ, in doing good to al[85] men, love, honor, and help especially, those that are of the houshold of faith. Ye are debtors to your neighbors of all that[86] ye have, or are able to

---

[77] Gen. 17.1
[78] Mat. 16.14
[79] Col. 3.12
[80] 1. Jhon 10
[81] Jho. 13.35.
[82] 1. Cor. 12 25
[83] Psal. 15
[84] Gala. 6.10
[85] 1. Pet. 4.10
[86] 1. Pet. 4.8

do, to be disposers of it with condition, that ye render[87] to God an account. Honor the graces of God in your brethren, and cover their infirmities by charitie, be quicke to heare, but slowe to speake, and slow to wrath. For the wrath of man worketh not that which is righteous in the sight of God. Do not desire, hope, or imagine any other means to prosper by, than by the blessing of God. And do not looke, that hee should advaunce by the ayde of his blessing, that which he hath accursed by his mouth. So go forward in the amendment of your lives, that this day may passe yesterday. Seale to the puritie of the doctrine, with the holines of your life, that the ignorant seing your[88] blameles conversation, and esteming [Q4ʳ 116] you by your good workes, may glorifie God,[89] and imbrace the gospel with you, when it shall please G O D to call them. Have mind of that great curse pronounced[90] by the high Judge, against such as offend any of the very least. Furthermore, rejoyce in the Lord, indevour to be perfect, be comforted, be of one consent,[91] live in peace, and the God of love and peace shall be with you. But as it is God which worketh in us both to will, and in worke to accomplish according to his[92] good pleasure. So above all thinges imploy your selves to pray fervently and continually. Prayer (saith *Chrysostome*) is the soule of our souls. For it also is the soule which quickneth al the actions of the children of God. It was the lifting up[93] of *Moses* hands to heaven, which strengthned *Josuah* and his army, and gave him victorie over the *Amalekites.* And in deede, without the grace of God, the which we obtaine by prayer, all that we do is but vanitie. Faith is the key that openeth the coffers of the treasures of our God. Prayer is the hand to draw it out to inrich our selves. Prayer lifteth up [Q4ᵛ] our hearts from earth to heaven; it renueth the memorie of the promises of God to confirme us; it assureth us against all that wee can feare, it obtaineth all that we can desire. It giveth rest and contentment to our soules. It keepeth and strengtheneth the feare to offend God. It increaseth the desire to go unto him, whom in praying we feele to be the spring and heape of all good things. It ingendreth in us a stedfast despising of the world, and renouncing of the flesh: it representeth unto us the heavenly and everlasting felicitie, that we may aspire to the injoying of them. There is nothing to bee more desired, than to be conversant with him, without whome we can not be happy. But he that wil alwayes be with G O D, he must alwaies eyther

---

[87] Jam. 1.19
[88] 1. Pet. 2.12
[89] Luke 7.1.
[90] 2. Cor. 13 11
[91] Phil. 2.13
[92] 6. To pray to God.
[93] Exo. 17.11

pray or reade. For when we pray we talke with God: and when[94] wee reade, God talketh with us. The more we are exercised in prayer to God, the more we increase in godlines. Therefore also we may not be weary or faint-hearted in prayer, although the Lord deferre to make us feele the fruite [Q5r 117] of our prayers. For we have a promise of him that can not lie, that whatsoever we aske of GOD in the name of Jesus Christ, it shalbe given us. If he deferre, for some time, to make us feele the fruit of our praiers, it is for our greater benefite. Let us continue still and waight, knowing assuredly, that he, who according to his fatherly love and bounty, desireth our good, can (according to his infinite power) give that which we aske of him, and according to his truth will hear us: he also according to his wisdome knoweth the fittest time, as is before said, and the meanes most apt to make us feele the fruite of our praiers. When we aske of God (saith S. *Bernard*) even those thinges that concerne this present life: our praiers are not so soone gone out of our mouth, but they are written in his booke: and we ought (saith he) to be assured, that hee will either give the thing it selfe which we have asked, or other things which hee knoweth to bee more profitable for us. To conclude, Praier is the most mightie and fruitfull worke of charitie, seeing by it we helpe [Q5v] our neighbors present and absent, knowen and unknowen, great and little, and that both with spirituall and corporall good things, drawing by our praiers the blessing of God upon them. And in this confidence my very deare and worshipfull Brethren, I will continue in this dutie and office of charitie, earnestlie to pray to God for you, and particularlie I will water with my praiers to God this Exhortation, which I have directed unto you, beseeching him with all my heart, that beeing comforted and strengthened thereby, in the doctrine of the truth, which yee have received, yee may continue constantly in it, sealing it by the works of godlinesse and charitie, comforting your selves in the Lord, in that yee are his welbeloved Children in Jesus Christ: and surmounting al temptations and assaults, to the ende, that by the power of the holy Ghost departing Conquerors out of all conflicts, ye may attaine at the last, to the crowne of glorie, which God hath prepared to all his children, through Jesus Christ our Lord. Now[95] the GOD of peace sanctifie you [Q6r 118] throughout, and preserve your whole spirit, and soule, and bodie blamelesse, untill the comming of our Lord Jesus Christ. He that hath called you is faithfull, who also will doo it. I also beseech you (my brethren) to imploy your selves more and more in fervent and continuall praiers, for

---

[94] *Aug. in Psal.* 85.
[95] 1. *Thess.* 5.23

the preservation, prosperitie and advauncement of his Church, so mightelie assailed on all sides; and particularlie to bee mindfull of mee in your prayers, that it may please the Father of light, from whence all good gifts doo come, to continue his mercies towards mee, and to guide mee alwaies with his holie spirit, with the increase of his giftes and graces to accomplish the rest of my life, serving faithfull and holilie to his glorie, and the advauncement of the Kingdome of our Lord Jesus Christ. *Amen.*

CHAP. 13.

O Lord God almightie, al good and all wise, we are confounded before thy holy majestie, not (ô Lord) for the troubles and extreame calamities wherewith we are oppressed in these daies full of tribulations, anguishes and teares: but forasmuch as we have offended thee, and for asmuch as our sinnes, our ingratitude, and rebellions have kindled thi wrath against us: and chiefly forasmuch as the wicked and infidels, take occasion by thy just judgements and corrections to blaspheme thy holy name. Alas Lord, wee yeelde our selves guilty before thee, confessing that we are inexcusable, and unworthie to be named thy children: yea, wee are worthie to bee rejected of thee, wee are worthie of hel, and to be creatures accursed for ever. For (ô our good God) when we were the children of wrath, thine enemies, abandoned to all evil, thou hadst [Q7r 119] pitie uppon us poore and abhominable sinners. Thou hast cast the eyes of thy favour uppon us. Thou hast given thy welbeloved Sonne Jesus Christ to the shameful and cursed death of the crosse for us. Thou hast given us thy holy gospell, that blessed and joyfull tidings of our salvation: Thou hast accompanied it with thy spirit to lighten us, to draw us unto thee, to make us partakers of the treasures of thy Kingdome and of eternall life. Thou hast stretched out thy hand from heaven to the depth of hell, to pul us backe, and to make us thy happie children. Thou hast done according to the good pleasure of thy will, inasmuch as thou shewest mercie on whom thou wilt shewe mercie. Alas Lord, ought not we to acknowledge the daye of thy visitation, and the time of salvation? Ought not we to feele the abundant riches of thy incomprehensible grace towards us, to love, serve, praise, and adore thee? to renounce our selves, the world and the flesh, and all that which is contrarie to thy glorie: yea to abhorre all that doth displease thee? to walke as [Q7v] the children of light, and to consecrate our selves unto thee, to bring foorth fruites worthie of thy Gospell, and becomming the Children of such a Father: to be as bright lights in this darke world, to give light to the poore ignorant ones, to drawe them with us into the way of salvation. But alas, ô Lord our God, we (quite contrarie) having brought into thy Church the world and the flesh, have kept in our selves these enemies of thy glory, these plagues of our soules, and have served them. Our infidelitie and our flesh have made us love the earth more than the heaven, the world more than thy kingdome, the filthines and dust of vaine riches, more than the treasures of heavenlie and eternall good things, the smoke of humane honors, more than the glorious estate to be thy children, and brethren of thy sonne Jesus Christ. Covetousnes the roote of all evill, hath hardened our harts to despise thy poore ones, even Jesus Christ in his members. Wee have slaundered thy holy Gospell by fraudes, deceipts, and robbings: occupying our traffique and doing our affaires, as people having no knowledge of thee. [Q8^r 120] The aire in the Cities where thy word hath bin preached, hath bin stinking and infected, with the whoredomes, adulteries, and other infamous acts that there have bin committed. Gluttonie and drunkennes have made brutish those, that for thy blessings and bountie ought to have praised thee. Everie man thinking onlie how to profit and advance himself in this world, to the despising of thy holy service, and the building of thy Church. The profession of thy holy religion hath served many, but for the cloke of their iniquities. Wee have put our trust in the arme of flesh, and in broken reeds, seeking comfort for thy Church of the enemies of it, in forsaking the fountaine of living waters, and the almightie. Crimes, trespasses, blasphemies and iniquities have bin winked at and supported, in defiling the seate of thy justice, without punishment: thy threatnings and promises rejected as vanities, the holy Ministerie of thy Word despised, the chastisements which thou hast exercised on our brethren neglected, without thinking what our selves have deserved. Wee have not felt sorow for the afflictions of thy [Q8^v] children, to mourne with them, and to feare thy judgements. And what shal we say more, ô Lord? Our iniquities are as mountaines, our ingratitude and rebellions, as the great deepe, our whole life, before thee, being nothing else but a continuall sinne and despising of thy holy Majestie. If they who never heard speak of thy sonne Jesus Christ, and that have not knowen thy will, are justly punished in thy wrath; what judgement, what condemnation, what hells and cursses have we deserved, having so villainously, so long, so obstinately, despised thy holy instructions, thy promises, thy threatenings, and the examples of thy judgements, which thou hast exercised before our eyes. Also the voyce of our ingratitude is ascended before thee: our iniquities have, and doo crie vengeance against us. These are the procurers and advocates of thy justice, soliciting these judgements against us. Our sinnes have strengthned our enemies, and have made them conquerours over us. We have sowen iniquitie, and we have reaped afflictions: as thou seest, ô Lord our God, [R1^r 121] that thy children are banished, spoyled, and impovrished, that they are cruellie dealt withall, trodden under foote, and exposed to the laughter of thine enemies. Our persecuters make a scorne of those, over whom thy name is called on, and they make their boast of the evill that they doo: They scatter thy flockes: They throwe downe the scepter of thy sonne Jesus Christ: They deprive thy children of the pasture of thy word. Those temples (O Lord) those temples where not long since, thy praises did sound, in which thy holie Gospell was preached, the Sacraments purelie ministred, thy name religiouslie called on: These temples, O Lord, are now defiled with Idols and idolatrie, the abominable Masse is established againe, false tales and lies are preached. These temples where thy people assembled in so great number to praise thee, and to behold thy loving countenance, are now filled with people blaspheming thy holie name, and treading under their feete the bloud and glorie of thy [R1^{v}] sonne Jesus Christ. This youth of orphanes, fondlings, and others that went to schoole, being brought up in the knowledge of thee, and nourished in thy feare, is now given up to the enemies of thy trueth, to be instructed in the damnable doctrine and service of Antichrist. O good God, our sunne is turned into darknes, the Moone into bloud, our health into sicknes, our life into death: And yet, if thou shouldest punish us yet more rigorouslie, than hetherto thou hast done, and that for one stripe wee should receive an hundred. If thou shouldest transport the kingdome of thy sonne from us, to the Turkes, and the Jewes: If thou shouldest send such a famine of thy word, as running through the forrests to have some refreshing, and finding none, our soules should faint: Yea Lord, if thou shouldest throw us down into hell: we confesse that it were verie right, and yeeld our selves guiltie, acknowledging that we have well deserved it. Notwithstanding, O good God and father, there is mercie with [R2^{r} 122] thee, yea thy mercies are infinite to swallowe up the multitude and grievousnes of our sinnes. Thou art a God gracious and pitifull, slowe unto wrath, abounding in mercie and trueth, keeping mercie for thousands, pardoning iniquitie, transgression and sinne. Thou hast said that thou wilt not the death of a sinner, but rather that hee turne and live. Convert us then, O Lord, that we may be converted, and that we may live before thee. We are poore sinners, we confesse it: but yet thy sonne Jesus Christ came into the world to save sinners. Behold us then, O Lord, not in our selves (for wee are unworthy of thy grace) but behold us in the face of thy sonne Jesus Christ, and for his sake, bee at tone with us, and be mercifull and favourable unto us: that in the multitude of our sinnes the greatnes of thy grace may shine: if thou regard our iniquities, who is he that is able to stand before thee? Wee have been unfaithfull, but thou remainest still faithfull. Thou canst not renounce thy mercie and [R2^{v}] goodnes: we have forsaken thee, but thou hast promised not to forsake us. Wee have forgotten thee, but thou hast said, that though a mother should forget her childe, yet wouldst not thou forget us. Thou hast made a covenant with us, wherein thou hast promised to pardon our sinnes, and to remember our iniquities no more. Thou hast promised, that though our sins were as red as scarlet, thou wouldest make them as white as wooll: if they were as red as crimson, that they should be made as white as snowe. We are heavie laden, and labour with our iniquities. But Jesus Christ hath called us to him, and hath promised to refresh us. Have pitie then on us, O Lord, have pitie upon us. Let our miseries move the bowells of thy mercie. Forgive us (O our GOD) forgive us for thine owne sake, for the glorie of thy name, and for thy sonne Jesus Christs sake: Impute unto us the goodnes that is in him, that the evill that is in us may not be imputed. Thou hast punished the just, that thou mightest [R3^{r} 123] pardon the wicked: Accept thou the merites of his death and passion, for satisfaction of all that is in us, worthie of thy wrath and indignation: and make us to feele the fruites of our reconciliation with thee. If thou wilt afflict our bodies, have yet pitie of our soules. If thou wilt impovrish us on the earth, deprive us not yet of the riches of heaven. If thou wilt take away the bread of our bodies, yet leave us the spirituall bread of our soules. Though wee bee in reproach among our enemies, yet let not thy name be blasphemed. Though we bee accursed of the world, yet let us bee blessed of thee. Though the world hate us, yet let thy love abide upon us. O Lord we are thine, forsake us not. Thou hast saide, I am the Eternall, this is my name, I will not give my glorie unto Images, nor my praise unto another. For thine owne sake then, even for thine owne sake have mercie upon us. For why shall thy name bee blasphemed for our sakes? Not unto us Lord, not unto us, but unto thy name give [R3^{v}] glorie and honour, in shewing foorth the riches of thy graces, of thy truth, and of thy might. Thou art the God of glorie, sanctifie thy name, in drawing light out of our darknes, and life out of death, making perfect thy power in our infirmitie, and thy great grace in our unworthines, to thy praise and glorie. Heare the blasphemies of thine enemies, boasting them selves in their counsels and their forces, triumphing and rejoycing in our confusion: as if we were not thy people, thy children, thy Church: as if wee were cast off of thee: as if thou were not able to helpe or keepe us. Neverthelesse, thou art our creatour, and wee are the worke of thy hands: Thou art our shepheard, wee are thy flocke: Thou art our father, wee are thy children: Thou art our God, wee are thine inheritance: Thou art our redeemer, wee are the people whome thou hast bought. It is thou also (O our God) who by thy word alone, hast created the heaven and the earth, the sea and al that is in them: it is by thee [R4^{r} 124] that all things live, be, and have their moving: it is of thee, by thee and for thee, that all things are. It is thou which dooest whatsoever thou wilt. And there is neither counsell, wisedome, nor strength against thee. Represse then, O Lord, the rage and furie of thine enemies, breake their forces, dissipate their counsels, confound them in the bold enterprises which they have taken in hand against thee, and thy sonne Jesus Christ. Maintaine the rest of thy flocke, which thou hast kept untill this day. Establish againe the Churches that are ruined and dispersed. Suffer not the memorie of thy name to be abolished from the earth: rather let thy word sound, and thy Gospell bee preached, where it hath not yet been heard, to gather thine elect unto thee, and to magnifie thy name: And that so wee may see it florish more and more, and the kingdome of thy sonne Jesus Christ our Lord to bee advanced for ever more. *Amen.*

[S1r] The necessitie and benefite
of affliction.

GReat trouble and vexation
the righteous shall sustaine
By Gods determination,
whilest heere they doo remaine:
Which grievous is and irksome both
for flesh and bloud to beare.
Because by nature we are loath
to want our pleasure heere;
And eke because our enemie
that auncient deadly foe
Satan, with cruell tyrannie
the worker of our woe,
Doth still provoke the wicked sort
in sinne which doo delight,
To please themselves and make great sport,
to vexe us with despite.
Yet doo the righteous by the crosse
moe blessed things obtaine,
Than anie waie can be the losse,
the dolor, or the paine.
[S1v] *The losse is that, which in few daies*
would passe, fade and decay
Even of it selfe: the gaine alwaies
can no man take away.
All earthly estimation
the crosse may cleane deface,
But heavenlie consolation
the soule dooth then imbrace.
Afflictions worldly pleasures will
abandon out of minde:
Then is the soule more earnest still
the joyes of heaven to finde.
These worldly riches, goods and wealth,
by troubles may depart:
Then inward joyes and saving health
may wholly rule the heart.
In trouble friends doo start aside,
as cloudes doo with the winde:
But Gods assistance doth abide
to cheare the troubled minde.

If we should feele these losses all,
at once, by sudden change:
We may not be dismaid withall,
though it seeme verie strange.
Job *lost his frends, he lost his wealth,*
and comfort of his wife:
[S2r] *He lost his children and his health,*
yea, all but wretched life.
When all was gone, the Lord above
did still with him remaine,
With mercie, kindnes and with love
asswaging all his paine:
Teaching him by experience,
that all things fickle be
(Which subject are to humane sence)
and yeeld all miserie.
But godlinesse within the heart
remaineth ever sure.
In wealth and woe, it is her part,
true comfort to procure.
Affliction turn'th these worldly joyes
to greater paine and woe,
Because the love was linck'd with toyes:
religion is not so.
For when mans heart doth most delight
in pleasure, wealth, and pride:
Religion then will take her flight,
she may not there abide.
Whereby our soules in wofull plight
continually remaine:
Yet have not we the grace or might
from such lusts to refraine.
[S2v] *In which estate most willingly*
(though tending right to hell)
We compt our chiefe felicitie,
and love therein to dwell.
Therefore the Lord which is above,
regarding us below
With mercie, pitie, grace and love,
that alwaies from him flow,
Doth mix with griefe these earthly things
wherein we doo delight:
Which to our soules all sorow brings,

or else remoov'th them quite.
Then dooth the holie word of God
most comfortable seeme:
Which we (before we felt the rod)
mere follie did esteeme.
The world which earst most pleasant was
now loathsome seem'th to be:
It doth appeare (as in a glasse)
all fraught with miserie.
Then feare we hell, then flie we sinne,
then seeke we heaven the more:
To use good meanes we then begin,
which we despisde before.
Then can we pray, then can we call
to God for strength and grace:
[S3r] *Which things before might not at all*
with us have anie place.
Then heare we with attentivenes,
then read we with all care:
Then pray we with great ferventnes,
no travaile then we spare.
Then shall we see, feele and confesse
the state wherein we dwelt,
To be nothing but wretchednes:
though worldly joyes we felt.
Because the soule by godlinesse
more comfort doth receave
In one day, than by worldlinesse,
for ever it can have.
Then we with David *shall confesse,*
that God from heaven above
(By humbling us) doth well expresse
his mercie and his love.
For ere we felt the scourging rod,
we er'de and went astray:
But now we keepe the law of God,
and waite thereon alway.
Then for religion love the crosse,
though it doo bring some paine:
The joy is great, small is the losse,
but infinite the gaine.

FINIS.

Textual Notes

The two extant copies of the *Sermons of John Calvin* (1560), F and L, have been collated and all the variants noted. Lock usually follows the 1562 printed French edition of the *Sermons*; translations based on the 1557 manuscript version, and those that diverge from the French texts, are so indicated. Unless noted to the contrary, biblical citations in the basetext (F) are correct. Sonnet numbers are an editorial addition, not found in the original text.

The four extant copies of *Of the Markes* (1590), HN, F, L, PN^{2}, have been collated and all the variants noted; only substantive variants in the subsequent editions are indicated. When individual copies of a single edition differ from one another, they are distinguished by library location using the abbreviations from the second edition of *The Short Title Catalogue* (e.g., 1608L and 1608O^{28}; see page lxxix). Unless noted to the contrary, biblical citations in the basetext (HN) are correct. Translations that diverge from the French text are noted. Unless otherwise indicated, the verso running-title is "*Of the markes*" and the recto running-title is "*of the children of God.*"

1560 Dedicatory Epistle to the Duchesse of Suffolke

	except for lines 2, 206, and 207 the text is printed in italics
6	IT] woodcut I
90	wretched] wretehed F, L
120	ignoraunt] iguoraunt F, L
133	safetie] safctie F, L
161	by cruell] hy cruell F, L
174	Ezechias] EZechias F, L
190	atteined] attemed F, L
A8^{v}	blank

Running-titles

A2^{v}–A8^{r}	THE EPISTLE. Periods omitted A2^{v} and A7^{v}. No page numbers.

The First Sermon

2	symbol of a hand pointing to the right
5	*I shall not see the Lorde, the Lorde*] follows the 1557 manuscript. 1557: Je ne verray plus le Seigneur, voire le Seigneur; 1562: Je ne verray plus le Seigneur
8	AS] woodcut A
8	we oughte] follows the 1557 manuscript. 1557: nous fault il; 1562: vous faut-il
9	honored] n partly obscured by woodcut F, L
10	during] r partly obscured by woodcut F, L
14	specially] speacilly F, L
15	note #1, *2. Pet. 5.*] correct citation is 2 Pet. 1:14–15
38–39	sinne of infidelitie.] mistranslation of French "signes d'infidelite" or printer's error
56	What] what F, L
78	the good king Ezechias] adds "good" to "le Roy Ezechias"
84–85	seconde epistle] follows the 1562 edition identifying the quotation from 2 Cor., but follows the 1557 manuscript omitting the verse number. 1557: 5e chapitre de la premiere aux Corinthiens; 1562: 5. chapitre de sa seconde aux Corinthiens, v. 4,
92	to lyve,] to to lyve, F, L; last word of line repeated as first word of subsequent line
105	instinction and feling] doublet created from "impression"
116	Christ] Chrst F, L
120	Moreover] moreover F, L
125	and the world] and the the world F, L; last word of line repeated as first word of subsequent line
134	sin.] sin, F, L
144	the first chap. to the Philip.] follows the 1557 manuscript. 1557: premier chapitre des Philipiens; 1562: premier chapitre des Philippiens, v. 23,
163	revelation of the heavenly life,] follows the 1557 manuscript. 1557: revelation de la vie celeste; 1562: revelation celeste,
179	man.] man F, L
316	note #13, *Psalm. 73.*] . [frisket bite] F
367	earth] carth F, L
370	sheweth] follows the 1557 manuscript. 1557: monstre; 1562: nostre
402	us) we maye] us) We maye F, L
406–407	in a small portion.] follows the 1557 manuscript. 1557: en une petite portion; 1562: en petite portion.

406	C2^{r}] B.2. F, L
423	that we] we that L
425	to blesse] ts blesse F, L
430	Howe] no indentation F, L
435	(I saye) we shalbe] (I say) we shall shalbe L
451	of Moyses,] f Moyses, [frisket bite] F
452	xxv.] xv. [frisket bite] F
452	yeares.] yeares, F, L
516	And] no indentation F, L
519–520	beynge verye well assured that it shall farre, surmonte and exceade] beynge assured that it shall very well surmount farre, and exccade L
519–520	surmonte and exceade] doublet created from "surmontera"
520	exceade] exccade F, L

Running-titles

B1^{r}–C4^{r}	The first sermon. Period is omitted on B4^{r}, C1^{v}, C2^{v}, C3^{r}, C4^{r}

The Seconde Sermon

3	symbol of a hand pointing to the right
3	*as a shepeherds lodge.*] follows the 1557 manuscript. 1557: comme une loge d'un bergier; 1562: comme la loge d'un berger.
11	EZechias] woodcut E
93	streightly,] streighly, F, L
115	fourtie Chapter of Esay.] adds "of Esay" to "quarantieme chapitre."
122	beynge in] beynge in in F, L; last word of line repeated as first word of subsequent line
153	It is] no indentation
174	bowyng] boyng L
176	And] and F, L; catchword on C8v is capitalized; no indentation
180	note #5, *Psal. 23.*] correct citation is Ps. 32:3–4
253	wrapped in, and tangled,] doublet created from "entortillez"
259	well ynoughe.] wcll ynoughe. F, L
265–266	until night, he meaneth that he cast his accompt,] follows the 1557 manuscript. 1557: jusques à la nuìct, c'est qu'il faisoit son conte. 1562: omitted
292	note #8, *Esay. 103.*] correct citation is Ps. 103; possible reference to Isa. 38:13

316	temtations] tẽtations F, L; temtations or tentations
346	in these batails and perplexities,] omits "in these troubles" from "en ces combats, en ces troubles et perplexitez"
361	almyghty,] aimyghty, F, L
374	and we can never] follows the 1557 manuscript. 1557: et jamais nous ne pourrions; 1562: et aussi jamais nous ne pourrions
390–391	to satisfie his creditour that which he oweth,] adds "his creditour" to "satisfaire à ce qu'il doit"
407	prayers and requestes unto God,] adds "unto God" to "prieres et oraisons:"
442	prayers?] prayers? , F, L
496–497	these broken unprofit tales,] adds "tales" to complete onomatopoeic "ces propos rompus,"
509–510	a true patience] follows the 1557 manuscript. 1557: une vraie patience; 1562: vraye patience

Running-titles

C5^{v}–D8^{r}	The seconde sermon. Period is omitted on D1^{v}, D2^{v}

The Thirde Sermon

3	symbol of a hand pointing to the right
5	*shall be notable*] *shall he notable* F, L
9	WE] woodcut W
15–16	well feleth] wcll feleth F, L
35	*easily or softly*] doublet created from "doucement"
35	*as a man whose pride is abated,*] adds "pride" to "comme un homme abbatu,"
63	sicke,] sitke, F, L
66	rele and stagger.] doublet created from "chanceler"
79	corrections,] corrcctions, F, L
87	let us] Let us F, L; catchword on E2^{r} is lowercase
218	me. When] me. when F, L
235–237	Bicause he ... of the shortnes.] omits "and also he does not identify those who live," from "Pource qu'il ne parle point yci des annees au commencement du verset, et aussi qu'il n'exprime point ceux qui vivront, voyla qui cause la briefveté:"
253	edification.] edifieation. F, L
344	serveth his processe] substitutes "his" for "our" in "nostre proces"
364	reson.] reson F, L

388 F1^{r} 50] correct page number is 65; incorrect numbering continues to the end of Sermons; convention of even-numbered verso pagination and odd-numbered recto pagination is ignored through F3^{r}

401 set the cart before the horse,] substitutes proverbial "cart" and "horse" for "charrue" [plow] and "boeufs" [oxen] (Tilley C103; see also P434).

413 when we so speake,] omits "of God" from "quand nous parlons ainsi de Dieu"

414 before God.] bcfore God. F, L

430–431 as in the Popes ... and confession,] omits "that when God forgives our sins" from "Comme en la Papauté nous voyons d'un costé qu'ils disent que quand Dieu nous pardonne nos pechez, ce n'est sinon qu'avec repentance et confession,"

436 Loe] Lo^{e} L

447 essence] ossence F, L; French: essence

453 and jangled] & inagled F; and iugle L; French: jargonnent

456 know] kuow F

505 F3^{v} 56] convention of even-numbered verso pagination restored by skipping 55 and assigning an even number to F3^{v}

510ff blank. 25 lines of inverted text in F; see Introduction, pages lxx–lxxi

Running-titles

E1^{r}–F3^{r} The thyrde sermon.

F3^{v} The thirde sermon.] The fourth sermon. F

The Fourth Sermon

1 F4^{r}] no page number

3 symbol of a hand pointing to the right

11 IT] woodcut I

18 F4^{v} 57] pagination resumes with incorrect number; convention of even-numbered verso pagination and odd-numbered recto pagination is ignored on F4^{v} and F5^{r}

45 For-thy] Fourthly F, L; French: Car cependant que

52 vi. Cha. of Esay)] adds "of Esay" to "sixieme chapitre)"

65 F5^{v} 60] convention of even-numbered verso pagination restored by skipping 59 and assigning an even number to F5^{v}

110 F6^{v} 61] pagination duplicated (61 for both F6^{r} and F6^{v}); convention of even-numbered verso pagination and odd-numbered recto pagination is ignored on F6^{v} and F7^{r}

158	F7^{v} 64] convention of even-numbered verso pagination restored by skipping 63 and assigning an even number to F7^{v}
181	So] incorrect catchword "So" on F7^{v}; no indentation
182	to pleade wyth God] adds "wyth God" to "plaider,"
203	F8^{v} 65] pagination duplicated (65 for both F8^{r} and F8^{v}); convention of even-numbered verso pagination ignored
203	There] no indentation
209	exercise] experuse F, L; French: s'exerce
224	G1^{r} 67] convention of odd-numbered recto pagination restored by skipping 66 and assigning an odd number to G1^{r}; numbering is sequential (but incorrect) to the end of the Sermons
318	so long as] so long as as F, L; last word of line repeated as first word of subsequent line
338	Nowe] no indentation
375	repetition] repetion F, L
379	affection,] affcction F, L
385	another.] another F, L
459–460	gave hym thys remedye, lyke to a fyre that burneth a man.] omits "because it is a sore as painful as any [caused] by the plague," from "donner ce remede: car c'est une playe aussi douloureuse qu'il en soit point que la peste: c'est comme un feu qui brusle l'homme."
469	But] but F, L
480	It] no indentation
514	to blesse] to to blesse F, L; last word of line repeated as first word of subsequent line
523	peoples] peopes F, L
G7^{v}–G8^{v}	blank

Running-titles

F4^{v}–G7^{r}	The fourth sermon.

Sonnets

1	leaf woodcut
Aa1^{v}	blank
11	Aa2^{r}] A.ii. F, L
14	THe] large roman T
29	With] with F, L
84	leaf woodcut
87	HAve] large roman H
217	*and the bones*] *ad the bones* F, L

220	*rejoyse.*] *rejoyse* F, L
286	*sinners*] *sinnes* F, L
287	*tourned*] *tourued* F, L
295	Have] Hyve F, L
357	*the walles*] *th walles.* F, L
372	*Then shall*] *then shall* F, L
Aa8^{v}	blank

Running-titles

Aa2^{v}	The Prefaee.	
Aa3^{r}	The Preface.	
Aa3^{v}–Aa7^{v}	A meditation of a sinner	verso
Aa4^{r}	upon the. 51. Psalme.	recto
Aa5^{r}–Aa8^{r}	upon the. li. Psalme.	recto

Latin Poem

3 colore] colore' with a ligature in the manuscript (see also Sylva' [Sylvam]; Medicu' [Medicum]; omne' [omnem]); despite ligature, must be "colore" not "colorem" as object of the preposition "in," modified by "viridi," and to avoid the juxtaposition of two consonants in "colorem tenet"

1590 Title Page

6–7 omitted 1634

14 The third Edition. 1634

22 *LONDON.* 1599, 1608, 1609, 1615, 1634

22–25 Imprinted at London by *Richard Field* for *Thomas Man*. 1591.

23–25 Printed by *Robert Robinson* for Thomas Man. 1597.

Imprinted by *Felix Kingston* for *Thomas Man*, dwelling in Pater noster Row, at the signe of the Talbot. 1599.

Printed by *T. E.* for *Thomas Man* dwelling in Paternoster-Row at the signe of the Talbot. 1608.

Printed by *T. C.* for *Thomas Man*, dwelling in Paternoster-Row, at the signe of the Talbot. 1609.

Printed by *Thomas Snodham*, for *Thomas Man*, dwelling in Paternoster-Row, at the signe of the Talbot. 1615.

Printed by the assignes of THOMAS MAN, PAUL MAN, and JONAH MAN; and are to be sold by JOHN GRISMOND in *Ivie-Lane* at the signe of the *Gun*. 1634.

A1^{v} Blank; Lock omits the note to the reader as well as the two poems and epigram found in the French edition on A1^{v} and A2^{r}. The French originals are given below, followed (in square brackets) by a line-for-line English translation.

Au Lecteur.

Amy Lecteur estant adverti, que la seconde Edition de ce petit livret estoit presque toute vendue, et que plusieurs faisoyent instance de l'avoir en Flamen: Je l'ay reveu et augmenté en plusieurs endroits: Et mesmes y ay adjousté deux chapitres nouveaux, ascavoir le troisieme et quatrieme: Esperant que par ce moyen il servira plus amplement à la gloire de Dieu, et à ta consolation et salut. Et comme c'est le seul but de ce mien petit labeur: Ainsi je prie Dieu me l'octroyer au nom de son Fils Jesus Christ.

A Harlem, ce xv. d'Octobre, 1588.

[Being informed, dear Reader, that the second edition of this little book has been almost sold out, and that several people have been given authority to translate it into Flemish: I have, therefore, revised and augmented it in several places: and I have also added two new chapters, namely the third and the fourth: hoping that in this way, it will better serve to the glory of God and for your consolation and salvation. This alone is the purpose of my modest labor: Thus I pray God to grant me in the name of his son, Jesus Christ.

At Haarlem, 15 October 1588.]

Prophetie ou Prediction de l'estat de l'Eglise jusqu'à la fin du monde.

QUand du monde pervers la hayne cessera
Contre les saincts de Christ cheminans en justice:
Quand entre les enfans aymez de Dieu sera
L'homicide Serpent sans envie et malice:
Quand les esleus en terre on trouvera sans vice
(Subject de chastiment): Quand Dieu plus ne voudra
Accroistre l'heur aux siens souffrans pour son service,
L'Eglise lors sans croix de repos jouira.

[The Prophecy or Prediction of the estate of the Church until the end of the world.

When the perverse world will cease its hatred
Against the saints of Christ who walk in righteousness:
When among the children loved of God will be found

The murderous serpent without envy or malice:
When those who are exalted on earth are found without vice
(Subject to chastisement): When God will not wish
To increase the blessings of those who suffer for his service,
Then the Church will enjoy a rest from the cross.]

Prophetie ou Prediction de l'estat de l'Eglise apres la resurrection.
QUand les membres de Christ eslevez es hauts cieux
Cesseront de voir Dieu face à face en sa gloire:
Quand en delaissant Christ et les Anges heureux
Ils reviendront mourir en ce bas territoire:
Quand des bienfaits de Christ le fruict et la memoire
Seront aneantis: Quand au ciel defaudront
La joye et charité, comme un bien transitoire,
Lors les enfans de Dieu d'estre heureux cesseront.

[The Prophecy or Prediction of the estate of the Church after the resurrection.
When the members of Christ who are exalted in high heaven
Cease to see God face to face in his glory:
When in abandoning Christ and the blessed Angels
They return to die in this low country:
When the fruit and memory of Christ's blessings
Are destroyed: When in heaven joy and love
Become unnecessary, like transitory goods,
Then the children of God will cease to be blessed.]

A Dieu ta vie, en Dieu ta fin.
[To God your life, in God your end.]

1590 Dedicatory Epistle to the Countesse of Warwicke

5	FOrasmuch] woodcut F
17	compted] counted 1597, 1599, 1609, 1615, 1634
19–20	pleasure, . . . God)] pleasure) . . . God, 1597
37	themselves, their] themselves and their 1615
45	especiallie] specially 1597
47	to your] unto your 1615
47	and to those] and those 1591, 1599, 1634
50	my sex,] the sexe, 1597
52	of that Jerusalem,] of Jerusalem, 1591, 1599, 1634
64	what building] what buildings 1599

66	walls] walkes 1597
70	dwel] well 1591
84	this] his 1597
93	Handwritten inscription, "April, 11 1597" 1597
94	humble] humbly. 1608, 1609, 1615

Running-titles

A2^{v}–A5^{v}	THE EPISTLE	verso
	DEDICATORIE.	recto

Taffin Preliminaries

	Lock reverses the order of French Preface and Table of Contents
3	I*T*] woodcut I
3	*without reason*] French adds marginal citations: 2. cor. 10.4; 1. tim. 1.18; Jan. 16.21; Apoc. 12.2; Marc. 4.39; Psal. 129.3
7–8	dissipations, assailed] disputations, assaulted 1591, 1597, 1599, 1608, 1609, 1615, 1634
8–9	*of all calamities)*] *of all (calamities* 1615
23–24	*in the middest*] *in middest* 1609
33–34	*15. September*] 15. of *September* 1608, 1609
A7^{v}	blank
42	OF] large O
42–68	Handwritten page or folio numbers HN, 1597, 1608L, 1609F, 1634
51	the true religion,] true religion, 1597
63	Other] Of the 1634

Running-titles

A6^{v}	To the faithfull
A7^{r}	of the Low Countrie.

Chapter One

3	*consolations in their afflictions.*] Comforts in Afflictions. 1608, 1609, 1615
4–5	To the faithfull of the Low Countrie.] Published for the good and benefit of the *Elect children of God in Christ* 1634
6	*of the everlasting*] of everlasting 1609, 1615
6–7	*Of the great and incomprehensible felicitie of the everlasting life promised to the children of God.*] in Table of Contents: OF the

	great and incomprehensible happines of the life everlasting promised to the children of God. French (in both places): De la grande et incomprehensible felicité de la vie eternelle promise aux enfans de Dieu.
6–8	Heading and chapter number reversed in 1634
9	SAint] woodcut S
16	*if it were it,*] if it were 1615
17	This happines] new paragraph 1609, 1615
36	note #10, The first degree of life.] adds "of life" to "Premier degré"
38	note #12, Philip. 4.7.] Phil. 7.4. 1591, 1599, 1634
39	God his] Gods 1615
47	note #16, The second degree of life.] adds "of life" to "Second degré"
49	For even] new paragraph 1608, 1609, 1615
53	note #17, Esay. 57.1.] correct citation is Isa. 57:2
56	entreth] Handwritten note, "2 Degree." L
65	note #21, The third degree of life.] adds "of life" to "Troisieme degré"
65–66	The third] new paragraph 1615
69	image of the glorious bodie of Jesus] image of Jesus 1615
72	note #27, 1. Thess. 4.17.] 2. Thess. 4.17 1591, 1597, 1599, 1608, 1609, 1615, 1634
73	the accomplishment] that accomplishment 1634
89	note #35, Reve 21.18.] citation omitted 1634
97–98	saith Saint *Paule*,] substitutes "Saint *Paule*" for "l'Apostre"
107–108	Then shall] new paragraph 1608, 1609, 1615
119	a Priest,] Priest 1591, 1599, 1634
130	note #39, Psal. 34.9.] correct citation is Ps. 34:8
133	note #41, 1. Cor. 15.18.] correct citation is 1 Cor. 15:28; French: 1. Cor. 15.28.
138	note #43, Jhe. 17.22.] Joh. 17.22. 1608, 1609, 1615, 1634
165	note #46, Ephe. 2.15.] Eph. 2.13. 1608, 1609, 1615
170	And indeed] new paragraph 1608, 1609, 1615
179	note #52, Matth. 25.21.] Matth. 25.12 1608, 1609, 1615
197	What then shall be] What joy then shall be 1591, 1599, 1634
205	this elect] the elect 1608, 1609, 1615
250	note #59, Of the eternitie of the life to come] adds "to come" to "De l'eternité de la vie"
261	note #66, Heb. 2.14.] Hebr. . 124. 1609
268	note #68, Joh. 16.22.] Joh. 15.22. 1591, 1597, 1599, 1608, 1609, 1615, 1634
272	note #70, Psal. 36.10.] correct citation is Ps. 36:9

Chapter Two

1	*How we shall knowe that we are the children of God.*] in Table of Contents: How wee knowe that wee are the children of God. French (in both places): Comment nous cognoissons, que nous sommes enfans de Dieu.
3	OF] woodcut O
16	Now, wee] new paragraph 1608, 1609, 1615
24	accompted] accounted 1591, 1597, 1599, 1608, 1609, 1615, 1634
37–38	Now, Jesus] new paragraph 1608, 1609, 1615
39	to bee] of 1634
42	note #14, Act. 14.3.] Act. 1.4.3. 1634
42	note #15, Act. 13.26.] Act. 13. 6 1634
50	note #18, Act. 22.5.] correct citation is Acts 22:16
51	note #20, Gal. 3.27.] G l. 3.27. 1634
55	Lords supper.] substitutes "Lords supper" for "saincte Cene"
64	note #25, Gen. 12.7.] correct citation is Gen. 12:8
66	note #27, Psal. 14.4.] Psal. 13.4. 1615
73	note #29, Mat. 18.19.] Mat. 28.19 1608, 1609, 1615
77	accompt] account 1597, 1608, 1609, 1615, 1634
113–114	First he] new paragraph 1608, 1609, 1615
125	note #37, Rom. 8.28.] correct citation is Rom. 8:29–30
129	For all] new paragraph 1615
135	are elected] and elected 1608, 1609, 1615
138	note #38, Rom. 8.30.] correct citation is Rom. 8:31
150	handwritten mark, "X" 1599
153	From hence] new paragraph 1608, 1609, 1615
168	feare of God,] feare God, HN, F, L, PN^2; French: la crainte de Dieu
174	children] childen HN, F, L, PN^2

Chapter Three

1–2	*How everie member of the Church ought to applie unto himselfe the tokens of it, to assure himselfe of his adoption and salvation.*] in Table of Contents: How everie member of the Church ought to applie to himselfe the markes of it, to assure himselfe of his adoption and salvation. French (in both places): Comment chacun membre de l'Eglise doit s'appliquer les marques d'icelle, pour s'asseurer de son adoption et salut.
4	NOw,] woodcut N
24	handwritten mark, "X" 1599

42	Now, the] new paragraph 1608, 1609, 1615
63	Moreover, he] new paragraph 1615
66	the soule,] our Soule 1608, 1609, 1615
67	might] may 1608, 1609, 1615
77	Now, faith] new paragraph 1608, 1609, 1615
92	note #8, Esay. 9.5.] Esay 6.5. 1615; correct citation is Isa. 9:6; French: Isai. 9.6.
107	note #11, Joh. 3.39.] correct citation is John 3:33; French: Jan. 3.33
107	I am come] I come 1597
108	Marie] Mary 1591, 1599, 1608, 1609, 1615, 1634
117	unto me] unto men HN, F, L, PN^2
123	And to] new paragraph 1608, 1609, 1615
126	handwritten mark, “X” 1599
147	But let] new paragraph 1608, 1609, 1615
151	to put thee,] put to thee, 1591, 1597, 1599, 1608, 1609, 1615, 1634
156	note #19, Gal. 3.27.26.] Gal. 3.27.28. 1615; Gal. 3.26.27 1634
163	note #20, Joh. 6.55.56.] Joh. 5.55 56. 1608, 1609, 1615
168	If the] new paragraph 1608, 1609, 1615
189	But these] new paragraph 1608, 1609, 1615
192	compt] count 1591, 1599, 1608, 1609, 1615, 1634
202	compt] count 1591, 1599, 1608, 1634; account 1609, 1615
202–203	that justlie] justly 1608, 1609, 1615

Chapter Four

1–3	*How although the markes of our adoption bee in us but small and feeble, yet wee ought, and may assure our selves that we are the children of God.*] in Table of Contents: How wee ought and may assure our selves that wee are the children of G O D, although the markes of our adoption be in us but small and weake. French (in both places): Comment ores que les marques de nostre adoption soyent en nous petites et foibles, toutesfois nous devons et pouvons nous asseurer d’estre enfans de Dieu.
5	I See] woodcut I
10	The unfaithfull] new paragraph 1609, 1615
11	note #1, temptation] temptations 1634
18	And indeed,] new paragraph 1615
18	note #4, Rom. 8.23.] correct citation is Rom. 8:24
20	handwritten mark, “X” 1599

20	Christ] Jesus Christ 1608L, 1609, 1615
21	We heare] new paragraph 1608O[28]
32	note #7, Rom. 8.25.] correct citation is Rom. 8:26
33	Againe, none] new paragraph 1608, 1609, 1615
44	are sorrowfull] art sorrowfull 1608, 1609
52	What devises] new paragraph 1608, 1609, 1615
52	make] makes 1608, 1609, 1615
55	deadlie:] daily: 1597
60	handwritten mark, "X" 1599
61	forsaken me] forsaken HN, F, L, PN[2], 1597, 1608; French: ma-il debouté
61	note #10, Psal. 77.8,9 10,11,vers.] vers. omitted 1615; correct citation is Ps. 77:7–10
69	note #11, Psal. 42.12.] correct citation is Ps. 42:11
71	handwritten mark, "X" 1599
72	If these] new paragraph 1615
74	note #13, John 6.69.] Joh. 16.69 1609, 1615; French: Matt. 6.69.
76	note #16, Luk 24.11] French: Jan. 24.11
77	(acknowledge] (acknowledging 1591, 1599, 1634
82	And also] possible new paragraph 1615
82	note #22, Luk. 22.32] Luk. 2.23 1608, 1609, 1615; refers to Peter's denial of Christ, line 78
91	note #26, Rom. 1.17.] .17. [frisket bite] 1599
97	note #27, Mar. 8.29.] correct citation is Mark 8:24; French: Marc. 8.24
99	afterward cleared.] afterwad cleare. 1597
111	so is] so it is 1591, 1597, 1599, 1608, 1609, 1615, 1634
122	But thou] new paragraph 1615; possible new paragraph 1608, 1609
125	that (following] (that following 1608, 1609, 1615
133	of our eye,] of the eye, 1608, 1609, 1615
136	He who] new paragraph 1608, 1609, 1615
147	saith Saint *John*,] (saith Saint *John*) 1615
152	There are] new paragraph 1615
159	flee] flye 1608, 1609, 1615
165	note #33, Rom. 8.5] omitted 1609, 1615
170–171	And indeed] new paragraph 1615
179	note #38, *Aug. ad Bonif. lib.* 3. *ca.* 7.] *'ug. ad Bonif.* *b.* 3 *cap.* 7. [frisket bite] 1599
205	had] hath 1634
209	toward] towards 1634

228	crie wyth] crie out wyth 1634
240	note #51, Matt. 9.13.] Mat. 9.63. 1597
241	note #53, Rom. 7.22] French: Rom. 7.
242	as is] as it is 1608, 1609, 1615
250	But thou] no paragraph 1591, 1597, 1599, 1608, 1609, 1634
250	note #54, because the] because rhe HN, F, L, PN^2
250	have of long] have long 1609, 1615
252	manner of fruite] manner fruit 1609, 1615
254	note #55, Psa. 69.4] correct citation is Ps. 69:3
271	especially] specially 1608, 1609, 1615
273	by his promise] by promise 1608, 1609, 1615
277	note #61, John 5.14.] correct citation is 1 John 5:14; French: 1 Jan. 5.14
282	note #62, Esa, 65.24] Esay 65.42. 1591, 1599, 1634; Esa. 85.24. 1609, 1615
282	note #63, Psal. 65.3] correct citation is Ps. 65:2
287	The fruites] new paragraph 1615
290	thought] though 1597
291	handwritten note, "Zacharie" L
300	will may bee] will bee 1608, 1609, 1615
306	The *Jewes*] posssible new paragraph 1608, 1609, 1615
308	note #67, Act. 4.6.] French: Act. 1.6.
316	note #69, Heb. 5 7.] Heb. 5.˙ [frisket bite] 1615; French: Hebr. 5.7. printed twice
331	commodities] commoditie 1591, 1599, 1634
342	therin] their 1608, 1609, 1615
350	note #73, Mar. 17.5.] Matth. 17.5. 1591, 1597, 1599, 1608, 1609, 1615, 1634; correct citation is Matt. 17:5; French: Mat. 17.5
360	note #77, Ro. 12.12.] Rom. 12. 1634
364	note #78, Psal. 141.2.] Psal. 14.1.2. 1597
394	or of spirite,] or spirite 1608, 1609, 1615
399–400	notes #81 and #82, Psal. 10.17; Psa. 38,10.] duplicated citations, E12^v repeats E12^r 1634
400	note #82, Psa. 38,10.] correct citation is Ps. 38:9
409	note #84, increas of grace] omits "of God" from "advancement es graces de Dieu"
412	note #85, Mat. 13.19.] Matth. 13. 1634
414–415	exercises,] excrcises HN, F, L, PN^2
418	yet much] yet 1591, 1599, 1634
423	[G1^r 41] word of God,] [G1^r 41] read and heare the word of God, L, 1597; G1$^{r–v}$ has been replaced in L with a leaf from

the 1597 edition; see also G8^{r}–^{v} in Chapter Five
423 alwaies that God] alwaies that *G*od L, 1597
425 holie spirit to profite to his glorie and thy] holy spirit to profit to his glory & thy L, 1597
426 sicke] siεke L, 1597
426 tast,] taste, L, 1597
427 eating:] eating*:* L, 1597
428 note #86, Psalm. 119.103.] Psal. 119.102. L, 1597
429 note #87, Psal. 19.11.] Psal. 11.11 1615; correct citation is Ps. 19:10
429 saith.] sayth. L, 1597
430 receive] receyve L, 1597
431 word] worde L, 1597
432 tast or appetite:] taste or appetite*:* L, 1597
434 by and by,] by & by, HN, F, PN^2
435 thy soule] the soule 1608, 1609, 1615
435 bodie:] bodye: [black-letter colon] L, 1597
436 digest and abide] digest & abide HN, F, PN^2
436 die (catchword)] dy: L, 1597
437 meat] meate L, 1597
437 day: So] day*:* *S*o L, 1597
438 word,] worde L, 1597
439 anie] any L, 1597
440 passe away:] passe away, L, 1597
441 bodie:] bodie*:* L, 1597
441 spiritual] spirituall L, 1597
441 soule.] soule. [black-letter period] L, 1597
442 sermon] *S*ermon L, 1597
442 passeport,] passport, L, 1597
444 conduct thee by,] conduct thee by L, 1597
445 reade] read L, 1597
446–447 (as thou] *(*as thou L, 1597
448 profite:] profite*:* L, 1597
448–449 exercises. This] exercises*:* this L, 1597
450 thine [G2^{r} 42] adoption,] thine a- [G2^{r} 42] doption, HN, F, PN^2; thine ad- [G2^{r} 42] option L, 1597
465 nor] or 1597
472 had it,] hidde it 1609, 1615
475 note #89, Matt. 26.74] Matth. 26.47 1591, 1599, 1634
476 On the] new paragraph 1608, 1609, 1615
477 note #90, Luk. 22.31] Luk. 22.3 1634; correct citation is Luke 22:32

480	offences,] offence, 1597
485	Yea, but] new paragraph 1615
485	(wilt thou] thou wilt 1615
490–491	make me] make me. HN, F, L, PN^2
492	upon other,] upon others, 1615, 1634
493	Wee denie] new paragraph 1609, 1615
510, 513	notes #94 and #95, Gen. 39.; Gen. 45.] Gen. 45.39. 1634
523	vanished and gone.] doublet created from "esvanouis"
536	Following this] new paragraph 1608, 1609, 1615
542	his holie spirit] his spirit 1591, 1599, 1634
553	beare the crosse] French adds marginal citation: Luc. 9.23.
570–571	those who have faith, are assured,] omits "the mother of a good conscience and the nurse of the fear of God" from "qui ont la foy mere de la bonne conscience, et nourrice de la crainte de Dieu, sont asseruez"
572–573	yet it can] yet can 1591, 1597, 1599, 1608, 1609, 1615, 1634
576	foule and grosse] doublet created from "lourdes"

Running-titles

F3^v–F5^v *Of the markes of* verso

Chapter Five

1–3	*That the Apostacie and revolt of some having made profession of the true religion, ought not to make us call in doubt neither our religion nor our adoption.*] in Table of Contents: That the Apostacie and revolt of some who have made profession of the true religion, ought not to cause us to call in doubt either the doctrine, or our adoption. French chapter heading: Que l'Apostasie et revolte d'aucuns ayans faict profession de la vraye religion, ne doit faire revoquer en doute, ni la doctrine, ni nostre adoption. French Table of Contents: Que l'apostasie et revolte d'aucuns qui ont fait profession de la vraye religion, ne doit point faire revoquer en doute ni la doctrine, ni nostre adoption.
5	WE] woodcut W
8	principallie,] principall, 1615
10–11	horrible offence or stumbling blocke] doublet created from "l'horrible scandale"
22	troubles,] troubles L, 1597; G8^r–^{v} has been replaced in L with a leaf from the 1597 edition; see also G1^r–^{v} in Chapter Four
23	whither he] whether he L, 1597

23 And] And L, 1597
25 al] all L, 1597
25 note #1, Of the cer-
taintie of
the doctrine
notwith-
standing
the revolts.]

Of the certain-
tie of the do-
ctrine notwith.
standing the
revolts. L, 1597
26 concerning] cōcerning HN, F, PN^2; concerning L, 1597
26 us:] us: L, 1597
27 foretold] foretolde L, 1597
27 wherwith the church] wherewith the Church L, 1597
28 called,] called L, 1597
28 saith Jesus Christ,] saith Christ, 1608, 1609, 1615
28 note #2, Matt. 20.16] Mat. 20.16. L, 1597; Mar. 20.16. 1591, 1599, 1634
30 shal heare] shall heare L, 1597
30 note #3, Matth. 13.] first words of line are "shal heare" HN, F, PN^2; first words of line are "much a doo" L, 1597
30 Gospel, shall] Gospell, shal L, 1597
31 S. *Paule*] S. [black-letter period] *Paule* L, 1597
31 note #4, 1. Tim. 4.1.] first word of line is "foretold" HN, F, PN^2; first words of line are "shall heare" L, 1597
32 shal fall] shall fall L, 1597
32 from the faith.] omits "that is to say the doctrine of the gospel" from "de la foy, c'est à dire de la doctrine de l'Evangile."
32 note #5, Act. 20.30.] Acts. 20.30. L, 1597
32 *Ephe.*] *Ephes.* L, 1597
34 note #6, 1. Cor. 11.19.] notes #6 and #7 combined L, 1597
34 church] Church L, 1597
35 divisions,] devisions, L, 1597
35 Saint] *S*aint L, 1597
36 (saith] *(*saith L, 1597
36 Israel,] Israell, L, 1597
38 errours,] errours L, 1597
38 manie shal] manie shall L, 1597

38	whom] whome L, 1597
39	Now, we] new paragraph 1609, 1615
39	thinke] think L, 1597
41	church] Church L, 1597
41	note #8, Gen. 6.] first words of line are "of God" HN, F, PN^2; first word of line is "floud," L, 1597
41	times.] black-letter period L, 1597
42	flood,] floud, L, 1597
42	onlie] only L, 1597
42	found] foūd HN, F, PN^2; found L, 1597
44	note #9, Gen. 9.25.] first word of line is "cast" HN, F, PN^2; first word of line is "posteritie" L, 1597; Gen 9:15. 1608, 1609, 1615
44	accursed.] accursed? L, 1597
45	church] Church L, 1597
46	*Abraham,*] *Abraham,* L, 1597
46	being] beeing L, 1597
47	idolatrie.] Idolatrie. L, 1597
47	*Elias*] *Elias*, L, 1597
47	note #11, 1. Reg. 19. 10.] 1. Reg. 19.10. L, 1597; 1. Reg. 19.16 1634
48	Lord] Lorde L, 1597
50	principal] principall L, 1597
77	unto] to 1591, 1597, 1599, 1608, 1609, 1615, 1634
84	did them,] did the 1634
85	to them] unto them 1609, 1615
91	note #19, Psal. 101.] Psal. 102. 1609, 1615
102	great] greater 1615
114	then] them 1599
115	were more] was more 1597
129	in intermedling] intermedling 1597
140	This then] new paragraph 1615
141–142	the Monke.] a Monke. 1615
147	hath set] saith set 1597
151–152	and so with fervent praiers] omits "in humility" from "et ainsi en humilité avec prieres ardentes"
167	that he] as he 1591, 1597, 1599, 1608, 1609, 1615, 1634
169	Papist, and] Papist, 1597; Priest, and 1609, 1615
171	note #23, Gal. 1.] correct citation is Gal. 1:8; French: Gala. 1.8.
173	of our God,] of God 1608, 1609, 1615
179	note #26, Esai. 8.18.] Esay 3.18. 1634
191	note #27, revolts.] revolt. 1615

192 these revoltes,] their revoltes 1597
211 the Sacraments,] his Sacraments 1608, 1609, 1615
218 But this is,] But that is, 1591, 1597, 1599, 1608, 1609, 1615, 1634
220 note #32, Matt. 15.13] Matth. 25.13. 1634
221 note #33, Matt. 13.] Mar. 13. 1608, 1609, 1615
226 choake] choakes 1634
245 to live] to love 1609, 1615
250 toward] towards 1608, 1609, 1615
254 note #37, Rom. 12.1.] Rom. 12 [frisket bite] 1609, 1615
258 note #38, 1. John 3.3.] 1 Joh. 3. [frisket bite] 1609, 1615

Chapter Six

1–2 *That afflictions ought not to make us to doubt of our adoption, but rather confirme us.*] in Table of Contents: That afflictions ought not to make us doubt of our adoption, but rather to confirme us. French chapter heading: Que les afflictions ne nous doivent faire douter de nostre adoption, ains plustost nous y confermer. French Table of Contents: Que les afflictions ne doivent point nous faire douter de nostre adoption, ains plus-tost nous y confermer.
1 *to doubt*] *doubt* 1615
4 LET] woodcut L
9 other kinsfolk] kinsfolke 1608, 1609, 1615
33 note #1, 2. Tim 3 12] 1. Tim 3.12. 1634
39 bee the verie] bee verie 1591, 1599, 1634
42 true] tue 1597
43 thereby,] theretby 1597
53 were)] were 1608, 1609

Chapter Seven

1–2 *That the afflictions that happen unto us, have beene foretolde, and therefore they ought to confirme us in the assurance of our adoption.*] in Table of Contents: That the afflictions which come unto us were foretold, and therfore they ought to confirme us in the assurance of our adoption. French (in both places): Que les afflictions qui nous adviennent, ont esté predites, et pourtant nous doyvent confermer en l'asseurance de nostre adoption.

1	*have*] *hath* 1608, 1609, 1615
4	THE] woodcut T
8–9	notes #1 and #2] reversed order 1615
19	of the Heaven.] of heaven. 1591, 1599, 1634
22	hundred] hundreth 1609
26	afflictions)] affliction) 1591, 1597, 1599, 1608, 1609, 1615, 1634; French: l'affliction
29	note #5, Psal. 34.20] correct citation is Ps. 34:19
34	note #6, Prophecies] The prophecies 1634
35	Above all,] new paragraph 1615
37	(saith he) to his Apostles,] (saith he to his Apostles), 1597, 1615
38	amongest] among 1597, 1615
45	Againe, Verelie,] new paragraph 1609, 1615
47	True it] new paragraph 1608, 1609, 1615
48–49	sayeth Saint *Peter*,] (saith Saint *Peter*) 1591, 1599, 1615, 1634
50	note #13, 2. Thes. 3.7] correct citation is 1 Thess. 3:3; French: 2. thes. 3.2
57	hath] had 1615
59	Now this] new paragraph 1615
62	note #17, Jhon 16.1.] omitted 1599
69	this behalfe.] that behalfe. 1608, 1609, 1615
69	For] Far 1599
77	But if] new paragraph 1615
84	thy king] the king 1609, 1615
85	note #20, *Dan.* 9 26] Dan. 9.29. 1599
88	they would have] they have 1591, 1599, 1634
92	note #21, *Rom.* 8.17] correct citation is Rom. 8:29; French: Rom. 8.29
92	conformable] comfortable 1609, 1615
94	and testimonies,] and testimonies, , HN, F, L, PN^{2}
98	addeth,] addetth, HN, F, L, PN^{2}
101	holie Virgine] Virgine 1591, 1599, 1634
125	note #24, Act. 14.22.] Actes. 14. 1591, 1597, 1599, 1608, 1609, 1615, 1634
126	note #25, Matt. 7.13.] omitted 1634

Chapter Eight

1–2	*That the Children of God have alwaies been afflicted, and yet still beloved of God.*] in Table of Contents: That the children of

GOD have at all times been afflicted, and yet beloved of God. French (in both places): Qes les enfans de Dieu ont esté de tout temps affligez, et cependant aymez de Dieu.

4 THis] woodcut T

17–18 to put him out] French adds marginal citation: Exod. 2.

27 eyes. Did they escape] eyes, they did escape 1591, 1599, 1608, 1609, 1615, 1634

38 note #12, 2. King. 25] 2. Reg. 25. 1591, 1634

44 note #15, Esa. 46.7.] correct citation is Isa. 49:7; French: Isa. 49.7.

47 returned] turned 1597

59 Againe, Thou] And againe, Thou 1609, 1615

63 Also comparing] new paragraph 1609, 1615

63 note #20, Psalm. 80.] omitted 1597; Psal. 81. 1599

70 In like] new paragraph 1615

77 seditions] seditious HN, F, L, PN^{2}, 1597; French: seditions

94 note #27, *Euse. lib.* 8. *chap.* 11.] Euse. li. 18. cap. 11 1609, 1615; *Euse. lib. chap.* 11. 1634

95 As touching] new paragraph 1608, 1609, 1615

96 tormens] torments 1591, 1597, 1599, 1608, 1609, 1615, 1634

106–107 into the Lime] into Lyme 1608, 1609, 1615

111 or thirst.] and thirst. 1615

133 him, with his] him, his 1608, 1609, 1615

135 note #35, Gen. 34.] omitted 1634

138 By this] new paragraph 1608, 1609

148 Among the] new paragraph 1615

151 people *Israel*,] people of *Israel*, 1591, 1597, 1599, 1608, 1609, 1615, 1634; French: peuple d'Israel

155 the sonne of *Pharaos* daughter,] French adds marginal citation: Heb. 11.24

156 *Ægypt*.] *Ægypt*: L

157 the commandement of GOD,] French adds marginal citation: Exod. 5.

164 note #43, Num. 12.1.] Numb. 12. [frisket bite] 1615

174 mockings] mocking 1597

177 sheepe] sheepes 1591, 1597, 1599, 1608, 1609, 1615, 1634

183 Now, this] new paragraph 1608, 1609, 1615

187 *Marie*.] Mary 1634

197 note #54, Mat. 11.19] Mat. 11.39 1615

198 note #55, Mat. 27.63.] Matth. 17.63 1591, 1599, 1634

205 note #59, Act. 9.16.] Ads. 9.16. L

213–214 I suffered] I have suffered 1608, 1609, 1615

221	Now, let] new paragraph 1615
221	When the] new paragraph 1608, 1609, 1615
225	have not] hath not 1615
226	crosse are] crosse and 1597
230	welbeloved one,] welbeloved ones, 1591, 1599, 1608, 1609, 1615, 1634
230	note #62, Esay. 41.8. and 49.15.] Esay. 41.8. and 49.25 1608, 1609; Esay 41.8. and 42.25 1615
248	note #66, 2. Cor. 11.23.] 2. Cor. 11.13. 1599
268	knew] know 1608, 1609, 1615
270	note #71, Mat. 5.12] Mark. 5.12. 1634
277	other] owne 1615
278	note #72, Rom. 8.28] correct citation is Rom. 8:29
281	note #73, 2. Tim. 2.11] 2. Tim. 2.1 [frisket bite] 1615
296	Now let] new paragraph 1608, 1609, 1615
299	though] although 1609, 1615
301–302	although] though 1609, 1615
304–305	hee also] also hee 1609, 1615
318	heigth,] height, 1597, 1608, 1609, 1615

Chapter Nine

1–3	*That the faithfull have the common afflictions of the children of Adam, because of the excellent fruites of them, testimonies of their adoption, and of the love of God toward them.*] in Table of Contents: That the common afflictions of the children of Adam, are to the faithfull, because of the excellent fruites of them, testimonies of their adoption, and of the love of GOD towards them. French (in both places): Que les afflictions communes aux enfans d'Adam sont aux fideles, à cause des excellens fruicts d'icelles, tesmoignages de leur adoption, et de l'amour de Dieu envers eux.
4	CAP. 9.] CAP. 7. 1597
5	TO] woodcut T
7	First, for] new paragraph 1615
14	The children] new paragraph 1615
15	but they] yet they 1615
20	*Manasses*] new paragraph 1615
22	at the last] at last 1634
30	that affliction;] this affliction 1608, 1609, 1615
33	And this] new paragraph 1615

34 remaining] remaineth 1634
39 See now] new paragraph 1615
42 *Ezechias*] *EZechias* HN, F, L, PN^2
46 and in putting] and putting 1608, 1609, 1615
48 note #9, 2. Sam. 16.22] 2. Sam. 26.22 1609, 1615
49 note #10, 2. Sam. 12 11] 2. Sam. 12.10. 1599
52 Now as] new paragraph 1615
56 conscience,] Consciences, 1609, 1615
64 world,] woɹld, HN, F, L, PN^2
67 cut in] cut me in 1608, 1609, 1615
69 note #15, 1. Cor. 12.32.] correct citation is 1 Cor. 11:32; French: 1. Cor. 11.32.
73 note #17, Psa. 119 71] omitted 1615
84 to keep] te keep 1591
95 note #18, 2. In] 3. In 1591, 1597, 1599, 1608, 1609, 1615, 1634
96 Furthermore,] new paragraph 1615
101 or mingleth] mingleth 1599
103 sheweth,] shewes, 1608, 1609, 1615
110 To be short,] new paragraph 1615
113 wake] make 1615
115 note #19, John 15.] John 5. HN, L, PN^2
119 so God] God 1615
126 The Prophet] new paragraph 1615
134 afflictions,] affliction, 1615
137 scribbles in margin 1591
142 of the flesh,] the flesh, 1608
145 note #21, In confidence.] In coufidence 1634
152 us to feele] us feele 1608, 1609, 1615
155 note #22, 2. Cor. 1.9.] 1. Cor. 1.9. 1597; omitted 1634
158 This is it] no paragraph 1608, 1609, 1615
159 in the first chapter of his first Epistle and the seaventh verse,] French omits phrases but includes a marginal citation: 1. Pier. 1.7
162 tribulations.] tribulation. 1591, 1597, 1599, 1608, 1609, 1615, 1634
163 at his ease,] at ease, 1591, 1597, 1599, 1608, 1609, 1615, 1634
172 overturn] overcome 1609, 1615
174 From hence] new paragraph 1615
175 of the name] on the name 1615
178 comfort in the] comfort on the 1609, 1615
182 The historie] new paragraph 1608, 1609, 1615
184 to G O D,] unto God, 1609, 1615

184 note #24, Psal. 78.34.] Psal. 18.34 1608, 1609, 1615

187 high and mightie GOD] doublet created from "Dieu Souverain"

188 note #25, Ose. 5.15 and 7.1.] correct citations are Hos. 5:15 and 6:1; French: Ose. 6.15. et 7.1.

192 note #26, Luk. 15.11.] Luke 15. 1634

194–195 Furthermore, our] new paragraph 1609, 1615

201 note #30, Ro. 10.13.] Rom. 10.| [frisket bite] 1609; Rom. 10.1. 1615

204 compt] count 1591, 1599, 1608, 1609, 1615, 1634

205 matter] matters 1615

211–212 to subject] subject 1591, 1597, 1599, 1608, 1609, 1615, 1634

213 trie us and] trye and 1609, 1615

221 note #36, Psal. 39.10.] Psal. 30.10. 1608, 1609, 1615; correct citation is Ps. 39:9

234 note #38, father and redeemer.] reverses terms in "Redempteur et Pere"

238 beareth us,] beareth, 1634

240 It is] new paragraph 1608, 1609, 1615

246 also it is] also is 1597

250 onlie true father,] onely father, 1608, 1609, 1615

252 his will,] his holy Will, 1609, 1615

261 note #42, 2. Sam. 15.16.] 2. Sam. 15.26. 1615; correct citation is 2 Sam. 15:26; French: 2. Sam. 15.26.

264 as *Abraham*] *Abraham* 1597

264 To bee] new paragraph 1608, 1609, 1615

266 If then afflictions] If afflictions 1597; If then affliction 1608, 1609, 1615; French adds marginal note: Conclusion.

272 toward] towards 1608, 1609, 1615, 1634

275 note #45, Heb. 12.6.] Heb. 12.9. 1634

276 If you] If yee 1615

280 accompteth] accounteth 1608, 1609, 1615, 1634

284 appertained] appertayneth 1615

289 Carpenters] Carpenter 1615

290 pieces of wood] a piece of wood 1591, 1599, 1608, 1609, 1615, 1634

293 lift up] lift 1634

293–294 hatchets] hatches 1599

Chapter Ten

1	*Of the afflictions for the name of Christ, and of their fruites.*] in Table of Contents: Of the afflictions for Christes sake, and of the fruites of them. French (in both places): Des afflictions pour le nom de Christ, et des fruicts d'icelles.
3	TRue] woodcut T
9	for the Church,] the church 1597
18–19	Blessed are they which are persecuted for righteousnes sake: Also,] omitted 1597
18	note #9, of God.] of the God HN, F, L, PN^2; French: *de Dieu*
20	note #10, Mat. 5.10.] omitted 1634; correct citation is Matt. 5:11
23	Now, if] no paragraph 1591, 1599, 1634
25	untollerable] intollerable 1591, 1599, 1609, 1615, 1634
31–32	They that] new paragraph 1608, 1609, 1615
48	Now, the] new paragraph 1608, 1609, 1615
56	doo not we] doe we not 1608, 1609, 1615
61	In the] new paragraph 1608, 1609, 1615
62	this blessing] the blessing 1608, 1609, 1615
68	the end] thee end 1597
70	glorie,] gloty 1634
75	note #20, Psal. 37.16.] Psal. 37. [torn page] 1597
85	hundred] hnndred 1634
87	note #22, Rom. 8.31.] om. 8.31. [torn page] 1597; correct citation is Rom. 8:32
92–93	the pupils,] Pupils, 1608, 1609, 1615
93	portion:] proportion: 1591, 1599, 1634
96	seeke first] first seeke 1634
97	promise] promises 1609, 1615
103	dispose,] propose, 1634
109	bondslaves] bondslave 1591, 1599, 1634
110	note #24, Col. 3.24] omitted 1634
111	great] grear 1597
118	a house,] an house, 1608, 1609, 1615
122	dignities] dignitie 1591, 1599, 1634
145	his death;] death; 1608, 1609, 1615
153	this reward] their reward 1591, 1597, 1599, 1608, 1609, 1615, 1634
157	note #31, 2. Cor. 4.17] .Cor. 4.17. [frisket bite] 1599
160	And to] new paragraph 1615
174	note #32, John 9.] omitted [torn page] 1597

181 note #33, 2. Sam. 16 12] 2. Sam. 12.16 1591, 1597, 1599, 1608, 1609, 1615, 1634
183 note #34, Reve. 1.6] Rene. 1.6. HN, F, L, PN^2
184 note #35, Heb. 2.12] Heb. 2.21 1597; correct citation is Heb. 2:11; French: Hebr. 2.11
189 God giveth us] French adds marginal citation: Apoc. 21.
193 consider] confesse 1609, 1615
199 note #36, Psal. 56.9] correct citation is Ps. 56:8
200 numbred my] numbred thy 1597
203 father, mother, lands] omits "wife" in "pere, mere, femme, champs"
211–212 our afflictions] afflictions 1591, 1597, 1599, 1608, 1609, 1615, 1634
217 note #39, 2. Co. 4.18.] 1. Cor. 4.18. 1591, 1599, 1634
221 note #40, Gen. 47.9.] omitted [torn page] 1597
221 had been] have been 1591, 1599, 1634; hath bin 1597, 1608, 1609
222 they few,] thy fewe, 1597
229 How?] Now, 1615
234 note #43, 1. Joh. 2.18] 4. Ioh. 2.18. 1608, 1609, 1615
237 1587. yeres,] this section apparently was added to the augmented edition
241 of man:] of a man: 1591, 1597, 1599, 1608, 1609, 1615, 1634
249 note #44, 1. Pet. 3.8.] correct citation is 2 Pet. 3:8; French: 2. Pier. 3.8
252 note #45, Psal. 90.4.] omitted [torn page] 1597
252 before god] substitutes "before" for "the eyes of" in "les yeux de Dieu"
253 80. yeres] 80. 1591, 1597, 1599, 1608, 1609, 1615, 1634
266 note #50, 1. Co. 15.28] 2. Cor. 15.28. 1599
268 as also S. *Paul* saith,] French adds marginal citation: 2. Tim. 1.10.

Chapter Eleven

1 *Other fruites of the afflictions for the name of Jesus Christ.*] in Table of Contents: Other fruites of the afflictions for the name of Christ. French chapter heading: Autres fruicts des afflictions pour le nom de Jesus Christ. French Table of Content: Autres fruicts des afflictions pour le nom de Christ.
3 BEsides] woodcut B

3	these,] those 1591, 1599, 1634
3	note #1, 1. Fruit,] ite, [torn page] 1597; First fruit, 1634
13	note #4, Rev. 17.6.] Revel. 7.6. 1634
22	for his name.] of his name. 1599
22	when] when when HN, F, L, PN^2; last word of line repeated as first word of subsequent line
25	renowme,] renowne, 1591, 1599, 1608, 1609, 1615, 1634
29	(as it were)] as it were 1597
30	against those] against them 1615
38	note #7, declaring] decla- [$O1^r$ 97] claring HN, F, L, PN^2; declaring and [$O1^r$ 97] claring 1597
38	note #7, shewing] shewiug 1591
45	with our] with out 1634
50	supposts] suppost 1591, 1597, 1599, 1608, 1609, 1615, 1634
57	I can doo] *I doe* 1608, 1609, 1615
65	the course,] a course 1597
66	in the combat,] in Combat, 1608, 1609, 1615
69	note #12, the body] tht body 1599
79	he hath] he had 1591, 1597, 1608, 1609, 1615, 1634
81	note #13, Mat. 28.29] correct citation is Matt. 28:20
81	which hath] which was 1608, 1609, 1615
90	least] lest 1634
100	there were] there was 1634
102	goodlie] godlie 1591, 1599, 1608, 1609, 1615, 1634
103	note #19, Phil. 1.12] Phil. 12.19. 1591, 1597, 1599, 1634
105	bandes] hands 1609, 1615
110	daunted of any,] danted an any, 1608; daunted at any, 1609, 1615
120	the honours] honours 1591, 1597, 1599, 1608, 1609, 1615, 1634
120	and life] and the Life 1608, 1609, 1615
128	with them,] French adds marginal citation: Ps. 91.15.
134	setteth] sitteth 1599
138	so excellent] excellent 1591, 1599, 1634
143	by his Spirite,] by the Spirit, 1634
154	compteth] counteth 1591, 1597, 1599, 1608, 1609, 1615, 1634

Chapter Twelve

1–4	*An exhortation to persevere constantly in the truth of the Gospell in the time of persecution, not to feare death, to keepe us from apostacie and dissimulation, to use the holy Ministerie, to walke in the feare of God, and to pray to him.*] in Table of Contents:

An exhortation to persever constantlie in the trueth of the Gospell, in the time of persecution: not to feare death: for man to keepe himselfe from Apostacie and dissimulation: To use the holie Ministerie: To walke in the feare of God, and to pray unto him. French (in both places): Exhortation à perseverer constamment en la verité de l'Evangile au temps de persecution: à ne craindre la mort: à se garder d'apostasie et simulation: à user du sainct Ministere: à cheminer en la crainte de Dieu: et à le prier.

4 *to pray*] *pray* 1591, 1597, 1599, 1608, 1609, 1615, 1634

6 BY] woodcut B HN, F, L, PN^{2}, 1591, 1597, 1599, 1608, 1634; large B 1609, 1615

7 or to be] or be 1591, 1597, 1599, 1608, 1609, 1615, 1634

8 note #2, of the felicitie] of of the felicitie HN, F, L, PN^{2}; last word of line repeated as first word of subsequent line

10 race, all runne,] omits "sayth Saint Paul," in "Quand on court la lice, dit sainct Paul, tous courent"

17 mad] made 1599

38 accompt] account 1597, 1608, 1609, 1615, 1634

42 note #5, *Gal.* 6.17.] 6.17. [torn page] 1597

43 vile or base things,] doublet created from "choses viles:"

46–47 shall not it] shal it not 1591, 1599, 1608, 1609, 1615, 1634; shall not 1597

47 accompt] account 1591, 1597, 1599, 1608, 1609, 1615, 1634

53 nor shaken] not shaken 1599

55 note #6, *Philip.* 1.28] Psal. 1.28. 1634

57 it is as a] it is a 1591, 1597, 1599, 1608, 1609, 1615, 1634

58 drunke] drunge 1599

63 note #7, 2. *Thess.* 1.5] 2. Thess. 15. 1599

65 affliction] afflictions 1615

66 Angels] Gngels 1597

68 obeyed] obeying 1608, 1609, 1615

75 note #8, *Ja.* 5.11.] Jam. 5.1. 1591, 1597, 1599, 1608, 1609, 1615, 1634

78 note #9, *Gen.* 37.39.] correct citation is Gen. 37 and 39; French: Genes. 37. et 39.

80 but let us see] French adds marginal citation: Genes. 41.

85 so be] be so 1615

90 (will we say)] (will we say 1608

91 handleth] handles 1615

92 the resurrection to the death:] the death to the resurrection: 1608, 1609, 1615

97	would not shout] should not shout 1591, 1597, 1599, 1608, 1609, 1634
104	that should] what should 1597
113	pleasure,] pleasures 1615
114	*Lazarus*,] *LaZarus*, HN, F, L, PN^2
118	compt,] count, 1591, 1599, 1608, 1609, 1615, 1634
118	condition] conditions 1609, 1615
118–119	Lazarusses] *Lazarusse* 1597
120	note #12, Psal. 94.12.] Psal. 94.10 1615
124	note #13, 2. Not] 3 Not 1615
126	after a great travaile, the haven desired] omitted 1597
128	sicknes,] sicknesses, 1609, 1615
135	note #15, Phil. 1.23.] Phil. [torn page] 1597
139	the bodie:] Body: 1608, 1609, 1615
141	beeing then] then beeing 1609, 1615
143	It is] new paragraph 1608, 1609, 1615
145	against] great 1609, 1615
152	Let us put off] Let us cut off 1591, 1597, 1599, 1608, 1609, 1615, 1634
163	note #17, Psal. 31.16] correct citation is Ps. 31:15
164	There is] new paragraph 1609, 1615
165	to man,] unto man, 1609, 1615
166	note #18, Mat. 13.39] Mat. 13.19 1609, 1615
167	note #20, Job 1. and 2.] Job. 1. and [cropped page] 1609
173	saith ... *Samuel,*] (saith ... *Samuell,* 1609; (saith ... *Samuell,*) 1615
173	note #22, 1. Sam. 2.3] 1. Sam. 2. [cropped page] 1609
177	as *David* saith,] (as *David* sayeth) 1608, 1609, 1615
183	his infinite] the infinite 1597
186	note #25, Rom. 8.30.] om. 8.30. [cropped page] 1609
188	Saint *Paule,*] new paragraph 1608, 1609, 1615
191	note #27, Ro. 12.36.] Rom. 11.36. 1591, 1599, 1634; correct citation is Rom. 11:36
197	into the land] in the land 1591, 1597, 1599, 1608, 1609, 1634
204	saith Jesus Christ,] (sayth Jesus Christ) 1608, 1609, 1615
204	note #29, Luk. 12.24] correct citation is Luke 12:4–5
208	In like] new paragraph 1608, 1609, 1615
218	note #30, Mat. 14.13] correct citation is Matt. 24:13
219	you to] yo tou 1599
220	note #31, our] o [torn page] 1597
233	unto the end.] to the end. 1597
234	*Nicodemites,*] *Nicodemoies*, 1591, 1597, 1599, 1608, 1609; *Nico-*

demies, 1615; *Nicodemus's* 1634

235 untollerable)] intollerable) 1591, 1599, 1634

236 Will the] new paragraph 1608, 1609, 1615

241 note #33, 2. Cor. 7.1] Cor. 7.1 [torn page] 1597; Cor. 17.1 1608, 1609; 1 Cor. 17.1 1615

249 note #35, Joh. 6.27.] Joh. 6.24. 1608, 1609, 1615

250–251 it that] that it 1591, 1599; that which 1608, 1609, 1615; that that it 1634

256 note #36, Col. 3.16] 6 [torn page] 1597

256 note #37, Psa. 1.2.] omitted [torn page] 1597

257 note #38, Act. 17.11 Deut. 6] omitted [torn page] 1597

257 note #39, Psa. 119] Psal. 116 1597

265 this mother,] his Mother, 1608, 1609

268 In ancient] new paragraph 1608, 1609, 1615

268 note #43, Act. 11.26] 11.26 [torn page] 1597

274 note #47, Ephe. 2.19] Eph. 2.10. 1615

275 note #48, 2. Cor. 3.8] 2 Cer. 3.8. 1615

292 note #52, Psal. 27.] correct citation is Ps. 27:4; French: Ps. 27.4.

321 anie] auy 1634

321 note #58, Rom. 6] m. 6 [torn page] 1597

322–333 of [$Q1^r$ 113] iniquitie] of [$Q1^r$ 113] of iniquitie HN, F, L, PN^2

324 note #59, Rom. 6.18] Rom. 6 [torn page] 1597

328 note #61, Gal. 5.24] Gal. 5.22 1599

329 note #62, Gal. 5.25] omitted 1591, 1634

331 if ye] if we 1597, 1599

332 sanctification.] sanctification HN, F, L, PN^2

332 If yee] If wee 1597, 1599

333 note #64] 1. Jho. 3. 2 3] 1. Joh. 3.23 1608, 1609, 1615; correct citation is 1 John 3:2–3

334 shall see] can see 1609, 1615

338 note #67, 1. Pet. 1.15] 5 [torn page] 1597; 2. Pet. 1.15. 1609, 1615

338 note #68, 2. Cor. 6] 6 [torn page] 1597; 1. Cor. 6. 1609, 1615; correct citation is 2 Cor. 6:14–17; French: 1. Cor. 6.

339 saith Saint *Paule,*] (saith Saint *Paul*) 1608, 1609, 1615

341 beleeving] Beleever 1608, 1609, 1615

344 touch] couch 1608

344 The ende] new paragraph 1608, 1609, 1615

352 note #70, Col. 2.13] correct citation is Col. 1:13

356 note #71, Phil. 2.15] Phil. 2.1. [crease in repaired page] 1597

361 lusts,] lust, 1591, 1597, 1599, 1608, 1609, 1615, 1634

362	the world] this world 1609, 1615
364	note #74, Eph. 5.11] French: Ephe. 5.12.
365–366	reproofe] proof 1591, 1597, 1599, 1608, 1609, 1615, 1634
366	note #75, Job. 28.28.] omitted 1608, 1609, 1615
375	God, and to suffer himselfe quietlie to] omitted 1591, 1634
378	than it,] that it, 1608
378	note #78, Mat. 16.14] correct citation is Matt. 16:24
379–380	hate ye] French adds marginal citation: Rom. 12.9
381	note #79, Col. 3.12] C l. 3.12 [damaged page] 1597
381	Procure things] French adds marginal citation: 2. Cor. 8.21
382	be possible,] French adds marginal citation: rom. 12.18
383	yee] we 1591, 1597, 1599, 1608, 1609, 1615, 1634
384	bowells] bowell 1591, 1599, 1608, 1609, 1634
386	have a quarel] hath a quarrel 1615
386	note #80, 1. Jhon 10] .Jhon. 10 [frisket bite] 1591; correct citation is 1 John 3:10; French 1. Jan. 3.10
389	the true disciples] the Disciples 1608, 1609, 1615
392	If yee] new paragraph 1609, 1615
397	note #84, Gala. 6.10] 10 [torn page] 1597
398	note #85, 1. Pet. 4.10] 1. Pet. 10. 1591, 1597, 1599, 1608, 1609, 1615, 1634
399	note #86, 1. Pet. 4.8] 1. Pet. 8.4. 1597, 1599; 2. Pet. 4.8. 1615
409	note #88, 1. Pet. 2.12] Pet. 2.1 [torn page] 1597
410	note #89, Luke 7.1.] correct citation is Luke 17:1–2; French: Luc. 17.1.
412	offend] offended 1591, 1597, 1599, 1608, 1609, 1615, 1634
429	heape] heade 1597, 1599
434	note #94, *Aug*.] g. [torn page] 1597
436	handwritten inscription, "Francis Clarke his book 1691" 1597
438	prayers.] prayers, HN, F, L, PN^{2}
461	your] our 1597, 1599
465	to all] for all 1615
466	note #95, 1. *Thess*. 5.23] 1. Thes. 5.25. 1599; 1. The. 5. [frisket bite] 1608; 1. Thes. 5. 1609, 1615
474	mercies] mercy 1615
476	faithfull] faithfully 1591, 1597, 1599, 1608, 1609, 1615, 1634

Chapter Thirteen

1	*Holie meditations and praiers.*] in Table of Contents: Holie meditations and praiers. French chapter heading: Meditations

	sainctes et prieres. French Table of Contents: Meditations sainctes et priere.
3	O] woodcut O
4	the troubles] thy troubles 1591, 1597, 1608, 1609, 1615
6	forasmuch] as much 1591, 1608, 1609, 1615, 1634; in asmuch 1597, 1599
7	thi wrath] his wrath 1591, 1597, 1599, 1608, 1609, 1615, 1634
11–12	wee are worthie to bee rejected of thee,] omitted 1591, 1597, 1599, 1608, 1609, 1615, 1634
15	favour] omits "mercy" in "misericorde et faveur"
33	our God,] ô God 1591, 1597, 1599, 1608, 1609, 1615, 1634
46	adulteries,] adulterie, 1609, 1615
47	have made] hath made 1608, 1609, 1615
50	thy Church.] the Church. 1615
56	thy Word] the word 1591, 1597, 1599, 1608, 1609, 1615, 1634
64	that have not] that not 1597
82	religiouslie] righteously 1599
90	given up] given us 1608, 1609; given as 1615
93	into death:] unto death: 1597
108	Behold us] new paragraph 1615
110	at tone] at one 1591, 1597, 1599, 1608, 1609, 1615, 1634
117	not thou] thou not 1609, 1615
119	that though] that although 1609, 1615
122	us to him,] us unto him, 1609, 1615
131	of our soules.] on our soules. 1615
143	our darknes,] darknes, 1597
143	life] lift HN, F, L, PN^2
144	unworthines,] worthines, 1597
152	the people] thy people 1634
154	by thee] omitted 1608, 1609, 1615
159	the bold] their bolde 1608, 1609, 1615
162	ruined] renewed 1597; ruinated 1609, 1615
165	that so wee] that we 1597
R4^{v}	Blank

The necessitie and benefite of affliction

Lock substitutes her poem on affliction for Taffin's quotations from the New Testament and poetic paraphrases of Augustine's *De civitate Dei.* The biblical passages, entitled "Prieres extraictes des Epistres de Sainct Paul," are prayers taken from the following Pauline epistles: Eph. 1:17–20; 3:14–

19; 2 Cor. 4:6; 1 Thess. 5:23–24; Col. 1:9–11; 1 Thess. 3:12–13; 2 Thess. 2:16–17; Rom. 15:13; 2 Thess. 3:5. The quotations follow the French Geneva version (Geneva: [Jeremie des Planches], 1588) with grammatical changes to personalize the prayers and occasional word substitutions that reflect the earlier Olivetan translation (Neuchatel: Pierre de Vingle, 1535). The two selections from *De civitate Dei*, probably translated by Taffin himself, are from Book I, chapter 8; they are followed (in square brackets) by a line-for-line English translation.

L'Eternel a voulu selon sa sapience
Preparer à ses saincts des biens à l'avenir,
Dont les meschans n'auront aucune jouissance,
Et des maux aux meschans, que les justes souffrir
Ne pourront nullement. Mais quant à eeste [ceste] vie,
Des biens communs à tous il y a et des maux:
Afin que ni ces biens l'homme de bien n'envie
Communs aux plus meschans, et que de ces travaux,
Dont les enfans de Dieu justes, saincts, et fideles
Nous voyons affligez plus ordinairement
Que l'injuste courant aux peines eternelles,
Se soustraire et garder ne vueille laschement.
Aug. lib. I. de Civit. Dei. c. 8.

[The Eternal has desired according to his wisdom
To prepare for his saints future blessings,
Which the wicked will not enjoy,
And to prepare evil things for the wicked, which the righteous will suffer
Not at all. But as for this life,
Good things are common to all, and also those things that are evil:
So that neither should the righteous man desire the good
Which is common to the most wicked, nor these troubles,
Which the children of God who are just, holy, and faithful
We see more often afflicted with than
The unjust who incur eternal punishments,
Should they wish to escape and avoid with cowardly weakness.]

Qui craint Dieu ne s'esleve en sa prosperité,
Et jamais abbatu n'est en adversité.
Aug. lib. I. de Civit. Dei. c. 8.

[The one who fears God neither elevates himself in prosperity
Nor is ever beaten down in adversity.]

	woodcut border on top of page
1	G*Reat*] large G
33	*These*] *The* 1591, 1597, 1599, 1608, 1609, 1615, 1634
35	*Then*] *The* 1591, 1597, 1599, 1608, 1609, 1615, 1634
37	*start*] *stænd* 1597
75	*compt*] *count* 1599, 1608, 1609, 1615, 1634
84	*remoov'th*] *removes* 1615
88	*mere*] *more* 1591, 1597, 1599, 1608, 1609, 1634
90	*seem'th*] *seemes* 1615
99	*not at all*] *not all* 1597
108	*we*] *be* 1609, 1615
112	*for ever it can have.*] *in many we atchieve:* 1591, 1599, 1634; *more folly did esteeme:* [copies line which is directly oppposite on the verso page: *more follie did esteeme.*] 1597; *which they full soone shall leave.* 1608, 1609, 1615
124	*infinite the gaine.*] *infinite is the gaine.* 1591, 1597, 1599, 1608, 1609, 1615, 1634
$S3^v$	handwritten inscription, "John dan" HN
$S3^v$–$S4^v$	blank; S4 lacking in HN, PN^2

Running-titles

$S1^v$–$S3^r$	The benefite	verso
	of Affliction.	recto

Explanatory Notes

These notes include definitions, explanations of idioms and proverbs, biblical citations not annotated in the text, and patristic and historical sources. Usages predating the earliest citation found in the second edition of the *Oxford English Dictionary* are noted. Elided forms with "the" (e.g., thold, thend) are not individually noted. Archaic words that occur more than one time are glossed when they first appear in both *Sermons* and *Markes*.

The following authors are cited more than once in *Of the Markes*:

Augustine	St. Augustine, Bishop of Hippo (354–420)
Bernard	St. Bernard of Clairvaux (1090–1153)
Chrysostom	St. Chrysostom, Bishop of Constantinople (c. 347–371)
Cyprian	St. Cyprian, Bishop of Carthage (c. 200–258)

1560 Dedicatory Epistle to the Duchesse of Suffolke

6	falleth out] happens (*OED v.* 94g, lists first use in 1568).
17	suffisance,] abundance (*OED* 3).
20–21	above measure] excessively (*OED* "above" *adv.* B7, lists first use in 1611).
21	greves] physical pains (*OED* "grief" *sb.* 6).
27	sicke stomacke of mynde,] literal bodily organ and figurative seat of the emotions paralleling "soul" (*OED* "stomach" *sb.* 6a).
36	skilfull men by arte, or honest neyghbours] probably a distinction between university-trained licensed physicians and unlicensed practitioners of medicine.
42	receipt,] prescription (*OED sb.* 1a).
43	appaired,] impaired (*OED ppl. a*).
47	compounded,] mixed by an apothecary (*OED v.* 3); see Sermon Four, line 444.
48	bounden and humble] i.e., bounden and humble servant.
54	conversation] manner of life (*OED* 6).
58	Ezechias] Hezekiah; earlier form used in the Vulgate and Coverdale Bibles.
60	naturall] innate (*OED a.* 1); possibly unregenerate (*OED a.* 4a).

61 easie] not very good (*OED a.* 15).

62 overheale] heals over the surface of the wound in a superficial way (*OED v.*, cites Lock as first usage).

66 perfite] skilled (*OED* "perfect" *a.* B2a).

69 determined] ordained (*OED ppl. a.* 4).

70 ordreth and disposeth . . . truste in him?] Rom. 8:28.

83 in heavye case] in a distressing condition (*OED* "heavy" *a.*[1] 25a).

85 conserve] a medicinal preparation (*OED sb.* 4); see Suffolk Epistle, line 181.

87 brooke] digest (*OED v.* 2).

97 the soule which sinneth shall die,] Ezek. 18:4,20.

99–100 to begge and borrowe others Virgins oyle] Matt. 25:1–13.

104 stuffe] liquid medicine (*OED sb.*[1] 6b, lists first use in 1611).

104 soulesleaers] those who kill the soul (not in *OED*); probably coined by analogy with "manslayer."

107 deceived] deluded (*OED ppl. a.*, lists first use in 1569; *OED* "deceive" *v.* 2, lists first use in 1320).

112 selly] miserable (*OED a.* 6).

115 th'everlasting Chaos] Luke 16:26 (Vulgate); see Sonnets, line 139.

120 poisonous] venomous (*OED a.* 1, lists first use in 1573).

120 corrupted] defiled (*OED ppl. a.*, lists first use in 1563; *OED* "corrupt" *v.* 3, lists first use in 1300); see Sonnets, line 301.

127 oyle of the same scorpion] a medicinal remedy (*OED* "scorpion" 1e, lists first use in 1594; Tilley S153).

130–136 He knoweth . . . weaknes of man.] Rom. 8:29–39.

132 tentation] temptation (*OED sb.*).

135 alknowynge and alworking] omniscient and providential (*OED* "all" *adv.* E7, lists first usage in 1588); see "all sufficing" (Sonnets, line 73) and "allpearcing" (Sonnets, line 146).

139 everabiding] eternal (*OED* "ever" *adv.* 10a, lists first use in 1586).

146 fits,] attacks of illness (*OED sb.*[2] 3a).

146 passions,] painful bodily disorders (*OED sb.* 4a).

146 alterations,] distempers (*OED* 3, lists first use in 1621).

147 disposition of body] physical constitution (*OED* 8).

156 Ezechias,] for accounts of Hezekiah's sickness and recovery see 2 Kings 20:1–11, 2 Chron. 32:24, and Isa. 38.

164 gastly] death-like (*OED a.* 2a, lists first use in 1581).

165 lyvely moisture] life-giving humors (*OED sb.* 2c).

166 yeldyngly] submissively (*OED* "yieldingly" *adv.*, cites Lock as

first usage; *OED* "yield" *v.* B 14a (b), lists first use in 1300); see Sonnets, lines 75 and 315.

166–167 struglinglye] in a struggling manner (*OED adv.*, cites Lock as first usage).

169 chappes,] jaws (*OED sb.*[2] 2).

179 merciful Samaritans oyle,] Luke 10:25–37.

181 conserve] a medicinal preparation (*OED sb.* 4); see Suffolk Epistle, line 85.

183 unstedy] not secure (*OED a.* 1, lists first use in 1598).

189–190 prescribeth.] orders the use of a medicine (*OED v.* 3a, lists first use in 1581; used as a technical medical term in William Turner, *A new booke of spirituall physic* ([Emden], 1555; STC 24361, K1^{v}).

200–201 tyme that shall excede all extent of yeares,] eternity (*OED* "extent" *sb.* 4c, lists first use in 1671).

203 rendred] translated (*OED v.* 6, lists first use in 1610).

205 good parte.] i.e., in good part.

The First Sermon

2–7 *The writinge . . . lodge.*] Isa. 38:9–12.

2 *Ezechia kinge of Juda,*] for other accounts of Hezekiah's sickness and recovery see 2 Kings 20:1–11 and 2 Chron. 32:24.

28 shake our eares] pay no attention (*OED* "shake" *v.* 6c, lists first use in 1580; Tilley E16).

42–43 gave the bridle] abandoned control (*OED sb.* 1c).

88 affection,] attachment (*OED sb.* 6a).

94 curse of God,] Gen. 3:19.

95–96 death is come upon the world by sinne,] Rom. 5:12.

105 instinction] instinct (*OED* 2).

115–116 Jesus Christ hath repared] Rom. 5:17.

122–123 to mannage them,] to train them as one might train a horse (*OED v.* 7, lists first use in 1594).

123 to make them to fetch their compasses] to take a circuitous course (*OED* "compass" *sb.*[1] 11d).

124–125 our life is nothing els but a course,] Heb. 12.1.

125 course,] race (*OED sb.* 18).

125 world is but a shadow,] Job 8:9; Pss. 102:11; 144:4.

127 by low] on earth (*OED* "below" *adv.* 2a, cites Lock as first usage).

135 note #3, *Rom. 7.*] Rom. 7:21–24.

137	note #4, *2. Cor. 5.*] 2 Cor. 5:6–7.
144	note #5, *Philip. 1.*] Phil. 1:23–24.
148	affection] disposition (*OED sb.* 5).
156	adoption bring the inheritance?] Rom. 8:15–17.
166	note #6, *Math. 22*] Matt. 22:32.
175	note #7, *Num. 23*] Num. 23:10.
179	refused] rejected (*OED ppl. a.*, cites Lock as first usage; *OED* "refuse" *v.*^{1} 4a, lists first use in 1390); see Sonnets, line 47.
188	gage] pledge; security (*OED sb.*^{1} 1).
197	note #8, *Gene. 25.35.49.*] Gen. 25:8; 35:29; 49:33.
199	I wyll put my truste in thy salvation, my God.] Gen. 49:18.
208	note #9, *Psalm. 6.*] Ps. 6:2–5.
209	note #10, *Psalm. 30.*] Ps. 30:9.
212	note #11, *1. Reg. 2*] 1 Kings 2:10.
213	note #12, *1. Par. 29.*] 1 Chron. 29:28.
217	hels] hell, probably plural by analogy with "les enfers."
220	disputation] debate; possibly doubt (*OED* 1 and 3).
225	on slepe] asleep (*OED* "on" *prep.* 10a [a]).
269	accombred] overwhelmed (*OED ppl. a.*).
279–280	the grounde of the evill.] figurative translation of "la vraye source du mal" (not in *OED* or Tilley).
280	the leprosie] figurative translation of "l'hypocrisie" (*OED* 1b, lists first use in 1598); possible printing error for "hypocrisy."
286	sleyghtes] cunning tricks (*OED sb.*^{1} 6).
308	ordred] punished (*OED v.* 4).
316	note #13, *Psalm. 73.*] Ps. 73:4–14.
316	jolitie,] indulge in dissipations; be indulgently self-confident (*OED* 2, 3, 4).
322	kinge Ezechias:] for accounts of Hezekiah's reign see 2 Kings 18–20 and 2 Chron. 29–32.
334	slipt here of the henges] became morally disordered (*OED* "hinge" *sb.* 5, lists first use in 1611; Tilley H473).
338	pastime] to entertain themselves (*OED v.* 1).
339–341	*I have sayd ... Lorde.*] Isa. 38:10–11.
344	delicates,] luxuries (*OED sb.* B2a).
358	lighten] enlighten (*OED v.*^{2} 3).
381	note #14, *Esay. 5.*] Isa. 5:12.
384–385	the lump that maketh up the heape of evell] figurative translation of "le comble [height] du mal" (not in *OED* or Tilley).
405–407	we shal beholde ... portion.] 1 Cor. 13:12.
435	note #15, *Psalm. 31.*] Ps. 31:5.
436	note #16, *Luke. 23.*] Luke 23:46.

443 note #17, *Jonas. 2.*] Jon. 2:7.
449 note #18, *Psalm. 90*] Ps. 90:3–10.
452 xiiii. yere of his raigne,] 2 Kings 18:13.
473 attributeth] yields [to God] as his right (*OED v.* 1).
477–478 When he saith . . . *lyving:*] Isa. 38:10–11.
479 conversant] living among (*OED a.* A2a).
482 confusely myngled] promiscuously intermixed (*OED* "confusely" *adv.* 2).
494 hardelye] harshly (*OED adv.* 4).
501 startynge hoales:] shelters in which animals take refuge (*OED* "start" *sb.*[2] 12, lists first use in 1624).
501–502 of necessitie the case muste passe wyth hym.] he will necessarily dismiss the legal case (*OED* "pass" *v.* 59, lists first use in 1641).
512 drowsinesse,] moral lethargy (*OED* 2, lists first use in 1575).

The Seconde Sermon

3–10 *My lyfe . . . done it.*] Isa. 38:12–15.
11 yesterdaye was entreated of,] was discussed yesterday, i.e., Friday, 5 November 1557 (*OED* "entreat" *v.* 3b, lists first use in 1561).
18 note #1, *Math. 6.*] Matt. 6:25–34.
48 note #2, *2. Corin. 5.*] 2 Cor. 5:4.
49 transitory,] i.e., a transitory moment.
85 *From the morninge . . . to naught.*] Isa. 38:12.
93 handle them streightly,] deal with them strictly (*OED* "straitly" *adv.* 5).
96 corde be straite,] noose is tightened (*OED* "strait" *a.* 1b, lists first use in 1561).
105 note #3, *Psal. 104.*] Ps. 104:29.
114 note #4, *Esay. 40.*] Isa. 40:6–8.
128–129 *he chattered . . . a Dove.*] Isa. 38:14.
154 throughly] thoroughly (*OED adv.*).
170 abide us:] i.e., abide for us.
171 to make oure partye good,] to better our condition (*OED* "party" *sb.* 4).
172 think straunge] i.e., think it strange; be surprised at (*OED* "strange" *a.* 10b, lists first use in 1585).
177 a water that is powred out and spilt.] 2 Sam. 14:14.
180 note #5, *Psal. 23.*] Ps. 32:3–4.

186 note #6, *Psal. 39.*] Ps. 39:1–3.

191–193 even as a fyre . . . out in a flame,] variation on proverb "fire that's closest kept burns most of all" (Tilley F265).

215 strongly fournished.] very clever (*OED* "furnished" *ppl. a.* 1).

246 note #7, *Roma. 8.*] Rom. 8:26.

263–265 *That he made . . . of a Lyon.*] Isa. 38:13.

280–281 to recken without our hoste,] to come to conclusions without taking into consideration all the facts (*OED* "host" *sb.*^{2} 2b; Tilley H728).

284 sclender.] slender; slight (*OED a.* 7).

292 note #8, *Esay. 103.*] Ps. 103; see also Isa. 38:13.

351 with mouth.] i.e., with the mouth.

355–356 if the mountayns tremble before him and melt away,] Ps. 46:2, 3, 6.

378–380 Lorde, the payne . . . sayde it.] Isa. 38:14–15.

382 God helpe,] i.e., God's help.

398 advertised] formally warned (*OED v.* 4b).

411–412 and what . . . done it.] Isa. 38:15.

422 enterlace] become entangled (*OED v.* 5b).

422 note #9, *Psal. 39.*] Ps. 39:1.

429–430 And in Job we see many suche lyke complayntes.] Job 6:24; 40:4–5.

435–436 that we may be unburthened, as it is said in the Psalme.] Ps. 39:3.

464 let to conclude,] stop (*OED* "let" *v.*^{1} 12a).

465 lettes] hindrances (*OED sb.*^{1} 1).

479 stayes,] obstacles (*OED sb.*^{3} 5).

490 dispayres,] despairs (*OED sb.* 1b, cites Lock as first usage of plural).

494 from the depest bottomes.] Ps. 130:1.

496 unprofit] i.e., unprofitable.

503 in the mydwaye.] at the halfway point (*OED sb.* 1).

The Thirde Sermon

3–8 *What shall . . . thy back.*] Isa. 38:15–17.

23 Accordyng as he . . . done it,] Isa. 38:15.

32 let us kepe oure mouthe close as it is sayd in Job:] Job 40:4–5.

34–36 *That all . . . his soule.*] Isa. 38:15.

43 niggardly] sparing (*OED a.* 1, lists first use in 1571).

47 (as it is sayd unto the Prophet)] Jer. 30:21.

61 in effecte,] in fact (*OED sb.* 8, lists first use in 1588).

105 wylde,] angry (*OED* 11a, lists first use in 1653); possibly rebellious (*OED* 5). French: revesches.

113–114 that the bitternes . . . in his prosperitie.] Isa. 38:17.

127–140 For we have seene . . . careles and negligent.] for accounts of the siege of Jerusalem and its deliverance see Isa. 36–37; 2 Kings 18:13–19:37; 2 Chron. 32:1–23.

150 daseled] confounded (*OED v.* 4, lists first use in 1561).

161 I have sayde . . . no more be shaken.] Ps. 30:6.

165 He had bene persecuted of the people,] for accounts of David's exile see 1 Sam. 20–30.

170 ravished unto God,] drawn forcibly unto and therefore dependent upon God (*OED v.* 1c); see Sermon Four, line 31.

171–173 It was of . . . was troubled.] Ps. 30:7.

181–182 Lorde thou hast hyd thy face and behold I was troubled.] Ps. 30:7.

184 astonishment] consternation (*OED* 3, lists first use in 1586).

191 under his wynges,] Ruth 2:12; Pss. 17:8; 36:7; 57:1; 61:4; 63:7; 91:4.

195–197 He sayth . . . from the grave.] Isa. 38:17.

215 Lord (saith he) thou hast loved my soule:] Isa. 38:17.

217 shadow,] i.e., a shadow.

219 eye] i.e., his eye.

230–231 Lorde, they that . . . hath bene prolonged.] Isa. 38:16.

241 to purpose.] the point at issue (*OED sb.* 5).

244 shal never be put under fote,] shall never be forgotten (not in *OED* or Tilley).

245 Before he said] Isa. 38:15.

247 largelier] more largely (not in *OED*).

255–261 Lord (said he) . . . they shalbe abashed.] Ps. 35:26–28.

265 For (saieth he) thou hast cast me on slepe.] Isa. 38:16.

283–287 and that praise . . . by many.] 2 Cor. 1:8–11.

306–307 God hathe cast his sinnes behynd his backe.] Isa. 38:17.

321 sargeant] common soldier (*OED sb.* 2a).

330 wype our mouthes.] probably in contrast to a more thorough cleaning (not in *OED* or Tilley).

336 that he breaketh our bones as a Lyon:] Isa. 38:13.

344 serveth his processe] indicts (*OED* "process" *sb.* 7b).

389 soveraigne] greatest (*OED a.* II2).

424–425 Happie is the man (saith David) whose sinnes are pardoned.] Ps. 32:1–2.

425–427 Saint Paule . . . summe therof.] Rom. 4:3–8.

445 *Thou haste caste my sinnes behinde thy backe.*] Isa. 38:17.
448–449 like as when it is said . . . bottom of the sea,] Mic. 7:19.
453 jangled] babbled (*OED v.* 4).
462 commoditie] benefit (*OED* 2c, lists first use in 1571).
463 warely] prudently (*OED adv.*).
466–467 contrariant,] antagonistic (*OED a.* B2, cites Lock as first usage).

The Fourth Sermon

3–10 *For the grave . . . of the Lorde?*] Isa. 38:18–22.
31 ravished] drawn forcibly (*OED v.* 1c); see Sermon Three, line 170.
36–38 And S. Paul . . . alway avaunced.] Phil. 1:21–26.
45 For-thy] for this reason (*OED conj.* 1a).
48 note #1, *2. Cor. 5.*] 2 Cor. 5:6.
51–53 And we knowe . . . the holy.] Isa. 6:2–3.
59 to emprow his lands,] to improve his lands so as to make a profit (*OED* "improve" *v.*[2] 3).
73 the living, the lyving shall praise God.] Isa. 38:19.
97 gnashynge of teethe,] Matt. 8:12; 13:42; 22:13; 24:51; 25:30; Luke 13:28.
98 note #2, *Psal. 51.*] Ps. 51:15.
100 note #3, *Psal. 40.*] Ps. 40:3.
108 sayinge that the dead shall not praise god,] Isa. 38:18.
119–121 in the lxxxviii. Psalme . . . what God is.] Ps. 88:5.
125 at randon] carelessly (*OED* "random" *sb.* 3a, lists first use in 1565).
126 note #4, *Job. 3.*] Job 3:17–19.
126 carefulnesse,] concerns (*OED* a).
127 verlet] servant (*OED* 1).
150 at adventure,] at random (*OED sb.* 3b).
151–152 measurable sorowes, and complaintes] unmeasurable sorrows and complaints; French: regrets et complaintes . . . qui excederont mesure.
158–162 And we see . . . god hathe preserved us.] Ps. 115:17–18.
176–177 the example . . . by death.] Phil. 1:20.
179 oughte to be suspicious] considered suspect (*OED a.* 1).
180 kepe measure] restrain ourselves (*OED* "measure" *sb.* 12c).
181 The dead shall not prayse God,] Isa. 38:18.
182 consequent] logical conclusion (*OED* "consequent" *a.* 2, lists first use in 1638).

182 profe,] a written document so attested as to form legal evidence (*OED sb.* BI 1b).

184 in the vi. Psalme,] Ps. 6:4–5.

186 dissipation] dissolution by death (*OED* 3, lists first use in 1597).

187 tempted as if] i.e., were tempted to believe as if.

187–188 utterly disclaime in them,] renounce them (*OED* "disclaim" *v.* 2a, cites Lock as first usage).

204 ravished] utterly impressed (*OED v.* 3c).

204–207 as it is saide . . . it were astonyshed.] Ps. 40:5, 12.

221 affiaunce,] assurance (*OED sb.* 2).

223 a sacrifice of thankesgeving] Pss. 107:22; 116:17.

231–233 The lyving, . . . thy vertue.] Isa. 38:19.

233 vertue.] usually translated "truth"; French: verité. See Sermon Four, lines 6, 234, 237, 252, 255, 275, 302, 318, 327.

235 indifferently] indiscriminately (*OED adv.* 1).

237–238 When Jacob . . . of the Lorde.] Gen. 49:18.

274–275 that Ezechias sayeth . . . the treweth of God.] Isa. 38:19.

276–277 Moreover, where as he . . . leane unto it.] Isa. 38:18.

299 incharge] as a responsibility (*OED* "charge" *sb.* 13b).

306 wil discharg them selves of theyr duties,] fulfill their obligations (*OED* "discharge" *v.* 2b, lists first use in 1586).

308 geve them the bridle] abandon control (*OED* "bridle" *sb.* 1c; Tilley B671).

311–312 for they lift . . . shall be more deadly] variation on proverb "the higher standing the lower fall" (Tilley S823; see also C414, F131, M1211, T489).

320–323 Shall I hyde . . . in my ordinances:] Gen. 18:17–19.

329–330 The Lorde it is that shall save me.] Isa. 38:20.

343 minishe] reduce (*OED v.* 1).

344 coloure] pretext (*OED sb.*[1] 12d).

351 The Lorde it is that saveth us.] Isa. 38:20.

358 The mercye of God is more worth than all lyves,] Ps. 63:3.

361 warrant] protect (*OED v.* 1).

367–368 And we wyll singe . . . house of the Lord.] Isa. 38:20.

371 acknowledgement] confession (*OED* 1, lists first use in 1594).

378 a sodein braide,] a short time (*OED* "sudden" *a.* 8, lists first use in 1561 and "braid" *sb.* 2).

393 fire of stubble,] 1 Cor. 3:12–13 (*OED* "stubble" *sb.* 2b, lists first use in 1591).

398 When he sayeth, In the house of the Lorde.] Isa. 38:20.

404 his] i.e., those who are his.

405 perticulerly] individually (*OED adv.* 1a).

417 note #5, *Jonas. 2.*] Jon. 2:7.

423–424 that the Prophet Esay . . . upon his wounde,] Isa. 38:21.

426–427 Ezechias also demaundeth . . . the diall of Achas.] Isa. 38:7–8.

443 to confirme] to strengthen spiritually (*OED v.* 4).

444 compound] a compounded drug (*OED sb.*[1] 2a, lists first use in 1611); see Suffolk Epistle, line 47.

445 ripe] bring to a head (*OED v.*[1] 3).

448–450 God promiseth . . . threateneth us raine.] Gen. 9:11–17.

457 credit] credibility (*OED sb.* 2a, lists first use in 1574).

467 pitiful] compassionate (*OED a.* 2).

502 note #6, *Judj. 6.*] Judg. 6:36–40.

502 motion] prompting from God (*OED sb.* 9b).

517 in acknowledgyng] in acknowledgment (*OED vbl. n.*, lists first use in 1561; *OED* "acknowledge" *v.* 1, lists first use in 1553).

Sonnets

12 passioned] grieved; afflicted (*OED ppl. a.* 2, lists first use in 1591; *OED* "passion" *v.* 2, lists first use in 1491).

15 febled] weakened (*OED ppl. a.*, lists first use in 1566; *OED* "feeble" *v.* 1, lists first use in 1225).

18 disteined] defiled (*OED ppl. a.*, lists first use in 1590; *OED* "distain" *v.* 2, lists first use in 1406).

21 dobleedged sworde,] Ps. 149:6; Heb. 4:12; Rev. 1:16; 2:12.

22 dimmed] rendered dim (*OED ppl. a.*, lists first use in 1590; *OED* "dim" *v.* 1, lists first use in 1300).

24 bryne] tears (*OED sb.* 3, lists first use in 1592).

25 grefefull] sorrowful (*OED* "griefful" *a.*).

30 groveling in the myre,] 2 Pet. 2:22.

32 abounding] abundant (*OED ppl. a.* 1, lists first use in 1684; *OED* "abound" *v.*[1], list first use in 1382).

37 gnawing] consuming (*OED ppl. a.*, lists first use in 1567; *OED* "gnaw" *v.* 2, lists first use in 1530).

42 shreking] piercing (*OED ppl. a.*, lists first use in 1586; *OED* "shriek" *v.* 1a, lists first use in 1577. Cognate *OED* "shriking" *ppl. a.*, lists first use in 1583; *OED* "shrike" *v.*, lists first use in 1200).

47 refused] rejected (*OED ppl. a.*, cites Lock as first usage; *OED* "refuse" *v.*[1] 4a, lists first use in 1390); see Sermon One, line 179.

50 damned vessell] Rom. 9:22; 2 Tim. 2:20.

51 beknowyng] knowing (not in *OED* as *ppl. a.*; *OED* "beknow" *v.* 2, lists first use in 1325).

58 of grace my senslesse cheare,] my inability to feel grace (*OED* "cheer" *v.* 1a).

64 by conscience] possible printer's error for "my conscience."

70 presuming] presumptuous (*OED ppl. a.*, lists first use in 1604; *OED* "presume" *v.* 5, lists first use in 1430).

73 crummes] for accounts of the Syro-Phoenician woman see Matt. 15:21–28; Mark 7:24–30.

73 all sufficing] completely sufficient (*OED* "all" *adv.* E7, lists first usage in 1588); see "allpearcing" (Sonnets, line 146) and "alknowywnge and alworking" (Suffolk Epistle, line 135).

75 yelding] submissive (*OED ppl. a.* 3, lists first use in 1578; *OED* "yield" *v.* B 14a (b), lists first use in 1300); see Sonnets, line 315 and Suffolk Epistle, line 166.

77 oft repeted] reiterated (*OED ppl. a.* 1, lists first use in 1611; *OED* "repeat" *v.* 1a, lists first use in 1375).

80 wrekefull] vengeful (*OED a.* 2).

103 sinking] drowning (*OED ppl. a.* 2, lists first use in 1676; *OED* "sink" *v.* 1, lists first use in 975).

139 My Chaos] probably a reference to the gulf between heaven and hell; see Suffolk Epistle, line 115.

146 allpearcing] thoroughly piercing (*OED* "all" *adv.* E7, lists first usage in 1588); see "all sufficing" (Sonnets, line 73) and "alknowynge and alworking" (Suffolk Epistle, line 135).

151 sharpned] made sharp (*OED ppl. a.*, lists first use in 1594; *OED* "sharp" *v.* 5a, lists first use in 1425).

152 splat] slit open (*OED v.*[1] 1).

152 ripped] slit (*OED ppl. a.* 1, lists first use in 1823; *OED* "rip" *v.*[2] 2a, lists first use in 1530).

161 behight] promised (*OED v.* B1).

167 during] enduring (*OED ppl. a*).

172 sede] semen (*OED sb.* 4).

178 juyse] a multiple pun indicating sap (*OED* "juice" *sb.* 1.a.), the essence of human nature (*OED* "juice" *sb.* 4.a.) and possibly judgement (*OED* "juise")

185 sooth,] truth (*OED sb.* 1).

186 trutheles] false (*OED a.* 3, lists first use in 1567).

186 visour] mask (*OED sb.* 3a).

214 threates and thonders of the law,] Exod. 19:16; 20:18; Heb. 12:18–19.

219 pearce myne eares,] Ps. 40:6.

227 beknowe,] confess (*OED v.* 2).

230 whelmed] engulfed (*OED ppl. a.*, lists first use in 1819; *OED* "whelm" *v.* 5b, lists first use in 1553; *OED* "overwhelmed" *ppl. a.*, lists first use in 1440).

248 reeling] tottering (*OED ppl. a.* 1, lists first use in 1577; *OED* "reel" *v.*[1] 5, lists first use in 1477).

252 pight] fixed (*OED* "pitch" *v.*[1] B6).

270 reft,] pulled up (*OED* "reave" *v.*[2] 3).

284 gaping] wide open (*OED ppl. a.*, lists first use in 1588; *OED* "gape" *v.* 1b, lists first use in 1375).

299 Assoile] pardon (*OED v.* 1).

300 ingrowyng] innate (*OED ppl. a.*, lists first use in 1869; not in *OED* as verb).

301 corrupted] defiled (*OED ppl. a.*, lists first use in 1563; *OED* "corrupt" *v.* 3, lists first use in 1300); see Suffolk Epistle, line 120.

304 revengyng] avenging (*OED ppl. a.*, lists first use in 1568; *OED* "revenge" *v.* 1a, lists first use in 1375).

305 joying] joyful (not in *OED* as participle; *OED* "joy" *v.* 2, lists first use in 1300).

315 yeldyng] submissive (*OED ppl. a.* 3, lists first use in 1578; *OED* "yield" *v.* B 14a (b), lists first use in 1300); see Sonnets, line 75 and Suffolk Epistle, line 166.

330 vaprie] consistency of vapour (*OED a.* 1, lists first use in 1598).

333 pease] appease (*OED v.* 2).

334 sufficing] sufficient (*OED ppl. a.*, lists first use in 1606; *OED* "suffice" *v.* 1, lists first use in 1340).

335 at one] possibly a pun on "atone."

337 hoste] sacrifice; allusion to Eucharistic bread (*OED sb.*[4]); see Phil. 4:18; 1 Pet. 2:5.

343 tastlesse] unable to taste (*OED a.* 1, lists first use in 1591).

343 languor] disease (*OED sb.* 1).

343 lingring] painfully protracted (*OED ppl. a.* 1b, lists first use with specific reference to a disease in 1593; *OED* "linger" *v.* 3, lists first use in 1534).

352, 372 humbled] abased (*OED v.*[1] 4, lists first use as participle in 1600; *OED* "humble" *v.*[1] 2, lists first use in 1484).

352 wise.] fashion (*OED sb.*[1] II 1b).

360 myning] undermining (*OED ppl. a.* 1, lists first use in 1561; *OED* "mine" *v.* 4b, lists first use in 1412).

369 brute] report (*OED* "bruit" *sb.* 2).
372 yelden] submissive (*OED* "yolden" *ppl. a.* 1).
377 deface:] blot out of existence (*OED v.* 3b).

Latin Poem

2–5 elegiac meter, resembling an epic simile.
3–5 Luminaque, colore, exculta, repleta] rhetorical terms; an extended pun comparing the sylvan setting and the doctor's rhetorical skills.

1590 Dedicatory Epistle to the Countesse of Warwicke

16 under the crosse.] Rom. 8:17.
20–21 if God chastise ... whom he receiveth,] Prov. 3:11–12; Heb. 12:5–6.
21–22 every member ... fashioned like unto the head,] Eph. 4:15–16.
24 sure pledges of their adoption:] Rom. 8:15–16.
32 theefe in the night,] Matt. 24:43; 1 Thess. 5:2,4; 2 Pet. 3:10.
44–45 light upon ... unto manie,] Matt. 5:14–16.
46–47 comfortable] helpful (*OED a.* 2).
48 Everie one in his calling] 1 Cor. 7:20.
51–52 brought my poore ... of the walles] Neh. 3–4.
52 walles of that Jerusalem,] Gal. 4:26; Heb. 12:22; Rev. 3:12; 21:2; see also Eph. 2:11–22.
56 vaine imaginations,] Rom. 1:21.
62 bewitch the minds] Gal. 3:1.
65–67 whose pavement ... orient pearles?] Rev. 21:19–21.
67–70 what Citie ... in happinesse for ever?] Rev. 5:6–14; 21:2–3.
67 replenished] abundantly supplied (*OED v.* 1).
71–72 child of so ... kingdome;] Rom. 8:16–17.
72–74 where neither time ... endles and incomprehensible?] Matt. 6:19–20.
76–77 but by the same ... by the crosse:] Heb. 2:9.
77–82 why (casting off ... throne of God?] Heb. 12:1–2.
82–83 if as *Esau*, ... sold his birthright)] Heb. 12:16–17.
85–86 which Christ ... hath purchased for us.] 1 Cor. 6:20; 7:23; 1 Pet. 1:18–19.
87–89 while it is saide ... shall have end.] Heb. 4:7–11.

Taffin Preface

17 *voiage from* Germanie] probably the 1586 trip from Leiden to Haarlem.

Chapter One

13 butt,] end (*OED sb.*[4] 4a, lists first use in 1594).

14 note #2, Aug. Enarrat. 2. Psal. 26. Tom. 8.] Augustine, *Enarrationes in Psalmos*, Ps. 26, second part, para. 8 (Vulgate numbering). Vol. 8 (Tom. 8) of Frobenius's edition of Augustine's *Opera*.

26 make curtesie] deprecate (*OED* "courtesy" *sb.* 7).

88 note #34, Bern. meditation. 9.] Bernard, *Meditationes* (spurious), ch. 9.

132 note #40, *Cipri. de ascen. Christi*] Cyprian, *De Ascensione Christi* from *Ad Cornelium Papam, de cardinalibus operibus Christi usque ad ascensum eius ad Patrem* (spurious).

134 note #42, *August. lib.* 80. *quæst.* 69. *and lib. de trinit.* 1. *cap.* 8.] Augustine, *Quaestiones Veteris et Novi Testamenti* (spurious), qs. 69 and *De Trinitate*, bk. 1, ch. 8.

181 note #53, *Aug. in manuel. cap.* 35.] Augustine, *Manuale* (spurious), ch. 35.

190 superabounding] excessive (*OED ppl. a.*, lists first use in 1598; *OED* "superabound" *v.* 2, lists first use in 1520).

217 note #54, *Bernard in tract. de diligendo deo.*] Bernard, *Liber de diligendo Deo*, ch. 1, para. 1.

230–241 Now (to returne . . . the fulnes of this joye.] Augustine, *Manuale* (spurious), ch. 35.

264–267 The mercie of GOD . . . hath no ending.] Bernard, Epistle 107, para. 5 addressed to Thomas, Provost of Beverley.

Chapter Two

34 sticketh not at all,] is not reluctant (*OED* "stick" *v.*[1] 15).

124 gradation] series of successive stages (*OED* 2).

133 lightened] enlightened (*OED v.*[2] 3).

138 note #39, *Bern. ser.* 5 *in dedica. templi.*] Bernard, *De dedicatione templi* (*In dedicatione ecclesiae*), serm. 5.

149 note #40, *Aug. Hom. in Joan.* 35.] Augustine, *Tractatus in evangelium Joannis*, serm. 35, para. 9.

Chapter Three

28–31 But it is not . . . in Jesus Christ.] Rom. 10:6–8.

31 of credite,] trustworthy (*OED sb.* 2a).

51–52 interposeth] intervenes (*OED v.* 4a, lists first use in 1603).

115 conclusion:] logical term denoting the final proposition in a syllogism derived from two former premisses (*OED* 5b); here the syllogism is "Christ saves sinners, I am a sinner, therefore Christ saves me."

149 note #18, *August in Joan. hom.* 89.] Augustine, *Tractatus in evangelium Joannis*, serm. 80, para. 3.

170 communication of the holie supper.] observance of Holy Communion (*OED* "communication" 9, lists first use in 1610).

Chapter Four

20 apprehension.] anticipation (*OED* 11, lists first use in 1603).

35 motions] promptings of God (*OED sb.* 9b).

53 saith S. *Augustine*,] Augustine, *Tractatus in evangelium Joannis*, serm. 52, para. 9.

76 principall rest] main support (*OED* "rest" *sb.*^{1} 12a, lists first use in 1609).

179 note #38, *Aug. ad Bonif. lib.* 3 *ca.* 7.] Augustine, letter to Boniface, governor of the province of Africa, in *Contra duas epistolas pelagianorum ad Bonifatium*, bk. 3, ch. 7.

184–185 as the same author saith,] Augustine, letter to Boniface, bk. 3, ch. 7.

193 saith S. *Augustine*,] Augustine, commonplace observation; for example, *Enarrationes in Psalmos*, Ps. 92, para. 3 (Vulgate numbering).

304 as Saint *Augustine* saith:] Augustine, commonplace observation; for example, *Tractatus in evangelium Joannis*, serm. 7, para. 12.

372 originall,] origination (*OED sb.* B1a).

372 note #79, Chrisost. Homil. of the Canaanit.] Chrysostom, *Monitum in homiliam de Chananæa* (spurious), ch. 10.

397 let] prevent (*OED v.*^{2} 1).

397–398 desire is praier before God, saith Saint *Augustine*;] Augustine, *Enarrationes in Psalmos*, Ps. 37, para. 14 (Vulgate numbering).

438 leesing] losing (*OED vbl. n.*^{1}).

Chapter Five

121–122 *John Haren*] prominent French-speaking reformed pastor in Bruges, who repudiated his Protestant profession in a public recantation before the Society of Jesus on 9 March 1586. The following year he published *Brief discours des causes justes et équitables, qui ont meves M. Jean Haren, jadis Ministre, de quitter la Réligion prétendue Réformée*, and in 1599 published three more tracts against Protestantism. He was imprisoned from 1602 to 1609 for speaking on behalf of Protestant churches and made a public recantation of his Roman Catholic profession on 7 March 1610. This recantation was published in French and translated that same year into Dutch and English (*The repentance of John Haren priest* [STC 12769]).

124–125 as a hireling, . . . flocke.] John 10:12–13.

125 what letters I writ] apparently not extant.

127 colour] specious reason (*OED sb.*[1] 12a).

142 as saint *Augustine* sayth:] Augustine, Epistle 22 to Bishop Valerius (c. 392).

226 so as it like thornes, choake] so these, like thornes, choake; French: tellement que cela comme espines estouffe.

247 note #36, Aug. de correct. and gra. ca. 12. to. 7.] Augustine, *De correptione et gratia*, ch. 12, para. 36. Vol. 7 (to. 7) of Frobenius's edition of Augustine's *Opera*.

Chapter Six

[no explanatory notes for this chapter]

Chapter Seven

67–68 entertainment] treatment (*OED* 5).

73 gospel of velvet] gospel without cost (*OED* "velvet" *sb.* 1c, lists first use as figurative term in 1592).

Chapter Eight

38 unkindlie] with unnatural cruelty (*OED adv.* 1b).

84 note #23, *Henrie of Erford.*] Henry of Huntingdon, historian and Archdeacon of Huntingdon (c. 1084–1155), *Historia Anglorum,* first printed in Sir Henry Savile's collection of the

Rerum Anglicarum Scriptores post Bedam præcipui (1596); bk. 1 exonerates Hadrian but attributes severe persecutions to Diocletian and Herculius Maximian. Taffin's incorrect allusion to Hadrian suggests he knew Huntingdon's work from references in other sources.

86 note #24, *Oros. lib. 7. chap.* 25.] Paulus Orosius, historian and friend of St. Augustine (early 5th century), *Historiarum adversum paganos*, bk. 7, ch. 25.

87 note #25, *Ursperg.*] Burchard of Biberach [Burchardus Urspergensis of Lichtenau] (twelfth century–1230), *Chronicon abbatis Urspergen*, a history of the world from King Ninus of Assyria to 1229, sometimes wrongly attributed to Conradus, Abbot of Ursperg.

89 carried to the mettals,] condemned to the mines (*OED* "metal" *sb.* 4, lists first use in 1660).

90 note #26, *Vincent. in his mirrour lib.* 12. *chap.* 136.] Vincent of Beauvais, encyclopedist (c. 1190–1264), *Speculum Historiale*; part 3 of the *Speculum Majus*, ch. 136 details cruelty at Trenios and the Mosel river.

92–93 *Fasciculus temporum,*] Werner Rolevinck, Carthusian theologian and historian (1425–1502), the *Fasciculus temporum*, a popular history of the world.

94 note #27, *Euse. lib.* 8. *chap.* 11.] Eusebius, Bishop of Caesarea (c. 260–c. 340), *Historia ecclesiastica*, bk. 8, ch. 11.

120 mischievouslie] wickedly (*OED adv.* 2).

158 incontinently] immediately (*OED adv.*[2]).

163 plaints] complaints (*OED sb.* 2).

220 combereth] distresses (*OED* "cumber" *v.* 2).

245 conversant] living among (*OED a.* A2a).

303–306 Let us saie boldlie . . . see him as hee is.] 1 John 3:2.

Chapter Nine

7–8 reliques] remnant (*OED* 3a).

37 blockishnesse] great stupidity (*OED sb.*).

63 note #14, *Prosper in sen. ex. Aug.* 5.] Prosper Tiro of Aquitane (c. 390–c. 463), *Liber sententiarum ex operibus S. Augustini delibatarum*, bk. 1, para. 5.

66–67 S. *Bernard*] Bernard, quotation is not in the genuine works.

76–77 as also S. *Augustine* saith,] Augustine, *Enarrationes in Psalmos*, Ps. 102, para. 20 (Vulgate numbering).

147 gage] pledge; security (*OED sb.*^{1} 1).

148 traffiques,] business (*OED sb.* 2a).

161 fining pot] crucible (*OED* "fining" 3, lists first use in 1611).

196 G O D his assistance,] God's assistance. French: l'assistence de Dieu.

265–266 in following G O D, . . . to call us.] used in different context in 1 Cor. 7:20.

265 note #44, *Sen. de vita beata. cap.* 15.] Lucius Annaeus Seneca (c. 4 B.C.–A.D. 65), *De beata vita*, ch. 15, para. 5.

288 note #47, *Grego. Nazian.*] Gregory of Nazianzus (329–389), quotation is not in the genuine works.

Chapter Ten

25 an untollerable impudencie] shameless effrontery (*OED* "impudency" 2b, lists first use with article in 1624).

55–56 mouth of our faith] the expanse of our faith; literal translation of "la bouche de nostre foy."

71–72 delicates,] luxuries (*OED sb.* B2a).

123 favourits.] intimate companions of a superior (*OED* A2, lists first use in 1599).

127 note #25, *August.*] Augustine, the Homily on John 6:53, the table of the Martyr St. Cyprian.

133 contentation] contentment (*OED* 3b).

134 note #26, *Manuel. Aug. cha.* 3] Augustine, *Manuale* (spurious), ch. 3.

136–137 As also he saith in another place,] Augustine, *Meditationum liber* (spurious), ch. 18.

197 Tutor,] guardian of a ward (*OED sb.* 2b).

199 rents] sources of income (*OED sb.*^{1} 1a).

200 fleetings,] unsteady movements; wanderings (*OED v.*^{1} 6).

203 flittings,] flight; exile (*OED vbl. n.* 2).

Chapter Eleven

24 supposts,] followers (*OED* a).

25 renowme,] renown (*OED sb.* 1); possibly reputation (*OED sb.* 3c, lists first use in 1611).

68 note #11, *Bernar. in Can.*] Bernard, *Sermones super Cantica Canticorum*, serm. 27, para. 8.

75 slights,] deceptions (*OED* "sleight" *sb.*^{1} 1).

107–108 *Justine* in his communication with *Triphon*] Justin Martyr (c. 110–c. 165), *Dialogus cum Tryphone*, ch. 110.

124–125 the blood of the Martyres is the seede of the Church.] Quintus Septimius Florens Tertullian (c. 160–ca. 220), the *Apologeticum*, ch. 50, para. 13.

141 proposition] riddle (*OED sb.* 3b).

Chapter Twelve

17 at all adventure] at random (*OED sb.* 3c).

56–57 (sayth Saint *Augustine*)] Augustine, quotation is not in the genuine works.

135 to be dissolved,] to die (*OED* 6).

147–148 Saint *Chrisostome* saith] Chrysostom, *Homiliae 21 de statuis ad populum Antiochenum*, serm. 5, para. 11.

149 visours.] masks (*OED sb.* 3a).

186 If God be for us, who shall bee against us.] Rom. 8:31.

234 *Nicodemites*,] those who remained within the Roman church while privately denouncing its errors or working for its reform; coined by John Calvin in *Excuse de Jehan Calvin, à Messieurs les Nicodèmites* (1544).

259 the assemblie:] the congregation (*OED* 6a, lists first use in 1600).

266 conduct] guidance (*OED sb.*[1] 1a).

297 ravished] drawn forcibly (*OED v.* 1c).

309 subscribe with his hande,] write his signature as a testimony (*OED* "subscribe" *v.* 6).

335 file] defile (*OED v.*[2] 1).

336 band] obligation; bond (*OED sb.*[1] 8).

345–346 melodie and consent] agreement, but literally melody and harmony (*OED* "concent" *sb.* 2).

365 conversation] manner of life (*OED* 6).

390 parts-taking] taking sides (*OED* "partaking" *vbl. n.* 2).

407 that this day may passe yesterday.] so that you may do better today than yesterday; literal translation of "que le jourd'huy surmonte celuy d'hier."

417 (saith *Chrysostome*)] Chrysostom, *In Philemon homiliae*, serm. 3, vs. 25.

434 note #94, *Aug. in Psal.* 85.] Augustine, *Enarrationes in Psalmos*, Ps. 85, para. 1 (Vulgate numbering).

446 (saith S. *Bernard*)] Bernard, *Sermones in Quadragesima*, serm. 5, para. 5.

473–474 Father of light, from whence all good gifts doo come,] James 1:17.

Chapter Thirteen

7 thi] archaic form of "thy."
23–24 as thou shewest mercie . . . shewe mercie.] Exod. 33:19; Rom. 9:15.
40–41 Covetousnes the roote of all evill,] 1 Tim. 6:10.
70 procurers] prosecutors (*OED* 1e).
88 youth of orphanes,] young orphans; literal translation of "jeunesse d'orphelins."
88 fondlings,] foundlings (*OED* 1).
91–92 our sunne is turned into darknes, the Moone into bloud,] Rev. 6:12.
96–97 a famine of thy word,] Amos 8:11.
102–104 Thou art a God . . . transgression and sinne.] Exod. 34:6–7.
105–106 Thou hast said . . . turne and live.] Ezek. 18:23; 33:11.
108 Jesus Christ came into the world to save sinners.] 1 Tim. 1:15.
110 at tone] reconciled (*OED* "at one" *adv.* 2).
112–113 if thou regard . . . before thee?] Ps. 130:3.
116–117 that though a mother . . . forget us.] Isa. 49:15.
117–118 thou hast promised . . . no more.] Jer. 31:34.
119–121 that though our sins . . . white as snowe.] Isa. 1:18.
121 heavie laden,] Matt. 11:28.
137–138 I am the Eternall, . . . praise unto another.] Isa. 42:8.
140–141 Not unto us . . . and honour,] Ps. 115:1.
143–144 making perfect thy power in our infirmitie,] 2 Cor. 12:9.
153–154 hast created the heaven . . . in them:] Ps. 146:6; Acts 4:24; 14:15.
154–155 it is by thee . . . have their moving:] Acts 17:28.
155–156 it is of thee, by thee and for thee, that all things are.] Rom. 11:36.
156 It is thou which dooest whatsoever thou wilt.] Isa. 37:26; 46:11.
156–157 And there is neither . . . against thee.] Prov. 21:30.

The necessitie and benefite of affliction

3 *determination*,] appointment (*OED* 5, lists first use in 1594).
8 *want*] miss (*OED* *v.* 2a).

16 *despite.*] malicious acts (*OED sb.* 3).

20 *dolor,*] sorrow (*OED* 2).

25 *estimation*] value (*OED* 1).

26 *deface,*] destroy (*OED v.* 2); possibly to outshine by contrast (*OED v.* 6).

30 *out of minde:*] from memory (*OED* "mind" *sb.*[1] 2f).

37 *start aside,*] desert (*OED v.* 7).

39 *assistance*] presence (*OED* 1).

55 *sence)*] faculties of the senses as opposed to the mind (*OED sb.* 1c); possibly the senses as channels for gratifying the flesh (*OED sb.* 4a, lists first use in 1597).

63 *toyes:*] foolish trifles (*OED sb.* 5).

64, 67, 121 *religion*] reformed Protestantism (*OED* 4b).

86 *comfortable*] comforting (*OED a.* 6).

Index of Biblical Texts

All marginal citations as well as unglossed references to biblical texts are included in this index, listed by section and line numbers. Marginal citations are indicated by an asterisk; erroneous references have been corrected (see the textual notes). Marginal citations included in the French version, but not in the English text, are indicated by a dagger. Psalm citations follow the numbering of the English Bible.

Old Testament

Genesis

Judges

Ruth

1 Samuel

2 Samuel

1 Kings

2 Kings

1 Chronicles

2 Chronicles

Nehemiah

Job

Psalms

Mark

Luke

John

Romans

1 Corinthians

2 Corinthians

Galatians

Ephesians

Philippians

James

1 Peter

2 Peter

1 John

Revelation

Editorial Committee for *The Collected Works of Anne Vaughan Lock*
Elizabeth Hageman, Chair
Steven May
Anne O'Donnell

The Renaissance English Text Society was established to publish literary texts, chiefly nondramatic, of the period 1475–1660. Dues are $25.00 per annum ($15.00, graduate students; life membership is available at $500.00). Members receive the text published for each year of membership. The Society sponsors panels at such annual meetings as those of the Modern Language Association, the Renaissance Society of America, and the Medieval Congress at Kalamazoo. General inquiries should be addressed to the president, Arthur Kinney, Department of English, University of Massachusetts, Amherst, Mass. 01002, USA. Inquiries about membership should be addressed to M. Di Cesare, Windrush, 101 Booter Road, Fairview, North Carolina, 28730.

Copies of volumes X–XII may be purchased from Associated University Presses, 440 Forsgate Drive, Cranbury, NJ 08512. Members may order copies of earlier volumes still in print or of later volumes from XIII, at special member prices, from the Treasurer.

FIRST SERIES

VOL. I. *Merie Tales of the Mad Men of Gotam* by A. B., edited by Stanley J. Kahrl, and *The History of Tom Thumbe,* by R. I., edited by Curt F. Buhler, 1965. (o.p.)

VOL. II. Thomas Watson's Latin *Amyntas,* edited by Walter F. Staton, Jr., and Abraham Fraunce's translation *The Lamentations of Amyntas,* edited by Franklin M. Dickey, 1967.

SECOND SERIES

VOL. III. *The dyaloge called Funus,* A Translation of Erasmus's Colloquy (1534), and *A very pleasaunt & fruitful Diologe called The Epicure,* Gerrard's Translation of Erasmus's Colloquy (1545), edited by Robert R. Allen, 1969.

VOL. IV. *Leicester's Ghost* by Thomas Rogers, edited by Franklin B. Williams, Jr., 1972.

THIRD SERIES

VOLS. V–VI. *A Collection of Emblemes, Ancient and Moderne,* by George Wither, with an introduction by Rosemary Freeman and bibliographical notes by Charles S. Hensley, 1975. (o.p.)

FOURTH SERIES

VOLS. VII–VIII. *Tom a' Lincolne* by R. I., edited by Richard S. M. Hirsch, 1978.

FIFTH SERIES

VOL. IX. *Metrical Visions* by George Cavendish, edited by A. S. G. Edwards, 1980.

SIXTH SERIES

VOL. X. *Two Early Renaissance Bird Poems,* edited by Malcolm Andrew, 1984.

VOL. XI. *Argalus and Parthenia* by Francis Quarles, edited by David Freeman, 1986.

VOL. XII. Cicero's *De Officiis,* trans. Nicholas Grimald, edited by Gerald O'Gorman, 1987.

VOL. XIII. *The Silkewormes and their Flies* by Thomas Moffet (1599), edited with introduction and commentary by Victor Houliston, 1988.

SEVENTH SERIES

VOL. XIV. John Bale, *The Vocacyon of Johan Bale,* edited by Peter Happé and John N. King, 1989.

VOL. XV. *The Nondramatic Works of John Ford,* edited by L. E. Stock, Gilles D. Monsarrat, Judith M. Kennedy, and Dennis Danielson, with the assistance of Marta Straznicky, 1990.

Special Publication. *New Ways of Looking at Old Texts: Papers of the Renaissance English Text Society, 1985–1991,* edited by W. Speed Hill, 1993. (Sent *gratis* to all 1991 members.)

VOL. XVI. *George Herbert, The Temple: A Diplomatic Edition of the Bodleian Manuscript (Tanner 307),* edited by Mario A. Di Cesare, 1991.

VOL. XVII. *Lady Mary Wroth, The First Part of the Countess of Montgomery's Urania,* edited by Josephine Roberts. 1992.

VOL. XVIII. *Richard Beacon, Solon His Follie,* edited by Clare Carroll and Vincent Carey. 1993.

VOL. XIX. *An Collins, Divine Songs and Meditacions,* edited by Sidney Gottlieb. 1994.

VOL. XX. *The Southwell-Sibthorpe Commonplace Book: Folger MS V.b.198,* edited by Sr. Jean Klene. 1995.

Special Publication. *New Ways of Looking at Old Texts II: Papers of the Renaissance English Text Society, 1992–1996,* edited by W. Speed Hill, 1998. (Sent *gratis* to all 1996 members.)

VOL. XXI. *The Collected Works of Anne Vaughan Lock,* edited by Susan M. Felch. 1996.

MRTS

MEDIEVAL & RENAISSANCE TEXTS & STUDIES
is the major publishing program of the
Arizona Center for Medieval and Renaissance Studies
at Arizona State University, Tempe, Arizona.

MRTS emphasizes books that are needed —
texts, translations, and major research tools.

MRTS aims to publish the highest quality scholarship
in attractive and durable format at modest cost.